HUMANS IN THE CYBER LOOP

Humans in the Cyber Loop

Perspectives on Social Cybersecurity

Dorota Domalewska

Aleksandra Gasztold

Agnieszka Wrońska

Haymarket Books
Chicago, IL

First published in 2025 by Brill Academic Publishers, The Netherlands
© 2025 Koninklijke Brill NV, Leiden, The Netherlands

Published in paperback in 2026 by
Haymarket Books
P.O. Box 180165
Chicago, IL 60618
773-583-7884
www.haymarketbooks.org

ISBN: 979-8-88890-806-8

Distributed to the trade in the US through Consortium Book Sales and
Distribution (www.cbsd.com) and internationally through Ingram Publisher
Services International (www.ingramcontent.com).

This book was published with the generous support of Lannan Foundation,
Wallace Action Fund, and the Marguerite Casey Foundation.

Special discounts are available for bulk purchases by organizations and
institutions. Please call 773-583-7884 or email info@haymarketbooks.org for more
information.

Cover design by Jamie Kerry and Ragina Johnson.

Printed in the United States.

Library of Congress Cataloging-in-Publication data is available.

Contents

Acknowledgments

The completion of this book was greatly facilitated by the invaluable support and resources provided by several academic institutions: War Studies University, the University of Warsaw, and NASK – National Research Institute. The encouragement and administrative support from the faculty have been fundamental to the successful realization of this project. Many colleagues have also contributed through valuable discussions and support. We would like to extend our special gratitude to one colleague in particular, Professor Danuta Kaźmierczak, whose thorough review of the manuscript and insightful feedback greatly enhanced the quality and coherence of the book.

We would also like to express our gratitude to Prof. David Fasenfest, the Editor of Studies in Critical Social Sciences, who provided invaluable guidance. Additionally, we thank the editors at Brill for their continuous support and meticulous attention to detail, which have been essential in preparing this manuscript for publication.

In developing the book, the editing process was facilitated and supported by artificial intelligence. Tools such as ChatGPT, Paperpal, Grammarly, and DeepL were used to improve the readability and language of the manuscript, as well as to ensure accuracy and precision in English. After using these tools, the authors proofread and edited the content with the assistance of a professional proofreader, Terry Deal. The authors take full responsibility for the content of the publication. The integration of AI in our methodology reflects the broader theme of the book and emphasizes the potential of technology to support human efforts in securing cyberspace.

The project was co-financed by the state budget funds, awarded by the Minister of Science in Poland under the "Excellent Science II" program (project number MONOG/SP/0015/2024/02). We also gratefully acknowledge the support received from the Ministry of Science and Higher Education in Poland under the "Science for Society II" program (project number NdS-II/SP/0381/2024/01), War Studies University and the University of Warsaw.

Abbreviations

CAAS	cybercrime-as-a-service
CSAM	child sexual abuse material
CTS	Critical Terrorism Studies
DDoS	distributed denial-of-service attacks
ENISA	European Union Agency for Network and Information Security
GPG	global public good
GWOT	Global War on Terrorism
HEAT	high-end asymmetric threats
IoT	Internet of Things
LAWS	lethal autonomous weapons systems
LLM	large language model
NFT	non-fungible token
PIU	problematic internet use
PPI	pay-per-install
RaaS	Ransomware-as-a-Service
VoIP	voice over internet protocol

Introduction

> The advancement of technology is like a razor:
> you can use it to shave,
> but you can also cut your throat with it.
> Stanisław Lem

∴

The internet and Web 2.0 technologies have connected billions of devices and users worldwide. High-tech advancements have created a complex and dynamic digital ecosystem that has significantly increased human activity in cyberspace. Many traditional vulnerabilities and threats have also migrated to the digital world, where they have intensified and now pose significant risks to individuals and society. Traditional tactics, such as social engineering, can now be effectively executed on a massive scale with far greater efficiency. Similarly, fabricated and manipulated disinformation can be easily created and disseminated to influence public perception and gain competitive advantages. Deceptive practices can now be precisely targeted at vulnerable individuals through sophisticated algorithms and big data analytics. The scope and pace of ongoing socio-technological developments are enormous, especially with the rapid advancements in artificial intelligence. What is more, ongoing armed conflicts have been demonstrating that cyber operations are integral to conventional warfare. Disruptive cyber tools are increasingly being used in the context of great power rivalry. Consequently, cybersecurity challenges have expanded far beyond the technical domain of protecting systems and data. Present-day cyber challenges now encompass broader social, economic and political dimensions.

Cybersecurity threats have wide-reaching social implications that not only affect individual users but also entire communities and societies. Economically, cybercrime results in significant financial losses. Politically, activities such as state-sponsored cyber attacks and disinformation campaigns undermine democratic processes, increase global tensions and contribute to polarization and radicalization. Socially, the proliferation of malicious content, such as extremist material and disinformation, deepens societal divisions and weakens social cohesion. Additionally, the emotional and psychological effects of exposure to harmful content such as hate and cyber pornography, can cause lasting damage to mental health. Cyber terrorism and cybercrime are not only criminal issues but also significant national security concerns that may escalate social and political tensions. They demonstrate the profound impact of cybersecurity on individual well-being, societal stability and national security. The human-centered approach recognizes the complex nature of cyber threats and their broad implications. It also recognizes the need for a multidisciplinary approach to cybersecurity that integrates insights from various fields to understand and address human factors in cybersecurity. As cyberspace continues to evolve, so must our understanding and managing of cybersecurity to ensure adequate protection not only of systems and networks but also of people and society. The expansion of challenges has given rise to the field of social cybersecurity, which addresses the critical intersection of human behavior, social interactions and digital security. In its early days, cybersecurity was primarily concerned with technical defenses against malicious software, unauthorized access and data breaches. Tools and techniques such as firewalls, antivirus software, encryption, and intrusion detection systems were developed to protect individual computers and network infrastructures. Social cybersecurity, however, recognizes that human actions and vulnerabilities are central to the security of digital environments. It shifts the focus from merely protecting technological infrastructures to understanding and mitigating the risks associated with human behavior in cyberspace. Humans are no longer viewed as passive users but as active participants who actively shape the digital ecosystem and who need protection.

As humans are at the center of the digital ecosystem and the primary factor that makes cybersecurity complex, a human-centered approach to cybersecurity is essential. This strategy ensures that they are firmly integrated in the cyber loop. Many cyber threats arise due to human actions, whether intentional or accidental. Human beings are the weakest link in the context of cybersecurity. Human errors, insufficient risk awareness and poor security practices often become easy targets for cyber criminals. People may fail to update software regularly and be susceptible to social engineering tactics. These factors significantly increase the likelihood of cybersecurity breaches. People are, therefore, both part of the problem and the solution,[1] which reflects the complexity of cybersecurity. Individuals are not merely passive elements in the digital ecosystem but are actively involved in both the origins and mitigation of cybersecurity challenges. This dual role justifies the need for a holistic approach to cybersecurity that integrates technological solutions

---

1   Verena Zimmermann and Karen Renaud, "Moving from a 'Human-as-Problem' to a 'Human-as-Solution' Cybersecurity Mindset", *International Journal of Human-Computer Studies* 131 (2019): 169–87, https://doi.org/10.1016/j.ijhcs.2019.05.005.

with comprehensive educational and behavioral interventions. Humans are in the cyber loop and are central to both the creation and resolution of cyber issues. Addressing evolving cyber threats requires interdisciplinary strategies that encompass technical, psychological and organizational perspectives. By acknowledging and addressing the human element, social cybersecurity aims to create a more resilient and secure digital ecosystem. A human-centered approach to cybersecurity is essential for understanding and mitigating the social, political and ethical consequences of digital activity.

With this book we hope to contribute to the wider debate on the evolving nature of cybersecurity by emphasizing the importance of a human-centered approach. The book examines the complex interplay of factors that define the field of social cybersecurity. While it was not possible to examine an exhaustive range of case studies, we aim to provide representative examples that point out key concepts and trends. We also seek to identify key factors that influence both individual and collective behavior and perceptions of cybersecurity. Topics such as the impact of disinformation on democratic processes, the role of social media in shaping public opinion, algorithmic decision-making, and the socio-economic effects of digital transformation are explored to demonstrate the importance of building societal resilience to cyber attacks and to better understand specific needs and challenges in this domain. We analyze the interplay between technological advancements and social dynamics to shed light on the evolving nature of cyber threats. We also address the ethical aspects of cybersecurity, such as privacy concerns, algorithmic biases and the responsibilities of digital content creators. Our intention is not only to identify problems but also to provide a comprehensive analysis that enhances understanding of digital security issues and highlights the importance of fostering a more secure and inclusive cyberspace. Through comprehensive analysis, we aim to emphasize the significance of protecting not only technical infrastructures but also the human and societal elements in the digital ecosystem.

This volume situates itself in the broader discourse on cybersecurity, offering a fresh perspective on its societal dimension. It addresses the evolution of cyber threats and redefines the role of humans in cyberspace through the analysis of how digital interactions and advancements shape and are shaped by societal, economic and political factors. The book systematically explores social cybersecurity, beginning with foundational concepts and the human-centered approach, examines modern challenges such as cybercrime, information warfare and the power of algorithms, and concludes with a synthesis of key findings and a justification of the adopted framework.

In the first chapter, the book outlines the transformation of cybersecurity from traditional, technology-focused cybersecurity to a more holistic, human-centered approach. As digital technologies evolve, the focus shifts from protecting infrastructure to ensuring the safety and security of users against digital threats. Social cybersecurity emerges as a discipline that not only integrates cybersecurity and human behavior but also addresses the socio-cultural and political outcomes of digital interactions. This chapter explores the redefinition of human roles and security in the rapidly developing cyberspace, emphasizing the importance of integrating human factors into cybersecurity strategies to enhance societal and individual resilience against a spectrum of digital threats.

The second chapter focuses on the evolution of cybersecurity into a critical component of modern warfare. It explores how cyber operations have become essential tools of political strategies and influence global power dynamics. As cyber threats grow more sophisticated, understanding their potential impact on national security and international relations is crucial.

Chapter 3 gives an overview of modern information warfare and disinformation that is used to destabilize governments, influence public opinion and erode trust in democratic institutions. The spread of disinformation is driven by technological advancements, political agendas and changing media consumption habits. Social networking sites and algorithms in particular amplify its reach. The chapter also outlines how repressive governments maintain power by using legal and technological means to allegedly combat disinformation whereas in fact they aim to censor and shape public narratives to maintain governmental power.

The fourth chapter critically examines the pervasive role of algorithms in shaping online experiences and their broader societal implications. As algorithms filter and curate vast streams of data, they significantly influence our perceptions by determining the information we encounter online. While algorithms drive various technological advancements, they also have the potential to reinforce existing social inequalities and generate unforeseen consequences. This chapter considers the roles of algorithms in the broader contexts in which they are applied to fully understand their impact.

Further on, chapter five investigates the societal and economic changes driven by rapid technological advancement. It discusses how digital technologies are reshaping retail, business operations and the job market. The chapter investigates effective marketing strategies enabled by social media, such as customer communication, recommendation algorithms and data collection to boost website traffic. It also addresses ethical challenges like privacy issues, the privacy paradox, profiling, and surveillance.

The sixth chapter explores the power of social media influencers and other stakeholders in cyberspace, examining their impact on public opinion and behavior. It critically investigates ethical concerns, such as content monetization, the promotion of low-quality content, idealized lifestyle, and unsustainable consumption. Additionally, the chapter discusses the risks faced by kidfluencers, specifically related to their economic, physical and psychological abuse. Finally, the chapter assesses the accountability of influencers, particularly when they engage in unethical behavior, and calls for more responsible practices.

Chapter 7 addresses the psychological and social consequences of digital content, examining issues such as information overload and the rise of infotainment, which is often characterized by shallow and commercial content. Next, the darker aspects of digital interactions like hate speech and cyber bullying are discussed focusing on the freedom of expression dilemma and the threat to democratic values posed by hate speech. Finally, the chapter presents multidisciplinary approaches to combating hate speech that integrate education, regulations and social initiatives.

In chapter 8, the phenomenon of problematic internet use (PIU) is explored and likened to substance addiction with significant impacts on both the individual and society. It also discusses how digital design exploits psychological vulnerabilities and social dynamics, leading to compulsive behaviors.

Finally, the concluding chapter discusses digital ecosystems and emphasizes the need for a human-centered approach to cybersecurity. It explores the multidimensional factors and the dynamic interplay between technology, its users and the evolving norms in cyberspace under the significant influence of broader socio-political and economic contexts. Digital ecosystems are not confined to virtual spaces; they are crucial infrastructures that underpin various societal functions and cater to diverse social needs. Through the lens of Urie Bronfenbrenner's ecological systems theory, the chapter illustrates how digital and real-world interactions are deeply intertwined and impact human behavior and societal structures. The chapter further discusses how different layers of the ecosystem, ranging from personal digital interactions to global socio-economic trends, shape user experiences and contribute to the ecosystem's evolution.

The book engages with contemporary debates on cybersecurity and cyber threats. However, in contrast to previous studies that have primarily focused on technical infrastructure, the volume introduces a new perspective on the need for multidisciplinary and interdisciplinary approaches. Adopting a socio-ecological approach allows us to understand the trends of many interrelated layers of digital ecosystems with human beings in the cyber loop. In an age of advanced machines and systems, the human factor remains crucial to ensuring safety and solving the problems generated by the technologies themselves. Therefore, it is extremely important to pay attention to the need for an ethical and humanistic approach to technological development. Consequently, understanding and integrating human aspects into cybersecurity strategies are essential to strengthening individual and societal resilience to digital threats, a key element in building a secure and sustainable digital ecosystem. Given the increasing reliance on digital systems, discussions on social cybersecurity are crucial not only as part of academic research but also in broader public discourse. Recognizing and addressing these issues is fundamental to ensuring a sustainable and secure digital environment for everyone.

Social Cybersecurity: from Technology to a Human-Centered Approach

In an era of intensive digitalization and technological progress, user activity in cyberspace has significantly increased. Digital transformation calls for a revision of our approach to cybersecurity from its traditional focus on protecting technical infrastructure and data to ensuring the safety of users from complex digital threats that were once confined to the physical world. The scope of cybersecurity has therefore spread beyond its traditional boundaries to include aspects of human and societal security. This chapter introduces social cybersecurity, a paradigm that focuses on the nexus between cybersecurity and human behavior as well as the social, cultural and political consequences that result from digital interactions. The primary goal of social cybersecurity is to adopt a human-centered approach that empowers humans in the digital world. Such an approach ensures that people, who are in the loop of the digital ecosystem, are well protected and that the digital environment is a secure and supportive space that fosters, rather than constrains, positive human interactions and the overall functioning of society.

1   Redefining the Human Role and Security in the Evolving Cyberspace

The rapid development of cyberspace, made possible by the emergence of Web 2.0 technologies, has led to a much greater human presence online and revolutionized the roles people take. Interactive features, such as social networking sites and user-generated content, have facilitated collaboration, sharing and social interaction. Users have been empowered to contribute to the digital ecosystem by sharing information, expressing thoughts and actively engaging in various communities, political campaigns and social movements. The evolution of methods of communication and collaboration has brought about a transformation of social practices and norms. Networks are no longer used to merely transmit information and symbolic content, they also enable the production of new forms of action, interaction and social relations. Their influence can be seen in the consolidation of power and the strengthening of various actors. They may be used by some to gain an advantage or to exclude others.[1] They have thus become part of the social infrastructure that at the same time connects and divides people, amplifies their messages, influences their individual experience and shapes the socio-political environment.

The transition of public goods and services to the digital space as well as increased human activity online has redefined cybersecurity. As digitalization progresses, human and societal security is also migrating to the digital space, which has direct implications for individuals and communities. Vulnerabilities that were once confined to the physical world have migrated to cyberspace,[2] often with increased force and in an unexpected way, threatening both the individual and society. Discriminatory algorithms, for example, operate covertly to treat users unequally and even exclude individuals from access to information, services or groups. Hence, the evolution of the internet goes hand in hand with the evolution of cyber threats. Traditionally, they included viruses and malware designed to damage systems or steal sensitive information. More recently, cyber threats have transformed into a full spectrum of sophisticated human-targeted threats, such as social engineering and disinformation. They are spreading on a global scale and increasing their reach and influence. The financial losses incurred as a result of cybercrime are staggering as they impact the individual, the organization and the state. Furthermore, social networking sites are often criticized for their roles in increasing ethnic violence and deepening religious nationalism, boosting the popularity of authoritarian leaders, spreading disinformation campaigns, and impeding public debate on important issues.[3] Social networks are also used by terrorist organizations as an effective tool for recruiting new members, planning attacks and spreading terror, which not only poses a direct security threat but also contributes to the spread of extremism and radicalization online.

Given the evolution of cyberspace, the role of human beings within it has been significantly redefined. People are not just passively present in cyberspace, but are actively engaged through extensive human-computer interactions and human-human connections. They play a critical role in cybersecurity.[4] This

---

1   Manuel Castells, *The Internet Galaxy: Reflections on the Internet, Business and Society* (Oxford: Oxford University Press, 2002), 83.

2   Joëlle Klein and Kamrul Hossain, "Conceptualising Human-centric Cyber Security in the Arctic in Light of Digitalisation and Climate Change", *Arctic Review on Law and Politics* 11 (2020): 9, https://doi.org/10.23865/arctic.v11.1936.

3   Siva Vaidhyanathan, *Anti-Social Media. How Facebook Disconnects Us and Undermines Democracy* (Oxford: Oxford University Press, 2018), 10–12.

4   Myriam Dunn Cavelty and Andreas Wenger, "Cyber Security Meets Security Politics: Complex Technology, Fragmented Politics, and Networked Science", *Contemporary Security Policy* 41, no. 1 (2020): 5–32, https://doi.org/10.1080/13523260.2019.1678855; Hugo Loiseau,

paradigm shift towards human-centered cybersecurity recognizes that the actions, behavior and vulnerabilities of individuals have a direct impact on the security and integrity of cyberspace. Humans are no longer merely seen as potential aggressors who can carry out attacks, or as victims of these attacks. Instead, they are now understood as valuable resources that need protection.[5] The change in the perception of the role of humans, i.e., recognizing them as integral components of the digital ecosystem, can strengthen security in cyberspace. Cybersecurity efforts can be better directed towards protecting their well-being and ensuring that their online identities are protected. Therefore, a wide approach to cybersecurity needs to be taken in order to include the broader social and cultural contexts in which cybersecurity operates.

Cybersecurity threats have wide-ranging implications that extend beyond individual users and organizations, but impact entire communities and society as a whole. The social implications of exposure to harmful online content, such as disinformation and extremist material, intensifies societal divisions, fuels intolerance and undermines social cohesion. Emotional or psychological effects of exposure to cyber pornography and grooming can have long-term effects on mental health and erode trust in communities. Furthermore, there are ethical concerns about privacy and surveillance as well as threats to democracy that are related to the evolving media and information landscape. Cybersecurity threats, such as those resulting from cybercrime, also have significant economic impacts ranging from direct financial losses to broader economic instability. Political consequences of state-sponsored cyber attacks and disinformation campaigns can destabilize governments and influence electoral outcomes. However, when analyzing the political dimension of cybersecurity, it is important to underline the difficulty in precisely and unambiguously defining the nature of threats. The challenge arises from the inhomogeneity of dangers and risks caused by the diverse activities of state and non-state actors. The peculiarities of cyberspace operations are influenced by the fact that an increasing number of resources depend on security in the virtual world. Actions carried out in cyberspace can have effects in the real world, although their effectiveness is determined by different factors. Technological monoculture benefits the cyber threat actor because the methods and

---

Daniel Ventre and Hartmut Aden, eds., *Cybersecurity in Humanities and Social Sciences: A Research Methods Approach* (Hoboken, NJ: Wiley, 2020); Jonathan Andrew and Frédéric Bernard, eds., *Human Rights Responsibilities in the Digital Age: States, Companies and Individuals* (Oxford: Hart Publishing, 2021).

5 Rossouw Von Solms and Johan Van Niekerk, "From Information Security to Cyber Security", *Computers & Security* 38 (2013): 97–102, https://doi.org/10.1016/J.COSE.2013.04.004.

resources of any operation can be freely moved to and launched from any-where to any target. Costs are limited to the acquisition of necessary hardware and software, whereas skills can be developed through accessible online attack scenarios and do not require specialized knowledge. Furthermore, there are no geographic or material limitations. Factors such as distance and time are not barriers. The only requirement is the technical ability to enter the system, i.e., cyberspace. Conflict transferred to cyberspace significantly balances the power of state and non-state international actors, thereby reducing the disparity between them. Often it is more beneficial to the weaker party and described as a force equalizer.[6]

As cyber threats are diverse and intricate, they can easily disrupt societal norms and impact security. On a structural and societal level, cyber terrorism, cybercrime and hostile operations in cyberspace all pose a threat to national security. They increase social and political tensions in societies and undermine social stability. They can significantly change social and political structure, lead to a shift in power dynamics and potentially cause unrest and conflict. These threats can undermine a nation's core values, including freedom of speech and the right to information. Cyberspace can be manipulated and used to silence dissent and spread fabricated information. Cyber threats erode trust in governmental and financial institutions as well as increase societal divisions. Consequently, they threaten democratic processes. Additionally, cyber threats strengthen the capabilities of malicious actors to disrupt societal norms and functions. Disinformation campaigns destabilize the position of a state in the global community, pose a threat to the stability and integration of international organizations like the European Union, and undermine national democratic systems. They can lead to polarization, radicalization and increased tensions, all of which lead to social disruption. Algorithmization also poses a serious threat to society, especially in the sphere of privacy and social equality. Personalized algorithms, frequently used in targeted advertising and content recommendations, can create filter bubbles that isolate individuals in a customized digital environment.[7] By limiting exposure to diverse perspectives and information, filter bubbles can foster a distorted perception of reality, deepen social inequalities and discriminate against or restrict individuals based on unclear or complex factors. From an instrumental perspective, social cyber threats require more effective cybersecurity strategies with a

---

6   E. Anders Eriksson, "Viewpoint. Information Warfare: Hype or Reality?", *The Nonproliferation Review* 6, no. 3 (1999): 60, https://doi.org/10.1080/10736709908436765.

7   Eli Pariser, *The Filter Bubble. How the New Personalized Web is Changing What We Read and How We Think* (London: Penguin Books, 2011).

strong emphasis on awareness, resilience and international cooperation. It is therefore crucial to understand the nature and mechanisms of these threats to effectively develop and implement countermeasures.

2   Social Cybersecurity

The development and spread of the internet and technological progress in general have made it possible for citizens to play an active role in economic, social and political activities. At the same time, heavy reliance on digital infrastructure and increased human presence online have also increased their vulnerability to cyber threats. The rapid development of cyberspace both empowers individuals but also makes them targets of cyber attacks and exposes them to other adverse impacts such as privacy breaches and manipulation. Consequently, the concept of cybersecurity expands beyond traditional boundaries. The traditional perception of cybersecurity, defined as "a collection of defensive technologies (hardware/software), processes and practices designed to protect networks, computers, programs and information from attack, damage or unauthorized access in order to secure systems that are connected to the internet",[8] has evolved. It used to be described as a reduction in the risk of malicious attacks on software, computers and networks with various tools such as intrusion detection, antivirus software, access control, and encryption.[9] It was understood as a type of praxis and information code designed to protect individuals, communities, states, and international organizations from external threats. Cybersecurity meant protecting critical systems and sensitive information from malicious attacks with the use of various forms of malware, such as spyware, viruses, worms, trojans and rootkits. In practical terms, cybersecurity was perceived as the art of protecting networks, devices and data from unauthorized access or criminal use, and the practice of ensuring the confidentiality, integrity and availability of information. Thus, it was a purely technical problem that could be solved with better technologies and stricter controls. However, this perspective does not fully embrace the interdisciplinary nature of cybersecurity, the multitude of ongoing cyber threats and the human element. What is more, it overlooks how cybersecurity is framed and defined in a wide range of policies as well as state and non-state actor

---

8   John Wu Chwan-Hwa and J. David Irwin, *Introduction to Computer Networks and Cybersecurity* (Boca Faton, FL: CRC Press, 2013), 29.
9   Edward Amoroso, *Cyber Security* (New Jersey: Silicon Press, 2006).

practices, which makes it naive, outdated and incomplete for addressing the complexity of cyber threats.[10]

The progression of economic, social and political digitalization resulted in the development of the information society but also led to the emergence of new types of cyber threat. Hence, cybersecurity has acquired a broader meaning. It entails the protection of society and human behavior in the new digital world, which requires a comprehensive and nuanced understanding of cybersecurity. Since cyber threats have evolved to include transmission of communicative content across information systems and surveillance activities, cybersecurity encompasses expressive and symbolic content, which broadens the scope beyond the narrower understanding of cybersecurity solely as the protection of networks and critical infrastructure that facilitate communicative exchanges.[11]

Similarly, Dan Craigen et al.[12] propose a broader definition of cybersecurity as "the organization and collection of resources, processes, and structures used to protect cyberspace and cyberspace-enabled systems from occurrences that misalign de jure from de facto property rights", which emphasizes the need to protect against a range of threats, both intentional and accidental incidents that can affect property rights in cyberspace. It also acknowledges the multifaceted nature and complexity of cybersecurity, which entails human – computer interactions and extensive interconnectedness in cyberspace. When we recognize that humans are an integral part of cyberspace, it becomes necessary to protect not only infrastructure and data, but also the individuals who use and contribute to it. This approach involves understanding how human behavior and psychology impact security, thus there is a need for a multidimensional approach that combines education, technology and organizational culture to mitigate human-related security risks effectively.

Furthermore, the human element in cybersecurity means that users are not just end-users or potential victims, but integral components of the cyber ecosystem that actively contribute to its defense. Human behavior plays a crucial role in cybersecurity, both as a source of potential vulnerabilities and as a key component of defense. In this context, we can point out four mutually interrelated aspects of the human-centered approach: cybersecurity awareness, risk culture, user-friendly security, and behavioral insights. The first component

---

10   Tim Stevens, *Cyber Security and the Politics of Time* (Cambridge: Cambridge University Press, 2015), 23.

11   Stevens, 8–9.

12   Dan Craigen, Nadia Diakun-Thibault and Randy Purse, "Defining Cybersecurity", *Technology Innovation Management Review* 4, no. 10 (2014): 17.

underlines that people are often the first line of defense against cyber threats. Improving knowledge and skills through cybersecurity education and training programs is essential to strengthen this line of defense. The risk culture aspect refers to the collective effort to foster a security culture characterized by shared responsibility and proactive attitudes towards cyber threats. Understanding the threats and their origins promotes preventive attitudes toward risk, threats and safety that emphasize the importance of balancing necessary risks with ensuring protection and safety. Next, the user-friendly security aspect promotes intuitive security interfaces and processes that make it easier for individuals to adhere to best practices and facilitate digital hygiene. Finally, behavioral insights refers to human choices. By understanding how people make decisions, more effective strategies can be designed, thereby improving their effectiveness. Central to this analysis is Ulrich Beck's concept of "risk society", which assumes that modern society's methods of production and distribution are intricately linked to environmental and societal risks. The risks are a part of a global economy that depends on scientific and technical expertise. They contribute to the structuring and turmoil of societal systems. Therefore, societies are threatened by the side effects of scientific and technological development. "The risk society is thus not a revolutionary society, but more than that, a catastrophic society. In it, the state of emergency threatens to become the normal state".[13] In this context, the normative goal of security becomes managing the non-security or threats that arise, as society transitions into a "risk society" that increasingly engages in discussing, preventing and controlling the risks it generates.

Human behavior, as a source of both potential vulnerabilities and defense, plays a significant role in the dynamic digital ecosystem. A key aspect of this approach is recognizing the role of technology in human-centered cybersecurity. Technology acts as both an enabler and a support system that enhances overall security measures. Furthermore, understanding human behavior, decision-making processes and interactions with technology is crucial for identifying and mitigating various socio-political and psychological threats, including hybrid and information warfare, digital manipulations such as disinformation, societal disparities, such as digital divide, and various forms of cyber hostility. Incidents such as influence operations and malicious use of big data reveal the significant impact of cyber activities on society and prove that social and psychological factors need to be incorporated into cybersecurity strategies.

---

13   Ulrich Beck, *Risk Society: Towards a New Modernity* (London; Newbury Park, Calif: Sage Publications, 1992), 78–79.

The human factor, frequently regarded as the most vulnerable aspect in cybersecurity due to its susceptibility to manipulation or error, must be recognized and adequately addressed. In this context, the human-centered approach to cybersecurity transcends the conventional focus on security systems and data, focusing on the individual. As David M. Beskow and Kathleen M. Carley argue, the change was driven by two significant factors. First, technological advancements have eliminated the need for physical proximity to be able to influence society, which means that individuals or groups can influence or launch cyber attacks from anywhere in the world without having to be physically present at the place being targeted. The range of potential threats has therefore increased. It is also more difficult to track and counter them. Second, the decentralization of information flows has reduced the cost of entry into the cyberspace. Information is no longer controlled by a few centralized entities, but is dispersed across different platforms and networks.[14] Therefore, it is easier for individuals or groups to spread information or misinformation and influence public opinion or launch cyber attacks.

This evolution gives rise to a new field of study, social cybersecurity, which is an emerging subdomain of national security "focused on the science to characterize, understand, and forecast cyber-mediated changes in human behavior, social, cultural, and political outcomes, and to build the cyber infrastructure needed for society to persist in its essential character in a cyber-mediated information environment under changing conditions, actual or imminent social cyber threats, and cyber-mediated threats".[15] Social cybersecurity is a separate field from traditional cybersecurity. While the latter is concerned with protecting machines such as computers and databases from being compromised, the former is more people-centered as it addresses the ways in which individuals can be manipulated, influenced or marginalized. Unlike cybersecurity professionals who need to be well-versed in technology, computer science and engineering, social cybersecurity experts should have a deep understanding of social communication, community building, statistics, social networking, and machine learning.[16]

Social cybersecurity is also different from cognitive security. Cognitive security focuses on human cognition and how messages can be designed to take

---

14   David M. Beskow and Kathleen M. Carley, "Social Cybersecurity an Emerging National Security Requirement", *Military Review* 2 (2019): 117–27.

15   Beskow and Carley: 118.

16   Kathleen M. Carley, "Social Cybersecurity: An Emerging Science", *Computational and Mathematical Organization Theory* 26, no. 4 (2020): 365–81, https://doi.org/10.1007/S10588-020-09322-9.

advantage of cognitive limitations. Social cybersecurity, on the other hand, is about individuals in their social contexts and how the digital environment can be altered to change both the community and the narrative. While cognitive security experts need a strong foundation in psychology, social cybersecurity professionals are expected to have a broader range of knowledge in the social sciences.[17]

Adopting a human-centered approach to cybersecurity can help change the perception of humans as the weakest link in the cybersecurity chain. Understanding human behavior in the digital world (including human motivation, needs, emotion-driven behavior, and cognitive bias) and the societal impact of digitalization can empower users and "lift [them] to be the strongest link in the cybersecurity space".[18] Social cybersecurity centers on the role of human behavior and social interactions in the digital space. It deals with understanding, predicting and counteracting behavior that occurs in the context of cybersecurity, information security and online communities. Therefore, social cybersecurity refers to the protection of cyberspace, digital culture and digital life, with a focus on the human aspects and social impact of cybersecurity.

A human-centered approach to cybersecurity is a holistic and proactive strategy that prioritizes the needs, behaviors and capabilities of individuals and organizations in the face of cybersecurity challenges. It recognizes that humans are both users and the potential weak links in the security chain. The goal is to develop and implement cybersecurity measures that are not only user-friendly and culturally sensitive but also aligned with the way people engage with and use technology. New threats in cyberspace point to the need to move away from the traditional state-centric perspectives on security. This approach does not entail a redefinition of security, but calls for a more dynamic consideration of various determinants, contingencies and interactions in the security system(s).

Furthermore, given the problem of human rights violations in cyberspace, including surveillance, algorithmic filtering, online censorship, and manipulation, social cybersecurity has become increasingly focused on the protection of human rights. Digital violations of human rights undermine human autonomy, empathy and dignity. The regression of the norm, according to Aaron Brantly, is extremely progressive. He observes,

---

17   Carley, "Social Cybersecurity: An Emerging Science".
18   Marthie Grobler, Raj Gaire and Surya Nepal, "User, Usage and Usability: Redefining Human Centric Cyber Security", *Frontiers in Big Data* 4 (2021): 16, https://doi.org/10.3389/FDATA.2021.583723.

The result is that human autonomy in digital spaces is increasingly not a right, but a privilege secured through either payment to firms, or complex security practices learned and implemented by individuals. Through algorithms, networks, data collection and analysis, and platforms that shift the perceptions of others, technologies are increasingly attacking the foundations of empathy that enable recognition of autonomy within others. The combined result of the degradation of both human autonomy and empathy through digital means is the undermining of human dignity.[19]

Cybersecurity is, therefore, not just about protecting systems and networks, but also about protecting people and their interactions in the digital world. It is a multidimensional field that requires a comprehensive approach encompassing technical, human, regulatory, risk management, incident response, legal, ethical, technological, supply chain, cultural, and international dimensions. An effective cybersecurity strategy considers and integrates these dimensions to create a robust defense against cyber threats. In response to the growing range of threats and challenges that affect not only the state as an institution but also other entities, the means and methods of eliminating them and shaping resilience are continually evolving. Consequently, there is a subject, object and spatial expansion of security, which also includes the humanitarian, economic, energy, ecological, and cyberspace domains. Today's security, while still retaining its traditional dimension, is increasingly linked to new developments and technologies, including artificial intelligence, virtual and augmented reality, the Internet of Things (IoT), the technology cloud, and blockchain, which affect the lives of individuals. Hence, cybersecurity, like the term security itself, is a subjective need, that is, it can affect various entities, from individuals to large social groups, including organizational structures and various groups such as states, societies, nations, and the international system. It entails ensuring certainty in the existence and survival, state of affairs, and operation and development of various entities. Certainty arises not only from the absence of threats (their non-existence or elimination), but is formed primarily as a result of the creative activity of actors and is variable over time, that is it has the nature of a social process. Social digital security should therefore be studied through the prism of human values.

---

19   Aaron Brantly, "Utopia Lost – Human Rights in a Digital World", *Applied Cybersecurity & Internet Governance* 1, no. 1 (2022): 49, https://doi.org/10.5604/01.3001.0016.1238.

3   Cybersecurity as a New Frontier in Security Studies

Cybersecurity is a distinct sector in the broader field of security studies, focusing on addressing threats and referent objects in the digital environment. It stands apart from other security domains due to its unique referent objects, types of threats and specific securitization processes. The essence of security studies is inherently interdisciplinary, manifesting itself at the intersection of numerous areas and fields. Traditionally, security has been perceived simplistically as a state of absence of threats. This negative definition focuses on the entity that is threatened and the one that nullifies the threats, often making the state a key player. Security is related to military science, strategic studies, international law, international relations, and political science. The military-strategic approach is useful in analyzing both technological progress and defense and protection capabilities, but it does not show the complex problem of human behavior in an innovative world. In this context, the human security paradigm challenges the traditional notion of security and may prove beneficial because it focuses on the safety of the individual.

It entails the assumption that security is a universal concept that is best achieved through preventive measures. Additionally, the paradigm is characterized as human-centered, that is, it recognizes the importance of addressing the needs and well-being of individuals. Furthermore, it emphasizes the interdependence of various components in the human security framework. In this perspective, the world is interconnected, and a fundamental aspect of human security lies in recognizing the intricate interconnectedness of the modern era: a threat to individuals in one region can jeopardize security globally because threats can have far-reaching and debilitating impacts on societies worldwide. The concept, loosely defined by the United Nations Development Program's Human Development Report,[20] implies that when individuals confront threats, international security is also implicated. This approach emphasizes shared vulnerability and the collective nature of global security concerns.

Adopting the human-centered approach to security has sparked a controversial debate in academic circles over the scope of the concept and its inclusiveness. Critics argue that the all-encompassing nature of human security, including everything from disease to political repression, results in a lack of prioritization, making the framework inoperable. Such a broad interpretation is criticized for diluting focus and making it difficult to establish connections between various threats. Methodologically, this approach is challenged for

---

20   UNDP Report, "Human Development Report 1994" (New York, NY: Oxford University Press, 1994).

combining dependent and independent variables, making it difficult to identify threats. The broad definition of human security renders it a "meaningless and analytically useless" concept.[21] The practical goal of improving the quality of life for individuals competes with visions of security in international politics. Additionally, concerns have been raised about prioritizing threats based on the interests of powerful rather than weaker actors. Critics argue that powerful states and international organizations may exploit the human security discourse to justify intervention in weaker states. There have also been allegations that development agencies adopt a human security framework to present development issues as security issues, which helps attract more funding.[22]

Edward Newman[23] argues that human security possesses normative allure but lacks analytical strength. Under the human security framework, anything posing a critical threat to life is considered a security threat, regardless of its origin. If individual security is treated as a variable, attempting to identify and categorize every physiological aspect becomes impractical and generates an unmanageable array. Simultaneously, establishing arbitrary boundaries for including or excluding specific threats raises issues. The academic discourse on human security hinges on this fundamental conceptual challenge. Disagreements over what qualifies as a human security threat, or decisions based on arbitrary criteria, complicate the task of ensuring the reliability of human security or variations therein. Consequently, Newman questions the analytical usefulness of this concept. He also underlines the relationship between human security and non-traditional security studies that challenge neorealist orthodoxy, but often from more sophisticated theoretical perspectives. However, the human security approach focuses on meeting the basic needs of individuals and practices how to achieve global security. Hence, it expands the traditional view of security through the prism of protection (and defense) against threats, focusing on individual human needs. An approach to cybersecurity that emphasizes the human aspect employs the human security paradigm to protect values derived from humanitarianism. Incorporating the human security framework can provide added value in discerning the needs, concerns, and challenges arising from digitalization. Traditional approaches to cybersecurity often overlook the day-to-day concerns and problems of

---

21   S. Neil MacFarlane and Yuen Foon Khong, *Human Security and the UN: A Critical History* (Bloomington: Indiana University Press, 2006), 247.

22   Natasha Lindstaedt, *Human Security in Disease and Disaster* (London and New York: Routledge, 2022), 18.

23   Edward Newman, "Critical Human Security Studies", *Review of International Studies* 36, no. 1 (2010): 82, https://doi.org/10.1017/S0260210509990519.

individuals related to digitalization and new technologies. A human-centered approach to cybersecurity, which aligns in part with the principles of human security, offers a more comprehensive understanding of the effects of digitalization. This approach adopts a people-centric perspective, placing the individual firmly in the cyber loop as the central point of security.[24]

When considering (cyber) security issues, three dimensions can be distinguished: subject, object and process. In the first dimension, security means the certainty of the existence and survival of a given social actor. This implies that the focus is on ensuring the security and continuity of entities or actors, such as organizations, individuals or nations, in the face of security threats. The second dimension refers to the state of possession, including identity and opportunities for development. Such an approach suggests that security is not only about protecting the subject but also about safeguarding the assets, resources and opportunities that the subject possesses. Lastly, the process dimension concerns functioning over time and space, representing a sequence of evolving states. It means that security is a dynamic process that evolves and adapts over time, reflecting the changing nature of threats and vulnerabilities. Together, the three dimensions (subject, object and process) provide a comprehensive framework for understanding and addressing (cyber) security issues comprehensively. It helps clarify who or what needs protection and how security measures are implemented and maintained over time. By considering all three dimensions, organizations and individuals can develop a more holistic and effective approach to security.

Viewed through this lens, cybersecurity could be seen as a public good, or an asset for which there can be no rivalry; in this case, it cannot be an excludable good. According to Paul Samuelson's concept, public goods are enjoyed by all without explanation and in equal share. General public goods are those that are non-rivalrous and non-excludable when consumed.[25] However, access to digital innovation and the ongoing challenges of digital exclusion contradict this. Moreover, cybersecurity encompasses both private and public aspects, making it a complex bundle of goods. Treating cybersecurity as a public good prioritizes the need for collective responsibility. This approach assesses the implications of managing cybersecurity in a dynamic and uncertain digital

---

24   Mirva Salminen, Gerald Zojer and Kamrul Hossain, "Comprehensive Cybersecurity and Human Rights in the Digitalising European High North", in *Digitalisation and Human Security*, eds. Mirva Salminen, Gerald Zojer and Kamrul Hossain, New Security Challenges (Cham: Springer International Publishing, 2020), 21–55, https://doi.org/10.1007/978-3-030 -48070-7_2.

25   Paul A. Samuelson, "The Pure Theory of Public Expenditure", *The Review of Economics and Statistics* 36, no. 4 (1954): 387, https://doi.org/10.2307/1925895.

environment. It introduces a framework for evaluating the "publicness" of goods, focusing on criteria related to decision-making, distribution of benefits and consumption. A literature review shows that there are different arguments in favor of treating cybersecurity as a public good. Several studies have integrated this perspective into game-theoretical analyses, which capture essential characteristics of decision-making to protect assets in an environment.[26] Adopting this approach can help establish a comprehensive policy framework for defining objectives and means, bringing coherence to various sector-specific policies and programs. It emphasizes the importance of preemptive action by identifying and rectifying fundamental vulnerabilities in security frameworks, while also focusing on forecasting and mitigating emerging threats through timely implementation of preventive measures. At its core, this perspective is about strengthening resilience mechanisms.

The collective approach to cybersecurity as a public good aligns with the broader challenges faced by other global public goods (GPG s), as discussed by Inge Kaul. The researcher examines the underprovision of critical GPG s such as climate change mitigation, financial stability, global health, and cybersecurity. This deficiency poses threats to both developed and developing regions as well as to global sustainability. Kaul puts forward a framework for future research and discussion that aims to develop a novel sector of public policy.[27] The proposed model would not only offer well-founded guidance on how to reconcile the interests of individual states and non-state actors, including concerns related to national sovereignty, while simultaneously fulfilling the requirements for providing GPG s. It also seeks to shed light on the current state of policymaking, understand the factors that impede or facilitate GPG provision and potentially inspire policymakers to embrace creative policies that improve the management of interdependence, promote development and contribute to global sustainability.

---

26   Paul Rosenzweig, "Cybersecurity, the Public/Private 'Partnership,' and Public Goods", SSRN Scholarly Paper (Rochester, NY, 2011), https://papers.ssrn.com/abstract=1923869; Mariarosaria Taddeo, "Is Cybersecurity a Public Good?", *Minds and Machines* 29, no. 3 (2019): 349–54, https://doi.org/10.1007/s11023-019-09507-5; Mazaher Kianpour, Stewart James Kowalski and Harald Øverby, "Advancing the Concept of Cybersecurity as a Public Good", *Simulation Modelling Practice and Theory* 116 (2022): 102493, https://doi.org/10.1016/j.simpat.2022.102493.

27   Inge Kaul, "Global Public Goods and Governance for Addressing Sustainability", in *The Palgrave Handbook of Development Economics*, eds. Machiko Nissanke and José Antonio Ocampo (Cham: Springer International Publishing, 2019), 833–65, https://doi.org/10.1007/978-3-030-14000-7_24.

Furthermore, in a broader social context, security is related to securing the needs of existence, survival, certainty, stability, identity, independence, and protection of quality of life. Thus, it is the supreme need of human beings, social groups, states, and international systems. Lack of security, on the other hand, causes anxiety and a sense of insecurity. Unfulfilled human needs cause a deficiency which generates threats to existence, shelter, possession, development, environment, and personal dignity, etc. Hence, a threat is the opposite of security and attracts more attention when it comes from outside. Moreover, it pertains to a specific tangible occurrence that is regarded as unfavorable or hazardous. Every entity strives to shape its external environment to mitigate, neutralize, or, at the very least, delay threats, as well as to alleviate its concerns, apprehensions, and uncertainties.[28] Threats play a crucial role as they are perceived as processes or conditions that disrupt the certainty of existence and development of an entity. As processes, they unfold over time, while as conditions/circumstances they reflect what is happening at a given moment in the process. Threats can be considered as actions or a sequence of events that (1) threaten drastically and over a relatively brief period to degrade the quality of life for the inhabitants of a state or (2) threaten significantly to narrow the range of policy choices available to a state government, or private, non-governmental entities (persons, groups, corporations) in the state.[29]

Threats and vulnerabilities can emerge across a wide spectrum, encompassing both military and non-military domains. However, to be categorized as security concerns, they must meet specific criteria that set them apart from general political issues. Furthermore, they are framed as existential threats to a specific subject, orchestrated by an actor engaged in securitization. Such framing justifies the adoption of emergency measures that go beyond ordinary rules and constraints.[30] In theory, the human approach to cybersecurity should shift priorities from the aspirations of nation-states to those that are more focused on the needs of the most vulnerable groups and individuals in society. Such a shift would require not only identifying who is the most vulnerable but also understanding why. Thus, more than ever, there is a greater need for a societal perspective that recognizes the interconnectedness between people, new

---

28   Ryszard Zięba, *The Euro-Atlantic Security System in the 21st Century*, Global Power Shift (Cham: Springer International Publishing, 2018), 55–56, https://doi.org/10.1007/978-3-319 -79105-0.

29   Richard H. Ullman, "Redefining Security", *International Security* 8, no. 1 (1983): 133, https:// doi.org/10.2307/2538489.

30   Barry Buzan et al., *Security: A New Framework for Analysis* (Lynne Rienner Publishers, 1998), 5.

technologies and cyber threats, while taking into account the developmental factors that influence vulnerability to cyber threats.

Barry Buzan's concept of "societal security" is distinct from traditional notions of security, which often focus on military threats and state security. Instead, it emphasizes the security of a society as a whole. It shifts the focus from the security of the state or its institutions to the security and well-being of the society or people in a state. It considers the impact of various non-military threats on the stability and functioning of a society. Threats can include a wide range of challenges, such as environmental degradation, economic crises, pandemics, political instability, terrorism, drug trafficking, and more. In this sense, societal security preserves society's cohesion, culture and identity.[31] Buzan's approach involves analyzing security concerns at multiple levels, from the individual to the global.

Societal security is not only freedom from threats that undermine societal stability and well-being, but also the presence of real guarantees for individual development. It results from social processes and phenomena. Development is viewed as sustainable and progressive process, closely linked with improving the quality of life in socio-economic terms.[32] From this perspective, it is treated as an integral component of national security identified with the state. In the traditional view, security has been treated as an existential need of the state, provided through political and military means. Hence, the international system has been conceptualized through values related to the state, such as survival, autonomy and territorial integrity, rather than values related to individual human well-being. Although the needs and interests of states are represented by the power exercised by specific individuals, they concern the state as a supreme being. For decades, the importance of the human factor was overlooked, although interactions in the international environment affected the population living in a given state territory.[33] The gradual and

---

31   Dritero Arifi and Ngadhnjim Brovina, "Kosovo Society: Coexistence, Challenges and Opportunities", in *Social Security in the Balkans – Volume 3: An Overview of Social Policy in Serbia and Kosovo*, ed. Marzena Żakowska (Boston: Brill, 2022), 225–27, https://doi.org/10.1163/9789004500068.

32   Marzena Żakowska and Dorota Domalewska, "Social Security in the Balkans: Lessons and Recommendations", in *Social Security in the Balkans – Volume 3. An Overview of Social Policy in Serbia and Kosovo*, ed. Marzena Żakowska (Boston, Leiden: Brill, 2022), 257–58, https://doi.org/10.1163/9789004500068_011.

33   Marzena Żakowska and Dorota Domalewska, "Social Security in the Balkans", in *Social Security in the Balkans – Volume 1: An Overview of Social Policy in Croatia, Albania, Bosnia and Hercegovina, Greece, Romania and Bulgaria* (Leiden, Boston: Brill, 2021), 1–8, https://doi.org/10.1163/9789004466579.

uneven integration of human rights into international law, epitomized by the Universal Declaration of Human Rights (1948), marks the first manifestation of the reconciliation between values represented by states and human values.[34] Nonetheless, the authorities that legislate these rights also decide who should and can respect them. One regression of human rights in favor of state values is the increasing tendency to control and regulate the digital sphere.[35]

The concept of societal security acknowledges that what is considered a threat may vary depending on the level of analysis and for different groups in society. Furthermore, societal security concerns can undergo securitization in the same way as traditional military concerns, integrating them into a broader understanding of what constitutes a security threat.[36] Similarly, cyber-security involves a comprehensive analysis of cyber threats, the process of securitization, and their broader implications. According to Lene Hansen and Helen Nissenbaum, this field is characterized by various security modalities such as hypersecuritization, everyday security practices and technifications, which respectively deal with large-scale instantaneous disaster scenarios, the securitization of citizens' lived experiences and reliance on expert technical knowledge for issue resolution37. Cybersecurity is often associated with the recognition of cyber attacks as significant threats in the digital age, and its study extends the Copenhagen School's securitization theory to address critical debates surrounding the politics and epistemology of securitization and the desecuritization process. The latter involves transitioning from security-based logic to more political or technical approaches. By defining and exposing a challenge as a "security issue," it gains more importance than it could do without such a reference, making it possible to take extraordinary measures in the name of ensuring security. Hypersecuritization in the context of cybersecurity refers to the extreme or intensified securitization of the entire digital network and information technology infrastructure. It draws parallels with environmental security discourse, particularly in terms of the severity and urgency attributed to the threats, often framed as existential or irreversible. However, the rapid pace at which cyber threat scenarios evolve and the

---

34   Louis Henkin, "Law and Politics in International Relations: State and Human Values", *Journal of International Affairs* 44, no. 1 (1990): 183–208.

35   Milton Mueller, *Will the Internet Fragment? Sovereignty, Globalization, and Cyberspace* (Cambridge: Polity Press, 2017).

36   Barry Buzan, *People, States and Fear: An Agenda for International Security Studies in the Post-Cold War Era* (London: Harvester Wheatsheaf, 1991).

37   Lene Hansen and Helen Nissenbaum. "Digital Disaster, Cyber Security, and the Copenhagen School". *International Studies Quarterly* 53, no. 4 (2009): 1157–58. https://doi.org/10.1111/j.1468-2478.2009.00572.x.

challenges associated with visualizing threats distinguish cybersecurity from environmental security. This distinction influences the dynamics of political interventions in response to cyber threats. The discourse about cyber threats may amplify the potential of insecurities leading to an exaggeration of the necessary countermeasures.

4 The Evolution of Cyber Threats

The expanded interpretation of cybersecurity, which includes both technological and human elements, is increasingly acknowledged in contemporary research and reports. The 2022 Threat Landscape Report by the European Union Agency for Network and Information Security[38] reflects a wider perspective on cybersecurity and identifies the following elements as threats: ransomware, malware, social engineering, data threats (i.e., unauthorized access, disclosure or manipulation of data, which may be intentional data breaches or unintentional data leaks, and can serve as a basis for other threats such as ransomware and denial-of-service attacks), threats against availability (denial-of-service or internet threats), disinformation/misinformation, and supply chain attacks. Most of these threats relate to the integrity of networks or computer systems with the human element as a secondary factor or a background. They affect individuals, but the main security focus is on the network or online tool. Since 2017, ENISA reports have identified social engineering as a cyber threat that exploits fundamental human vulnerabilities to gain unauthorized access or extract sensitive information. Additionally, since 2021, ENISA reports have recognized the significance of cognitive threats against humans through disinformation and misinformation campaigns that directly target and manipulate individuals. The 2023 ENISA report further identifies emerging threats that include the escalation of cyber attacks due to geopolitical tensions and the rise of hacktivism with the emergence of new groups, an onslaught of DDoS and ransomware attacks, and the growing problem of information manipulation. Social engineering attacks enabled by the development of artificial intelligence and novel techniques have also increased, although phishing remains the most common attack method. State-nexus groups continue to use dual-use tools to maintain stealth and embed malicious code in well-known software packages. Cyber criminals have increasingly shifted their focus to cloud infrastructures

---

38   ENISA, "ENISA Threat Landscape 2022", (Athens: European Union Agency for Network and Information Security, 2022), https://www.enisa.europa.eu/publications/enisa-threat -landscape-2022.

and demonstrated geopolitical motivations in 2023, expanding their extortion activities beyond ransomware to directly target users.[39] The political implications of cybercrime are extensive as cyber criminals influence politics, access national security sensitive data or disrupt critical infrastructure. In particular, such risks are associated with the use of ransomware with double and even triple extortion tactics to increase the likelihood that targets will pay. In such attacks, cyber criminals exfiltrate large amounts of data before encrypting files and demanding a ransom. They then use the threat of releasing the sensitive data as a kind of 'insurance policy' in case the target follows best practices, such as maintaining up-to-date backups. The triple extortion tactic involves demanding payment from customers, partners and other third parties. It is particularly effective in the not-so-tight supply chain of services to the government sector. Numerous cyber criminals have shifted tactics, moving away from ransomware to quieter attacks like crypto-jacking, IoT malware and encrypted threats. SonicWall's report reveals a record surge in crypto-jacking attacks, reaching 332 million in 2023, a 399% increase, in contrast to just 66.7 million in the corresponding period of the previous year. IoT malware attacks are also increasing dramatically in a variety of sectors including aviation, water supply, rail transport, robotics, and industrial control systems.[40]

The expanding range of threats requires a comprehensive approach to cybersecurity that addresses both the technological infrastructures and the human elements susceptible to exploitation. Technological threats such as data theft, malware and access blocking represent one part of the challenge. Social threats are equally significant. They include exposure to illegal content such as exploitative material, online violence and content that promotes self-harm or extremist behavior. In addition, there are risks associated with harmful internet contacts, such as grooming and cyber bullying, as well as sexting and the misuse of personal data. Risks extend into more specific groups and include exposure to illegal and harmful content, such as violence, physical injury and cruelty towards humans and animals; content that encourages self-destructive behavior such as self-harm, suicide and substance abuse; content that incites intolerance, hostility or animosity; child pornography and child sexual abuse material (CSAM). Furthermore, social threats also include dangerous contacts, for example child grooming; risky behavior, in particular sexting, cyber

---

39   ENISA, "ENISA Threat Landscape July 2022 to June 2023", (Athens: European Union Agency for Network and Information Security, 2023), https://www.enisa.europa.eu/pub lications/enisa-threat-landscape-2023.

40   "Sonicwall Cyber Threat Report: Charting Cybercrime's Shifting Frontlines" (Sonicwall, 2023), https://www.sonicwall.com/2023-cyber-threat-report/.

bullying, problematic internet use; and a broad spectrum of cybercrime activities.[41] Each category is complex and contains numerous sub-elements that affect users differently, ranging from personal psychological impacts to broader societal implications. This typology points to the need to address both the direct attacks on cybersecurity infrastructure and the various methods by which technologies are exploited to harm individuals. Additionally, concerns such as problematic internet use and cybercrime, including financial and identity theft, indicate the complexity and diversity of challenges in cybersecurity.

Building on this understanding, cyber threats can be categorized into the following types:

- Technical/technological threats related to ICT crime that undermine the integrity and confidentiality of digital systems: malicious software (malware), ransomware, information protection breaches, computer intrusions, unlawful data acquisition or destruction, document fraud, copyright infringement and cracking;
- Social engineering threats including exploiting human vulnerabilities to gain unauthorized access to systems and sensitive information and tricking victims into opening malicious documents and visiting compromised websites. Techniques include phishing, vishing, SMSishing, and spoofing;[42]
- Online disinformation threats characterized by the deliberate and consistent dissemination of false or manipulated information that misleads recipients, distorts reality and affects decisions and opinions;
- Threats to physical and mental health, i.e., visual and hearing impairment, musculoskeletal problems, wrist and thumb problems, and mental health disorders, such as self-injury, self-harm, suicide related to cyberspace activities, and other psycho-physical conditions;

---

41   Mariya Stoilova, Sonia Livingstone and Daniel Kardefelt-Winther, "Global Kids Online: Researching Children's Rights Globally in the Digital Age", *Global Studies of Childhood* 6, no. 4 (2016): 455–66, https://doi.org/10.1177/2043610616676035; Stefan Lehne, "After Russia's War Against Ukraine: What Kind of World Order?", 2023, https://carnegieeurope.eu/research/2023/02/after-russias-war-against-ukraine-what-kind-of-world-order?lang=en¢er=europe.

42   Phishing is the practice of impersonating a legitimate institution or individual to extract data and confidential information, such as bank account numbers or login passwords. Vishing (voice phishing) is a voice-based variation of phishing where scammers use automated voice calls or synthetic speech to trick individuals into revealing sensitive information. SMSishing involves sending text messages that appear to come from trusted sources to lure recipients into providing personal data or downloading malware. Spoofing refers to disguising communication from an unknown source as being from a known, trusted source (e.g., legitimate businesses or authorities).

- Excessive use of devices (laptops, smartphones), addiction to computer games and problematic use of the internet;
- Social threats, including cyber bullying and online aggression, online gambling, hate speech, interpersonal contact disorders, social alienation and weakening of family ties, escape from the real world, illegal or harmful content access, including pathological content, racist, xenophobic content, glorification of chemical substances, drugs and weapons;
- Moral hazards: cyber pornography, online prostitution, cyber sex, sexting, proliferation of child sexual abuse material (CSAM);
- Risky online interactions, including online grooming, solicitation of harmful or illegal behavior, virtual world cults, sex and organ trafficking. The digital environment can also contribute to mental health issues such as eating disorders (anorexia), bigorexia, sextortion, access to pathological and "toxic" cults, youth subcultures or extremist and criminal groups;
- Threats to intellectual development, including disorders of cognitive functions, such as perceptual distortions, reduced fluidity of attention, reduced or lost capacity for logical thinking, intrusive thoughts, memory disorders due to lack of memory training, forming a false or fragmented view of the world, impaired verbal and written skills, predominance of concrete and pictorial thinking over abstract thinking, a reduced ability to synthesize, generalize, analyze, and perceive relationships, and, consequently, a reduced ability to reason and understand;
- Cultural risks associated with the spread of linguistic errors, cultural uniformity, increased cultural conflicts, threats to cultural identity, and cultural manipulation influencing views and attitudes.

Cyberspace is a constantly multiplying realm of opportunities and threats. As on-demand access to ubiquitous data and information platforms is growing, hackers are using sophisticated technologies such as artificial intelligence and machine learning to launch increasingly complex attacks. Simultaneously, systemic solutions, including regulations implemented by national and regional organizations, struggle to keep pace with high-tech advancements. All cybersecurity efforts involve seeking answers regarding the architecture of cyber development. Emerging technologies such as virtual reality and artificial intelligence are increasingly being used in strategic contexts, where they shape the perceptions and influence the decisions of policymakers in economic, social, political, and even military domains. Understanding and managing these processes require dialogue with the scientific community as well as manufacturers of new technologies.

The issue of interdependence is crucial. The human-focused approach helps analyze a wide range of security threats, such as hybrid threats, information warfare, cyber terrorism, cybercrime, and hate speech by examining their origins, specificity and broader implications. Furthermore, the evolving cyberspace should also be considered in the context of the ongoing reconfiguration of the international order. Discussions in Western international politics have revolved around advocating for a liberal and rules-based global order built on the principles of market economics, democracy and multilateral diplomacy. The United States and the EU have positioned themselves as primary proponents of this order, advocating for its widespread adoption worldwide. However, confidence in this vision has significantly waned in recent years. The shift aligns with the global erosion of democracy and a pragmatic reassessment of the "rules-based order" to make it more inclusive and adaptive to global realities.[43] John Mearsheimer, the creator of offensive realism, interprets these changes as the end of what he calls "liberal delusions".[44] In such a view, the war in Ukraine is not only a regional conflict but a broader confrontation between the West, led by the U.S. in defense and expansion of the existing liberal international, and Russia, backed by authoritarian regimes like China, and politically supported by other significant players in global politics such as India, Brazil, South Africa, and the broader Global South. The outcome of the war will have consequences for the new international order, including the architecture and governance of cyberspace.

---

43   Lehne, "After Russia's War Against Ukraine: What Kind of World Order?".

44   John J. Mearsheimer, *The Great Delusion: Liberal Dreams and International Realities* (New Haven and London: Yale University Press, 2018).

Cybersecurity: from Crime to Warfare in the Digital Age

Given the rapid flow of information in the digital world, the famous words of Joseph S. Nye Jr. "The world is shrinking"[1] ought to qualify as an accomplished fact, i.e., the world has shrunk. The ongoing digital revolution resulting from computerization and the implementation of new technologies is reshaping societal structures and changing social dynamics. Knowledge and information, along with capital and labor, have become strategic resources. However, the dependence on the reliability of information and communication technologies, as well as their trans-sectoral nature, poses significant challenges. Cyberspace, with its civilian and military dimensions, requires collaborative public-private partnerships to enhance cybersecurity. Strengthening digital defenses requires new impulses from governments, effective work by security institutions, engagement with non-governmental organizations, dialogue with the scientific community, and, above all, cooperation with the IT sector. As threats like cyber terrorism and cybercrime evolve, the definition of security expands, as do the tools nations use to enforce it. At the same time, technological developments have made information warfare an integral part of political strategies. The rivalry and confrontation between global actors have extended to cyberspace, which has brought about complex interplay between technology, politics and security.

1   Cyber Terrorism

Defining terrorism, and subsequently cyber terrorism, is complicated as a result of the multiplicity of forms and trends as well as the constant evolution of organizational structures and *modi operandi*. Explaining this term is challenging owing to the lack of uniformity. It is difficult to distinguish terrorism from other forms of political violence. Furthermore, definitions often lack objectivity due to inherent bias influenced by political inconsistencies. There are wide discrepancies in how specific incidents are labeled and recognized as terrorist

---

1   Joseph S. Nye, *Understanding International Conflicts: An Introduction to Theory and History* (New York: Harper Collins, 1993), 1.

acts, and they are often interpreted through the lens of certain moral judgements. Moreover, many definitions do not include all forms of violence used by modern terrorist organizations and individual perpetrators. They typically focus on acts of terror carried out by non-state actors, effectively illustrating the challenge of creating a comprehensive and universally accepted definition.

Another challenge is the use of terrorism as a hybrid warfare tactic, which in some ways is also difficult to analyze and apply in practice. Hybrid terrorism operations can be conducted by both state and non-state actors, which makes these activities even more complex to understand and address, particularly taking into consideration the fact that there are various levels of state involvement in supporting or sponsoring terrorist organizations or individuals.[2] Possible scenarios include inspiring an organization or individual to commit acts of terrorism, conducting false flag attacks and engaging in mercenary activities. The violence in these acts is premeditated, aimed at instilling profound fear. The brutality of the attack serves multiple purposes: it manifests demands, creates fear and communicates messages. However, a critical aspect of hybrid terrorism is the concealment of the true perpetrator (a hostile actor), which makes it difficult to attribute and respond effectively. Furthermore, recognizing terrorism as a crucial component of hybrid warfare waged by both state and non-state actors calls for a new approach to understanding terrorism in a broader framework.[3] This approach entails the establishment of institutions (centers and think tanks) to enable coordination and an effective response to terrorism and hybrid threats, with a particular focus on cybersecurity and the protection of critical infrastructure. Examples include the European Center of Excellence for Countering Hybrid Threats established in 2017, the Center Against Hybrid Terrorism and Hybrid Threats in the Czech Republic, also established in 2017, the UK National Cybersecurity Center established in 2016, and the Swiss National Center for Cybersecurity, which has been operational since 2019. The new analytical bodies have been set up as part of an integrated effort in the European Union and its member states to counter modern terrorism and hybrid warfare.

Terrorism may be understood as a phenomenon that involves the use of violence or the threat of its use against persons or property to force authorities into making certain concessions or political decisions. The desired effect is to create a state of unrest and insecurity. The psychological effect of acts of

---

2   Aleksandra Gasztold and Przemysław Gasztold, "The Polish Counterterrorism System and Hybrid Warfare Threats", *Terrorism and Political Violence* 34, no. 6 (2022): 1260–61, https://doi .org/10.1080/09546553.2020.1777110.

3   Gasztold and Gasztold, 1261.

terrorism is to sow terror. It can be characterized as a strategy of action with several elements: violence, the object or victims of the attack and the purpose of the action. Violence is undertaken premeditatedly to provoke extreme fear; it is designed to affect a wider community than the victims of direct violence. It often involves a random selection of victims and usually occurs at locations that hold symbolic value. Violence serves multiple purposes. It is used to express opposition to and protest against the community in which the attack was carried out. The atrocity of the attack serves three functions simultaneously: (1) a manifestation of demands, (2) creation of fear and propaganda, and (3) communication with the audience – the victims and the authorities. Regardless of the ideological motivation (national liberation, religious, right wing, left wing, one-issue) alluded to by the entity employing the terrorist strategy (individual, group, state), it refers to systemic elements regulated by public authority. The term "terrorism" itself is charged with value because of political inconsistency in recognizing or disregarding specific events as acts of terrorism.[4]

Contemporary research into terrorism has been criticized for its superficiality, overgeneralization, subjective selection of threats and specific events, its focus on the study of terrorist behavior and motivation as well as relying mainly on descriptive methodologies and secondary sources like media reports instead of source materials. Additionally, research carried out in terrorism studies tends to focus on jihadist terrorism. Scholarly analysis often coincides with counterterrorism policy trends and is dependent on state funding. The way terrorism is conceptualized and fought influences public perception of terrorist threats and the politics of terrorism information. Therefore, there has been a progressive marginalization of other forms of political violence, such as far-right, supremacist, leftist, and national liberationist threats, while the study of groups like Al-Qaeda and the so-called Islamic State has dominated discussions on political violence, the problem of radicalization and behavior that leads to violent extremism. The lack of objectivity in terrorism studies has been further manifested through the U.S. "war on terror" campaign, which is often reflected in academic research. The bias in research on political violence is evident among scholars from Europe and the United States, influenced by their distinct historical experiences with counter-terrorism. Framing terrorism in terms of war or crime influences these scholars' perspectives and, by extension, their strategic culture. The difference is often referred to as the

---

4 Gasztold and Gasztold, 1260–64.

Atlantic divide.[5] Criticism of the political narrative on terrorism, as applied in scientific analysis, was inspired by Richard Jackson[6] and led to the development of Critical Terrorism Studies (CTS). Researchers in this field focus on examining the role of the state as a causal agent and on assessing counterterrorism policies.[7]

In terrorism studies, the antiterrorism approach became dominant after the 9/11 attacks. George W. Bush's Global War on Terrorism (GWOT) intensified the dichotomy between Christianity and Islam, which reflects Carl von Clausewitz's conceptualization of war and Carl Schmitt's formulation of political identity based on a friend – enemy opposition. However, the approach to terrorism in the United States is not new and the paradigm of war can also be observed in the Israeli–Palestinian conflict and the Russian–Chechen military conflict. Generally, the counterterrorism paradigm is based on an approach to war derived from the counterinsurgency praxis during the Cold War era of decolonization.[8] The post-2001 U.S. campaign against Al-Qaeda, and more recent actions such as the 2023 Israeli campaign against Hamas, have associated terrorist acts with moral judgements and efforts to punish perpetrators, marginalizing the sources, conditions and catalysts behind radicalization of opinions, attitudes and behavior contributing to terrorism. In contrast, European countries have mainly adopted a criminal justice approach to terrorism and treat it as a criminal act. The war paradigm has not fully proven itself and has generated problems, such as the rise of Al-Qaeda in Iraq, the bombings in Madrid (2004) and London (2005), and the establishment of the Islamic State in Iraq and Syria (ISIS) since 2014, as well as the most recent conflicts: Israeli vs. Hamas (since 2023) and Iran vs. Israel (2024).

The Global War on Terrorism led by President George W. Bush was replaced in 2009 by President Barack Obama, who introduced the term Overseas Contingency Operations. Despite a softening of rhetoric and increased efforts

---

5   Matan Chorev, "When in the Divide? Terrorism and the Future of Atlanticism", *Journal of International Affairs* 11, no. 1 (2006): 36.

6   Richard Jackson, "Security, Democracy, and the Rhetoric of Counter-Terrorism", *Democracy and Security* 1, no. 2 (2005): 147–71, https://doi.org/10.1080/17419160500322517; Richard Jackson, *Writing the War on Terrorism: Language, Politics, and Counter-Terrorism* (Manchester; New York: Manchester University Press, 2005).

7   Richard Jackson, Marie Breen Smyth and Jeroen Gunning, *Critical Terrorism Studies: A New Research Agenda* (New York: Routledge, 2009); Jacob L. Stump and Priya Dixit, *Critical Terrorism Studies: An Introduction to Research Methods* (London; New York, NY: Routledge, 2013).

8   Joshua D. Kertzer, "Seriousness, Grand Strategy, and Paradigm Shifts in the 'War on Terror'", *International Journal: Canada's Journal of Global Policy Analysis* 62, no. 4: 971, https://doi.org/10.1177/002070200706200414.

for dialogue with Muslim nations, the military approach continued to view terrorism through the paradigm of war.[9] The armed approach to counterterrorism aims to triumph over the enemy, leading to their defeat or even complete elimination. The assumed success of military efforts depends on three factors: the will of the people, political leadership and the outcome on the battlefield. Initially, the GWOT campaign received significant support; President Bush was a political leader whose intentions and rhetoric in response to terrorist events were strong and almost pioneering. However, the unfolding battlefield results, specifically the campaigns in Afghanistan and Iraq, demonstrated the weakness of this narrative and intensified the dichotomy between the West and Dar al Islam (the land of Islam). The expected success of spreading democratic values did not materialize.

The Global War on Terrorism mentality established counterterrorism as the main focus of foreign policy. Additionally, President George W. Bush stressed that terrorism targets civilians, which gave his policy a moral depth. Blending morality and politics, which are usually two distinct dimensions, redirected the media, global attention and America's allies towards aspects related to protecting life, civilian populations and condemning attacks. Consequently, morality gained dominance in global discourse and American messianism became incomprehensible to many cultural circles. Reports often reflect more about the issuer than the events themselves, a trend likely catalyzed by the 9/11 attacks. Over time, the perspective on reporting terrorist incidents has evolved, but their classification has been subordinated to shifting trends in counterterrorism policy.

The G.W. Bush administration imposed a certain interpretation on the threat of Islamic terrorism (in the European Union, jihadist since 2010), but looking at TE-SAT reports issued by EUROPOL since 2007, ethnic and nationalist organizations have been the main actors in terrorist incidents in the EU. Hence, recent European analyses, such as the reports from the International Center for Counter-Terrorism, point at Russia's support for racially or ethnically motivated violent extremism (REMVE), including cyber operations.[10] It is believed that Russia not only attempts to destabilize and fuel violence but also recruits individuals, both online and offline, to carry out attacks in NATO states. The annexation of Crimea in 2014 is perceived as a catalyst for far-right mobilization with the emergence of the phenomenon of far-right

---

9   Trevor McCrisken, "Ten Years on: Obama's War on Terrorism in Rhetoric and Practice",
      International Affairs 87, no. 4 (2011): 781–801, https://doi.org/10.1111/j.1468-2346.2011.01004.x.
10   Kacper Rękawek, *Foreign Fighters in Ukraine: The Brown-Red Cocktail*, (London; New York:
      Routledge Taylor & Francis Group, 2023).

foreign fighters traveling to conflict zones.[11] However, Western public opinion tends to perceive jihadism as the greatest threat it faces, often overlooking domestic separatist organizations, anarchist movements, left- and right-wing tensions, and the societal polarization (and further radicalization) potential in their own countries. The U.S. is believed to be the catalyst behind the threats emanating from the Middle East, while ignoring the entire spectrum of organizations, trends and individuals that have become radicalized in other political and social currents and pose a real threat to the security of other regions.

The problem of terrorism escalated with the increasing use of the internet as a communication tool. However, the relationship between technology and political violence has a long tradition. The spread of innovations has enabled ordinary individuals to access weapons of mass violence once controlled by states. Additionally, non-state actors are now capable of mass mobilization, force projection and systems integration, functions previously reserved for state militaries.[12] As a phenomenon, terrorism consists of various criminal acts; cyberspace is merely another platform for criminal behavior. Al-Qaeda, for instance, has used online tools to spread the call for jihad, creating a new unlimited mujahideen movement through digital libraries, platforms for radical preaching, networking hubs for radical discourse and others. The strategy of swarming has been adopted by other organizations as well. "[T]he Internet has come to serve as a choice means of communications outreach on the part of Al Qaeda and its regional affiliates, for its pronounced, digitalized multiplier effects on jihadist consciousness-raising, recruitment, training, fund-raising, and operational activities".[13]

The proliferation of jihadist ideology, in cyberspace too, is an example of the triumph of cognitive warfare over conventional methods. This phenomenon is evident in the Taliban's success in Afghanistan, the final withdrawal of American troops from the country in 2021 and the overall failure of the Global War on Terrorism following the 9/11 attacks. Non-state actors, in particular Al-Qaeda, have consolidated against the anti-terrorist coalition and expanded

---

11   Christian Kaunert, Alex MacKenzie and Sarah Léonard, "Far-Right Foreign Fighters and Ukraine: A Blind Spot for the European Union?", *New Journal of European Criminal Law* 14, no. 2 (2023): 247–66, https://doi.org/10.1177/20322844231164089; Claudia Wallner, "The Global Far Right and the War in Ukraine: Initial Reactions and Enduring Narratives" (Global Center on Cooperative Security, 2023), https://www.jstor.org/stable/resrep48741.

12   Audrey Kurth Cronin, *Power to the People. How Open Technological Innovation Is Arming Tomorrow's Terrorists* (Oxford: Oxford University Press, 2019).

13   Martin Rudner, "Electronic Jihad: The Internet as Al Qaeda's Catalyst for Global Terror", *Studies in Conflict & Terrorism* 40, no. 1 (2017): 11, https://doi.org/10.1080/1057610X.2016.1157403.

terrorist groups across various regions. This model was copied and developed by ISIS, which used online platforms to advocate globally for jihadism and fighting with crusaders. The strategic use of cyberspace and online platforms by violent extremist groups plays an important role in recruiting young people and minors.[14] Recruitment is facilitated through the spread of propaganda, the reinforcement of certain ideologies and identification of vulnerable individuals. The decentralized nature of the internet allows for anonymous access or dissemination of any content. Information spreads faster, in greater volumes, and in various designs with very little governmental control. The increase in the number of cyber users makes it possible for radicals and extremists to interact with an audience through cheap, flexible and user-friendly platforms regardless of traditional constraints of time and space.[15] The culture of terrorism exploits the basic values of the internet, namely freedom and equality, based on the assumption that everyone can participate. The information culture, fundamental for intercultural exchange, also fosters terrorism.[16]

Definitional problems and counterterrorism policies also influence how activities defined as terrorism in the cyber domain are interpreted. Cyber terrorism is typically classified as non-kinetic terrorism in the infosphere. However, psychological operations, which exhibit a violent nature, can also be conceptualized in this manner. Marco Marsili notes the existence of two prevailing definitions of cyber terrorism: "a very narrow definition of cyber terrorism, relating to deployment by known terrorist organizations of disruption attacks against information systems for the primary purpose of creating alarm, panic, or physical disruption, or a broader definition, which includes cybercrime".[17] The nature of terrorist activity, such as fundraising and recruitment, blurs the clear line between terrorism and other forms of crime. Political motivation should clearly separate these concepts, but it becomes problematic when examining the impact of drug cartels in Latin and South America, the criminal activities of oligarchs in Eastern Europe, or mafia operations in Southern Europe on the political world. If the defining feature of terrorism is the

---

14   Álvaro Vicente, "How Radicalizing Agents Mobilize Minors to Jihadism: A Qualitative Study in Spain", *Behavioral Sciences of Terrorism and Political Aggression* 14, no. 1 (2022): 22–48, https://doi.org/10.1080/19434472.2020.1800063.

15   Dounia Bouzar, Christophe Caupenne and Sulayman Valsan, "La Métamorphose Opérée chez le Jeune par les Nouveaux Discours Terroristes" (Lille: CPDSI, 2014).

16   Jonathan Matusitz, "The Role of Intercultural Communication in Cyberterrorism", *Journal of Human Behavior in the Social Environment* 24, no. 7 (2014): 775–90, https://doi.org/10.1080/10911359.2013.876375.

17   Marco Marsili, "The War on Cyberterrorism", *Democracy and Security* 15, no. 2 (2019): 173, https://doi.org/10.1080/17419166.2018.1496826.

cultivation of fear to achieve a desired psychological impact and political outcome, such as influencing authorities and their decision-making, then international crime organizations also exhibit such tendencies in certain regions. The lines between transnational criminal syndicates and terrorist groups are increasingly blurred as they learn from each other and adapt to changing conditions. The evolution of terrorism and organized crime is parallel, even though the academic discourse about these phenomena is separate. The historical focus on terrorism, particularly after the 9/11 attacks, has overshadowed concerns about organized crime. Terrorism and organized crime can intersect, overlap and create spaces where the boundaries between terrorism and mafia-style organized crime disappear. Moreover, terrorist organizations also tend to create illicit economies driven by both ideology and criminal administration. An example is the entire economy of the Islamic State, with its oil trade, slave trade, tribute, etc.[18]

The term cyber terrorism is commonly misused to describe any politically motivated activity prohibited by law. However, it specifically refers to acts of terrorism or organized crime that involve the use of digital technology, primarily the internet and computer systems, with the primary goal of causing widespread disruption, undermining the political order or causing significant harm to the collective interests of an authority, nation, state, or international organization. The goal is also to instill fear, anxiety and trepidation in the civilian population. The attacks are carried out by individuals, groups or state-sponsored entities driven by political, ideological, religious, or social motivations. Therefore, cyberterrorist acts are characterized by a teleological element that involves a political agenda aimed at altering the constitutional order or destabilizing a legitimately elected government. Cyber acts also contain an instrumental element, involving methods to spread terror in people's minds, typically through indiscriminate attacks with potential real-world consequences, such as threats to life, health or critical infrastructure. The choice of methods used in cyberterrorist operations depends not only on motives and resources but also the desired impact. They do not always target ICT systems, but may encompass broader activities such as financing, promotion of content inciting violence, recruitment and training.

Differentiating cyber terrorism from other forms of cyber attacks, such as cybercrime and hacktivism, can be challenging due to overlapping techniques

---

18   Patrick Blannin, "Islamic State's Financing: Sources, methods and utilization", *Counter Terrorist Trends and Analyses* 9, no. 5 (2017): 13–22.

and impacts.[19] The main difference lies in the motivation behind the attack and the intention to incite terror or significant societal disruption. Cyber terrorism is distinguished by its collective focus on national interests rather than individual targets and is organized in nature, involving structured groups with access to resources and the capacity to plan and execute operations over time. An act can be defined as cyber terrorism when it includes a clear connection to the violation or threat to the constitutional order, a demonstration of a political agenda and the potential for significant, widespread harm. As cyber terrorism poses a significant threat to national security, governments, law enforcement agencies and cybersecurity experts work diligently to prevent and respond to such attacks.

Recent research on cyber terrorism faces persistent challenges as already discussed above: conceptual ambiguity and a scarcity of uncontroversial instances of realized threats. Current literature often relies on analogical reasoning, exercises simulating consequences and speculative projections of future threats due to the absence of clear-cut cases. Some scholars explore worst-case scenarios, emphasizing potential gains for terrorists, while others adopt a more skeptical perspective, noting significant governmental attention to cybersecurity and the risk of threat exaggeration in this complex domain. A significant theme in contemporary scholarship is the examination of measures to counter cyber terrorism. Legal studies often focus on the regulation of internet technologies, considering challenges posed by varying national jurisdictions and the limitations of international law. Related research addresses the political challenges of global cybersecurity governance. At the micro-level, studies explore the preparedness and resilience of individuals, both as citizens and employees, to potential cyber attacks. However, discussions on enhancing individual computer security hygiene and awareness are recognized as more suitable for high-frequency, low-level incidents rather than the catastrophic scenarios often associated with cyber terrorism discussions. Another significant area of research is the feasibility of deterrence, especially in the face of the challenge of attributing attacks. Since some terrorist organizations persistently seek to use any means, including cyber attacks, deterrence efforts are crucial for policymakers and military planners.[20]

---

19   Dorothy E. Denning, "Activism, Hacktivism, and Cyberterrorism: The Internet as a Tool for Influencing Foreign Policy" (Global Problem Solving Information Technology and Tools, 2000), https://nautilus.org/global-problem-solving/activism-hacktivism-and-cyberterrorism-the-internet-as-a-tool-for-influencing-foreign-policy-2/.

20   Stuart Macdonald, Lee Jarvis and Simon M. Lavis, "Cyberterrorism Today? Findings From a Follow-on Survey of Researchers", *Studies in Conflict & Terrorism* 45, no. 8 (2022): 729–31, https://doi.org/10.1080/1057610X.2019.1696444.

Cyber terrorism produces political responses that differ from those generated by conventional terrorism. The distinction can be seen in the counter-terrorism policies and strategies implemented in countries affected by terrorist activity. The level of public support for retaliatory campaigns varies significantly depending on the type of terrorism experienced. Support for retaliatory attacks is notably lower among individuals who experience terrorist cyber attacks rather than conventional terrorist attacks, especially when the consequences of a cyber attack are not fatal. However, when cyber attacks result in fatalities, public support for retaliation is as high as it is for conventional terrorist attacks. Terrorist activities in cyberspace, especially brutal ones, may increase public support for restrictions on civil liberties and rights. Consequently, this could lead to amendments to counter-terrorism laws and strengthen the powers of agencies dealing with extremist groups. There seems to be a lethality threshold for the consequences of cyber terrorism, where the impact of an attack must reach a minimum level of destructiveness to elicit political responses comparable to those prompted by conventional terrorism. Comparative studies from the USA, UK and Israel reveal that the link between exposure to cyber terrorism and support for retaliation is mainly driven by anger. Exposure to terrorism generates an emotional response, which, in turn, propels political support for retaliation. This model suggests that anger, rather than fear or perceived threat, is the dominant variable linking political violence and militant attitudes. Terrorist attacks, including those in cyberspace, that directly violate norms on the use of force are particularly likely to provoke anger and, consequently, a desire for retaliatory attacks. While the threat may not be experienced personally, exposure to the event and knowledge about the victims significantly impact emotional states and directly affect the preference for retaliation.[21]

The key characteristics of cyber terrorism include the explicit intention to inflict significant harm, often on a large scale, by targeting critical infrastructure, financial systems, government institutions, or public safety. Broadly speaking, there is widespread consensus that technologically adept terrorists have shown remarkable adaptability in using online platforms, exploiting every new development, platform, and application to further their communicative and instrumental goals. Their online presence dates back to the late 1990s on websites, forums and chatrooms. Following the 9/11 attacks and subsequent antiterrorism efforts, many terrorist groups moved their operations to

---

21   Ryan Shandler et al., "Cyber Terrorism and Public Support for Retaliation – A Multi-Country Survey Experiment", *British Journal of Political Science* 52, no. 2 (2022): 850–68, https://doi.org/10.1017/S0007123420000812.

cyberspace, and they created a variety of websites to disseminate their messages and coordinate activities. When intelligence agencies, law enforcement and activists targeted and disrupted these websites, terrorist organizations started to use social media to spread propaganda, claim responsibility for attacks, issue calls to action, and solicit donations. For example, Al-Qaida had an official Twitter account created on 25 September 2013 under the handle @shomokhalislam in both English and Arabic. It was suspended after five days, after it was visited by over 3,000 people in this brief period. One of the most effective self-promoting organizations was Al-Shabaab. It operated a Twitter channel @HSMPress, which was frequently suspended and modified. Its activity served as an inspiration for other jihadi groups. The scale of online support for ISIS at the time the Islamic State was declared included approximately 90 000 accounts.[22] The X platform, more than Facebook, YouTube or Snapchat, is considered a significant public space that potentially amplifies the threats of terrorist propaganda dissemination and recruitment. X's popularity is due to its diverse functionalities, which support anonymous online identities, micro-blogging, sharing multimedia content, recruitment, and targeted messaging. Terrorist recruiters often engage in intimate communication designed to build relationships of complicity and friendship. They foster one-on-one dialogue with potential candidates to gradually introduce them to their new "brotherhood".[23]

Following the attacks in Europe in 2015 (the Charlie Hebdo Attack, Kosher Supermarket Siege, Bataclan Attack in Paris and the Copenhagen shootings) and 2016 (the Brussels Airport Bombing, Nice Truck Attack, and the Christmas Market Truck Attack in Berlin), repressive counter-strategies on social media were implemented. They mainly involved suspension or removal of accounts. Although a reduction in online activity was observed, suspensions were often interpreted by terrorist groups as oppression caused by their enemies and has become ingrained in the online identity of their followers as part of a historical pattern of aggression by "kuffar" (unbelievers) against Muslims. Rather than weakening pro-ISIS individuals, these actions often further strengthen their resolve. The ability to endure and recover from suspension is seen as a

---

22   J.M. Berger and Jonathon Morgan, "The ISIS Twitter Census Defining and Describing the Population of ISIS Supporters on Twitter", The Brookings Project on U.S. Relations with the Islamic World (2015), 9.

23   UNESCO, *School Violence and Bullying: Global Status Report* (UNESCO, 2017), 19–20, https://doi.org/10.54675/POIV1573; Elizabeth Pearson, "Online as the New Frontline: Affect, Gender, and ISIS-Take-Down on Social Media", *Studies in Conflict & Terrorism* 41, no. 11 (2018): 863, https://doi.org/10.1080/1057610X.2017.1352280.

manifestation of persistence and a symbol of the enduring spirit of the Islamic State – a celebration of resilience and defiance.[24]

Counter-radicalization efforts have encouraged terrorists to use other messaging applications such as Telegram, WhatsApp and Viber. Telegram hosts the channels of many internationally sanctioned terrorist organizations, including al-Qaeda, Hamas, Hezbollah, the Taliban, and ISIS.[25] YouTube, on the other hand, became an attractive platform for propaganda due to its video-promoting capabilities. It was widely used by many organizations, like Hezbollah, Hamas, the Tamil Tigers of Elam, and Shining Path.[26]

Social media differs from traditional media in terms of interactivity, reach, frequency, usability, immediacy, and permanence. It allows two-way communication, enabling anyone to publish or access information. The widespread availability of mobile and web-based networks creates highly interactive platforms that greatly increase the number of information transmitters. Terrorists are drawn to social media for several reasons. First, it is immensely popular with their target audience, which allows them to be part of the mainstream. Second, social media platforms are user-friendly, reliable and free of charge. Lastly, they enable targeted communication, which allows terrorists to reach specific segments of the public that share certain values, preferences, demographics, and beliefs. A targeted approach is instrumental in disseminating their messages directly to intended audiences.

Since 2014, terrorists and violent extremists have increasingly used popular social media platforms such as Facebook, YouTube, Twitter, and Instagram. They also engaged with online messaging apps such as WhatsApp and Telegram, explored new platforms like 4chan, 8chan and TikTok, used anonymous cloud storage, and navigated the Dark Net.[27] The phenomenon of live-streamed terrorism has shifted from traditional television channels to self-created narratives by terrorists on new media platforms. The transition involves the use of real-time video transmission across various channels, effectively amplifying the reach and impact of terrorist propaganda. Once a live stream is initiated, it can be shared, reposted and discussed across multiple platforms, reaching a far larger audience than traditional media could ever

---

24   Pearson, "Online as the New Frontline", 863.

25   "Terrorist on Telegram", The Counter Extremism Project, 2017, https://www.counterex tremism.com/terrorists-on-telegram.

26   Gabriel Weimann, "Terrorist Migration to Social Media", *Georgetown Journal of International Affairs* 16, no. 1 (2015): 180–87.

27   Gabriele Weimann and Roy Dimant, "The Metaverse and Terrorism: Threats and Challenges", *Terrorism and Counter-Terrorism Studies* 17, no. 1 (2023): 95, https://doi.org/10 .19165/ELIM4426.

achieve. Terrorist groups and individuals can now control their message and narrative without the mediation of traditional news outlets, allowing them to frame events in a manner that aligns with their ideological objectives and disseminate their propaganda more effectively. By simply using a GoPro camera during their actions, real-time broadcasts of violent acts are designed to maximize the psychological impact, spreading fear and panic among viewers. The assailant's attack may incorporate elements reminiscent of video games, such as live-streaming and first-person camera views, which create a virtual reality-like experience. The use of multiple weapons, music and erratic behavior during the attack mirrors popular video game themes and mechanics. The gamification of violence adds a surreal, game-like dimension to the real-life event.[28] The immediacy and graphic nature of live-streamed content can profoundly affect public perception and morale. Moreover, terrorists often employ elements of gamification to increase interactivity and participation among viewers. This can include real-time commentary, polls and the solicitation of viewer actions or responses, creating a sense of involvement and investment in the events that are being broadcast. Some terrorist organizations incorporate achievement systems akin to those found in video games. Participants may receive recognition, virtual badges or other forms of acknowledgment for their involvement, whether through spreading propaganda, contributing funds or engaging in acts of violence. Another gamification tactic is the creation of compelling narratives that allow individuals to adopt different roles. These narratives frequently depict terrorists as heroic figures, encouraging viewers to see themselves in similar positions and fostering a sense of identity and purpose aligned with the terrorist group's ideology. Additionally, live-streamed content often acts as a simulation and training tool for potential recruits. By broadcasting detailed accounts of attacks, including tactics and strategies, terrorist groups provide a virtual learning environment that can be used to educate and prepare future operatives. They have rapidly adopted the latest digital technologies, which suggests it is very likely that emerging spaces like the Metaverse will also be scrutinized, explored and potentially exploited. Terrorists have openly expressed their intentions to use platforms such as Facebook to disseminate content, mainly due to the ease with which they can reach large audiences. The user-friendliness and widespread popularity of social networks provides terrorists with an effective means to connect with their target audiences. Terrorists use tailored online pages, videos, chats,

---

28   Suraj Lakhani and Susann Wiedlitzka, "'Press F to Pay Respects': An Empirical Exploration of the Mechanics of Gamification in Relation to the Christchurch Attack", *Terrorism and Political Violence* 35, no. 7 (2023): 1593, https://doi.org/10.1080/09546553.2022.2064746.

images, and appeals to resonate with specific social groups, particularly targeting young people. The advent of social media technology offers technical advantages for terrorists, as modern smartphones and social media accounts are sufficient for sharing, uploading or downloading files and videos. They can instantly disseminate materials to large audiences in real time.[29]

The rapid development of AI technology has introduced new threats, as even non-tech-savvy terrorists can exploit AI in various ways. One significant area of concern is propaganda and media outreach. AI can create targeted content that optimizes messages and channels, effectively reaching larger groups potentially prone to radicalization. Moreover, advancements in deepfake technology allow terrorists to generate fake voice messages and other media that can be highly convincing and deceptive. Profiling potential sympathizers and members is another avenue where AI can be misused. By analyzing large datasets, terrorists can identify individuals who might be susceptible to their cause. This capability extends to recruitment and training, where visually appealing content in multiple languages can be produced to attract and indoctrinate new members. AI can also enhance data gathering and mapping of security systems, regulations, and vulnerabilities, thereby increasing logistical capabilities and facilitating more precise targeting. Furthermore, the weaponization of AI is particularly alarming. Terrorists can use AI to enhance cyber and physical attacks, including the design of weapons that can be 3D printed, as well as deploying advanced drones and autonomous vehicles.[30] Emerging technologies such as large language models (LLM s) like ChatGPT and Gemini are increasingly being used for online mobilization. They make it less costly to participate, lower the threshold for knowledge required for involvement, and empower small groups and individuals to commit crimes.

Generative Artificial Intelligence (GenAI) is being used for social engineering scams, disinformation, terrorist propaganda, and recruitment. Although many commercial tools have safeguards to recognize problematic content input, such as hate speech, terrorism and sexual assaults, they can be circumvented through techniques like prompt engineering and adversarial examples. Propaganda

---

29   Suraj Lakhani, "Video Gaming and (Violent) Extremism: An Exploration of the Current Landscape, Trends, and Threats" (Luxembourg: Publication Office of the European Union, 2021), https://home-affairs.ec.europa.eu/document/download/67db2a03-5b45-44f2-b0e9 -3b0544a08dfc_en?filename=EUIF%20Technical%20Meeting%20on%20Video%20 Gaming%20October%202021%20RAN%20Policy%20Support%20paper_en.pdf; Linda Schlegel and Rachel Kowert, eds., *Gaming and Extremism. The Radicalization of Digital Playgrounds* (London and New York: Routledge, 2024).

30   Katarzyna Maniszewska, *Towards a New Definition of Terrorism. Challenges and Perspectives in a Shifting Paradigm* (Cham: Springer, 2024), 74.

materials can be easily tailored to various age groups, ethnicities and individuals with varying levels of education and radicalization. Multiple messages can
be produced and adapted to diverse audiences in a relatively short time.[31] The
adoption of emerging tools, coupled with the emergence of lone wolf terrorism,
represents a significant trend. Lone wolf terrorism, in which the perpetrator
is not affiliated with any specific terrorist organization, is the fastest-growing
form of terrorism, especially in the West. Such attacks involve individuals
who have been radicalized, recruited, trained, and launched on social media
platforms.[32] However, AI also has significant potential for improving counter-
terrorism efforts.

Cyberterrorists use a wide range of "classical" cyber techniques, such as
hacking, distributed denial-of-service (DDoS) attacks, malware deployment,
and data breaches. Driven by political, ideological, or religious motivations,
cyberterrorists strive to advance their agendas, protest perceived injustices
or disrupt the operations of governments and organizations opposed to their
beliefs. The scope of cyber terrorism targets is extensive, ranging from government agencies and financial institutions to energy grids, transportation
systems, and healthcare facilities; essentially any organization whose disruption could have a significant societal impact. Apart from causing immediate
tangible damage, cyberterrorists also aim to create a profound psychological
impact by cultivating fear, mistrust and a pervasive sense of insecurity among
the general population. Additionally, cyberterrorists systematically employ
techniques to mask their identities and locations, which significantly complicates the efforts of authorities to attribute attacks to specific individuals or
groups. The deliberate obfuscation makes it even more complex to identify
cyberterrorists and hold them accountable.

Academic perspectives on cyber terrorism are diverse, reflecting varying
interpretations of the threat and differing opinions on whether incidents of
cyber terrorism have actually occurred. Evidence of this variability was found
in a research project led by Lee Jarvis, Stuart Macdonald, and Lella Nouri,
which analyzed academic views on cyber terrorism focusing on its definition,
perceived threat and response strategies. The study surveyed 118 researchers

---

31 UNICRI, *Algorithms and Terrorism: The Malicious Use of Artificial Intelligence for Terrorist
    Purposes. A Joint Report by UNICRI and UNCCT*, (Turin: United Nations Interregional
    Crime and Justice Research Institute, 2021), https://unicri.it/News/Algorithms-Terrorism
    -UNICRI-UNOCCT; Europol, *ChatGPT – The Impact of Large Language Models on Law
    Enforcement, a Tech Watch Flash Report from the Europol Innovation Lab* (Luxembourg:
    Publications Office of the European Union, 2023).
32 Gabriel Weimann, "Terrorist Migration to Social Media", *Georgetown Journal of Interna-
    tional Affairs* 16, no. 1 (2015): 181–82.

from 24 countries focusing on three main questions: (1) Is cyber terrorism a significant threat, and if so, against whom or what? (2) Has a cyber terrorism attack ever taken place? and (3) What are the most effective countermeasures, and are they different from traditional anti- or counterterrorism approaches? The findings showed a lack of consensus in the academic community regarding the threat of cyber terrorism, pointing to conceptual disagreements, definitional issues, and the contestability of the term itself. Despite these disagreements, the perceived threat of cyber terrorism is considered serious.[33] The study was revisited five years later, and both surveys revealed key aspects of cyber terrorism such as political/ideological motivation, the use of digital means or targets, and the intention to instill fear. Recent research has identified three noteworthy trends. First, there is a discernible shift towards greater agreement on the fundamental characteristics of cyber terrorism, despite ongoing conceptual disagreements. Second, there is an increasing concern among researchers about the cyber terrorism threat, which is seen as escalating, coupled with a recognition that such attacks may indeed have occurred. Thirdly, there is support for a range of countermeasures to address the threat, although there is a surprising lack of advocacy for extreme or draconian measures. One significant challenge in academic cybersecurity research remains the limited access to data,[34] which hampers the ability to conduct comprehensive studies and develop informed responses to cyber terrorism.

Cyberterrorist attacks, even non-lethal ones, can have profound psychological consequences for the people affected. A study by Michael L. Gross, Daphna Canetti and Dana R. Vashdi measured the fear of cyber terrorism among individuals, finding that exposure to such threats increases stress levels, threat perceptions and political militancy. The identity of the perpetrator influences people's attitudes, with attacks attributed to known terrorist organizations inciting greater fear and perceived threat. Additionally, they highlight the importance of addressing the human dimension of cyber terrorism, including risk communication, psychological intervention and cognitive behavioral therapy to mitigate anxieties induced by the attacks.[35] Overall, cyber terrorism can have significant psychological consequences that are comparable to conventional terrorism.

---

33   Lee Jarvis, Stuart Macdonald and Lella Nouri, "The Cyberterrorism Threat: Findings from a Survey of Researchers", *Studies in Conflict & Terrorism* 37, no. 1 (2014): 68–90, https:// doi.org/10.1080/1057610X.2014.853603.

34   Macdonald, Jarvis and Lavis, "Cyberterrorism Today?".

35   Michael L. Gross, Daphna Canetti and Dana R. Vashdi, "The Psychological Effects of Cyber Terrorism", *Bulletin of the Atomic Scientists* 72, no. 5 (2016): 284–91, https://doi.org/10.1080 /00963402.2016.1216502.

Taking into account the new challenges posed by cyberspace, it is worth mentioning that virtual economies are becoming alternative mechanisms of influence. Their rapid rise resulting from the advanced development of online games offers new opportunities to influence ideas, modes of operation, value hierarchies, and attitudes. Virtual economies offer mechanisms for building relationships based on benefits and boundless business prospects, also for terrorists. The challenge is to prevent the potential abuse of opportunities for money laundering and financing terrorism.[36] The Metaverse, with its reliance on cryptocurrencies and blockchain technology, introduces new challenges in combating the financing of terrorism. Terrorist organizations are looking for new methods of acquiring and transferring funds. Cryptocurrencies are one way to avoid financial oversight, especially when there is no consistent regulation in this area. Despite the risks associated with exchange rate volatility, the anonymity, ease and potential for immediate profit make cryptocurrencies appealing to terrorist groups.[37] The anonymity, immediate payment capabilities and cross-border transfers facilitated by cryptocurrencies raise concerns about their use in illicit activities in the Metaverse. It is difficult to trace transactions, so terrorist groups exploit financial opportunities, such as selling identity artefacts as non-fungible tokens (NFTs) for fundraising or engaging in online events to support extremism. Moreover, in the realm of financial terrorism, the cyberspace poses risks to traditional forms of financial cyber-crimes such as phishing and fraud scams, with cyber criminals using social engineering tactics to manipulate users and exploit their psychological vulnerabilities. Tactics such as "rug pulls", where developers abruptly abandon a cryptocurrency project and seize user funds, have become a threat, especially for investors. Furthermore, the potential misuse of fundraising campaigns and fake charity activities organized by terrorists and extremists adds another layer of concern. The dynamic interplay between state actors and online terrorists has evolved, with non-state actors playing a significant role on the virtual battlefield.[38] However, it is worth adding that terrorists do not have a monopoly on cyber attacks. Cyber criminals who use their own skills to destabilize, damage systems or steal data are an inhomogeneous group.

---

36   Annelieke Mooij, *Regulating the Metaverse Economy: How to Prevent Money Laundering and the Financing of Terrorism*, SpringerBriefs in Law (Cham: Springer Nature Switzerland, 2024), https://doi.org/10.1007/978-3-031-46417-1.

37   Seden Akcinaroglu and Moyan Shi, "Exploring the Impact of Cryptocurrency on Terrorism", *Terrorism and Political Violence*, 37, no. 1 (2023), 116, https://doi.org/10.1080/09546553.2023.2275057.

38   Weimann and Dimant, "The Metaverse and Terrorism", 100–101.

2   Cybercrime

Cases of cybercrime are on the rise worldwide. Attack scenarios are becoming increasingly technically sophisticated.[39] Advances in IT are also constantly changing the type and quality of the tools available for criminal activities. In addition, the techniques of anonymization, encryption and unlimited internet access greatly facilitate the proliferation of cybercrime. The darknet has encouraged and accelerated the emergence of criminal service providers in the form of "cybercrime-as-a-service" (CAAS). The accessibility and simplicity of cyber tools have contributed to the shift. As cybercrime has become exponentially profitable, hackers have found it more advantageous and less risky to sell their services. Consequently, the paradigm has shifted towards selling packaged CAAS, surpassing the direct commission of criminal acts.[40] Cybercrime has therefore evolved into a highly specialized and professionalized industry, where various services can be accessed easily through online platforms. Here, cyber criminals can buy, sell and exchange services and expertise so that even non-tech-savvy individuals can participate in cyber activities through simplified tools provided by these services. As a result, practically anyone can nowadays carry out cybercrime attacks. For instance, pay-per-install (PPI) services specialize in spreading malware through affiliates – individuals at the lower end of the cybercrime hierarchy who are responsible for actual malware distribution. They are paid per successful installation, which ties their income directly to their efficacy in spreading malicious software.[41] Ransomware-as-a-Service (RaaS) allows affiliates to use ransomware tools that are developed by more experienced hackers.

The increasing number of experts and novice malicious actors engaged in cyber criminal activities poses an ongoing challenge for governments and organizations. Cyber criminals flourish in nation-states where cybersecurity law enforcement is weak or where the government tolerates illegal activities. Since most cybercrime transcends international jurisdictions, the likelihood

---

39   Yuchong Li and Qinghui Liu, "A Comprehensive Review Study of Cyber-Attacks and Cyber Security; Emerging Trends and Recent Developments", *Energy Reports* 7 (2021): 8176–86, https://doi.org/10.1016/j.egyr.2021.08.126.

40   Thomas S. Hyslip, "Cybercrime-as-a-Service Operations", in *The Palgrave Handbook of International Cybercrime and Cyberdeviance*, eds. Thomas J. Holt and Adam M. Bossler (Cham: Springer International Publishing, 2020), 815–46, https://doi.org/10.1007/978-3 -319-78440-3_36.

41   Masarah Paquet-Clouston and Sebastián García, "On the Motivations and Challenges of Affiliates Involved in Cybercrime", *Trends in Organized Crime*, 2022, https://doi.org/10 .1007/s12117-022-09474-x.

of legal action is often low. Cyber criminals have incorporated data trading and ransomware into their arsenal. They rely on highly organized teams with technical expertise and specialized knowledge to execute criminal activities. The growing success of these operations perpetuates cybercrime as a sustainable business.[42]

Cybercrime is a broad term and there is no universally accepted definition. It is commonly understood to include all criminal offenses committed using or against information and communication technology. Cyberspace serves as a parallel world where real-world threats have also been transferred. The classification of cybercrime was formally discussed during the 10th UN Congress on the Prevention of Crime and the Treatment of Offenders in 2000. The framework, often used in law enforcement, distinguishes between two main categories: cybercrime in a narrow sense, often termed "computer crime," and cybercrime in a broad sense, referred to as "computer-related crime." The former includes crimes that directly target computer data and systems, such as data theft, hacking and denial-of-service attacks. The latter encompasses traditional crimes facilitated by digital technology, such as fraud, child exploitation and cyber bullying. Cybercrimes can involve any criminal acts conducted using electronic means or in an electronic environment.[43]

The Council of Europe's Convention on Cybercrime (ETS No. 185, also known as the Budapest Convention), the first international treaty on crimes committed via the internet and other computer networks, categorizes cyber-related offenses into four distinct titles for comprehensive legal handling. Title 1 addresses offenses against the confidentiality, integrity and availability of computer systems, detailing crimes like illegal access, interception, data interference, system interference, and the misuse of devices. Title 2 focuses on computer-related offenses, such as forgery and fraud, which involve manipulating computer data or systems for deceptive purposes. Title 3 refers to content-related offenses, specifically targeting the production and distribution of child pornography through digital means. Title 4 addresses offenses related to infringements of copyright and related rights.

---

42   Calvin Nobles, Sharon L. Burton and Darrell Norman Burrell, "Cybercrime as a Sustained Business", in *Advances in Information Security, Privacy, and Ethics*, eds. Festus Fatai Adedoyin and Bryan Christiansen (IGI Global, 2023), 104–6, https://doi.org/10.4018/978-1-6684-7207-1.ch005.

43   United Nations, "Tenth United Nations Congress on the Prevention of Crime and the Treatment of Offenders, Vienna 10–17 April 2000", 2000, https://www.unodc.org/documents/congress//Previous_Congresses/10th_Congress_2000/017_ACONF.187.10_Crimes_Related_to_Computer_Networks.pdf.

Cybercrimes are often categorized based on how computers are involved in the offenses, falling into three primary categories. First, "computer as a target" refers to crimes where the computer itself is the objective, such as in cases of hacking, malware distribution and denial-of-service attacks, where the aim is to infiltrate or damage information systems. Second, "computer as a weapon" involves using the computer as a tool to commit traditional crimes, including cyberstalking, phishing and fraud, often leading to identity or financial theft or spreading illegal content. Lastly, in the "computer as an accessory" category, the computer serves as a storage medium for illegal or stolen data, such as child pornography, details of criminal activities or data from unauthorized breaches.[44]

As of 2024, the most common cybercrimes worldwide include phishing, ransomware, non-payment/non-delivery, personal data breach, identity theft, cyber extortion, confidence fraud, tech support, investment, cyber espionage, and cryptojacking. Acts such as internet-based fraud, unauthorized acquisition of information (hacking), computer eavesdropping (sniffing), falsification of access to computer data, computer sabotage, dissemination of malicious programs, and cracking are criminalized and penalized. Furthermore, a separate category of offenses against public security includes acts that introduce danger to the life or health of many individuals, offenses against civil aviation, maritime trade, terrorist attacks, and unintentional interference with automatic information processing that leads to general danger, as well as attacks on critical infrastructure. Cybercrime involves activities such as hacking, data breaches, identity theft, and online fraud, categorized by using a computer as either a target or a weapon. Reasons for cybercrime include the capacity for compact data storage, easy accessibility, system complexity, negligence, and the potential loss of evidence. Methods of committing cybercrime range from unauthorized access and electronic information theft to email bombing, data diddling, salami attacks, denial of service attacks, virus/worm infections, logic bombs, Trojan attacks, internet time thefts, and web jacking. Cyber criminals vary from curious children and adolescents, to organized hackers with political agendas, professionals aiming for financial gain, and discontented employees seeking revenge.

Cybercrime has repercussions for individuals, businesses and societies. It manifests in various types of harm, including compromised assets, loss of

---

44   Ghulam Muhammad Kundi et al., "Digital Revolution, Cyber-Crimes And Cyber Legislation: A Challenge To Governments In Developing Countries", *Journal of Information Engineering and Applications* 4, no. 4 (2014): 62; Joshua B. Hill and Nancy E. Marion, *Introduction to Cybercrime: Computer Crimes, Laws, and Policing in the 21st Century* (Santa Barbara, CA: Bloomsbury Publishing USA, 2016), 57.

private data, tarnished reputation, increased costs of protection, lost sales, and disruptions in business operations. It can also negatively affect personal relationships, potentially causing long-lasting trauma to victims.[45] Increasing digitization is affecting all groups in society, including the most vulnerable – children. Among the risks with the most severe consequences are sexual exploitation and abuse. Cyberspace characterized by unlimited communication and a high degree of anonymity makes it possible for offenders to distribute child sexual abuse material (CSAM). Modern online communication technologies enable the live streaming of child abuse for financial gain. In the anonymous setting, children are often coerced or manipulated into producing exploitative material, which then circulates as a perverse form of currency.[46]

Preventive measures against cybercrime are essential to protect individuals and organizations from potential threats. They include the installation and regular update of antivirus and antispyware software, implementation of firewalls, application of cryptography for secure communication. It is also necessary to adhere to cyberethics and observe laws. Raising awareness about online security is another preventive measure that equips users with the knowledge and skills to minimize the risk of falling victim to cybercrime and encourage proactive behavior. Addressing the multifaceted nature of cybercrime requires a combination of technological solutions, legal frameworks, ethical considerations, and individual awareness to mitigate its impact on individuals, organizations and society at large.

3   Social Engineering

Social engineering is a set of techniques and strategies aimed at manipulating people in order to obtain information, influence their behavior or force them to take specific actions. The term, introduced in the 1920s, initially referred to methods of managing people in organizations. Over time, social engineering

---

45   Mihail Antonescu and Ramona Birău, "Financial and Non-Financial Implications of Cybercrimes in Emerging Countries", *Procedia Economics and Finance* 32 (2015): 618–21, https://doi.org/10.1016/S2212-5671(15)01440-9; Cecilia Cheng, Linus Chan and Chor-lam Chau, "Individual Differences in Susceptibility to Cybercrime Victimization and Its Psychological Aftermath", *Computers in Human Behavior* 108 (2020): 106311, https://doi.org/10.1016/j.chb.2020.106311; V Krishna Viraja and Pradnya Purandare, "A Qualitative Research on the Impact and Challenges of Cybercrimes", *Journal of Physics: Conference Series* 1964, no. 4 (2021): 042004, https://doi.org/10.1088/1742-6596/1964/4/042004.

46   Katarzyna Staciwa, "Wykorzystanie Seksualne Dzieci w Cyberprzestrzeni: Analiza Akt Postępowań Karnych ze Szczególnym Uwzględnieniem Roli Biegłych Powołanych w tych Postępowaniach" (Warsaw: NASK Państwowy Instytut Badawczy, 2023), 9–10.

has taken on new meanings, particularly in the context of information security, with the development of computer technology and the internet. Nowadays, social engineering also encompasses manipulative techniques criminals use to gain access to sensitive information such as passwords, financial data and personal information.

Christopher Hadnagy defines social engineering as "any act that influences a person to take an action that may or may not be in his or her best interest".[47] Therefore, social engineering in itself is neither good nor bad. Its ethical implications depend on the context in which it is applied, as it can serve various purposes.[48] Companies often use social engineering methods to test their own security systems. By simulating phishing attacks or fake breaches, they can evaluate the responsiveness of their staff and the effectiveness of their security protocols. Social engineering strategies can also be used to promote certain desirable behavior (e.g., encourage vaccination or healthy eating to benefit public health) or guide consumer behavior. Influencing an individual as a member of a particular social collective is crucial in the context of shaping public opinion, marketing and politics. In marketing, sociotechnical techniques are used to persuade consumers to purchase products or services. They use psychological mechanisms such as the rule of unavailability (the rarity of products increases their value) and persuasive techniques that influence brand and product perceptions.[49] Social engineering can motivate employees, build teams and manage conflict in human resource management. It uses techniques that influence employee commitment and loyalty by creating a sense of belonging and common purpose. In politics, social engineering shapes public opinion and influences election outcomes. Strategies of propaganda, disinformation and media manipulation can influence public attitudes and voting preferences, often without citizens being aware of it.

The most controversial and problematic uses of social engineering relate to cybercrime. Hackers and cyber criminals use sociotechnical techniques to break through security and access information systems and personal data. During a social engineering attack, the attacker uses social interactions and exploits human psychology rather than technical vulnerabilities to persuade

---

47   Christopher Hadnagy, *Social Engineering: The Science of Human Hacking* (Hoboken, NJ: Wiley, 2018), 7.

48   Hadnagy, *Social Engineering: The Art of Human Hacking*, 17.

49   Elliot Aronson and Anthony Pratkanis, *Age of Propaganda: The Everyday Use and Abuse of Persuasion. Revised Edition* (New York: Henry Holt and Company, 2001); Robert B. Cialdini, *Pre-Suasion: Channeling Attention for Change* (New York: Simon & Schuster, 2016); Robert B. Cialdini, *Influence, New and Expanded: The Psychology of Persuasion* (New York: HarperCollins, 2021).

the target to carry out a specific action such as opening a file or clicking a link. However, an attack may involve acquiring sensitive information about an organization, its activities or computer systems in order to infiltrate and compromise networks and systems. In more complex scenarios, content is crafted to draw the target into a situation that could lead to fraud or theft.[50] As a result, social engineering leads to significant financial, operational and reputational damage for individuals and organizations.

Social engineering attacks are a significant concern. Breaches involving social engineering and phishing are among the costliest, with social engineering attacks costing slightly less than malicious insider attacks but more than many other types of breaches. The average global cost of a data breach increased by 10% to USD 4.88 million, with social engineering being a significant contributor.[51] Specific social engineering attacks (excluding phishing) take 257 days on average to identify and contain. Phishing is the second most common attack, accounting for 15% of data breaches and had an average cost of USD 4.88 million.[52] Google blocks about 100 million phishing emails daily. In 2022, over half of phishing emails used '.com' domains, with '.net' as the next most common. Major domains targeted included Adobe, Google, and Weebly.[53]

Social engineering attacks can be categorized based on the entity involved, the method of execution, and the type of contact. When classified by the entity involved, attacks can either be human-based, involving direct interactions and manipulations like impersonation and pretexting, or software-based, where technical methods such as phishing and malware are used. In terms of method, social engineering attacks can be social, relying on personal interactions to deceive, technical, which exploit vulnerabilities in software or systems, or physical, where attackers gain unauthorized access through methods like tailgating and dumpster diving. Additionally, based on the contact type, attacks can be direct, requiring physical presence or face-to-face interaction, such as shoulder surfing and document theft, or indirect, where the attacker does not need to be physically present, as seen in phishing emails and ransomware

---

50   Michael Erbschloe, *Social Engineering. Hacking Systems, Nations, and Societies* (Boca Raton, Fl: CRC Press, 2020), 48–49.

51   IBM, "Cost of a Data Breach Report", 2024, 5, https://www.ibm.com/downloads/cas/1KZ3XE9D.

52   IBM, 5–6.

53   AAG, "The Latest 2024 Phishing Statistics (Updated June 2024)", 2024, https://aag-it.com/the-latest-phishing-statistics/.

attacks.[54] This comprehensive classification makes it possible to understand the various tactics used in social engineering to breach security.

Phishing attacks are the most common form of social engineering, where attackers attempt to fraudulently acquire sensitive information such as login credentials and financial details by masquerading as a trustworthy entity in electronic communications. Attacks often involve fake websites, emails or ads that prompt victims to reveal personal information. Variants include spear phishing, which targets specific individuals or groups by using personal information to make the attack appear legitimate. This approach often involves extensive research on the victim. Whaling is a form of spear phishing that targets high-profile executives or "big fish" in companies, aiming to steal sensitive business information. Vishing is voice phishing carried out over the phone, where attackers pretend to be from legitimate organizations to extract information. Interactive voice response phishing uses automated systems to trick victims into providing sensitive information as if they are interacting with a legitimate business.

Other social engineering attacks include pretexting, which involves creating a fabricated scenario to steal a victim's personal information. Attackers use believable pretexts to gain the victim's trust and obtain sensitive data. They may make phone calls, send emails or engage in in-person interactions, often using publicly available information or scenarios to enhance credibility. Baiting seduces victims with promises of free items or services to trick them into exposing personal information or installing malware. A common tactic is leaving infected USB drives in public places, hoping victims will plug them into their computers, triggering a malware infection. Tailgating, also known as piggybacking, entails an unauthorized person following an authorized individual into a restricted area. Attackers may ask victims to hold the door open, claiming they forgot their access card, or borrow devices to install malicious software. Next, ransomware encrypts a victim's data and demands a ransom for the decryption key. Attacks can cause severe financial damage, often more than the ransom itself, due to business interruption, loss of data and long-term operational impacts. Victims may have to choose between paying the ransom, attempting to restore data from backups or losing their data entirely. In reverse social engineering, attackers create a problem in a network or system and then pose as the only capable entity to resolve it. They first cause the issue, advertise their ability to fix it, and then exploit the situation to gain access to sensitive information. Other attacks involve malicious pop-ups that appear on

---

54   Fatima Salahdine and Naima Kaabouch, "Social Engineering Attacks: A Survey", *Future Internet* 11, no. 4 (2019): 89, https://doi.org/10.3390/fi11040089.

a victim's screen, prompting them to enter sensitive information or download malware. Pop-ups can mimic system alerts or enticing offers, tricking victims into reacting quickly and compromising their data. In phone or email scams, attackers contact victims via phone or email, often posing as legitimate entities, to extract specific information or manipulate them into breaking security protocols. Scams may promise prizes or request personal details under false pretenses. SMSishing, a variation of phishing conducted via text messages, is particularly effective due to the ubiquity of mobile phones. Robocalls involve automated phone calls delivering prerecorded messages to trick victims into providing information or performing actions. Attacks use voice over internet protocol (VoIP) to reach a large number of targets, often posing as legitimate service providers. Furthermore, attackers may pose as employees or authorities of help desk calls or network administrators to obtain information from help desks, usernames and passwords. They may collect sensitive information from discarded materials such as documents or old electronic devices (dumpster diving) or attempt to offer something desirable in exchange for information or access. Attacks may also involve redirecting deliveries to unauthorized locations (diversion theft), observing someone entering sensitive information (shoulder surfing) and redirecting web traffic to fake websites to steal information, often by exploiting vulnerabilities in DNS servers (pharming).[55]

Social engineering uses a sophisticated strategy involving multiple, nonlinear steps to ensure success. The initial phase, reconnaissance, involves collecting extensive information about the target. Attackers use a variety of methods, such as open-source intelligence, social media scrutiny, dumpster diving, and phishing, to gather data that typically includes details about the organization's structure, technological systems, employee roles, and communication patterns. Sensitive information helps identify potential vulnerabilities and key individuals that will be the targets of the attack. Hence, the next stage, the target selection process, involves identifying the individuals or groups who are most susceptible to exploitation. The following factors influence the decision: the roles and access privileges of potential targets, their psychological traits such as trustworthiness and susceptibility to manipulation and their relevance to the attacker's objectives. The next step, pretext development, entails crafting a believable and trustworthy persona or scenario to lower the target's defenses and increase their willingness to cooperate. The success of this stage depends on the attacker's ability to appear friendly and relatable, thus

---

55   Hadnagy, *Social Engineering: The Science of Human Hacking*; Salahdine and Kaabouch, "Social Engineering Attacks"; V. Ambika, H.L. Gururaj and V. Janhavi, *Social Engineering in Cybersecurity. Threats and Defenses* (Boca Raton, Fl: CRC Press, 2024).

easing the manipulation process. During the engagement phase, the attacker focuses on building rapport and trust with the target. Various manipulation techniques may be used to gain trust, maintain control over interactions and ensure the target remains oblivious to the underlying manipulative tactics. In the next phase, exploitation, the attacker manipulates the victim into performing certain actions, such as disabling security measures or accessing sensitive information. Alternatively, the attacker may discreetly extract further information through strategic questioning, active listening, and psychological manipulation, exploiting traits like reciprocity and authority. Finally, in the execution phase, the attacker uses the information or access obtained to launch a cyber attack. Therefore, they achieve their ultimate objectives while crafting an exit strategy that avoids detection by the target organization's cybersecurity defenses.[56]

Understanding the processes behind attacks is crucial for developing strong defensive measures. Regular and comprehensive training is the most effective strategy for recognizing and avoiding social engineering tactics, as educated individuals find it easier to identify early warning signs and potential manipulative indicators (the red flags of social engineering), thereby enhancing their ability to discern and resist attempts at manipulation. First, social engineers often create a sense of urgency to prompt quick decision-making without adequate reflection. Signs such as requests for immediate action, threats of negative outcomes or promises of exceptional rewards may suggest a manipulative intent. Second, attackers might impersonate authority figures like supervisors or trusted individuals to obtain compliance. Unusual or unexpected requests from these figures, especially those that bypass standard procedures, should sow suspicion. Third, social engineers typically engage in thorough information gathering to tailor their approaches and build credibility. Therefore, unsolicited requests for personal or sensitive information, particularly during casual conversations or friendly interactions, might indicate an attempt at social engineering. Fourth, inconsistencies in communications or requests, such as unusual email addresses, phone numbers or document discrepancies should raise doubt. Additionally, social engineers may communicate via unfamiliar platforms, social media or personal messaging instead of official channels in an attempt to evade security protocols and establish trust. Emotional manipulation is another tactic used to exploit feelings of empathy, sympathy or fear. Stories that evoke strong emotional responses, particularly those that seem disproportionate or overly dramatic, should be treated with

---

56   Cesar Bravo and Desilda Toska, *The Art of Social Engineering. Uncover the Secrets Behind the Human Dynamics in Cybersecurity* (Birmingham: Packt Publishing, 2023), 168–78.

caution. Unsolicited offers that promise significant rewards are also suspicious. Such offers are commonly used by social engineers to elicit information, make individuals perform specific actions or financial commitments without proper scrutiny. Furthermore, while not definitive, errors in grammar or spelling in communications may hint at a social engineering attempt as many cyber criminals originate from regions where different languages are spoken. Requests for sensitive information or financial details through unexpected channels should always be a red flag. Legitimate organizations typically adhere to established protocols for such requests. If something feels off or suspicious, it is wise to verify the details, seek second opinions or consult relevant authorities before acting. Social engineers rely on creating confusion, distractions or doubts to manipulate their targets. If a situation seems questionable, taking the time to verify the facts can prevent potential manipulation.[57]

Another crucial aspect of defensive strategies against social engineering attacks involves establishing and enforcing strong security policies and procedures. Using multi-factor authentication, secure communication protocols and clear procedures to verify identities can significantly mitigate the risk. Next, corporate guidelines for only sharing information with authorized parties should be implemented and executed. Finally, adopting AI and automation can enhance the speed of detection and response, potentially reducing both the costs and impact of breaches that result from social engineering.

4   Cyber War

Since the beginning of the 21st century, growing rivalry in the international arena has led to a reconfiguration of the global world order. The shift has been accompanied by a gradual increase in military expenditures by the major powers shaping global governance. Following a period of demilitarization in the first post-Cold War decade, international security has again been increasingly shaped by methods of force, which is demonstrated by successive Western military interventions: the 2008 Georgian war, Russia's annexation of Crimea and intervention in Donbas in 2014, followed by Russia's launch of a full-scale war against Ukraine in February 2022, and most recently, Israel's bloody pacification of the Gaza Strip after Hamas terrorist attacks on Israeli civilians. Furthermore, China's growing power is increasingly raising concerns in the

---

57   Bravo and Toska, *The Art of Social Engineering*, 181–82.

U.S. This concern is often described by the notion of the Thucydides Trap,[58] an ancient military concept suggesting an inevitable conflict between rising and established powers.[59] Not all rising powers inevitably come into conflict with established powers, and the Thucydides Trap is a cautionary concept rather than a deterministic prediction. Diplomacy, international cooperation and crisis management are key tools to avoid escalation and conflict. The nature of that rivalry will depend on how effectively superpower countries can navigate their relationships in the coming years. However, American neorealists, Kenneth Waltz and John J. Mearsheimer, predict a return to the old tried-and-true ways of competition by force in international politics under conditions of deepening anarchy.[60] The security dilemma is becoming topical anew,[61] accompanied by a growing sense of danger that a major war may occur. It arises from the fundamental challenges of uncertainty and lack of trust in the international system. It means that traditional patterns of power politics and the inevitability of war are being renewed.

The reconfiguration of the post-Cold War international order began when the U.S. waged a global "war on terror" following the 9/11 attacks. It was further accelerated by the global financial crisis and recession in 2008–2011, the Arab Spring, the Syrian civil war, and the COVID-19 pandemic. However, the threat of a major war between superpowers resurfaced in 2022 for the first time since the peaceful end of the Cold War when Russia launched an attack on Ukraine. The Russian–Ukrainian war saw the rapid evolution and dynamic nature of modern warfare, especially in cyberspace. It involved a wide range of state and non-state actors and created a complex and expansive battlefield with numerous ambiguous areas and emerging frontiers. Both countries involved in the conflict boast robust domestic IT industries and are renowned

---

58   Thucydides (*c.*460–*c.*400 BC) chronicled the Peloponnesian War between Athens and Sparta. He documented how the rise of Athens and the fear it instilled in Sparta led to a conflict that resulted in war. In modern geopolitics, the concept describes a situation where an established power (like Sparta) perceives a rising power (like Athens) as a threat to its dominance. The fear and competition between the two powers can escalate into a conflict, often with catastrophic consequences. As the rising power grows stronger, tensions rise and the established power may resort to measures to contain or counteract the rising power's influence. This can lead to a spiral of hostility and ultimately conflict.

59   Graham T. Allison, *Destined for War: Can America and China Escape Thucydides's Trap?* (Boston: Houghton Mifflin Harcourt, 2017).

60   Kenneth N. Waltz, "Structural Realism after the Cold War", *International security* 25, no. 1 (2000): 5–41, https://doi.org/10.1162/016228800560372; John J. Mearsheimer, *The Tragedy of Great Power Politics* (New York: Norton, 2001).

61   John H. Herz, "Idealist Internationalism and the Security Dilemma", *World Politics* 2, no. 2 (1950): 157–80, https://doi.org/10.2307/2009187.

as hubs for hackers, which further complicates the broader conflict. However, the Russian invasion of Ukraine has challenged existing theories about the role of cyber attacks in conventional warfare. Contrary to widespread expectations, cyber operations played a rather minor role in the initial stages of the invasion, generating various hypotheses and speculation to explain the limited cyber engagement. The constrained use of cyber attacks can be explained twofold: either Russia's attempts at cyber attacks were effectively countered, or Russia deliberately refrained from deploying them extensively.[62] Cyber war could become to the 21st century what Blitzkrieg was to the 20th, but as the example of Russian aggression has shown, we have not yet reached that stage. The cyber campaign against Ukraine has faltered and Russia's digital abilities have been overestimated. Despite the significant role of new technologies, such as AI-enabled systems of satellite imagery, drone footage, open-source data, facial recognition, transcription, and decoding systems, they do not determine victory per se. However, the ongoing war in eastern Europe illustrates what future wars might be like. It is a war fought on land in accordance with the strategy of war of Materialschlacht in which it boils down to the constant elimination of personnel, military equipment and economic resources. The arms industry, as traditionally understood, is still the basic element of victory. Emerging technologies, however, can affect battlefield outcomes. Their presence strengthens the position of new commercial actors in warfare, but they have not yet matched human "situational awareness".[63]

Attitudes regarding the impact of AI on warfare generally fall into three categories: enthusiasm, denial and pragmatism. The enthusiastic scenario argues that AI adoption will significantly reshape warfare, affecting its strategic, operational and tactical dimensions, and potentially even its fundamental nature over time. The distinct quality of AI, particularly its capacity to enhance autonomy across various military functions, is fueling expectations that technology could eventually supplant or augment human involvement in warfare. The pragmatic outline anticipates that while some changes will occur, they will likely be more modest and evolutionary rather than revolutionary. The denial perspective, on the other hand, contends that significant technical and organizational barriers will limit AI's impact, questioning its disruptive potential.

62   Kristen E. Eichensehr, "Ukraine, Cyberattacks, and the Lessons for International Law", *AJIL Unbound* 116 (2022): 145–49, https://doi.org/10.1017/aju.2022.20.

63   Alexander Kott, Norbou Buchler and Kristin E. Schaefer, "Kinetic and Cyber", in *Cyber Defense and Situational Awareness*, eds. Alexander Kott, Cliff Wang and Robert F. Erbacher, vol. 62, Advances in Information Security (Cham: Springer International Publishing, 2014), 29–45, https://doi.org/10.1007/978-3-319-11391-3_3.

Nonetheless, the prevailing sentiment among major military forces suggests that AI adoption will offer significant advantages to those who successfully integrate it, enabling superior decision-making, enhanced operational efficiency and effectiveness.[64] Relevant to these scenarios is the debate on lethal autonomous weapons systems (LAWS), particularly regarding the potential risk of nuclear operation.[65] The question of including a human in the loop in command-and-control systems is not always met with understanding, as evidenced by sessions of the Group of Governmental Experts (GGE) on Emerging Technologies in the Area of LAWS at the United Nations.[66]

The internet is an inferior substitute for conventional military force when it comes to achieving manipulation. Cyber war, by itself, cannot achieve conquest or coercion effectively. It often occurs in conjunction with conventional warfare or as a symbolic expression of dissatisfaction with an opponent. Cyber attacks alone are also unlikely to lead to a lasting shift in the balance of power unless they are accompanied by traditional military force or other actions. The main beneficiaries of cyber war are likely to be nation-states with established military prowess, rather than marginal groups or rising challengers. In this context, the internet is seen as an extension of existing international disparities in power and influence. In military strategy, tactical actions should align with strategic objectives, which, in turn, should align with overarching, grand strategic goals. When it comes to cyber war, there is no explanation regarding the internet's capability to serve as a stage for meaningful political conflict because it cannot function as the final arbiter of political differences in the way traditional physical violence has throughout history. Cyber war, while a growing concern, remains a relatively minor aspect of grand strategy.[67]

---

64 Erik Gartzke, "The Myth of Cyberwar: Bringing War in Cyberspace Back Down to Earth", *International Security* 38, no. 2 (2013): 72–73, https://doi.org/10.1162/ISEC_a_00136; Małgorzata Gawlik-Kobylińska and Marcin Rojek, "Artificial Intelligence in the Implementation of Didactic Principles in a Novel Mobility Platform: The Case of the eMediator Project", in *Reliability and Statistics in Transportation and Communication*, eds. Igor Kabashkin, Irina Yatskiv and Olegas Prentkovskis, vol. 913, Lecture Notes in Networks and Systems (Cham: Springer Nature Switzerland, 2024), 617–27, https://doi.org/10.1007/978-3-031-53598-7_55.

65 Austin Wyatt, "Examining Supply Chain Risks in Autonomous Weapon Systems and Artificial Intelligence", *Applied Cybersecurity & Internet Governance* 2, no. 1 (2023): 1–21, https://doi.org/10.60097/ACIG/162874.

66 The Group of Governmental Experts on Emerging Technologies in the Area of Lethal Autonomous Weapons Systems is a subsidiary body of the Convention on Certain Conventional Weapons (CCW).

67 Gartzke, "The Myth of Cyberwar", 72–73.

The insights gained from recent cyber warfare experience are already shaping the global understanding of cyber threats and are expected to be a prominent subject of study in cybersecurity for many years to come. Contemporary conflicts demonstrate the urgent need to establish and enforce international rules, not only for rare and very destructive high-impact cyber operations, but also for more frequent lower-level cyber activities that have consistently posed challenges, both in Ukraine and elsewhere.

5 Hybrid Warfare

To better understand the nature of modern conflicts, it is worth taking a closer look at the concept of new wars. According to Herfried Münkler, the new war economy (Ökonomie der neuen Kriege) emerged in the early 21st century and has primarily been associated with the breakdown or collapse of states. Münkler points out significant shifts in this evolution: transitioning from symmetrical confrontations among states to asymmetrical global power dynamics; shifting from national armies to increasingly private or commercial factions led by warlords, child soldiers, and mercenaries; moving away from traditional pitched battles to prolonged conflicts distinguished by minimal combat and predominant targeting of civilian populations. Changes in weapons technology, coupled with intricate economic factors, pose a tangible threat of perpetual simmering conflicts in the years ahead.[68] Contemporary conflicts tend to have a localized nature and are commonly orchestrated by non-state actors. However, they are typically influenced and overseen by more powerful actors that frequently engage private contractors. These conflicts are characterized by the diversity of actors involved with various combinations of state and non-state forces instead of regular armed forces; their goals based on identity politics; their methods supported by multiple tactics, such as guerrilla warfare and terrorism; and their innovative financing that links economics with the intention to wage conflict.[69]

Modern armed conflicts occur within a single state's borders rather than involving conflicts between different states. Moreover, they are situated against a backdrop of state collapse and societal changes fueled by globalization, the

---

68   Herfried Münkler, *Die Neuen Kriege. 6. Aufl.* (Reinbek bei Hamburg: Rowohlt, 2003).

69   Mary Kaldor, "In Defence of New Wars", *Stability: International Journal of Security and Development* 2, no. 1 (2013): 2–10, https://doi.org/10.5334/sta.at.

influence of liberal economic policies and rapid technological development.[70] Another distinguishing feature of contemporary conflicts is the privatization of war, which reduces and diversifies costs, disperses responsibility and weakens the state monopoly on violence.[71] Additionally, ethnic and religious disparities hold greater significance compared to political ideology. Civilian casualties and forced displacements increase significantly, mainly due to the deliberate targeting of civilians. The erosion of state authority in new wars blurs the line between individuals engaged in official state combat roles and private combatants.[72]

The relationship between politics and warfare has become increasingly complex as the nature of warfare is in a constant state of change. Today, warfare encompasses a wide spectrum of approaches. It may involve kinetic operations in combination with irregular military actions, as well as political and informational strategies aimed at destabilizing and weakening the targeted state to promote desired policies. On a global level, it involves disrupting or changing the international balance of power. In the context of hybrid warfare, political actors aim to introduce a state of global anarchy using a mix of both military strategies (such as irregular warfare, limited use of special forces, employing mercenaries and separatists) and non-military tactics (like shaping social attitudes, engaging in corruption, energy blackmail, propaganda, and using other political, diplomatic, social, psychological, and informational instruments).[73]

The concept of hybrid warfare was introduced by Frank Hoffman, who foresaw that the greatest threat was not conventional war or interstate conflict, but a type of conflict that constituted a peculiar mix of tactics and techniques. Blending them blurs the boundaries between conventional and unconventional warfare[74] and combines the lethality of interstate conflicts with fanaticism and prolonged fervor of irregular warfare to achieve political goals.[75] NATO defined hybrid threats in a communication dated August 25, 2010, as low-intensity

---

70 Antulio J. Echevarria, *Globalization and the Nature of War* (Carlisle, PA: Strategic Studies Institute, 2003).

71 Alex J. Bellamy, "Understanding and Regulating Contemporary War", *Australian Journal of Political Science* 42, no. 4 (2007): 704, https://doi.org/10.1080/10361140701689214.

72 Edward Newman, "The 'New Wars' Debate: A Historical Perspective Is Needed", *Security Dialogue* 35, no. 2 (2004): 173–89, https://doi.org/10.1177/0967010604044975.

73 Olga Wasiuta and Sergiusz Wasiuta, "Militarne i Niemilitarne Metody Prowadzenia Wojny Hybrydowej Rosji przeciwko Ukrainie", *Visnyk of the Lviv University. Series International Relations* 39, no. 3–17 (2016): 3–6.

74 Frank G. Hoffman, *Conflict in the 21st Century: The Rise of Hybrid Wars* (Arlington, VA: Potomac Institute for Policy Studies, 2007), 7.

75 Hoffman, *Conflict in the 21st Century*, 28.

threats that employ both conventional and unconventional means, depending on their objectives. They may include terrorism, piracy, organized crime, demographic challenges, resources security, retrenchment from globalization, and the proliferation of weapons of mass destruction.[76] The European Union's 2015 European Security Agenda identified hybrid threats and cyber terrorism as areas of growing concern requiring coordinated action. Subsequently, on April 6, 2016, a joint communication was issued to the European Parliament and the Council, which defined hybrid threats as "a mixture of coercive and subversive activity, conventional and unconventional methods (i.e., diplomatic, military, economic, technological), which can be used in a coordinated manner by state or non-state actors to achieve specific objectives while remaining below the threshold of formally declared warfare".[77] Hybrid warfare involves blending diverse methods of conflict to gain dominance in physical and psychological arenas through control of information and media. It employs various strategies to minimize vulnerability to undermine an adversary's resolve and weaken support for its legitimate authorities.[78] Additionally, a vast array of strategies can be combined or juxtaposed based on a nation's strategic culture, historical context, geographic conditions, and available economic and military resources. Hence, hybrid wars are complex and adaptable, as they do not adhere to a uniform template. They become elusive and increasingly challenging to define and operationalize.[79]

Hybrid warfare introduces complex dynamics to conflicts not only by using an extensive toolkit for undermining adversaries but also by enabling security challenges on many fronts simultaneously. The challenges are closely tied to their overarching objectives, which are not primarily aimed at the physical destruction of the enemy but rather its demoralization and asserting the aggressor's will over the citizens of the targeted nation. Such outcomes can be achieved by exerting the informational and psychological impact on individuals who are unprepared for a physical confrontation. Hybrid warfare employs various methods to weaken the opponent. It exploits contradictions such as ethnic, social, economic, and political divides in the targeted country. It also

---

76   NATO, "BI-SC Input for a New NATO Capstone Concept for The Military Contribution to Countering Hybrid Threats" (Brussels: NATO, 2010).

77   European Commission, "Joint Communication to the European Parliament and the Council. Joint Framework on Countering Hybrid Threats a European Union Response" (2016), https://eur-lex.europa.eu/legal-content/EN/TXT/?uri=CELEX%3A52016JC0018.

78   Guillaume Lasconjarias and Jeffrey A. Larsen, "Introduction: A New Way of Warfare", in *NATO's response to hybrid threats*, eds. Lasconjarias, Guillaume, Larsen, Jeffrey A. (Rome: NATO Defense College, 2015), 3.

79   Lasconjarias and Larsen, "Introduction: A New Way of Warfare", 3.

involves the use of "soft power" tools to disintegrate and influence the governance structures of enemy countries, effectively integrating them into the aggressor's sphere of influence. Hybrid warfare can be understood as a combination of battle spaces, types of operations – military or non-kinetic – and a blurring of actors with the scope of achieving strategic objectives by creating "exploitable ambiguity".[80]

Understanding hybrid warfare therefore offers key insights into the evolution towards hybrid threats, pointing at the range of aggressive measures in international relations. Hybrid warfare and hybrid threats represent two phases or perspectives of the same phenomenon.[81] Hybrid warfare concerns active actions taken by one actor against another actor. On the other hand, hybrid threats are passive, representing real or imagined threats of possible future actions. If hybrid threats are not detected and analyzed in time, the threshold between hybrid threats and hybrid warfare will be crossed. Threatening hybrid operations, which do not constitute hybrid warfare, can succeed if the opponent is intimidated enough to change political course or react in a harmful way to itself.[82] Similar to hybrid warfare, a variety of methods can be employed as hybrid threats, such as traditional capabilities, unconventional strategies, terrorist attacks with random violence and coercion, and criminal disorder.[83] The progressive growth of such threats is fostered by the deregulation of the liberal international order, globalization, the development of modern technologies, the evolution of the information and communication space, the nature of contemporary armed conflicts, and generational and cultural changes. A recognized range of hybrid tools does not limit the aggressor to their use alone.

The unpredictability and complexity of actions in hybrid warfare make it challenging to mount effective defenses against them. New threats are constantly evolving and have reached a stage where they differ significantly from the methods and capabilities seen in traditional and irregular conflicts. Nathan Freier labels emerging threats as high-end asymmetric threats (HEAT), as they rely on advanced technologies that hinder defense capabilities and

---

80   Rory Cormac and Richard J. Aldrich, "Grey Is the New Black: Covert Action and Implausible Deniability", *International Affairs* 94, no. 3 (2018): 490, https://doi.org/10.1093/ia/iiy067.

81   Mikael Weissmann, "Hybrid Warfare and Hybrid Threats Today and Tomorrow: Towards an Analytical Framework", *Journal on Baltic Security* 5, no. 1 (2019): 18, https://doi.org/10.2478/JOBS-2019-0002.

82   Olga Wasiuta, "Zagrożenia Hybrydowe", in *Vademecum Bezpieczeństwa Informacyjnego. Tom 2*, eds. Olga Wasiuta and Rafał Klepka (Kraków: Uniwersytet Pedagogiczny im. Komisji Edukacji Narodowej w Krakowie, 2019), 639.

83   Hoffman, *Conflict in the 21st Century: The Rise of Hybrid Wars*, 8.

disrupt the functioning of the state.[84] They also reveal weaknesses in the defensive strategies of democratic states, whose legal structures, traditions, ethos, or organizational cultures may not adequately address the dynamic security architecture and its threats. Nation-states, while strong, may lack the agility and adaptability of non-state adversaries. Success in conflict depends on their ability to adjust, innovate and navigate evolving threats effectively. In contrast, authoritarian states excel in using a wide range of resources and tools to project threats precisely, often facilitated by strong political leadership. Democratic states, on the other hand, face challenges in defending against the multifaceted and potentially extensive violence of hybrid threats due to their limited defense capabilities.[85]

Hybrid threats have been redefined, particularly due to the evolution of cyberspace. The cyber domain has become a new battleground where non-state transnational actors engage in asymmetric activities that challenge the modern security architecture. Hybrid operations in cyberspace cover a broad spectrum of activities that impact all aspects of integrated society, ranging from cyber attacks on critical infrastructure to social or sectarian threats, where internet and social media users may become passive witnesses or victims. The use of such operations gives a competitive edge to those who deploy them. Hybrid operations are also carried out to shape narratives desired by the aggressor. Activities bearing the hallmarks of cognitive warfare[86] are carried

---

84   Nathan Freier, "Hybrid Threats and Challenges: Describe ... Don't Define", *Small Wars Journal*, 2009.

85   Artur Gruszczak, "Hybrydowość Współczesnych Wojen – Analiza Krytyczna", in *Asymetria i hybrydowość – stare armie wobec nowych konfliktów*, eds. Witold Sokała and Bartłomiej Zapała (Warsaw: Biuro Bezpieczeństwa Narodowego, 2011), 17.

86   Cognitive warfare is an advanced and unconventional form of warfare that targets the cognitive abilities of populations and individuals to influence, manipulate and disrupt decision-making processes. This approach blends psychological, information and cyber operations. It uses the latest advancements in artificial intelligence and machine learning to extend its influence globally across both military and civilian sectors. The primary goal of cognitive warfare is to alter perceptions of reality, exploit mental biases and heuristics to achieve strategic objectives. Unlike traditional forms of warfare, the cognitive impact is the key objective rather than a secondary by-product (Bernard Claverie and François du Cluzel, "The Cognitive Warfare Concept" (Innovation Hub Sponsored by NATO Allied Command Transformation, 2022), https://innovationhub-act.org/wp-content/uploads /2023/12/CW-article-Claverie-du-Cluzel-final_0.pdf; D. Pappalardo, "'Win the War before the War?': A French Perspective on Cognitive Warfare" (War on the Rocks, 2022), https:// warontherocks.com/2022/08/win-the-war-before-the-war-a-french-perspective-on -cognitive-warfare/; Yvonne R. Masakowski and J.M. Blatny, "Mitigating and Responding to Cognitive Warfare" (NATO Science and Technical Organization, 2023). Cognitive warfare acts as a form of advanced propaganda that uses manipulated media to instill and

out as part of planned special operations against various actors in international relations. They are designed to influence, modify or distort perception and are primarily centered on influencing opinions, attitudes and behavior. Their objective is to capture attention, evoke or manipulate emotions, establish a particular "false" perspective as genuine and induce individuals to make decisions or behave in ways desired by the adversary. In addition to employing classical mechanisms of influence like diplomacy or economics, psychological manipulation is used as an effective tool to achieve desired outcomes such as fragmenting national unity, exacerbating polarization, fostering frustration that can lead to aggression, and undermining trust in one's own representatives. To attain specific objectives in cognitive warfare, a combination of cyber, informational, psychological, and socio-technical tools is deployed simultaneously. The internet and social media platforms serve as primary conduits for these operations.

The implications of hybrid warfare are multifaceted and can profoundly impact a nation across various domains. One of the most serious threats is the potential overthrow of governmental systems, which represents a severe threat to national security. This danger is compounded by the potential of various cyber incidents that could precede physical warfare and lay the groundwork for further conflict. Furthermore, beyond immediate security concerns, hybrid operations can severely damage a country's international reputation and its diplomatic relationships. The destruction or tarnishing of a nation's image on the global stage can have far-reaching consequences that lead to strained political and economic relations with other countries. Such repercussions may extend to human casualties and threats to public health and safety, which exacerbates internal chaos and disrupts the administration of the state. Malicious digital activities also have the capacity to undermine public confidence in governmental institutions and to erode trust in established religious, national and ethnic beliefs. The erosion of societal foundations further compounds the challenges faced by a nation in the aftermath of a cyber assault.

Hybrid warfare can profoundly impact national economies by using a variety of economic tools and strategies that destabilize a country's stability and development, such as energy dependence manipulations, exploitation of

---

perpetuate conflicting narratives for political or military purposes. The goal is to make people either overly trust or completely ignore certain information. Cognitive warfare strategically manipulates perceptions and exploits cognitive biases to cloud judgment and influences actions potentially fracturing societies and disrupting strategic alliances (Marco Marsili, "Guerre à la Carte: Cyber, Information, Cognitive Warfare and the Metaverse", *Applied Cybersecurity & Internet Governance* 2, no. 1 (2023): 1–11, https://doi.org/10.60097/ACIG/162861).

foreign trade vulnerabilities, and disruptions in human capital. These actions can affect multiple areas of resilience, including the military and logistics infrastructure crucial for both economic development and military operations.[87] For instance, a country's reliance on foreign aid or trade can be manipulated to coerce political concessions or influence policy decisions. The economic superiority of a hybrid aggressor amplifies the impact as it enables the aggressor to dictate terms and conditions that align with its strategic interests, often at the expense of the targeted nation's autonomy and economic health.[88] The efficiency of economic coercion points at the profound implications of economic dependencies on national sovereignty and development.

Economic tools are increasingly integrated with cyber operations. The ease of executing cyber attacks, their low cost and perceived minimal risk, makes them appealing for nations aiming to further their foreign and security policy objectives. The extensive destruction or disruption of vital cyber assets undermines the functionality of critical infrastructure, leading to widespread economic turmoil and instability. The cascading effects of cyber incidents magnify their impact too, converting a single cyber event into a sequence of widespread disruptions across various sectors. Compromising a nation's power grid, for example, could incapacitate traffic systems and disrupt emergency services. Hence, a single cyber attack may trigger extensive logistical disruptions well beyond the initial cyber intrusion. The domino effect not only escalates the initial harm but also poses significant risks to public safety and the broader economy.[89] As cyber tactics become more sophisticated, so does their potential for physical destruction. Their disruptive power could be compared to conventional military forces (even though critical infrastructures, particularly in large market economies, are more distributed, varied, redundant, and capable of self-repair, which makes them less susceptible to sustained damage).[90]

---

87   Maria Constantinescu, "Measuring Economic Resilience for the CEE and Black Sea Countries in the Framework of Comprehensive Defense", *Security and Defence Quarterly* 44, no. 4 (2023): 56; 63–64, https://doi.org/10.35467/sdq/175379.

88   Khayal Iskandarov and Piotr Gawliczek, "Economic Coercion as a Means of Hybrid Warfare: The South Caucasus as a Focal Point", *Security and Defence Quarterly* 40, no. 4 (2022): 50–51, https://doi.org/10.35467/sdq/151038.

89   Greg Simons, Yuriy Danyk and Tamara Maliarchuk, "Hybrid War and Cyber-Attacks: Creating Legal and Operational Dilemmas", *Global Change, Peace & Security* 32, no. 3 (2020): 4, https://doi.org/10.1080/14781158.2020.1732899.

90   James A. Lewis, "Assessing the Risks of Cyber Terrorism, Cyber War and Other Cyber Threats" (Center for Strategic and International Studies, 2002), 2; Myriam Dunn Cavelty, "Is Anything ever New? – Exploring the Specificities of Security and Governance in the Information Age", in *Power and Security in the Information Age*, eds. Myriam Dunn Cavelty, Victor Mauer and Sai-Felicia Krishna-Hensel (Aldershot: Ashgate, 2007), 139.

Addressing the complex challenges posed by hybrid threats is crucial for safeguarding national security and preserving the stability of nations in an increasingly interconnected world.[91] The response to hybrid threats must occur at multiple levels. First, there is the need for monitoring and assessing threats to enhance situational awareness. Centers for countering hybrid threats have been established worldwide (e.g., the European Centre of Excellence for Countering Hybrid Threats) to examine the application of hybrid strategies and contribute to the development of new concepts and technologies. Such initiatives are essential for bolstering member states' resilience against evolving threats. Building the resilience of critical infrastructure is paramount, hence it is essential to fortify energy networks, transportation and supply chains as well as the space domain. Strengthening defense capabilities, ensuring public health protection and food security are equally crucial. Financial systems must also be robust and capable to counter the financing of hybrid threats effectively. Efforts to build resilience against radicalization and violent extremism are also essential, as is strengthening cooperation with third countries and improving collaboration with NATO. Strategic communication also plays a vital role in countering hybrid threats. Monitoring both traditional media and online platforms is a proactive approach that enables the swift detection and mitigation of disinformation and narratives aimed at manipulating political discourse, destabilizing society and fostering radicalized attitudes.

---

91   Li and Liu, "A Comprehensive Review Study of Cyber-Attacks and Cyber Security; Emerging Trends and Recent Developments", 8177.

CHAPTER 3

Information Warfare and Disinformation: a Modern Challenge

The proliferation of digital communication tools has given rise to sophisticated forms of information warfare and disinformation campaigns. In this chapter, we argue that traditional cybersecurity approaches need to be reevaluated to address not only conventional cyber threats but also strategic information manipulation. Information warfare has evolved dramatically, with an extensive range of technologies now available to disrupt communication, influence public opinion, destabilize nations, and undermine trust in democratic institutions. Information operations often involve the manipulation of narratives, where truth and falsehood blend to shape public discourse. The proliferation of disinformation has become a potent tool that exploits the rapid dissemination capabilities of social media and takes advantage of vulnerabilities in the information ecosystem. This allows both state and non-state actors to influence electoral outcomes, disrupt economic stability and fuel unrest.

1   A Human-Centered Approach to Information Warfare

In today's digital age, the constantly changing field of cybersecurity and information warfare presents numerous challenges and opportunities. As our dependence on digital technology continues to grow, so does the complexity and sophistication of cyber threats and tactics for information manipulation. Information warfare involves the manipulation of information to influence opinions, disrupt societies and undermine trust. To effectively defend against threats and protect our digital world, it is imperative to adopt a human-centered approach that places people at the core of cybersecurity and information warfare strategies.

Information warfare refers to the use of information, disinformation, fake news, strategic leaks, and communication technologies to gain a strategic advantage in various domains, including military, political, economic, and social. It encompasses a range of tactics and strategies aimed at influencing the perceptions, beliefs and behavior of individuals, groups or nations. Key actors in information warfare may include governments, military organizations, non-state actors, or individuals, and it often operates in the realm of cyberspace and the media. However, one of the challenges in information warfare is the difficulty of attributing specific attacks or campaigns to particular actors. Attackers often employ anonymity techniques to conceal their identities and origins. The scale of manipulation, disinformation and information operations that target public opinion in democratic states is critical to the stability of societies and nations. The main objective of using information warfare is to influence social perceptions, i.e., how society or social groups perceive reality. The consequences of information manipulation can lead to panic, a hardening of positions on pressing social issues, a loss of trust in state institutions, and the creation of false senses of security or threats. Additionally, it can compel public authorities to take or refrain from specific actions. This impact is not limited to cyberspace, but includes political, economic, military, and non-military spheres. It can influence elections, political discourse and decision-making processes. In military contexts, information warfare may include efforts to mislead or deceive an adversary about one's intentions or capabilities. Thus, disinformation campaigns are not an ultimate goal but rather a means used to achieve broader political or financial objectives, much like cyber attacks that use malware, viruses and social engineering techniques to penetrate security systems.

Disinformation presupposes the existence of two sides in a conflict, where one (the aggressor) attempts to mislead the recipient by disseminating information that appears true but is in fact distorted or even false and harmful. The aim is to persuade the recipient to make decisions that are beneficial to the actor spreading disinformation. The presentation of information to the public and the monitoring of its dissemination are expected to influence social behavior with seemingly spontaneous reactions. The construction of an alternative reality is facilitated by undermining the credibility of authorities and the press as well as by multiplying various channels of information, including the spread of fake news through social media by political entities. These activities are inherently offensive because they serve an informational purpose and are intended to manipulate public perception. In contrast, when the message fosters community consolidation and ensures the integrity of the entity, it is defensive in nature. Attempts to persuade individuals or groups to adopt certain opinions and attitudes are persuasive and often complement the implementation of a disinformation operation.

Distorted information, when deliberately used against a specific entity or state, can be linked to other hybrid warfare tactics. Ambiguity can hinder the timely recognition of these threats. Information warfare typically involves the dissemination of false or misleading information to shape public opinion, create confusion or sow discord. Disinformation exploits human emotional vulnerabilities, cognitive biases and a general reluctance to critically analyze the incoming information. Trust is not a reliable guide in evaluating information because it is based on instinct. Instead, verification should be based on certain intellectual standards, knowledge, experience, data accuracy, reliability of the source, and adherence to scientific criteria. To effectively counter "post-truth", it is essential to understand its dynamics.[1] The objectivity of information is confronted with contradictory facts. Propaganda techniques, which use psychological vulnerabilities, are frequently employed to advance a particular narrative or agenda. These tactics often target the media, social media platforms and fake news websites to control narratives or spread disinformation. They can also involve the manipulation of search engine results.

Another aspect of information warfare involves manipulating economic data, trade policies or financial markets to gain an advantage in international trade or geopolitical rivalry. Disinformation shapes public awareness and influences sentiment. It can be a prelude to other activities, including those with political implications. It is a simpler tool than direct political or economic interventions. These activities can sow emotions, diversify opinions and change attitudes. Furthermore, cyber attacks are also carried out to disrupt or compromise the functioning of critical infrastructure, communication systems and government or military networks. Common methods include hacking, distributed denial-of-service (DDoS) attacks and malware deployment.

Information warfare can have far-reaching consequences, including destabilizing governments, undermining public trust, exacerbating conflicts, and impacting international relations. As technology continues to advance, the methods and tactics employed in information warfare are likely to evolve, making it an area of ongoing concern and study in the fields of cybersecurity, geopolitics and international relations.

The human-centered approach to cybersecurity and information warfare recognizes that technology alone cannot provide foolproof protection against threats. In a flurry of information, individuals seek security, understood as certainty, by choosing explanations that are consistent with their existing views and experiences. Modifications must not disrupt the comfort zone known as the ideological bubble. This tendency is fostered by a growing reluctance to engage in critical analysis when faced with an overwhelming amount of information, which hinders the ability to distinguish true information from false and leads to multiplying opinions and interpretations rather than facts. Traditional authority figures are being devalued, a trend supported by the rise

---

1   Lee McIntyre, *Post-Truth* (Cambridge, MA: The MIT Press, 2018), https://doi.org/10.7551/mit press/11483.001.0001.

of unreliable journalism and the proliferation of "experts" among celebrities, vloggers and bloggers. Consequently, public trust in content producers and information transmitters is evolving. These trends facilitate the intentional dissemination of crafted information, which enables anyone to participate and share information. On the one hand, individuals and grassroots movements find it easier to challenge established narratives and bring new perspectives to the forefront. On the other hand, it makes the internet susceptible to manipulation and the spread of misinformation. People searching for information among the multitude of sources available may accept certain information as true without objectively verifying its accuracy. The internet, by its very nature, is anarchic and allows an unrestricted flow of information without a gatekeeper to dictate what can or cannot be shared. Nevertheless, the internet also provides a platform for fact-checking, citizen journalism and the exposure of falsehoods. Social media platforms and news websites have integrated fact-checking mechanisms, which can help users discern what information is true. The collective efforts of internet users to debunk and expose disinformation have revealed many falsehoods. Moreover, various organizations and initiatives, both governmental and non-governmental, are actively working to combat disinformation by promoting media literacy and providing tools to identify unreliable sources. Collaboration with major tech companies makes it possible to further limit the spread of fake news. However, these efforts are inadequate given the potential for spreading post-truth.

Moreover, promoting media literacy and critical thinking skills is crucial in the fight against disinformation and fake news. Educating individuals on how to evaluate the credibility of information sources and question their content helps build resilience against information warfare. Furthermore, individuals should be empowered to control their digital footprint and privacy. Education in data protection and privacy practices empowers individuals to defend against information warfare tactics such as doxing[2] or social engineering.

---

2   Doxing (the term derives from the alternate spelling of 'docs', short for documents) is the act of publicly revealing personal data on an individual or group on the internet, most frequently addresses, phone numbers, email addresses, and information about family members, which can lead to harassment, stalking and vilification. It may be done as a means of seeking justice against perceived immoral or unfair behavior, exposing wrongdoing or for malicious purposes (Peter Snyder et al., "Fifteen Minutes of Unwanted Fame: Detecting and Characterizing Doxing", in *Proceedings of the 2017 Internet Measurement Conference* (IMC '17: Internet Measurement Conference, London: ACM, 2017), 432–44, https://doi.org/10.1145/3131365.3131385; Briony Anderson and Mark A. Wood, "Doxxing: A Scoping Review and Typology", in *The Emerald International Handbook of Technology-Facilitated Violence and Abuse*, eds. Jane

Governments, social media platforms and news organizations play key roles in information warfare. A human-centered approach involves holding these entities accountable for their actions and their decisions related to content moderation and information dissemination. Transparency and accountability are essential. The sharing and distribution of information allows citizens to oversee the government's performance. Enhanced transparency reduces information asymmetries and enhances public trust in politicians.[3] Furthermore, it ensures adherence to ethical standards, which prevents the abuse of power and mitigates the manipulation of information.

2   Disinformation

The widespread dissemination of false information is a significant global challenge that affects the public sphere and profoundly influences both public discourse and individual perceptions on various topics, from healthcare to politics. It is by no means a modern phenomenon as deception and deliberate spreading of falsehood have been used to an individual's advantage since the beginning of time. However, the rise of digital media has significantly accelerated the spread of disinformation campaigns and the circulation of fake news due to a combination of factors such as the ease of publishing, its broad reach, and the absence of effective gatekeeping mechanisms that traditionally ensured the reliability and credibility of information. Social media platforms have not only enabled an exponential increase in the volume of false news stories but also amplified their societal and individual impacts. They provide the infrastructure necessary for conducting effective disinformation campaigns through the use of fake accounts and bots, which can be inexpensively acquired online. In 2024, a network of fake accounts or engagements could be purchased for just a couple of dollars. The legality of such transactions makes these services easy to access. The availability of platforms like Facebook on the Tor network also supports anonymous interactions, further enabling the covert dissemination of false content.

Disinformation is a deliberate and systematic process of disseminating false or manipulated information designed to achieve political or economic

---

Bailey, Asher Flynn and Nicola Henry (Bingley: Emerald Publishing Limited, 2021), 206–7, https://doi.org/10.1108/978-1-83982-848-520211015).

3   Javier Cifuentes-Faura, "The Role of Accountability and Transparency in Government during Disasters: The Case of Ukraine–Russia War", *Public Money & Management*, 2023, 1–10, https://doi.org/10.1080/09540962.2023.2243131.

advantage while causing harm to the public. The European Commission defines disinformation as "verifiably false or misleading information that is created, presented and disseminated for economic gain or to intentionally deceive the public, and may cause public harm".[4] The European Parliament resolution from 23 November 2016 draws attention to the complex nature of disinformation campaigns, whose primary purpose is:

> distorting truths, provoking doubt, dividing Member States, engineering a strategic split between the European Union and its North American partners and paralysing the decision-making process, discrediting the EU institutions and transatlantic partnerships, which play a recognised role in the European security and economic architecture, in the eyes and minds of EU citizens and of citizens of neighbouring countries, and undermining and eroding the European narrative based on democratic values, human rights and the rule of law; ... one of the most important tools used is incitement of fear and uncertainty in EU citizens, as well as presenting hostile state and non-state actors as much stronger than they are in reality.[5]

The resolution points out that disinformation campaigns employ a wide range of strategies and tools to manipulate public opinion and undermine trust in democratic institutions. The tactics include using social media platforms and digital networks for rapid and targeted dissemination of false content as well as exploiting algorithms to amplify divisive narratives. In this process, the identity of the entity spreading the content and its underlying purpose are concealed.[6] A common method in spreading disinformation involves creating narratives that blend truths with lies or misleading conclusions.[7] Although disinformation might contain elements of truth, it is ultimately designed to mislead and

---

4   Claire Wardle and Hossein Derakhshan, *Information Disorder: Toward an Interdisciplinary Framework for Research and Policy Making* (Strasbourg: Council of Europe, 2017); European Commission, "Communication on Tackling On-line Disinformation: A European Approach", COM(2018)236 (2018), https://eur-lex.europa.eu/legal-content/EN/TXT/?uri=CELEX%3A5 2018DC0236.

5   European Commission, Communication on Tackling On-line Disinformation: A European Approach.

6   Manipulation of information is a specific form of propaganda, often termed "black propaganda" for its concealed motives and deliberately misleading content (Garth S. Jowett and Victoria O'Donnell, *Propaganda and Persuasion* (Thousand Oaks, CA: Sage, 2019).

7   Wardle and Derakhshan, *Information Disorder: Toward an Interdisciplinary Framework for Research and Policy Making*.

persuade audiences to accept a fabricated story. Disinformation strategies may also involve presenting facts taken out of context or combined with false information to achieve the disinformers' covert objectives. Fake news websites and pseudo-news agencies mimic legitimate news outlets and publish fabricated or biased information to mislead audiences. Additionally, automated bots and organized troll farms manipulate online discussions, create an illusion of consensus or popularity for specific viewpoints. Emerging technologies like deepfakes generate highly realistic yet entirely false images or videos, which further blur the line between truth and falsehood. Disinformation operations also manipulate search engine results to increase the visibility and perceived legitimacy of misleading content. Direct messaging and email campaigns also deliver false information directly to individuals, capitalizing on personal trust networks.

Fake news, defined as a single media post or item containing incomplete, false or misleading information, is a common tool in disinformation campaigns. The concept overlaps with misinformation, i.e., the inadvertent spread of false information, and malinformation, and the deliberate dissemination of true information with the intent to cause harm. Fake news mirrors misinformation through its false or manipulated content and resembles malinformation in its purposeful distribution to cause public harm. It also takes various forms depending on the strategies used in its creation, the sender's intentions, the degree of content falsification, the sender's objectives, its content and function, and distribution channels.

To summarize, disinformation is characterized by several key criteria. First, the content is either false or deliberately misleading. However, disinformation does not necessarily comprise entirely fictitious content; rather, it frequently involves selectively manipulated information mixed with factual elements. The blend of manipulated and true information makes it challenging to distinguish disinformation from authentic content. Second, disinformation usually concerns matters of public interest and is strategically disseminated to sow uncertainty, escalate tensions, incite hatred, and undermine democratic processes.[8] Thirdly, the dissemination process is systematic, using mass media channels to reach wide audiences.[9] Fourthly, the true identity of the entity

---

8 Judit Bayer et al., "Disinformation and Propaganda – Impact on the Functioning of the Rule of Law in the EU and its Member States" (Brussels: European Parliament, 2019), https://www.europarl.europa.eu/RegData/etudes/STUD/2021/653633/EXPO_STU(2021)653633_EN.pdf.

9 Vladimir Volkoff, *Dezinformacja: Oręż Wojny* (Warsaw: Delikon, 1991); Rubén Arcos, Irena Chiru and Cristina Ivan, eds., *Routledge Handbook of Disinformation and National Security* (Abingdon and New York: Routledge, 2024).

behind disinformation often remains concealed, which makes it difficult to trace and counteract these campaigns.

Building on this understanding, Eleni Kapantai et al.[10] have developed a framework for analyzing disinformation through three key dimensions: facticity, verifiability and motivation. Facticity assesses the extent to which content is based on factual accuracy, spanning from entirely factual to completely fabricated. This dimension is crucial for evaluating the truthfulness and reliability of information. Verifiability refers to the ability to confirm or validate information against credible sources, highlighting the crucial role of transparency and the challenge of distinguishing authentic from deceptive content. Motivation examines the intent behind disseminating information, whether for financial gain, ideological influence or psychological manipulation. Together, these dimensions provide a comprehensive tool for understanding and categorizing disinformation. Given its complexity and multi-layered nature, a nuanced and multi-faceted approach is necessary to address the challenges of misleading information and its impact on public discourse. The facticity – verifiability – motivation framework facilitates targeted interventions and enhances the capacity to mitigate the effects of disinformation by examining its content, authenticity and underlying motives.

3 The Viral Spread of Disinformation in Democratic Societies

Disinformation has proliferated in democratic societies due to a complex interplay of social, political and media factors. The problem has intensified with technological advancements and the evolution of the media as social networking sites have significantly changed how information is disseminated and consumed. However, various socio-political factors also play a critical role in the dissemination of disinformation. First, the spread of disinformation often starts with political actors, including state entities and individual politicians or political parties, who spread biased, incomplete or unverified information in order to shape the narrative and serve their political agenda.[11] In the post-truth

---

10 Eleni Kapantai et al., "A Systematic Literature Review on Disinformation: Toward a Unified Taxonomical Framework", *New Media & Society* 23, no. 5 (2021): 1301–26, https://doi.org/10.1177/1461444820959296.

11 Edda Humprecht, Frank Esser and Peter Van Aelst, "Resilience to Online Disinformation: A Framework for Cross-National Comparative Research", *Resilience to online disinformation: A framework for cross-national comparative research* 25, no. 3 (2020): 493–516, https://doi.org/10.1177/1940161219900126.

political culture, emotional tone is more important than factual accuracy. News content is primarily crafted to attract attention and its informative function takes a secondary role. As a result, narratives are created, and detailed explanations are minimized. Critical debate cannot be easily encapsulated in a concise format of a post or tweet; therefore, it often becomes replaced by more sensational content. This shift not only degrades the quality of debates and reduces rational thinking, but also contributes to a weakened societal structure where citizens distrust political elites and the media. Additionally, polarization in society, fueled by populist leaders[12] who appeal to popular emotions, makes citizens prone to accept information that confirms their biases and reject or ignore opposing views. Social media algorithms further amplify the dissemination of sensational and unreliable information. They prioritize engaging content over accuracy and prefer news that triggers strong emotional reactions. As a result, people become enclosed in echo chambers, where individuals are predominantly exposed to information that aligns with their worldview, reinforcing and amplifying their beliefs.

Another key factor responsible for dissemination of disinformation is the change in media consumption habits. The decline in trust in traditional media and the growing role of the internet as a primary source of information have contributed to the increased influence of digital content. However, this content is often dominated by sensationalism and a profit-driven model, where 'clickbait' content is designed to attract attention regardless of its quality. Increased entertainment and tabloidization of media and public discourse turns the user into a passive consumer of information who prefers light and enjoyable content over more substantial news. Most social media users access social platforms for entertainment rather than information, which reduces

---

12   Populism often consolidates power around leaders presented as infallible. It blends truth with falsehoods to reinforce existing biases and strengthen support. It strategically uses disinformation to target perceived enemies and maintain power, disregarding democratic norms. Such narratives are typically propagated by alternative media platforms that proliferate, particularly in right-wing circles. These platforms focus on contentious issues like immigration and climate change denial and promote conspiracy theories and fake news. The credibility and popularity of such narratives increase when they are endorsed by influential figures or the media, thus legitimizing a post-truth environment where misinformation is not only widespread but also weaponized to support populist agendas (H. Tumber and Silvio Waisbord, "Media, Disinformation, and Populism. Problems and Responses", in *The Routledge Companion to Media Disinformation and Populism* (Abingdon-on-Thames: Routledge, 2021). Furthermore, populist leaders distrust experts, and are convinced of the existence of a conspiracy directed against them and the ideology they support. Therefore, they frequently accuse the media of spreading fake news.

their willingness to critically evaluate news sources.[13] Overreliance on social networking sites leads to a general reduction in political knowledge as users interact more with misleading or shallow content.[14] Many users do not verify the accuracy of information they encounter because they are not particularly interested in the topics discussed. However, this lack of interest does not protect them from falsehoods and manipulation. Even a casually read, manipulated headline skimmed while scrolling through content can subconsciously influence a person's decisions and attitudes.

The shift in media consumption habits can be partly attributed to the decline in the traditional media's business model and the change in revenue generation strategies. Digital advertising is more profitable with easily digestible, cheap, and highly clickable content as advertisers pay per view and click and individual content creators are incentivized to create and disseminate fake news for financial gain. This phenomenon is well-documented, including a case where Macedonian teenagers translated Russian fake news into English and disseminated it on American websites[15] and where individual citizens published false information for profit.[16] As a result, disinformation is not only more accessible but also more appealing to social media users, who may spread it further, motivated by profit.

The decline of the traditional media business model has also led to reduced investments in investigative journalism. This transformation has weakened the role of journalists as gatekeepers of factual information. The rapid cycle of news production and the pressure to continuously publish new content is further hindering journalists' ability to verify information adequately, which contributes to the spread of disinformation. On social media, algorithms have taken over the role of gatekeepers, controlling the flow of information. At present, algorithms are responsible for content selection, but they may not be sufficiently effective in filtering out false information. As a result, quite a lot of unverified information keeps circulating in the public space. Algorithms also

---

13   Nic Newman et al., *Reuters Institute Digital News Report 2017* (Oxford: Reuters Institute for the Study of Journalism, 2017).

14   Adam Shehata and Jesper Strömbäck, "Learning Political News from Social Media: Network Media Logic and Current Affairs News Learning in a High-Choice Media Environment", *Communication Research* 48, no. 1 (2018): 125–47, https://doi.org/10.1177/00936 50217749354.

15   Samanth Subramanian, "Inside the Macedonian Fake-News Complex", 2017, https://www.wired.com/2017/02/veles-macedonia-fake-news/%0A.

16   Kalia White, "Report: Drug Mixing Killed Fake-News Writer Paul Horner", *USA Today*, 2017, https://eu.usatoday.com/story/news/nation-now/2017/12/06/report-drug-mixing-killed-fake-news-writer-paul-horner/928412001/.

tend to prioritize sensational, controversial or emotionally charged content that is likely to generate more user engagement. A feedback loop is hence created: the more a news item is shared, the more it is promoted by the algorithm. It becomes even more visible and further influences public perception and conversation. This dynamic can overshadow more important but less sensational topics and reduce the diversity of information and viewpoints in the public sphere.

At the same time, the waning dominance of traditional media as the main source of information and the falling circulation of print media has forced media companies to cut costs and explore new revenue methods. To enhance cost-efficiency, the preparation time for news has been significantly shortened and the convergence of media platforms has increased. These changes have reduced the diversity and independence of media outlets, which are essential for fostering informed civic attitudes and sustaining democracy. Public media, weakened by insufficient funding and continuous government oversight, struggles to broadcast critical information on national and global issues. Poorly informed media coverage affects the level of societal knowledge and the interpretation of reported issues, thereby increasing the public's susceptibility to persuasive influences. A society with lower political awareness and knowledge is more vulnerable to manipulation and disinformation. Time pressures and the need to continuously publish new content also make it difficult for journalists to verify every piece of information thoroughly, which can lead to manipulation and disinformation. Insufficient funding of public media outlets and substantial government control over a large part of this sector have significantly affected the quality of media content.[17] As a result of competition in the media market, newsrooms are forced to cut jobs. In such circumstances, a single journalist often covers topics across multiple sectors, and due to the overload of information, there is no time to verify their sources.[18] Consequently, mass media outlets, including reputable opinion-forming news agencies, publish fake news that is either generated by journalists, politicians and social media users or reprinted from other sources (such as statements from institutions, information agencies or other mass media). The main goals are, on the one hand, to attract the attention of readers and encourage them to click on links

---

17   Cherilyn Ireton, "Truth, Trust and Journalism: Why it Matters", in *Journalism, Fake News & Disinformation. Handbook for Journalism Education and Training*, eds. Cherilyn Ireton and Julie Posetti (Paris: United Nations, 2018), 35.

18   Public Dialog, "Raport: Fake News z Perspektywy Polskich Dziennikarzy", 2017, http://pub licdialog.home.pl/www_logotomia/wp-content/uploads/2018/07/Raport_Badanie-fake -news-23-05-2017.pdf.

leading to publications, and on the other hand, to attract as many advertisers as possible who wish to run their informational and promotional campaigns in specific media outlets.

Social media's popularity means that many individuals now acquire knowledge about the world from platforms where anyone can publish content, and the virality of information depends more on how often it is shared rather than its accuracy. In social media environments where algorithms play the role of gatekeepers, false information spreads more rapidly and widely than truthful content.[19] Users are overwhelmed with trivial, unwanted, unreliable, and low-value messages. Information overload can impair users' decision-making abilities and their capacity to identify reliable content. The changing media landscape has altered audience behavior too. A fragmented media aims to reach specific interest groups. Smaller audience clusters that typically consist of like-minded individuals are less likely to challenge false information or incorrect interpretations. Ultimately, a general decline in media trust, partly due to societal malaise, has made people more vulnerable to disinformation

---

19   False information tends to spread more extensively – farther, faster, deeper, and to more people – than true information. This finding contradicts common assumption that network structures and user characteristics favor the truth (David M.J. Lazer et al., "The Science of Fake News", *Science* 359, no. 6380 (2018): 1094–96, https://doi.org/10.1126/SCIENCE.AAO2998; Soroush Vosoughi, Deb Roy and Sinan Aral, "The Spread of True and False News Online", *Science* 359, no. 6380 (2018): 1146–51, https://doi.org/10.1126/SCIENCE.AAP9559; Erik C. Nisbet and Olga Kamenchuk, "The Psychology of State-Sponsored Disinformation Campaigns and Implications for Public Diplomacy", *The Hague Journal of Diplomacy* 14, no. 1–2 (2019): 65–82, https://doi.org/10.1163/1871191X-11411019). In fact, posts containing false information reach one hundred times more people than those about true events (truth rarely reaches more than 1000 users, while the most viral fake news has been received by up to 100,000 internet users). This phenomenon can be attributed to several factors. First, the novelty of false information attracts attention by providing new or controversial insights. False news also evokes stronger emotional responses, particularly surprise and disgust, driving greater user engagement and sharing. Additionally, false information exhibits higher structural virality, spreading extensively through peer-to-peer sharing rather than just via direct broadcasts, which allows it to penetrate deeper into social networks. Human behavioral tendencies further amplify this spread, as people are more inclined to share sensational or emotionally charged misinformation. Consequently, false information cascades are characterized by rapid diffusion, reaching vast numbers of users quickly and outpacing true information, often before factual corrections can be made. The rapid spread of false information creates complex challenges to mitigate the spread of misinformation on social media platforms (Vosoughi, Roy and Aral, "The Spread of True and False News Online").

as they turn to alternative media sources, including social media platforms,[20] which are less regulated and more prone to spreading false information.

The dissemination of disinformation in the media is a pressing concern, as shown by recent findings from a Pew Research Center survey of journalists. A significant number of journalists express concern over potential restrictions on press freedoms, reflecting broader anxiety about the environment in which they operate. Many journalists frequently encounter false information, yet a large number acknowledge having unintentionally propagated misinformation themselves. This indicates a troubling gap in their ability to manage false content effectively. Although journalists are generally confident in their ability to recognize false information, the survey reveals that most news organizations are ill-equipped to handle disinformation and they often lack formal policies or guidelines. Another problem is false statements made by public figures. Journalists must decide whether to report falsehoods or ignore them to avoid amplification.[21] These dynamics illustrate the complex challenges that newsrooms face in combating disinformation and point to the need for more robust mechanisms and strategies in the media industry to safeguard information integrity.

Mass media plays a crucial role in disseminating information, shaping public opinion and supporting a healthy democracy. However, when information is not verified, false narratives not only reach a vast audience and affect public opinion, but also erode trust in the media itself. Herein lies the critical role of journalists: to verify information sources, debunk disinformation and reliably inform the public. Regardless of the motives behind the publication of false, unreliable or biased information, the consequences are severe. Fabricated content can threaten public safety, disrupt global financial markets, incite hatred, stigmatize social groups, reinforce stereotypes and prejudices, sow chaos and social unrest, and ultimately undermine trust in the media and weaken democratic structures.

---

20   Michael Hameleers, Anna Brosius and Claes H. de Vreese, "Whom to Trust? Media Exposure Patterns of Citizens with Perceptions of Misinformation and Disinformation Related to the News Media", *European Journal of Communication*, 2022, https://doi.org/10.1177/02673231211072667.

21   Jeffrey Gottfried et al., "Journalists Highly Concerned about Misinformation, Future of Press Freedoms" (Pew Research Center, 2022), https://www.pewresearch.org/journalism/2022/06/14/journalists-highly-concerned-about-misinformation-future-of-press-freedoms/.

4   The Human Factor in Disinformation

Misinformation and disinformation thrive in the digital space because it is eagerly spread by individual social media users. The appeal of false and manipulated news is often due to its novelty and emotional impact, which tends to attract more user attention than less sensational but truthful information.[22] Furthermore, emotionally charged content can impair rational processing and encourage sharing by engaging intuitive, reactive thought processes rather than reflective ones.[23] This means that fake news designed to provoke shock or outrage is more likely to spread virally. Social media users frequently share shocking or dramatic stories to grab attention and get reactions from their friends. This creates a loop where the most attention-grabbing, but untrue, information gets shared the most. Consequently, false beliefs are reinforced, which hurts our ability to find the truth. Therefore, falsehoods diffuse faster, farther and more deeply across social networks than factual content,[24] which leads to a phenomenon called the "tyranny of trends" where the most popular or trending topics dominate public discourse, often at the expense of more nuanced or accurate information.[25] Therefore, individual preferences for engaging content significantly contribute to the viral spread of mis- and disinformation. Factors such as user personality, beliefs, and cognitive and emotional mechanisms play a key role in increasing the organic reach of falsehoods.

Certain personality traits such as extraversion, agreeableness, conscientiousness, neuroticism, and openness to experience correlate with different social media behavior patterns, affecting the spread of disinformation. Extraverts with large social networks may have a greater impact on information dissemination as they are more likely to be exposed to a variety of viewpoints, including those that are false or misleading. Those who are organized and conscientious are more likely to engage with political content. Reflective individuals with highly developed analytical skills make fewer mistakes in assessing the veracity of information, as these traits increase resistance to the influence of heuristics

---

22   Vosoughi, Roy and Aral, "The Spread of True and False News Online"; Sinan Aral, *The Hype Machine* (New York: Currency, 2020).

23   Cameron Martel, Gordon Pennycook and David G. Rand, "Reliance on Emotion Promotes Belief in Fake News", *Cognitive Research: Principles and Implications 2020 5:1* 5, no. 1 (2020): 1–20, https://doi.org/10.1186/S41235-020-00252-3; Gordon Pennycook and David G. Rand, "The Psychology of Fake News", *Trends in Cognitive Sciences* 25, no. 5 (2021): 388–402, https://doi.org/10.1016/J.TICS.2021.02.007.

24   Vosoughi, Roy and Aral, "The Spread of True and False News Online".

25   Aral, *The Hype Machine*.

and cognitive biases.[26] Conversely, those who are neurotic are more likely to post on social networking sites frequently,[27] whereas people open to new experiences often share a wider variety of content. They are more capable of changing their beliefs under the influence of rational arguments, which makes them less susceptible to fake news.[28] Belief in conspiracy theories and intuitive thinking reduce the ability to recognize false information.[29]

Gordon Pennycook and David G. Rand[30] argue that individual susceptibility to mis- and disinformation is influenced by several cognitive and social factors. Cognitive factors encompass personal beliefs, cognitive abilities and reliance on heuristic processing. A lack of critical or analytic thinking skills can increase vulnerability to disinformation as people might accept misleading information at face value, particularly when it aligns superficially with pre-existing biases or appears plausible. This is compounded by cognitive biases, such as cognitive dissonance, where individuals experience discomfort when they encounter information that contradicts their beliefs. To reduce this discomfort, they often reject contradictory information in favor of that which confirms their preexisting beliefs. This selective attention can significantly distort perception, leading to the reinforcement of false beliefs through the confirmation effect and skepticism towards conflicting information (the denial effect). Repeated exposure to the same false statements can increase their perceived truthfulness – a phenomenon known as the illusory truth effect. This effect is based on a heuristic where familiarity with content (regardless of its factual accuracy) leads to increased belief in it. Additionally, the credibility of the source from which news is received significantly influences the likelihood that people will believe it. Information from a source perceived as authoritative or trustworthy is more likely to be believed, even if it is false.

Social factors also play a crucial role in sharing and falling for misinformation. One significant social factor is the role of group identity and partisanship. Individuals tend to align their beliefs and the news they consume with their

---

26 Gordon Pennycook and David G. Rand, "Lazy, not Biased: Susceptibility to Partisan Fake News is Better Explained by Lack of Reasoning than by Motivated Reasoning", *Cognition* 188 (2019): 39–50, https://doi.org/10.1016/J.COGNITION.2018.06.011.

27 Jeffrey A. Hall, Natalie Pennington and Allyn Lueders, "Impression Management and Formation on Facebook: A Lens Model Approach", *New Media & Society* 16, no. 6 (2013): 958–82, https://doi.org/10.1177/1461444813495166.

28 Klaudia Rosińska, *Fake News. Geneza, Istota, Przeciwdziałanie* (Warsaw: PWN, 2021), 157–58.

29 Viren Swami et al., "Analytic Thinking Reduces Belief in Conspiracy Theories", *Cognition* 133, no. 3 (2014): 572–85, https://doi.org/10.1016/J.COGNITION.2014.08.006.

30 Pennycook and Rand, "The Psychology of Fake News".

political identity, which leads to selective exposure where people prefer information that reinforces their pre-existing beliefs (the confirmation effect). This alignment not only makes them susceptible to misinformation that supports their views but also makes them resistant to information that contradicts their ideological stance (the denial effect). Another crucial aspect is the influence of social networks. People are more likely to believe and share information that seems popular or that has been endorsed by others in their social circle. Social media platforms facilitate the formation of highly polarized communities where users mainly interact with like-minded individuals. Echo chambers reinforce and amplify misinformation through repeated exposure (the illusory effect) and social endorsements (such as likes and shares), which makes false information look more credible.[31]

The impact of social norms and the desire for social approval also play a key role in the dissemination of information. People often share content that they believe will garner approval or enhance their status in their social groups, regardless of the content's accuracy. Fake news is often perceived as more novel than the truth, which makes it more appealing to users who want to appear well-informed or having access to inside information (the novelty hypothesis). This social currency aspect of information sharing can drive the spread of fake news, as the desire for social validation often trumps the commitment to truth.[32]

All in all, the spread of disinformation is a complex interplay of social, cognitive and emotional factors where personal biases, media consumption habits, and network dynamics play crucial roles. Altogether these factors create fertile ground for misinformation, manipulated through both intentional disinformation campaigns and algorithmic gate-keeping[33].

5   State-Sponsored Propaganda and Disinformation Based on the Example of Russia

Repressive governments, despite their differences, commonly share key strategies to maintain power: they restrict electoral processes, limit freedom of

---

31   Pennycook and Rand, "The Psychology of Fake News".

32   Aral, *The Hype Machine*; Sinan Aral, "The Changing Face of Russia's Information War against Ukraine and other Democratic Countries: Lessons and Recommendations. Interview with Professor Sinan Aral", *Security and Defence Quarterly* 41, no. 1 (2023), https://doi.org/10.35467/SDQ/156264.

33   Algorithmic gatekeeping refers to the influence that automated systems exert on the curation and management of information in the digital ecosystem. This process involves the use of algorithms to select, write, edit, schedule, repeat, and modify online content.

the press and control media institutions. Russia serves as a prime example where these methods are used to reinforce governmental power. The evolution of mainstream media has undergone three significant phases: an era of absolute state control during the Soviet period, a phase of relative openness following the collapse of the Soviet Union, and the current hybrid model. In this model, the media have been taken over by private companies who align with the government's interests, with only a few independent media outlets existing. Since Russia's 2022 invasion of Ukraine, most independent TV channels and Western media have been banned or heavily censored. The government controls almost all media outlets, forcing them to follow Kremlin narratives and avoid critical reporting.[34]

Over the years the Kremlin has subtly shifted from overt coercion of journalists to a strategic reallocation of media assets to government allies, ensuring that media coverage supports official narratives. The acquisition of NTV by Gazprom Media in 2001 illustrates this trend. A critical independent channel transformed into an outlet focused primarily on entertainment, thereby weakening its oppositional stance towards the government. This pattern reflects a broader strategy of co-opting or silencing dissenting media voices and replacing serious political discourse with entertainment.[35] As a result, citizens are less informed and disengaged politically. Since they are discouraged from being interested in politics, individuals living under authoritarian regimes rely on superficial knowledge to make sense of political news. This leads to fluctuating perceptions of the regime, where citizens' attitudes may rapidly oscillate between criticism and support based on current circumstances.[36]

Russia uses a variety of legal and technological means to control both its domestic information infrastructure and the content published online. Technical actions include DDoS attacks, whereas legislative measures are aimed at censoring content considered harmful, such as laws passed in 2012 to protect minors from certain online materials. These measures are part of a broader effort to regulate the digital information space, using both technology and law to curb dissent and shape public perception, reflecting an ongoing trend towards tightening control over media narratives in Russia.[37] In fact, the Kremlin made use of global efforts to fight disinformation in order to pass

---

34   Reporters Without Borders, "Russia", 2024, https://rsf.org/en/country/russia.

35   Ulises A. Mejias and Nikolai E. Vokuev, "Disinformation and the Media: The Case of Russia and Ukraine", *Media, Culture & Society* 39, no. 7 (2017): 1027–42, https://doi.org/10.1177/0163443716686672.

36   Maxim Alyukov, "Making Sense of the News in an Authoritarian Regime: Russian Television Viewers' Reception of the Russia–Ukraine Conflict", *Europe-Asia Studies* 74, no. 3 (2022): 337–59, https://doi.org/10.1080/09668136.2021.2016633.

37   Mejias and Vokuev, "Disinformation and the Media".

laws that increased censorship. Seemingly to protect the information space from fake news and disinformation, the *Federal Law of July 27, 2006 N 149-FZ On Information, Information Technologies and Information Protection* provides a comprehensive legal framework for controlling the media and the information. It balances the rights to information freedom with the imperatives of national security and public order, while also seemingly protecting individual rights under a guise of legal legitimacy. Essentially, the law secures the freedom to search, receive, transmit, produce, and disseminate information, albeit through strictly legal channels defined by the state. It also enforces stringent restrictions aimed at safeguarding the constitutional order, public morality and the state's security and defense needs, which are frequently invoked to justify censorship and information control. Specifically, Article 9 of the legislation empowers federal executive bodies to identify and restrict access to information resources that pose a threat to critical state interests. The regulatory power significantly enhances the state's ability to control the media narrative and suppress dissent under the guise of protecting societal and state stability. Additionally, the law prohibits the dissemination of information that could incite war, hatred or discrimination, claiming this will maintain social harmony and security. However, in practice, these provisions have been used selectively to suppress opposition and maintain a state-controlled information ecosystem. By limiting the flow of information that challenges the Kremlin's viewpoints, the Russian government effectively silences the independent media and public dissent, ensuring that only state-approved narratives are circulated in the public domain. In the years that followed, particularly after the 2022 invasion of Ukraine, the Russian government intensified its use of legal instruments to tighten control over the digital information space. Amendments to existing legislation further broadened the definition of fake news. Lawmakers introduced penalties for the deliberate dissemination of false content and imposed obligations on internet service providers to block access to websites that spread disinformation. As a result, the dissemination of independent reporting has been further curtailed and freedom of speech increasingly restricted.

The system of repression also includes imprisonment for posting content on social media platforms such as Facebook, Instagram, YouTube, X, and Telegram that contradicts the official government line.[38] Russian legislation requires digital service providers to store content and associated metadata (including content transmitted through messengers, email and social media services)

---

38   Funk Shahbaz et al., "Freedom on the Net 2021" (Freedom House, 2021), 8, freedomon thenet.org.

and then make it accessible to authorities without a court order. Hence, any information circulated outside traditional media channels must be traceable with a clear identification of its source. This ensures that all disseminated content adheres to state standards and can be held accountable. Therefore, a controlled information environment is supported where any unverified or dissenting views can be easily targeted and suppressed.

Furthermore, regulations allow supervisory institutions[39] to block websites and social networks under the pretext of fighting against the supposed censorship of content from Russian state news media, which in reality are propaganda messages published by services such as RT, RIA Novosti, and Crimea 24.[40] In April 2021, Russia took steps to limit the activity of the Google search engine within its borders, accusing its owner of abusing its dominant market position.[41] With the onset of the war in Ukraine in February 2022, it blocked a number of websites and social networks.[42] These actions on the one hand, restrict freedom of speech and access to uncensored information, and on the other, serve to disseminate propaganda content.

Russian control of the media is highly effective with the Kremlin's narrative influential in shaping citizens' perceptions. In his study of Russian citizens' reception of the Russia–Ukraine war, Alyukov found that despite the diversity of opinions, when exposed to government narratives or politically loaded terms, individuals tended to echo the state's official stance, viewing Russia as a victim of aggressive Western policies, not as the aggressor. However, personal experiences and discussions sometimes led to the emergence of critical views, showing that citizens could shift from support to criticism depending on the context. Alyukov identified several thematic categories of opinion, including emotional burnout from excessive media focus on conflict, skepticism towards

---

39   Roskomnadzor is a special regulatory agency that acts as a media and internet watchdog with extensive censorship powers. While it officially claims to target "fake news," it can block websites and remove online content at will, without the need for investigation or a legal process. The agency can unilaterally not only remove certain content from the digital space but also block any media resources online. Unchecked authority allows Roskomnadzor to silence critical voices and restrict information access, creating a media landscape dominated by state-approved narratives (Grigoryan Astghik, "Russia: Russian President Signs Anti-fake News Laws", 2019, https://www.loc.gov/item/global-legal-monitor/2019-04-11/russia-russian-president-signs-anti-fake-news-laws/).

40   Shahbaz et al., "Freedom on the Net 2021", 15.

41   Reuters, "Russian Competition Watchdog Opens Case against Google over YouTube Curbs", *reuters.com*, 2021, https://www.reuters.com/technology/russian-competition-watchdog-opens-case-against-google-over-youtube-curbs-2021-04-19/.

42   Morgan Meaker, "Russia Blocks Facebook and Twitter in a Propaganda Standoff", Wired, 2022, https://www.wired.com/story/russia-ukraine-social-media/.

the government's portrayal of economic and social prosperity, and concerns about the war being driven by elite interests.[43] These findings point at the role of media in shaping public opinion and reveal a pattern where state narratives dominate due to their accessibility, but where personal experiences or discussions can activate critical perspectives. The presence of contradictory opinions within individuals exposes the influence of media narratives and the variability of political engagement among citizens. This dynamic suggests that state-controlled media in authoritarian regimes like Russia is highly effective mainly due to political disengagement and the lack of coherent political views among citizens rather than the persuasiveness of the media content itself.

The strategy of information operations has long been an integral part of Russia's international tactics, reflecting a long-standing belief in the power of information influence. Russia has long used messages crafted to suit its purpose in reshaping the international order and destabilizing adversaries. To this end, they blend modern technology with traditional psychological tactics.[44] The practice of disinformation draws from the theory and practice of reflexive control, developed by a Soviet psychologist and mathematician, Vladimir Lefebvre, in the 1960s. This strategic approach aims to manipulate an opponent's decision-making through delivering carefully tailored information to influence the opponent's decision-making processes. Techniques of reflexive control include displays of military power, the spreading of disinformation and direct interference in the opponent's decision-making processes.[45] Over time, "reflexive control" has evolved into what the West commonly refers to as "perception management," although in the Russian context, this involves more direct control rather than mere management.[46] The evolved strategy, while rooted in Cold War era tactics, now effectively makes use of digital platforms and social media to broaden its impact and efficiency. It is notable for spreading an overwhelming quantity of messages across numerous channels, coupled with a blatant readiness to spread misleading or wholly fabricated information. The modern tactics of Russian disinformation benefit from a vast and diversified media landscape, including state-controlled outlets, social networks and the use of bots and trolls (fake personas spreading hyperpartisan themes), which makes tracing the origins to government sources challenging.

---

43   Alyukov, "Making Sense of the News in an Authoritarian Regime".

44   Ryszard Szpyra, "Russian Information Offensive in the International Relations", *Security and Defence Quarterly* 30, no. 3 (2020): 31–48, https://doi.org/10.35467/SDQ/124436.

45   Timothy Thomas, "Russia's Reflexive Control Theory and the Military", *Journal of Slavic Military Studies* 17 (2004): 237–56, https://doi.org/10.1080/13518040490450529.

46   Christian Kamphuis, "Reflexive Control", *Militaire Spectator*, 2018, https://www.militaire spectator.nl/thema/strategie-operaties/artikel/reflexive-control.

Such coordinated campaigns help disseminate messages rapidly and repeatedly to a wide audience, according to the psychological principle that people tend to trust the familiar (the illusory truth effect). Additionally, manipulation by altering an adversary's perception aims to make them voluntarily act in Russia's interest, which demonstrates the sophisticated and deeply ingrained nature of Russian informational tactics.[47]

---

47   The case of the Russian media's response to the downing of the Malaysia Airlines flight MH17 illustrates a deliberate and sophisticated use of disinformation and media manipulation to influence public opinion, avoid international censure and maintain control over the narrative both domestically and internationally. Flight MH17, carrying 283, mostly Dutch, passengers and 15 crew members, was shot down by a Buk missile that came from the Russian 53rd Anti-Aircraft Missile Brigade in Kursk from Russian-controlled territory in eastern Ukraine on July 17, 2014, a fact proven by extensive international investigation including the Dutch Safety Board and the Joint Investigation Team (JIT) (Dutch Safety Board, "Crash MH17, 17 July 2014", 2015, https://onderzoeksraad.nl/en/onderzoek/crash-mh17-17-july-2014/; Landelijk Parket, "Update in Criminal Investigation MH17 Disaster", 2018). Since the incident, Russian media, under state influence, has employed various narratives to reshape the discourse and deflect blame. Initially, Russian outlets, echoing statements from pro-Russian separatists, mistakenly celebrated the downing of what they thought was a Ukrainian military aircraft. However, once it was revealed that the downed aircraft was a civilian plane, Russian media swiftly shifted its narrative to blame the Ukrainian military, suggesting without substantiated evidence that a Ukrainian fighter jet was responsible. These claims were later contradicted by detailed investigations which pointed to the involvement of a Russian missile system. In response, Russian media and officials adopted a new tactic, questioning the credibility of the investigations and promoting alternative theories through state-run defense companies like Almaz-Antey. These theories suggested that if a Buk missile had been used, it was an older model operated by Ukraine, not Russia. Russian narratives also emphasized alleged failures by Ukraine, such as not closing its airspace over a conflict zone, suggesting that it was Ukraine that was responsible for the tragedy. The shift in focus was supported by a broader strategy of using a mix of genuine data, manipulated information and outright falsehoods to foster confusion and discredit opposing narratives. Throughout the campaign, Russian media has relied on statements from supposed experts and manipulated data to lend credibility to its claims, while simultaneously discrediting Western media outlets and investigation teams by accusing them of bias. On top of that, Russian-language trolls ran 163 hashtag campaigns to manipulate political sentiment and promote inconsistent theories about Ukraine's responsibility. They mainly reshared information and used automation tools for hashtag amplification and spreading disinformation. This approach has been effective in shaping perceptions in Russia, where a significant portion of the population believes Ukraine was responsible for shooting down the plane (Oliver Boyd-Barrett, "MH17 as Free-Floating Atrocity Propaganda", in *Media, Ideology and Hegemony*, eds. Savaş Çoban (The Hague: Brill, 2018), 267–98, https://doi.org/10.1163/9789004364417; Mason Richey, "Contemporary Russian Revisionism: Understanding the Kremlin's Hybrid Warfare and the Strategic and Tactical Deployment of Disinformation", *Asia Europe Journal* 16, no. 1 (2018): 101–13, https://doi.org/10.1007/s10308-017-0482-5; Alexandr Vesselkov, Benjamin Finley and Jouko Vankka, "Russian Trolls Speaking Russian: Regional Twitter Operations and

The effectiveness of Russian information operations abroad has been well documented, revealing its concerted efforts to interfere in the U.S. 2016 elections. The U.S. Senate investigation proved that the Russian government was engaged significantly to target state and local election infrastructure. These actions, including extensive scanning of election systems and extracting data from voter registration databases, did not aim to change the 2016 election's outcome directly. Instead, they appeared to be an attempt to undermine the integrity of elections or prepare for future exploitations.[48] Further investigations in interference strategies reveal the multifaceted strategies used with the aim of destabilizing the electoral process and amplifying societal discord. The Internet Research Agency (IRA), funded by Russian oligarch Yevgeniy Prigozhin with connections to President Putin, initiated early interference through a calculated social media campaign whose goal was to increase political and social tensions in the United States. Numerous fake social media accounts were created to act as profiles of social and political activists in order to ignite discussions on social media platforms. A significant number of profiles impersonated stolen identities of citizens and published seemingly authentic posts that were culturally adapted to mimic the activity dynamics of active users. They frequently addressed controversial topics, such as issues of racial social injustice (e.g., using the hashtag #BlackLivesMatter to promote controversial statements), the right to own firearms, alleged cases of Sharia law being applied in America, and the attack on Democratic Party candidate Hillary Clinton.

By using various marketing strategies, troll accounts were promoted to the position of opinion leaders on both the right and left sides of the political scene. Their task was to engage in discussion on topics that polarized public opinion and to fuel social tension (e.g., by supporting radical groups and users criticizing the current social and political situation). Troll accounts worked

MH17", in *12th ACM Conference on Web Science* (WebSci '20: 12th ACM Conference on Web Science, Southampton: ACM, 2020), 86–95, https://doi.org/10.1145/3394231.3397898; Alec Luhn, "MH17: Vast Majority of Russians Believe Ukraine Downed Plane, Poll Finds", *The Guardian*, 30 July 2014, https://www.theguardian.com/world/2014/jul/30/mh17-vast -majority-russians-believe-ukraine-downed-plane-poll. Thomas Rid, *Active Measures. The Secret History of Disinformation and Political Warfare* (London: Profile Books Ltd., 2020); Francesco Bechis, "Playing the Russian Disinformation Game: Information Operations from Soviet Tactics to Putin's Sharp Power", in *Democracy and Fake News. Information Manipulation and Post-Truth Politics* (London and New York: Routledge, 2021), 107–18).

48   U.S. Senate, "Report of the Select Committee on Intelligence United States Senate on Russian Active Measures Campaigns and Interference in the 2016 U.S. Election. Vol. 1: Russian Efforts against Election Infrastructure with Additional Views", 2020, https://www .intelligence.senate.gov/sites/default/files/documents/Report_Volume1.pdf.

closely with semi-automatic (cyborgs) and automatic (social bots) accounts to increase the reach of posts and selected accounts. Combined with a personalized advertising campaign, Russia ran an extremely effective political campaign. Its effectiveness was further enhanced by the medium – social media platforms that enable mass persuasion.

Simultaneously, the Russian government engaged in another layer of interference through cyber hacks and information dissemination detrimental to the Clinton campaign, executed by the GRU.[49] The secondary form of interference involved hacking and the release of materials through channels like WikiLeaks in order to influence U.S. politics without direct involvement from U.S. citizens. Complex and coordinated strategies show the sophisticated nature of Russian interference and its profound impact on the U.S. electoral and political scene. Evidence was also found of online foreign interference in the 2020 U.S. presidential election. Trolls and superconnectors (highly networked accounts spreading messages quickly) were extremely active in specific online communities on social media, targeting both liberal and conservative audiences.[50]

Apart from the U.S., Russian disinformation campaigns have significantly increased during key political events and social movements all over the world, such as the Brexit campaign, the "yellow vest" protests in France, social protests against racial injustice linked to the Black Lives Matter movement, the independence referendum in Catalonia in 2017, elections to the European Union Parliament, and cyber attacks directed against EU states.[51] Many of Russia's activities are also directed against the Baltic states, the Nordic countries and Poland, such as conducting disinformation campaigns using historical disinformation, accusations of Russophobia, promoting anti-Ukrainian and

---

49 The Main Intelligence Directorate of the General Staff of the Russian Armed Forces.

50 William Marcellino et al., *Foreign Interference in the 2020 Election. Tools for Detecting Online Election Interference* (Santa Monica, CA: RAND Corporation, 2020), https://www.rand.org/pubs/research_reports/RRA704-2.html.

51 Bence Kollanyi, Philip N. Howard and Samuel C. Woolley, "Bots and Automation over Twitter during the U.S. Election" (Oxford: Data Memo 2016.4., 2016), https://comprop.oii.ox.ac.uk/research/working-papers/bots-and-automation-over-twitter-during-the-u-s-election/; Freedom House, "Freedom on the Net 2017: Manipulating Social Media to Undermine Democracy", 2017, https://freedomhouse.org/report/freedom-net/freedom-net-2017; Laura Rosenberger, "Disinformation Disorientation", *Journal of Democracy* 31, no. 1 (2020): 203–7; Oscar Barberà, "All Fake? Information Disorders and the 2017 Referendum in Catalonia", in *Misinformation in Referenda*, eds. Sandrine Baume, Véronique Boillet and Vincent Martenet (London and New York: Routledge, 2020).

anti-EU attitudes, creating a negative image of NATO, promoting a narrative of Western decadence, and general anti-Western attitudes.[52]

During the COVID-19 pandemic, Russia exploited the anxiety and uncertainty caused by the pandemic in order to disseminate disinformation to promote their strategic goals of increasing existing societal divisions and undermining trust in democratic processes and institutions. Through state-backed media outlets such as RT and Sputnik, Russia portrayed Western democracies as incompetent and corrupt as well as intensified pre-existing controversies across economic, healthcare and social domains. They promoted racially charged narratives in the United States and disseminated a mix of genuine concerns and outright fabrications related to public health management, political leadership and societal inequalities during the pandemic.[53] Furthermore, Russia targeted vaccine communication by spreading misinformation that contributed to vaccine hesitancy worldwide. Russian media outlets promoted narratives that questioned the safety and efficacy of Western-developed vaccines, suggesting they were rushed through approval processes and thus potentially dangerous. They amplified reports of minor side effects to sow doubt among populations already skeptical of government health directives. Russian campaigns often included exaggerated claims about alternative treatments and preventive measures to further confuse public understanding. This approach not only undermined public trust in health systems but also in the scientific community, effectively slowing down global vaccination efforts and prolonging the impact of the pandemic. Such tactics are part of a broader Russian disinformation playbook that seeks to capitalize on crises to weaken adversaries and shift international opinion in Russia's favor.[54]

Frequently used tactics include spear phishing[55] campaigns (conducted to gain access to data), data breaches and leaks, destructive attacks on

---

52   Kazimierz Wóycicki, Marta Kowalska and Adam Lelonek, "Rosyjska Wojna Dezinformacyjna przeciwko Polsce" (Warsaw: Fundacja im. Kazimierza Pułaskiego, 2017); Ivo Juurvee et al., "Falsification of History as a Tool of Influence", NATO Strategic Communications Centre of Excellence, 2020; NATO STO, "Military Aspects of Countering Hybrid Warfare: Experiences, Lessons, Best Practices. Volume 2: Information and Influence" (NATO STO, 2024).

53   Wesley R. Moy and Kacper Gradon, *COVID-19 Effects of Russian Disinformation Campaigns* (Homeland Security Affairs Journal, Special COVID-19 Issue, 2020), 10–14, https://www.hsaj.org/resources/uploads/2020/12/hsaj_Covid192020_COVID19EffectsRussianDisinformationCampaigns.pdf.

54   Karishma Sharma, Yizhou Zhang and Yan Liu, "COVID-19 Vaccine Misinformation Campaigns and Social Media Narratives", *Proceedings of the International AAAI Conference on Web and Social Media* 16 (2022): 920–31, https://doi.org/10.1609/icwsm.v16i1.19346.

55   Phishing involves impersonating a legitimate institution or individual to extract confidential information. Spearphishing is a more targeted type of attack, involving personalized

electoral infrastructure, and the use of the online environment for manipulation and dissemination of disinformation.[56] Furthermore, Russia uses its intelligence agencies, mainly the FSB (Federal Security Service), GRU (Main Intelligence Directorate), and SVR (Foreign Intelligence Service), to sponsor and orchestrate cyber attacks. These agencies actively support and collaborate with various hacker groups, including patriotic hackers and Russian cyber criminals, to conduct sophisticated cyber operations. Key activities include launching disruptive cyber attacks (with the aim of testing and refining cyber warfare capabilities). The involvement of Russian agencies in cyber warfare is evident from their operational tactics, which include the use of destructive malware, such as wipers, to irreversibly damage target systems. Cyber operations are aligned with Russia's broader strategy of hybrid warfare. Their aim is to destabilize societies and weaken state structures from within without engaging in open conflict. Notably, the GRU and FSB units play significant roles in intensifying cyber attacks synchronized with Russia's military objectives, particularly during the ongoing war in Ukraine. These attacks are not isolated incidents but are part of a continuous effort to exert influence and achieve strategic dominance in the cyberspace domain alongside physical military engagements.[57] Russian cyber criminals and political hackers operate with high levels of anonymity provided by cyberspace, which allows Russia to enhance its geopolitical influence without direct attribution. Hackers engage in a variety of disruptive activities, ranging from denial of service attacks that cripple critical infrastructure to espionage that steals sensitive information. It is extremely challenging to attribute their involvement directly to Russia.[58]

---

messages sent to carefully selected and previously researched groups. Whaling, another type of phishing, specifically targets high-level executives to steal sensitive information or authentication credentials.

56 Janne Hakala and Jazlyn Melnychuk, *Russia's Strategy in Cyberspace* (Riga: NATO Strategic Communication Centre of Excellence, 2021).

57 Dowództwo Komponentu Wojsk Obrony Cyberprzestrzeni, "Ukraina 2022 na Cyfrowym Froncie", 2022, https://www.wojsko-polskie.pl/woc/u/4c/d1/4cd11eaf-3567-405d-994f-f88 b6b45adob/ukraina_2022_na_cyfrowym_froncie.pdf; Marina Miron and Rod Thornton, "The Use of Cyber Tools by the Russian Military: Lessons from the War against Ukraine and a Warning for NATO?", *Applied Cybersecurity & Internet Governance* 3, no. 1, 2024, https://doi.org/10.60097/ACIG/190142.

58 Scott Applegate, "Cybermilitias and Political Hackers: Use of Irregular Forces in Cyberwarfare", *IEEE Security & Privacy Magazine* 9, no. 5 (2011): 16–22, https://doi.org/10.1109/MSP.2011.46; Mark Grzegorzewski, "Russian Cyber Operations: The Relationship between the State and Cybercriminals", in *Cyber Terrorism and Extremism as Threat to Critical Infrastructure Protection*, eds. Denis Caleta and James F. Powers (Ljubljana: Ministry of Defence Republic of Slovenia, 2020), 53–64.

CHAPTER 4

The Power of Algorithms: Understanding Their Impact in Social Cybersecurity

Algorithms shape our online experience – they filter and curate vast streams of data in cyberspace, including newsfeeds and ads thus framing our perceptions of the world. Consequently, algorithms have significant power: not only do they determine what information we encounter, but they also influence our offline experiences. This chapter investigates the dual roles of algorithms. On the one hand, algorithms can support various activities through technological advancements. On the other hand, they may reinforce existing inequalities and bring about many unforeseen consequences. To fully understand the role of algorithms as well as their ethical, cultural and political impacts, it is crucial to consider them in the broader systems they influence and the context in which they operate.

1   Algorithms

Algorithms are formalized sequences of actions or rules designed to solve a problem or achieving a desired result. They take input data, process it through a series of predefined steps to produce an output. In the field of computer science, algorithms are defined as abstract, formalized representations of computational procedures categorized by their operational functions and the types of problems they address. Thus, there are combinatorial algorithms that deal with counting and enumeration, numerical algorithms designed for equation-solving and probabilistic algorithms that produce results based on probabilities where outcomes are uncertain.[1] They have evolved from technical tools to dynamic agents that are present in virtually every aspect of cyberspace, influencing everything from social media interactions to financial transactions. The active role of algorithms in shaping our social realities demonstrates their performative nature. They not only construct the user digital experience but have become a part of social, cultural and political contexts with serious social and ethical implications. A large body of research has shown that algorithms

---

1 Paul Dourish, "Algorithms and their Others: Algorithmic Culture in Context", *Big Data & Society* 3, no. 2 (2016): 3, https://doi.org/10.1177/2053951716665128.

on social networking platforms reflect and reinforce social norms and cultural biases.[2] They are not just passive tools but active agents that can significantly alter social practices and relationships. For example, newsfeed algorithms filter, rank and recommend content based on user profiling thereby shaping users' understanding and interpretation of the world. Similarly, credit scoring algorithms do not merely assess financial credibility; they actively determine access to financial services and, as a result, can influence socioeconomic stratification. Algorithms in social media and dating apps choose whose profile is more salient thereby shaping users' social network online and affecting social relations.

In order to fully understand algorithms, they need to be examined in the broader systems they permeate and not as isolated entities independent of their design and application contexts. Hence, a holistic approach needs to be taken to examine the multifaceted interactions and interdependencies between algorithms and the various sociomaterial elements they engage with. Understanding algorithms helps to reveal how they are embedded in and shape our societal structures, norms and behavior. Recognizing this allows us to see their performative nature and the importance of considering the broader ethical, cultural and political dimensions they influence and are influenced by.[3]

2   Algorithmic Shaping of User Experience

Algorithms analyze user activity and digital footprint to develop predictive models of user behavior. They are highly effective in deciding on the content presented to the audience and displaying personalized advertisements. There are countless numbers of algorithms. On social networking sites they determine how content is filtered, ranked, selected, and recommended to users. They fall into different categories. Newsfeed algorithms are complex and constantly evolving systems that organize and rank content from the collective

---

2   Cathy O'Neil, *Weapons of Math Destruction* (New York: Crown, 2016); Safiya Umoja Noble, *Algorithms of Oppression: How Search Engines Reinforce Racism* (New York: New York University Press, 2018); Senjooti Roy and Liat Ayalon, "Age and Gender Stereotypes Reflected in Google's 'Autocomplete' Function: The Portrayal and Possible Spread of Societal Stereotypes", *The Gerontologist* 60, no. 6 (2020): 1020–28, https://doi.org/10.1093/GERONT/GNZ172.

3   Jack Andersen, "Understanding and Interpreting Algorithms: Toward a Hermeneutics of Algorithms", *Media, Culture & Society* 42, no. 7–8 (2020): 1479–94, https://doi.org/10.1177/0163443720919373; Vern L. Glaser, Neil Pollock and Luciana D'Adderio, "The Biography of an Algorithm: Performing Algorithmic Technologies in Organizations", *Organization Theory* 2, no. 2 (2021): 4–6, https://doi.org/10.1177/26317877211004609.

pool created by users' social networks connections (friends, followed pages and groups) and the various posts and interactions created from these connections. Algorithms are personalized based on numerous factors, including users' past behavior, the composition of users' network and their interactions in that network. They respond not just to explicit actions (such as likes, shares, keywords in posts) but also to more implicit user behavior (such as browsing habits and the duration of time spent on certain content). This complex analysis helps the algorithm determine user preferences. They use machine learning to 'learn' from user behavior and adapt over time. Hence, feedback loops are created between user behavior and future content exposure. As users interact with content, these interactions inform the algorithm, which then adjusts the content it shows, thus creating a cycle of interaction and adaptation.

Algorithms are optimized for certain outcomes, primarily user engagement. They ensure that users' media experience is as relevant and significant as possible.[4] That is why content likely to keep users engaged, such as posts that elicit likes, comments or shares, is more likely to be featured prominently in users' feed. It is the algorithm that decides what is newsworthy because it aims to keep users engaged and active on the platform. The more time users spend on social networking sites, the more opportunities there are to expose them to advertisements. To achieve this, the algorithm tailors the content in users' newsfeeds to be as relevant and engaging as possible. By analyzing users' behavior, preferences and interactions, the algorithm curates content that according to its predictions, will keep users interested and engaged. Tailored content includes not just posts from friends and family but also from pages, groups and advertisers.[5]

Another example is the algorithms that operate the recommendation system. They suggest new connections or content to users based on the users' preferences and the digital footprint they leave. These algorithms use simple link prediction methods, such as evaluating the number of shared connections between two users or their shared interests, offline familiarity or the likelihood of forming a future relationship. User suggestions might appear as "People You May Know" on Facebook, "Whom to Follow" on X or "For You Page" on TikTok. As a result, they decide with whom we interact and shape social relations. The recommendations made by algorithms determine how users engage with the

---

4   Akos Lada, Meihong Wang and Tak Yan, "How does News Feed Predict what You Want to See? Personalized Ranking with Machine Learning", 2021, https://tech.fb.com/news-feed-ranking/.

5   Lazer et al., "The Science of Fake News"; Kjerstin Thorson et al., "Algorithmic Inference, Political Interest, and Exposure to News and Politics on Facebook", *Information, Communication & Society* 24, no. 2 (2021): 183–200, https://doi.org/10.1080/1369118X.2019.1642934.

network. They dictate the kind of content users see, the discussions they participate in and the range of opinions they encounter.

Algorithms also take the role of a spam filter, which stops less valuable content.[6] They also ensure that inappropriate content is blocked. Platforms include extensive restrictions on nudity, vulgarity, harassment, hate speech, and other sensitive and unlawful content. Automatic systems quickly and effectively identify and block content that violates the platforms' terms of service. However, some benign content might be mistakenly categorized as inappropriate (false positives), leading to over-censorship.[7] Furthermore, they penalize behavior that is deemed inappropriate and that explicitly breaks the rules of the platform by imposing shadow banning[8] on certain accounts that excessively post promotional material, overuse popular hashtags to gain visibility, exhibit bot-like behavior or engage in abusive behavior.[9]

Algorithms tailor content to meet specific user needs. This aspect is particularly valued from a consumer perspective, where people want the best possible return on their investment in services like music or television streaming. Users expect the platform to intuitively understand and fulfill their preferences.[10] Algorithms are precise in organizing and filtering information, which reduces information overload and supports users in finding relevant news amidst the abundance of available information. They use machine learning to make predictions that surpass human analytical capabilities. They democratize access to a wide range of products, services and information.[11] Consequently, wide implementation of algorithms boosts the efficiency of information retrieval as users can easily navigate through vast amounts of data.

---

6   Nick Clegg, "You and the Algorithm: It Takes Two to Tango", 2021, https://nickclegg .medium.com/you-and-the-algorithm-it-takes-two-to-tango-7722b19aa1c2.

7   Jennifer Cobbe, "Algorithmic Censorship by Social Platforms: Power and Resistance", *Philosophy & Technology* 34, no. 2021): 739–66, https://doi.org/10.1007/s13347-020-00429-0; Elena Pilipets and Susanna Paasonen, "Nipples, Memes, and Algorithmic Failure: NSFW Critique of Tumblr Censorship", *New Media & Society* 24, no. 6 (2022): 1459–80, https:// doi.org/10.1177/1461444820979280.

8   Shadow banning is a method where a user's posts are made invisible to everyone except the user themselves. The technique ensures that the affected user remains unaware of the ban, leading them to continue posting to what they believe is their audience, rather than creating a new account due to the lack of external feedback (Laura Savolainen, "The Shadow Banning Controversy: Perceived Governance and Algorithmic Folklore", *Media, Culture & Society* 44, no. 6 (2022): 1091–1109, https://doi.org/10.1177/01634437221077174).

9   Savolainen.

10   Daniel Meyerend, "The Algorithm Knows I'M Black: From Users to Subjects", *Media, Culture & Society* 45, no. 3 (2023): 635, https://doi.org/10.1177/01634437221140539.

11   Meyerend, 636.

When designed and adjusted appropriately, algorithms on online social network sites have the potential to bridge the gaps between different groups and break down echo chambers. They can facilitate connections among users with diverse political viewpoints, which could play a significant role in promoting more constructive and inclusive political discussions. This could lead to a healthier, more balanced political discourse in the online space. Therefore, with careful tuning, algorithms could encourage exposure to a wider range of opinions, thereby enriching political conversations and reducing polarization.[12]

3   Censorship and Bias in Algorithmic Decisions

Although algorithms offer several advantages such as improved efficiency in information retrieval, enhanced user experience and support for decision-making processes, these benefits are frequently overshadowed by high societal cost such as perpetuating bias, manipulating content for the benefit of a third party or pushing a distorted image of the world. First, algorithms may push some content whilst suppressing other content. TikTok, for example, has been criticized for banning content perceived as supportive of gay rights, even in countries where homosexuality is legally accepted. The platform also restricted videos created by individuals with disabilities, facial disfigurements, Down's syndrome, autism, and other conditions that might attract bullying. The policy was criticized for being discriminatory and victimizing disabled users by limiting their visibility instead of confronting and addressing the perpetrators of bullying. Hiding users is not a solution for protecting them from cyber bullying.[13]

Much political content is censored. TikTok in China bans discussions on sensitive topics like Tiananmen Square, Tibet, and Falun Gong. Similarly, in Turkey, content about Kurdish separatism, portrayals of non-Islamic religious figures and criticism of political leaders are restricted.[14] In authoritarian regimes, political imperatives might play a significant role in driving censorship

---

12   Fernando P. Santos, Yphtach Lelkes and Simon A. Levin, "Link Recommendation Algorithms and Dynamics of Polarization in Online Social Networks", *Proceedings of the National Academy of Sciences* 118, no. 50 (2021): e2102141118, https://doi.org/10.1073/pnas.2102141118.

13   Leo Kelion, "TikTok Suppressed Disabled Users' Videos", *BBC*, 3 December 2019, https://www.bbc.com/news/technology-50645345.

14   Alex Hern, "TikTok's Local Moderation Guidelines Ban Pro-LGBT Content", *The Guardian*, 26 September 2019, https://www.theguardian.com/technology/2019/sep/26/tiktoks-local-moderation-guidelines-ban-pro-lgbt-content.

algorithms, in accordance with political priorities set by the state.[15] Algorithmic censorship could also have consequences for democratic discourse. The commercial interests of platforms may impact the diversity of political discourse. By potentially suppressing certain political content, platforms might influence the public political narrative and limit the exposure of users to a broader range of political views. This manipulation of the public sphere through exposure to selected information significantly affects voters' abilities to make well-informed decisions. Such microtargeting practices can effectively exclude individuals from a diverse 'marketplace of ideas,' leading to biases in voter perceptions and contributing to a fragmented political discourse. Political actors can easily either disseminate tailored messages to different segments of voters or exclude certain groups from getting the message. The integration of data-driven strategies into electoral campaigns, coupled with the influential role of social media platforms in shaping political beliefs and behavior, raises concerns about fundamental democratic values.

Another negative effect of algorithm activity is polarization. Even though user recommendation systems are primarily designed to connect users and enhance their experience through personalization, it inadvertently impacts opinion formation. By suggesting some content, they make users more exposed to certain (most frequently similar) perspectives. By favoring connections between users who are structurally similar (in terms of shared connections in the network), algorithms may reinforce existing viewpoints, limit exposure to diverse perspectives and diminish areas of consensus. Consequently, this can lead to the formation of more homogenous groups, reinforce existing beliefs and intensify opinion polarization in online social environments.[16] The growing divide is further increased by a rising erosion of trust in public institutions and media outlets,[17] which are themselves becoming more polarized. Media platforms increasingly cater to niche audiences holding extreme views, shaping content to align with polarized opinions, thereby contributing to the problem.

Such dynamics pose significant challenges to the foundational principles of democracy. A crucial aspect of a democratic society is being able to engage in constructive disagreements. A healthy democratic environment flourishes on a 'marketplace of ideas' where differing viewpoints are not only tolerated

---

15   Cobbe, "Algorithmic Censorship by Social Platforms".

16   Santos, Lelkes and Levin, "Link Recommendation Algorithms and Dynamics of Polarization in Online Social Networks".

17   Siva Vaidhyanathan, *Anti-Social Media. How Facebook Disconnects Us and Undermines Democracy* (Oxford: Oxford University Press, 2018), 11.

but valued for the diversity they bring to debates, which foster a dialogue that benefits democratic engagement. However, the current situation is one of divided perceptions, fueled by a 'splinternet'[18] where different groups, each with varying opinions, are segregated by platform algorithms into distinct digital ecosystems. The digital segmentation, compounded by affective political polarization and misinformation, makes finding common ground increasingly challenging, thereby undermining the core advantage of democracy – the 'marketplace of ideas'. As a result, social tensions rise and conflicts between various groups intensify, which poses a significant threat to the democratic process.[19]

On the other hand, exposure to homogenous content on social media is limited because users form friendships with a variety of people they encounter, regardless of ideological similarities. They are therefore exposed to a broader range of content through interactions with diverse users. In contrast, the content they encounter through specific pages or groups tends to be more homogeneous because users decide to follow certain pages or join specific groups based on shared interests or ideological agreement. Essentially, this means that users are more likely to follow pages and join groups that align with their political beliefs or ideologies, but they follow friends based on a combination of other factors, such as offline or online encounter, personal preferences, social influences, and algorithmic recommendations. The distinction is significant because it implies that the content users are exposed to through pages and groups is more likely to reinforce their existing beliefs, as these are spaces that they have self-selected based on ideological alignment. In contrast, the content shared by friends may present a more diverse range of viewpoints, as friendships on social networking sites may not always be formed based on political or ideological factors. As a result, the echo chamber effect, where one is exposed predominantly to views that reinforce one's own, may be more pronounced in the context of following ideologically aligned pages and groups than in the content shared by a more diverse group of friends.[20]

Echo chambers limit exposure to diverse content and viewpoints. When algorithms categorize and predict user preferences, they create echo chambers that not only contribute to increased polarization, as explained above,

---

18   Splinternet refers to "the breaking apart of social media and digital communication networks into unconnected groups, by dimensions like political ideology or geography" Sinan Aral, 22 January 2021, https://twitter.com/sinanaral/status/1352657222279557125.

19   Aral, "The Changing Face of Russia's Information War against Ukraine and other Democratic Countries: Lessons and Recommendations. Interview with Professor Sinan Aral".

20   Sandra González-Bailón et al., "Asymmetric Ideological Segregation in Exposure to Political News on Facebook", *Science* 381, no. 6656 (2023): 392–98, https://doi.org/10.1126/science.ade7138.

but also reinforce existing societal biases, such as racial stereotypes, e.g.: algorithms operating in dating apps prioritize same-race matches. Even if a user does not set a racial preference in their profile, the algorithm might still suggest matches from the user's own race. This occurs because the algorithm relies heavily on implicit data – the underlying patterns of user behavior and preferences observed across the platform. As a result, the recommendations provided by the algorithm reflect aggregated user behavior and racial bias, rather than respecting the individual's stated preferences.[21]

African American Netflix users reported seeing thumbnails that featured African American actors, even when these actors played minor roles or the films themselves were not focused on Black stories or themes. Using images of African American actors in minor roles to attract Black viewers can misrepresent the actual content of the film or show and create a superficial and potentially misleading representation of racial diversity. It can also oversimplify and stereotype racial identities and preferences.[22] The use of such data-driven personalization can create a feedback loop. As users interact with the content presented to them, their responses further influence the algorithm, which continues to refine its predictions and recommendations based on the interactions. If the algorithm initially presents content based on stereotypical assumptions, biases can get reinforced over time because the system interprets user engagement with such content as a confirmation of its assumptions.[23] Large language models trained on datasets with pre-existing gender biases (such as a model trained for image classification that consistently mislabels female doctors as nurses) showed an increased tendency to exhibit biases. Furthermore, when biased outputs were used as training data for subsequent models, the gender bias was further amplified.[24]

A large body of research reports algorithmic bias in the information that users receive. For example, the search query "Black girls" once returned pornographic images of Black women and searching for a term "Jew" led to anti-Semitic websites.[25] Furthermore, autocomplete features in search engines can reinforce negative stereotypes. Google's autocomplete once suggested

---

21   Karim Nader, "Dating through the Filters", *Social Philosophy and Policy* 37, no. 2 (2020): 237–48, https://doi.org/10.1017/S0265052521000133.

22   Meyerend, "The Algorithm Knows I'm Black".

23   Rohan Taori and Tatsunori B. Hashimoto, *Data Feedback Loops: Model-driven Amplification of Dataset Biases*, Proceedings of the 40th International Conference on Machine Learning, 2023, https://proceedings.mlr.press/v202/taori23a.html.

24   Taori and Hashimoto, Proceedings of the 40th International Conference on Machine Learning: 1.

25   Noble, *Algorithms of Oppression: How Search Engines Reinforce Racism*, 99, 143.

negative adjectives like "angry," "loud," and "mean" following searches related to certain races such as "Why are Black women so ...".[26] For a certain period of time, Google's image search returned images of African Americans wherever the search included the keyword "gorilla".[27] Autocomplete suggestions also reveal gender and age biases. Searches involving "older woman" often yielded results related to biological functions and physical attractiveness, while "older man" searches frequently referred to intimate relationships. The pattern in Google's search engine reinforces stereotypes, associating older women with loss of physical attractiveness, and in the case of men – reinforcing the belief in their agency and organizing their lives according to their needs and desires.[28] After the shooting in San Bernardino, USA, in 2015, carried out by Sye Rizwan Farook and Tashfeen Malik, there was a rapid increase in Google searches for the phrase "kill Muslims", which influenced biased search results for terms related to this ethnic group.[29] Although these suggestions have been corrected, they show how easily algorithms can spread harmful stereotypes and misinformation.

Bias present in online and mobile marketplaces can lead to discrimination offline, for example unequal employment opportunities. On platforms for freelance labor, such as TaskRabbit and Fiverr, which rank freelance labor candidates, user reviews and ratings of freelancers differ along racial and gender lines. The difference is visible even though users might have similar qualifications or experiences. Human bias (after all reviews are written by individual users) is complemented by algorithmic bias as search algorithms on digital platforms are influenced by gender and race, leading to different visibility for workers based on these characteristics. Algorithmic bias could perpetuate existing inequalities by affecting which workers are more likely to be contracted for a job. It is evident in candidate ranking – if an algorithm prioritizes candidates based on certain attributes or behavior that are more common in a particular group, it can result in underrepresentation of minority groups.[30]

26   Noble, 21.

27   Taina Bucher, *If ... Then. Algorithmic Power and Politics* (Oxford: Oxford University Press, 2018).

28   Roy and Ayalon, "Age and Gender Stereotypes Reflected in Google's 'Autocomplete' Function: The Portrayal and Possible Spread of Societal Stereotypes".

29   Matthew Williams, *The Science of Hate: How Prejudice Becomes Hate and what we Can Do to Stop It* (London: Faber & Faber, 2021).

30   Tom Sühr, Sophie Hilgard and Himabindu Lakkaraju, "Does Fair Ranking Improve Minority Outcomes? Understanding the Interplay of Human and Algorithmic Biases in Online Hiring", in *Proceedings of the 2021 AAAI/ACM Conference on AI, Ethics, and Society* (AIES '21: AAAI/ACM Conference on AI, Ethics, and Society, Virtual Event USA: ACM, 2021), 989–99, https://doi.org/10.1145/3461702.3462602.

This creates a feedback loop where certain groups are continually favored, and others are discriminated against.

Another example of algorithmic bias is evident in the automated selection process where female applicants may face discrimination. Amazon faced significant challenges with its AI recruiting tool, designed to automate the process of candidate evaluations. The tool was trained on a dataset composed of resumes submitted over the previous ten years, a period dominated by male applicants due to the existing gender imbalance in the tech industry. Consequently, the system learned to prefer male candidates and penalized resumes containing terms like "women's," such as those listing leadership roles in women's clubs or graduates from all-women's colleges. Efforts to neutralize biases by editing the terms were insufficient to guarantee fairness, as the system could potentially find other ways to discriminate. Ultimately, Amazon discontinued the project, recognizing the tool's limitations in providing a fair and effective screening process. Other online hiring tools are, however, widely used.[31]

Biased data and automated analyses may also discriminate against certain groups based on characteristics such as race, religion, income level, or education. In the United States, programs designed to calculate recidivism rates were criticized for perpetuating racial inequalities to the disadvantage of African Americans and ethnic minorities. These programs were based on data such as the age or criminal history of the accused, including details of previous offenses and frequency of arrests. Efforts have been made to eliminate biases in algorithms with the latest programs no longer encoding data related to race, ethnic origin and sexual preferences. However, indirect bias persists due to the disproportionate number of detentions and arrests among African Americans and Latinos compared to white individuals. Factors such as living in poor neighborhoods increase the likelihood of encounters with police, even for routine checks. Additionally, these communities often face higher rates of unemployment and increased exposure to drugs, alcohol and acquaintances with criminal backgrounds. All these factors are encoded in algorithms assessing recidivism probability.[32] Thus, race and place of residence still indirectly

---

31	Jeffrey Dastin, "Amazon Scraps Secret AI Recruiting Tool that Showed Bias against Women", *Reuters*, 11 October 2019, https://www.reuters.com/article/idUSKCN1MK0AG/; Elham Albaroudi, Taha Mansouri and Ali Alameer, "A Comprehensive Review of AI Techniques for Addressing Algorithmic Bias in Job Hiring", *AI* 5, no. 1 (2024): 383–404, https://doi.org/10.3390/ai5010019.

32	Cynthia Dwork and Deirdre K. Mulligan, "It's not Privacy, and It's not Fair", *Stanford Law Review* 66 (2013), https://www.stanfordlawreview.org/online/privacy-and-big-data-its-not-privacy-and-its-not-fair/; Lisa Herzog, "Algorithmic Bias and Access to Opportunities", in *The Oxford Handbook of Digital Ethics*, eds. C. Veliz (Oxford: Oxford University Press, 2024), 421.

influence algorithmic outcomes. Moreover, automated decision-making processes contribute to creating negative feedback loops and exacerbate negative effects, thereby deepening social inequalities.[33]

Algorithmic bias and errors frequently result from complex interrelated factors. First, algorithms are trained on historical data that may reflect biased past decisions, practices and societal norms. If an algorithm is trained predominantly on data from male-dominated fields, it may develop a bias that favors men, as seen with Amazon's AI recruiting tool. This perpetuates existing inequalities because the algorithm continues to project past biases into future decisions. Second, algorithms are designed to operate efficiently under specific conditions. Thus, they are inherently equipped with pre-programmed choices, values and motives to optimize performance.[34] This is particularly evident on platforms driven by profit motives, where algorithms prioritize content that maximizes user engagement and advertising revenue. Consequently, digital platforms may amplify content that is sensational or divisive, as it tends to generate more clicks and shares. On the other hand, search engine results reflect bias by favoring established theories and popular institutions and limiting visibility for non-mainstream content and new companies or organizations.[35] Similarly, content from or about minorities and underprivileged groups may be systematically suppressed. Next, algorithms can unintentionally inherit and perpetuate the prejudices of their developers. When algorithms are designed, they often incorporate subtle biases of their creators, which can lead to discriminatory outcomes.[36] Furthermore, algorithms can generate incorrect outcomes when they operate on flawed (fragmented, incorrect, outdated, or biased) data sets. Bias can also occur when the algorithm clashes with another algorithm. Such conflict may result in inaccurate or unforeseen decisions. Finally, algorithms tend to reduce complex human interactions and societal dynamics to quantifiable metrics and logical models. Non quantifiable values (such as fairness or emotions) might be eliminated from assessment leading to

---

33   Bernard E Harcourt, "Risk as a Proxy for Race: The Dangers of Risk Assessment", *Federal Sentencing Reporter* 27, no. 4 (2015): 237–43, https://doi.org/10.1525/fsr.2015.27.4.237; O'Neil, *Weapons of Math Destruction*, 54.

34   Dominique Cardon, "Deconstructing the Algorithm: Four Types of Digital Information Calculations", in *Algorithmic Cultures – Essays on Meaning, Performance and New Technologies*, eds. Robert Seyfert and Jonathan Roberge (New York: Routledge, 2016), 95–110.

35   Susan Gerhart, "Do Web Search Engines Suppress Controversy", *First Monday2* 9, no. 1 (2004), https://doi.org/10.5210/fm.v9i1.1111.

36   Donghee Shin, "Embodying Algorithms, Enactive Artificial Intelligence and the Extended Cognition: You Can See as Much as You Know about Algorithm", *Journal of Information Science*, 2021, https://doi.org/10.1177/0165551520985495.

misguided conclusions and decisions that do not accurately reflect real-world complexities.[37]

Serious challenges also arise from unresolved issues related to privacy and data security in big data ecosystems. Memoona J. Anwar and her colleagues identify four key categories of concern: (1) human factors such as lack of user consent, misuse of knowledge, unauthorized access, and inaccurate analyses; (2) technological errors including inappropriate use of data, gaps in technology, issues with data timeliness, origin, and the heterogeneity of devices and data formats; (3) data management issues related to the difficulties in storing and processing data from diverse sources, as well as its availability; (4) environmental factors including inadequate big data management systems, underdeveloped legal regulations, organizational resistance, and challenges in establishing a data-driven culture.[38] Algorithms may enable extensive monitoring and surveillance, which can infringe privacy and lead to a society where every action is monitored. Intrusive surveillance raises ethical and legal concerns about individual rights and freedoms. Finally, the increasing reliance on algorithms can exacerbate the digital divide and marginalize those without access to digital technologies or the skills to navigate them effectively.

4   Commercial Bias in Algorithmic Content Curation

Automatization in content recommendation often prioritizes commercial and corporate interests. Platforms may suppress certain types of content not necessarily because it is harmful or illegal, but because it could deter advertisers or provoke regulatory scrutiny, which could be detrimental to the platform's financial interests. This approach is largely driven by the desire to attract a broad, general audience and to present a responsible image to both policymakers and advertisers. Due to their emphasis on growth, market control and profitability, digital platforms aim to cater to a wide audience and maintain good relations with advertisers and policymakers, thereby avoiding the possibility of costly regulatory actions.[39] Susan L. Gerhart notes a tendency in search engine results to favor positive and non-controversial content. Online searches

37   Magdalena Szpunar, *Kultura Algorytmów* (Kraków: Wydawnictwo Uniwersytetu Jagiellońskiego, 2019), 34.

38   Memoona J. Anwar et al., "Secure Big Data Ecosystem Architecture: Challenges and Solutions", *EURASIP Journal on Wireless Communications and Networking* 2021, no. 1 (2021): 1–30, https://doi.org/10.1186/S13638-021-01996-2.

39   Cobbe, "Algorithmic Censorship by Social Platforms".

more frequently direct users to well-established theories and recognized institutions. Consequently, traffic directed to newly established companies and organizations is limited.[40]

The trend towards advertiser-friendly content is especially visible on social media platforms that have adopted a subscription-based model.[41] YouTube has begun prioritizing longer videos that feature well-known celebrities and established media outlets. Although these videos may not be as viral as user-generated content, they help build a wide user base and increase screen time, which, in turn, boosts advertising revenue. The shift has been heavily criticized by independent creators, whose short creative videos helped build the platform. However, the platform is now prioritizing mainstream, more commercially attractive content.[42] This change reflects a broader trend in the industry where platforms subtly adjust policies to make their environments more attractive to advertisers.

For the same reason as creating a more advertiser-friendly digital environment, social networking sites often marginalize minority or unconventional viewpoints.[43] There are several factors that contribute to this trend. First, content that features unique or minority perspectives tends to attract a limited audience, which, in turn, does not generate significant advertising income. Therefore, platforms promote mainstream content that is trending more.[44] Second, content related to disability often becomes a target for hate speech and cyber bullying.[45] Such negative interactions drive advertisers away as companies do not want their products to be associated with controversial or divisive content. Therefore, social platforms strive to maintain a safe environment for advertisers[46] by sometimes shadow banning or hiding from search results any content that might repel advertisers.

---

40   Gerhart, "Do Web Search Engines Suppress Controversy".

41   Leonardo Madio and Martin Quinn, "Content Moderation and Advertising in Social Media Platforms. Marco Fanno Working Papers – 297" (University of Padova, 2023), https://econpapers.repec.org/paper/padwpaper/0297.htm.

42   Julia Alexander, "The Golden Age of YouTube is over" (The Verge, 2019), https://www.theverge.com/2019/4/5/18287318/youtube-logan-paul-pewdiepie-demonetization-adpocalypse-premium-influencers-creators.

43   Cobbe, "Algorithmic Censorship by Social Platforms".

44   Alexander, "The Golden Age of YouTube is over".

45   Kelion, "TikTok Suppressed Disabled Users' Videos".

46   Madio and Quinn, "Content Moderation and Advertising in Social Media Platforms. Marco Fanno Working Papers – 297".

Digital advertising is very subtle. Targeted ads appear in newsfeed, sidebars, sponsored links, and is blended with user-generated content. It is meant to be more pleasing and less intrusive to the customer than traditional advertising, even though many users find it irritating, especially when targeted ads fail to meet the actual interests and needs of the customers.[47] At the same time, targeting strategies used by many advertisers may be invasive or opaque. They employ a variety of targeting parameters, many of which are not directly related to the product being advertised. A commercial may be tailored to match the individual's personality traits. After all, every person is different; therefore, what is convincing for one consumer may not be so persuasive for another. For instance, tailoring advertising to match aspects such as a customer's level of extraversion or introversion can significantly enhance the persuasive power of the message.[48] Similarly, matching computer-generated advice with a consumer's dominance level can increase the perceived credibility of the source and the likelihood that they will change their original opinions in response to the advice received.[49]

Online marketing often predicts the psychological profile of consumers based on the content they publish,[50] the language they use,[51] social media activities,[52] liked photos,[53] and content viewed. Predictive analytics powered

47   Minna Ruckenstein and Julia Granroth, "Algorithms, Advertising and the Intimacy of Surveillance", *Journal of Cultural Economy* 13, no. 1 (2020): 12–24, https://doi.org/10.1080/17530350.2019.1574866.

48   S. Christian Wheeler, Richard E. Petty and George Y. Bizer, "Self-Schema Matching and Attitude Change: Situational and Dispositional Determinants of Message Elaboration", *Journal of Consumer Research* 31, no. 4 (2005): 787–97, https://doi.org/10.1086/426613.

49   Sandra C. Matz et al., "Psychological Targeting as an Effective Approach to Digital Mass Persuasion", *Proceedings of the National Academy of Sciences of the United States of America* 114, no. 48 (2017): 12714–19, https://doi.org/10.1073/PNAS.1710966114.

50   Bernd Marcus, Franz MacHilek and Astrid Schütz, "Personality in Cyberspace: Personal Web Sites as Media for Personality Expressions and Impressions", *Journal of Personality and Social Psychology* 90, no. 6 (2006): 1014–31, https://doi.org/10.1037/0022-3514.90.6.1014.

51   Tal Yarkoni, "Personality in 100,000 Words: A Large-Scale Analysis of Personality and Word Use among Bloggers", *Journal of Research in Personality* 44, no. 3 (2010): 363–73, https://doi.org/10.1016/J.JRP.2010.04.001.

52   Jennifer Golbeck et al., "Predicting Personality from Twitter", *Proceedings – 2011 IEEE International Conference on Privacy, Security, Risk and Trust and IEEE International Conference on Social Computing, PASSAT/SocialCom 2011*, 2011, 149–56, https://doi.org/10.1109/PASSAT/SOCIALCOM.2011.33.

53   Crisitina Segalin et al., "The Pictures We Like Are our Image: Continuous Mapping of Favorite Pictures into Self-Assessed and Attributed Personality Traits", *IEEE Transactions on Affective Computing* 8, no. 2 (2017): 268–85, https://doi.org/10.1109/TAFFC.2016.2516994.

by artificial intelligence can assess a person's personality from their digital footprint more accurately than even their acquaintances can.[54] In fact, we now have a situation where the algorithm knows users better than they know themselves. It can understand users' unconscious values, desires, deep-seated fears, and dislikes. Armed with this knowledge, the algorithm can precisely direct specific content to customers to evoke specific emotions and create fertile ground for effective advertising of a product, politician or ideology.[55] Meanwhile, users remain unaware of the influence, just like in the example of individual discrimination discussed below.

The personalized content delivery algorithms used by digital platforms can significantly shape individual media experiences and trap users in filtering bubbles in which they are exposed to skewed ad distribution. Being exposed to certain content over an extended period of time can lead to misperceptions about the world based on the specific ads they see, which further reinforces social inequalities. Affluent users may see a world as depicted in advertisements for luxury goods and services directly targeted at them, which reinforces their sense of security and stability. On the other hand, users from less affluent backgrounds may often receive ads for budget services or inexpensive products projecting a narrative of financial constraint and limited opportunities. The delivery algorithm might also segment the ad audience based on racial or ethnic lines. Ads for apartments in certain neighborhoods might target certain racial groups, thus reinforcing residential segregation. Similarly, the delivery of job ads might be skewed along gender lines. High-paying tech job ads might be shown more often to male users, while ads for nursing or administrative positions might be more frequently shown to female users, leading to gender stereotypes and inequality in job opportunities. Ads for credit services, like loans or credit cards, might be delivered in a way that favors certain racial or economic groups, potentially leading to unequal access to financial resources.[56] Consider the following example: a young person from a low-income background receives advertising offers tailored to their financial situation. Therefore, the offers of services and goods are limited. Advertisers,

---

54   Wu Youyou, Michal Kosinski and David Stillwell, "Computer-Based Personality Judgments Are More Accurate than Those Made by Humans", *Proceedings of the National Academy of Sciences of the United States of America* 112, no. 4 (2015): 1036–40, https://doi.org/10.1073/PNAS.1418680112.

55   Yuval Noah Harari, *21 Lessons for the 21st Century*, Reprint Edition (New York: Random House Publishing Group, 2018), 103.

56   Muhammad Ali et al., "Discrimination through Optimization: How Facebook's Ad Delivery Can Lead to Biased Outcomes", *Proceedings of the ACM on Human-Computer Interaction* 3, no. CSCW (2019): 1–30, https://doi.org/10.1145/3359301.

who want the return on advertising expenditure to be as high as possible,[57] direct their offer only to a specific group of recipients, who may be defined among other things by their income. Thus, the decision to consider purchasing a product or a service is made for the customer by the advertiser or the algorithm. This situation can pose an even bigger problem in nations where educational and health services are mainly offered by the private sector. A low-income consumer will not receive educational offers from prestigious universities, whose degrees land high-paying jobs. Instead, they will be directed to offers from lower-tier educational institutions. After graduation, they will receive personalized job offers also tailored to their level of education. The advertiser and algorithm will decide which group of customers to grant a loan to or show the advertisement of a newly built residential complex, taking into account factors such as their race, income, religion, beliefs, and other sociodemographic factors.[58] Microtargeting is therefore an example of contemporary discrimination that exacerbates prejudices and leads to the dominance of privileged groups being strengthened.

Skewed ad distribution may result from different factors. First, advertisers can select specific targeting parameters (e.g., age, location, interests) offered by the platforms that may target or exclude specific groups. Second, optimization algorithms used by platforms, whose aim is to maximize relevance, engagement and other business objectives, can also contribute to uneven ad distribution.[59] It should be noted, however, that recent updates to digital platforms have reduced the availability of targeting options, which previously had made it possible for advertisers to engage in wide discriminatory ad

---

57   Pay-per-click is the most common pricing model in digital advertising where advertisers pay a fee each time their ad is clicked.

58   Joseph Turow, *Niche Envy: Marketing Discrimination in the Digital Age* (Cambridge, MA: MIT, 2008); Latanya Sweeney, "Discrimination in Online Ad Delivery", *Communications of the ACM* 56, no. 5 (2013): 44–54, https://doi.org/10.48550/arxiv.1301.6822; Anja Lambrecht and Catherine Tucker, "Algorithmic Bias? An Empirical Study of Apparent Gender-Based Discrimination in the Display of STEM Career Ads", *Management Science* 65, no. 7 (2019): 2966–81, https://doi.org/10.1287/MNSC.2018.3093; Emmanuel Martinez and Lauren Kirchner, "The Secret Bias Hidden in Mortgage-Approval Algorithms", *The Markup*, 2021, https://themarkup.org/denied/2021/08/25/the-secret-bias-hidden-in-mort gage-approval-algorithms.

59   Ali et al., "Discrimination through Optimization"; Basileal Imana, Aleksandra Korolova and John Heidemann, "Auditing for Discrimination in Algorithms Delivering Job Ads", in *Proceedings of the Web Conference 2021* (WWW '21: The Web Conference 2021, Ljubljana Slovenia: ACM, 2021), 3767–78, https://doi.org/10.1145/3442381.3450077.

targeting.[60] Despite these changes, the ad distribution may remain skewed due to the choice of business objectives set by advertisers, such as reach or conversion. A wide reach indicates that the ad was distributed to the widest possible section of the target audience, whereas conversion focuses on the advertiser's aim to encourage a large number of ad viewers to perform a certain action, such as visiting the website or doing a purchase. Therefore, advertisers who opt for high conversion rates might focus their efforts on specific demographic or interest groups, potentially excluding others and reinforcing existing disparities in ad visibility. Finally, other factors beyond the direct control of advertisers or platforms can lead to skew, such as differing online presence across demographics, time-of-day effects and varying competition for user attention among advertisers.[61]

On the other hand, a body of research proves that algorithmic advertising does not aim to understand or manipulate individuals through highly personalized and persuasive advertising tactics. On the contrary, it aims to group individuals effectively into broader categories based on shared characteristics and behavior. Advertisers' primary objective is to enhance customer loyalty, increase the likelihood of repeat purchases, and expand customer bases. Therefore, they use data to hone their marketing strategies, rather than carry out invasive personal surveillance.[62]

Regardless of the intentions behind advertising strategies, it is crucial to emphasize a significant underlying risk associated with these practices. Microtargeting, in particular, poses a unique threat to individual freedom. When discrimination targets a group (e.g., women or racial minorities), its members can organize and strive for social change. However, when an individual is limited by an algorithm, especially when this happens based on unclear factors (after all, the operational methods of algorithms are not widely known), it is not possible to identify a group of people discriminated against or organize a common protest. The cause of the discrimination remains unknown; it may involve a complex set of factors. To make matters worse, individuals may

---

60   Facebook, "Simplifying Targeting Categories", 2020, https://www.facebook.com/business/news/update-to-facebook-ads-targeting-categories; Scott Spencer, "Upcoming Update to Housing, Employment, and Credit Advertising Policies", 2020, https://blog.google/technology/ads/upcoming-update-housing-employment-and-credit-advertising-policies/.

61   Imana, Korolova and Heidemann, "Auditing for Discrimination in Algorithms Delivering Job Ads".

62   Thomas Beauvisage et al., "How Online Advertising Targets Consumers: The Uses of Categories and Algorithmic Tools by Audience Planners", *New Media & Society*, 2023, 14614448221146l, https://doi.org/10.1177/14614448221146174.

not even be aware that they have been subjected to discriminatory practices.[63] In fact, advanced machine learning models can process more variable types or dimensions than classical statistical methods, which increases the risk of unnoticed correlations to protected characteristics such as gender, age, ethnicity, religion, political viewpoint, sexual orientation, health status, and disability. Ongoing and unnoticed discrimination can increase the gap between different groups and erode social cohesion.

5   Political Microtargeting

Aside from commercial gains, targeted marketing is frequently used to gain political advantage and influence electoral outcomes in democratic societies. The information asymmetry between political actors and citizens, combined with the use of personalized microtargeting, raises concerns about voter manipulation. It also leaves users unaware that they are being microtargeted and manipulated,[64] which brings into question the integrity of political communication and its impact on informed voting decisions.

A large body of research indicates that political ads are more persuasive when tailored to individuals' psychometric profiles. Introverts tend to respond more positively to negative, fear-based ads, while extraverts are more receptive to positive, enthusiasm-based ads. Political campaigns frequently use emotional strategies to gain more extensive media coverage, to engage voters as well as shape their attitudes and voting preferences.[65]

Emotions influence how individuals process information; therefore, political messages are purposefully framed to increase their impact. Fear-based campaigns can heighten alertness, increase focus on current events, and make individuals more susceptible to persuasion. They encourage voters to engage in more deliberative thinking, look for more information and emphasize the importance of safety. Consequently, voters may even support policies

---

63   Harari, *21 Lessons for the 21st Century*, 100.

64   Brahim Zarouali et al., "Using a Personality-Profiling Algorithm to Investigate Political Microtargeting: Assessing the Persuasion Effects of Personality-Tailored Ads on Social Media", *Communication Research* 49, no. 8 (2022): 1066–91, https://doi.org/10.1177/009365 0220961965.

65   Marzena Żakowska and Dorota Domalewska, "Factors Determining Polish Parliamentarians' Tweets on Migration", *Czech Journal of Political Science* 3 (2019): 200–216, https:// doi.org/10.5817/PC2019-3-200; Charles Crabtree et al., "It Is Not Only What You Say, It Is Also how You Say It: The Strategic Use of Campaign Sentiment", *The Journal of Politics* 82, no. 3 (2020): 1044–60, https://doi.org/10.1086/707613.

that counter their typical political leanings if they believe these policies will improve their security.[66] In contrast, aversion-driven campaigns reinforce existing political biases, discourage further information gathering, and intensify voter polarization. Increased polarization often extends beyond ideological differences and can amplify negative sentiments and discriminatory attitudes towards those with opposing political views.[67] All in all, content that provokes a strong emotional reaction is likely to be more memorable and impactful in shaping users' perspectives.[68]

In a highly polarized political environment, voters are more prone to influence. They often rely on simplified views and ignore more substantive arguments. They are more affected by aversion and contempt for political opponents than by logical argumentation. Political actors may exploit this by igniting animosity, fear and hostility rather than relying on reasoned argumentation. These tactics can be particularly advantageous for political parties that lack specific agendas and instead aim to increase political polarization.[69]

---

66   George E. Marcus and Michael B. MacKuen, "Anxiety, Enthusiasm, and the Vote: The Emotional Underpinnings of Learning and Involvement during Presidential Campaigns", *American Political Science Review* 87, no. 3 (1993): 672–85, https://doi.org/10.2307/2938743; Bethany Albertson and Shana Kushner Gadarian, *Anxious Politics: Democratic Citizenship in a Threatening World* (Cambridge: Cambridge University Press, 2015), https://doi.org /10.1017/CBO9781139963107; Alessandro Nai, Yves Schemeil and Jean Louis Marie, "Anxiety, Sophistication, and Resistance to Persuasion: Evidence from a Quasi-Experimental Survey on Global Climate Change", *Political Psychology* 38, no. 1 (2017): 137–56, https:// doi.org/10.1111/POPS.12331; Piotr Żuk and Paweł Żuk, "'Euro-Gomorrah and Homopropaganda': The Culture of Fear and 'Rainbow Scare' in the Narrative of Right-Wing Populists Media in Poland as Part of the Election Campaign to the European Parliament in 2019", *Discourse, Context & Media* 33 (2020): 100364, https://doi.org/10.1016/J.DCM.2019.100364.

67   Sten Hansson, "Discursive Strategies of Blame Avoidance in Government: A Framework for Analysis", *Discourse & Society* 26, no. 3 (2015): 299, https://doi.org/10.1177/09579265145 64736; Jennifer McCoy and Murat Somer, "Transformations Through Polarizations and Global Threats to Democracy", *The Annals of the American Academy of Political and Social Science* 681, no. 1 (2018): 8–22, https://doi.org/10.1177/0002716218818058.

68   Joëlle Swart, "Experiencing Algorithms: How Young People Understand, Feel about, and Engage with Algorithmic News Selection on Social Media", *Social Media + Society* 7, no. 2 (2021): 1–11, https://doi.org/10.1177/20563051211008828.

69   James N. Druckman, Jordan Fein and Thomas J. Leeper, "A Source of Bias in Public Opinion Stability", *American Political Science Review* 106, no. 2 (2012): 430–54, https://doi.org /10.1017/S0003055412000123; James N. Druckman, Erik Peterson and Rune Slothuus, "How Elite Partisan Polarization Affects Public Opinion Formation", *American Political Science Review* 107, no. 1 (2013): 57–79, https://doi.org/10.1017/S0003055412000500; Anne E. Wilson, Victoria Parker and Matthew Feinberg, "Polarization in the Contemporary Political and Media Landscape", *Current Opinion in Behavioral Sciences* 34 (2020): 225, https://doi.org/10.1016/J.COBEHA.2020.07.005.

Regarding the role of newsfeed algorithms in shaping political attitudes, research studies offer mixed results. A large body of research indicates that algorithms play a significant role in influencing political opinions on online social networks.[70] The dynamics of political view formation are to a great extent influenced by the interactions on digital platforms, which are governed by both human activity and algorithmic decisions. Algorithms that recommend new connections based on structural similarities, such as mutual acquaintances, can lead to increased opinion polarization. They determine what content users see in their feeds, which is then amplified by user interactions such as sharing and reposting. Additionally, algorithms influence the composition of the networks. For instance, users with many politically active friends are more likely to be categorized as interested in politics, which in turn increases their exposure to political content.[71]

For many young individuals, who heavily rely on social media and algorithmically curated platforms for news and information, algorithms significantly influence their understanding of the world. Social networking sites use algorithms to curate news feeds. Curated exposure affects how young people perceive and understand current affairs and global issues. By personalizing content based on users' past behaviors and preferences, algorithms can create filter bubbles and echo chambers. Users may see content that reinforces their pre-existing beliefs and viewpoints, potentially limiting exposure to diverse perspectives and opinions. The selective exposure can skew users' understanding of the world, as they may not receive a balanced or comprehensive view of news and events. Seeing more news about certain issues can increase the perceived importance of those issues to the user. If algorithms prioritize sensational or unverified content, it can lead to misconceptions and a distorted view of reality. Furthermore, the emotional response elicited by such content can also influence users' engagement with certain topics.

---

70   Shoshana Zuboff, *The Age of Surveillance Capitalism: The Fight for a Human Future at the New Frontier of Power* (New York: Public Affairs, 2019); Santos, Lelkes and Levin, "Link Recommendation Algorithms and Dynamics of Polarization in Online Social Networks"; Swart, "Experiencing Algorithms: How Young People Understand, Feel about, and Engage with Algorithmic News Selection on Social Media"; Thorson et al., "Algorithmic Inference, Political Interest, and Exposure to News and Politics on Facebook"; González-Bailón et al., "Asymmetric Ideological Segregation in Exposure to Political News on Facebook".

71   Thorson et al., "Algorithmic Inference, Political Interest, and Exposure to News and Politics on Facebook".

6   Applying Algorithms and AI for the Public Good Based on the Example of Estonia

Algorithms, and more generally AI, are rapidly transforming our world. They automate many tedious and complex tasks and act as powerful tools that enhance and facilitate a wide range of services and decision-making processes. In healthcare, they analyze vast sets of patient data to predict the likelihood of specific diagnoses. In the financial sector, algorithms can assess a customer's creditworthiness or the potential for contract breaches. In industrial settings, they can identify vulnerabilities in machinery and prevent catastrophic failures. In social media, they may even identify individuals who promote radical political or religious ideologies.[72] These capabilities are all based on statistical learning. By analyzing vast datasets of past decisions and the factors influencing them, AI and advanced algorithms can not only uncover hidden patterns and trends, but also formulate their own decision rules based on complex correlations.

AI facilitates decision-making processes, which can revolutionize governance at the societal level. Estonia serves as a leading example, actively promoting AI use in both public and private sectors. The country has implemented numerous e-services to improve efficiency, enhance trustworthiness, and foster a competitive edge.[73] AI enables citizens to access essential services, submit applications, and receive approvals quickly and conveniently, all through a user-friendly digital platform. Such integration not only reduces extensive paperwork but improves operational efficiency. More importantly, human intervention is only necessary for final approval and oversight, which frees up valuable time and resources and improves user satisfaction. Estonia's commitment to developing and implementing e-services serves as a foundational pillar for the creation of a society that is open, digital, intelligent, and inclusive.[74] This approach exemplifies how the strategic application of AI and digital technologies can transform societal structures, making governance more accessible and responsive to the needs of its citizens.

---

72   Paola Pisano, Luca Macis and Marco Tagliapietra, "Insights from Practice: Applying the Integrated Gradient methodology to help explain AI predictions", 2024, https://www.unesco.org/en/articles/insights-practice-applying-integrated-gradient-methodology-help-explain-ai-predictions.

73   Ott Velseberg, "Estonia's AI Vision: Building a Data-Driven Society and Government", 2024, https://apolitical.co/solution-articles/en/estonias-ai-vision-building-a-data-driven-society-and-government.

74   Tiit Riisalo, "Artificial Intelligence Is Part of the Next Chapter in Estonia's Digital Story", 2023, https://tinyurl.com/25zftmp7.

Estonia's strategic approach to incorporating AI into its societal and governmental framework is structured around three fundamental pillars: a data-driven economy and society, an AI-driven government and society, and trustworthy, human-centric AI and data governance.[75] Estonia's #KrattAI initiative represents a groundbreaking approach to public service delivery in the age of AI. #KrattAI aims to revolutionize public service by integrating AI technologies such as chatbots and virtual assistants in both public and private sectors. The system is built on a distributed architecture, which serves the dual purpose of fostering the system's adaptability for ongoing development and enhancing resilience against cyber attacks, ensuring continued service availability.

By August 2022, Estonia had successfully implemented over 80 AI applications in its government operations. The Information System Authority uses machine learning to monitor and detect anomalies and incidents in the traffic of the nation's data exchange layer, known as X-Road, the backbone of Estonian e-services. The system strengthens national cybersecurity and facilitates the smooth operation of digital services across the country. Additionally, predictive analytics inform police deployment for traffic regulation, which optimizes resource allocation in city police forces, thereby increasing efficiency and safety in urban areas. This is an example of an activity that improves public safety through more focused and efficient operations. The Estonian Unemployment Insurance Fund uses AI to connect job seekers with suitable open positions. The system, further enhanced by job seeker profiling algorithms, aims to reduce unemployment and ensure a better fit between individual skills and available jobs. The Estonian Agricultural Registers and Information Board employs machine learning to analyze satellite images and detect land use changes, e.g.; mowing activity. Automatic monitoring ensures that farmers comply with regulations to qualify for government grants, which streamlines agricultural practices and promotes sustainable farming practices.[76]

AI is undoubtedly a significant technological advancement that increases efficiency, productivity and daily life. It is a transformative force comparable to past innovations, such as the printing press and the steam engine, both of which reshaped society and redefined social norms. However, AI differs from historical technologies in its rapid rate of adoption, expansive reach and profound impact on societal structures and ethical frameworks. The fast-paced

---

75 Velseberg, "Estonia's AI Vision: Building a Data-Driven Society and Government".

76 Siim Sikkut, Ott Velsberg and Kristo Vaher, "#KrattAI: The Next Stage of Digital Public Serviced in #eEstonia", 2020, https://e-estonia.com/wp-content/uploads/2020-april-facts-ai-strategy.pdf.

evolution often outpaces society's ability to fully assess and mitigate potential adverse effects. Cultural lag takes place as legal, social and cultural norms lag significantly behind technological advancements.

AI could become a double-edged sword. On the one hand, it can enhance daily life, productivity and governance. However, AI systems can inadvertently deviate from their original, benevolent purposes, posing risks to individual well-being and public safety. Furthermore, ethical problems around privacy, justice, autonomy, inclusivity, and responsibility arise.[77] Algorithms impact human lives and can perpetuate societal inequalities and bias, especially on the labor market, fostering discriminative decisions in recruitment.[78] Innovative tools together with rapid digitalization accelerate transformation, bringing with it risks and threats. Such potential for misuse or unintended consequences proves the need for proactive governance and ethical oversight of AI technologies. Hence, numerous efforts by international organizations have been made. The OECD's[79] human-centered AI Principles and UNESCO's[80] Recommendation on the Ethics of AI are prime examples. Similarly, the European Union's Ethics Guidelines for Trustworthy AI[81] reflect a global commitment to ethical AI practices. The OECD and UNESCO are also creating tools and assessments to address specific challenges and make these principles practical. New initiatives like the Global Partnership on AI and the UN's High-level Advisory Body have been launched to tackle specific challenges and make AI governance practical.

---

77   Judith Simon, Gernot Rieder and Jason Branford, "The Philosophy and Ethics of AI: Conceptual, Empirical, and Technological Investigations into Values: CEPE/IACAP 2021: Introduction to Topical Collection", *Digital Society* 3, no. 1 (2024): 10, s44206-024-00094-2, https://doi.org/10.1007/s44206-024-00094-2.

78   Päivi Seppälä and Magdalena Małecka, "AI and Discriminative Decisions in Recruitment: Challenging the Core Assumptions", *Big Data & Society* 11, no. 1 (2024): 20539517241235872, https://doi.org/10.1177/20539517241235872.

79   OECD, "AI Principles Overview", 2019, https://oecd.ai/en/ai-principles.

80   UNESCO, "Recommendation on the Ethics of Artificial Intelligence" (UNESCO, 2021), https://unesdoc.unesco.org/ark:/48223/pf0000381137.

81   European Commission, "Ethics Guidelines for Trustworthy AI", 2019, https://digital-strat egy.ec.europa.eu/en/library/ethics-guidelines-trustworthy-ai.

Social Cybersecurity in the Context of Societal and Economic Change

Technological advancements are transforming retail and business operations. The automation of complex tasks leads to increased efficiency and cost savings. Simultaneously, social media marketing has revolutionized customer engagement, brand management, advertising, and sales. This chapter examines the socio-economic implications of these changes and analyzes emerging concerns in social cybersecurity. As AI systems have become integral to daily life and the economy, the intersections between user data, privacy and security have been growing increasingly complex. The collection and use of vast amounts of personal data for recommendation systems and personalized marketing, for example, raise significant privacy concerns.

1 Reshaping Society and the Economy

Digital technology has profoundly transformed both society and the economy. It has enhanced connectivity and communication, which has improved customer service and reduced the costs of data storage, computation and transmission. High-tech advancements have reshaped economic activity, competitive strategies and business operations, which has led to increased market efficiency and competition.[1] Furthermore, digitalization has contributed to the globalization of businesses by opening new markets, products and services. Global market integration allows even smaller companies in developing countries to access international markets, which creates new opportunities for income generation and entrepreneurship.[2]

AI automates complex tasks, which leads to increased efficiency and cost savings for businesses. Undoubtedly, technological advancements enhance worker capabilities and efficiency by complementing human labor. Workers

---

1 Avi Goldfarb, Shane M. Greenstein and Catherine E. Tucker, *Economic Analysis of the Digital Economy* (Chicago: The University of Chicago Press, 2015).

2 Zofia Wysokińska, "A Review of the Impact of the Digital Transformation on the Global and European Economy", *Comparative Economic Research. Central and Eastern Europe* 24, no. 3 (2021): 79, https://doi.org/10.18778/1508-2008.24.22.

can therefore focus on higher-value tasks and improve overall productivity. The use of AI improves job quality across almost every sector and occupation by minimizing redundancies and optimizing operations. Hence, AI supports innovation and productivity as companies use the latest developments in machine learning to develop new products and services.[3] Automation may lead to the creation of new jobs with a simultaneous reduction of traditional roles, which results in a net increase in employment.[4] On the other hand, some argue that the rapid evolution of technology will eliminate more jobs than it generates. Automation means workers must reskill and adapt[5] but this process is often hindered by a significant disparity in digital skill levels among the workforce. Many workers lack the technological skills, educational background and training opportunities needed for reskilling. Furthermore, educational and social systems struggle to keep pace with technological developments, potentially leading to increased unemployment and greater social inequality. The mismatch between market demands and the digital skills gap points at the challenges of adapting to a rapidly evolving digital environment.[6] In fact, some forecasts suggest that the delays in cultural and educational adaptation may slow down workforce reductions. Erik Brynjolfsson and Andrew McAfee point to three main reasons why automation may not necessarily lead to job losses: (1) slow technological adoption owing to economic, legal and social barriers; (2) worker adaptability to new technologies by transforming tasks rather than replacing them entirely; and (3) the emergence of new job

---

3   Oriana Branon, "Why Artificial Intelligence is the Future of Growth" (Accenture, 2016), https://newsroom.accenture.com/subjects/technology/artificial-intelligence-poised-to -double-annual-economic-growth-rate-in-12-developed-economies-and-boost-labor-pro ductivity-by-up-to-40-percent-by-2035-according-to-new-research-by-accenture.htm; OECD, *OECD Employment Outlook 2023: Artificial Intelligence and the Labour Market*, OECD (Paris: OECD, 2023), https://doi.org/10.1787/08785bba-en.

4   Ashley Nunes, "Automation Doesn't Just Create or Destroy Jobs – It Transforms Them", *Harvard Business Review*, 2021, https://hbr.org/2021/11/automation-doesnt-just-create-or-des troy-jobs-it-transforms-them.

5   For example, there is a growing demand for AI-skilled workers. Between 2017 and 2019, employment growth for AI-skilled workers was 63%, while for the general workforce, it was only 3%. However, the increase in demand for AI professionals is primarily attributed to a rise in AI skills within existing occupations, not a change in the distribution of occupations (Andrew Green and Lucas Lamby, "The Supply, Demand and Characteristics of the AI Workforce across OECD Countries", OECD Social, Employment and Migration Working Papers, vol. 287, OECD Social, Employment and Migration Working Papers, 2023, https://doi.org/10.1787/bb17314a-en).

6   Anthony Larsson and Robin Teigland, *The Digital Transformation of Labor* (Abingdon and New York: Routledge, 2020).

opportunities driven by the demand for emerging technologies.[7] However, in certain industries and among certain groups (such as the senior population), digitalization may be occurring too fast for labor markets to adapt and keep pace with. For example, Kodak, a well-known photographic company with over 140,000 employees and a pioneer in the field of digital cameras, went bankrupt when digital photography moved to social media platforms such as Instagram. The shift towards digitalization failed to provide employment opportunities for the thousands of Kodak production workers who lost their jobs.[8]

The impact of AI on employment varies across industries and skill levels. Job polarization will intensify as AI causes growth in some sectors and job losses in others, especially transactional, data processing and customer interaction jobs that involve repetitive tasks and decision-making based on predefined criteria. Even complex and highly trained jobs could be automated, which may lead to labor concentration in occupations that are either extremely complex and require high skills or very basic with minimal training requirements.[9] AI progress is moving at a fast pace, automating a great number of tasks, including those that are more creative and less routine. Although automation and robotization affected low-skilled jobs the most, it did not lead to the complete exclusion of some professions. Take the production of factory-made furniture by large furniture manufacturers. Despite its profitability and popularity, the demand for handmade furniture continues, providing real employment opportunities for carpenters. However, market demands for skills are increasing, raising the entry barrier to jobs that were once considered low-skilled. Hence, these jobs will not be completely eliminated, but will require higher levels of craftsmanship and specialization to remain competitive.

Another concern is the potential increase in income inequality. Research shows that wealth distribution is becoming increasingly uneven, especially between highly skilled professionals and the rest of the workforce. Skilled individuals experience significant productivity gains, whereas low-skilled workers are particularly vulnerable to automation, which can lead to a decline in wages

7   Melanie Arntz, Terry Gregory and Ulrich Zierahn, "The Risk of Automation for Jobs in OECD Countries: A Comparative Analysis", OECD Social, Employment and Migration Working Papers, vol. 189, OECD Social, Employment and Migration Working Papers, 2016, https:// doi.org/10.1787/5jlz9h56dvq7-en; Erik Brynjolfsson and Andrew McAfee, *Race Against the Machine* (Lexington, MA: Digital Frontier Press, 2011).

8   Eli Noam, "Inequality and the Digital Economy", in *Digitized Labor. The Impact of the Internet on Employment* (Cham: Palgrave Macmillan, 2018), 117–40, doi: 10.1007/978-3-319-78420-5.

9   Wein K. Solos and Joel Leonard, "On the Impact of Artificial Intelligence on Economy", *Science Insights* 41, no. 1 (2022): 551–60, https://doi.org/10.15354/si.22.re066.

and increase the wealth gap.[10] However, the long-term effects of automation may differ as low-skilled work may become more productive over time, potentially limiting the extent of inequality. Nevertheless, those who own and control AI technologies and capital assets will gain the most significant economic benefits.

The impact of AI on income inequality is complex and influences different sectors and stages of economic growth both domestically and internationally. Technological development can lead to regional disparities, as high-skilled workers tend to concentrate in urban centers with better job opportunities. In the context of developing nations, the automation of labor may have far-reaching consequences. Industrial automation could reduce the costs of labor replacement, diminishing the economic advantages held by low-wage countries. As a result, wealthier countries may relocate production to automated plants closer to their domestic markets, which will have a negative impact on the economic growth of low-income countries that rely on labor migration from agriculture to urban factory work.[11]

Although a comprehensive analysis of economic digitalization is beyond the scope of this chapter, it is crucial to acknowledge the significant impact technological advancements have on social cybersecurity. As reliance on digital systems increases, both individuals and organizations are becoming increasingly susceptible to cyber threats. Heightened risk requires substantial investments in cybersecurity measures, such as security upgrades. Furthermore, businesses also need to incur additional costs to comply with national and international cybersecurity regulations. Failure to comply might jeopardize their ability for innovation and economic competitiveness on the global market.

All in all, increasing digitalization and dependence on technology makes individuals and organizations more vulnerable to cyber threats. Economic, technological and social progress are closely interrelated. Job polarization, job displacement and increased income inequality pose significant socioeconomic risks, which, in turn, can trigger social unrest and destabilize societies. Rapid and unpredictable changes are characteristics of modern society. Permanent positions are fragile and transient; they disappear before they have time to become established. Zygmunt Bauman's concept of "liquid modernity" captures this dynamic. The sociologist describes a world where structures and jobs

---

10   UNCTAD, *Digital Economy Report 2019. Value Creation and Capture: Implications for Developing Countries* (Geneva: United Nations, 2019); Wysokińska, "A Review of the Impact of the Digital Transformation on the Global and European Economy", 79.

11   Solos and Leonard, "On the Impact of Artificial Intelligence on Economy".

are not solid enough to last before they are inevitably replaced or transformed.[12] Insights into the changing dynamics of the economy and the threats posed by new technologies help policymakers make informed decisions and develop regulations and strategies to mitigate potential cybersecurity challenges, build resilience, address digital inclusion, promote life-long learning and ethical development, as well as ensure the overall stability and security of society.

2   The Attention Economy and Redefining Value

Technological progress has stimulated the evolution into an information society where information and knowledge are fundamental assets. The shift, inspired by Daniel Bell's concept of a post-industrial society, is characterized by the rise of the service sector, which now surpasses the agricultural and industrial sectors as the main source of employment.[13] In this context, machinery symbolizes progress and further development. The paradigm of the information society is based on the assertion that information technologies integrate the world into global networks of instrumentality. Economic, social and cultural systems are fundamentally reconfigured around digital information networks that interconnect and provide access to vast amounts of data. It is necessary to reconsider the economic implications of such ubiquitous information accessibility. Michael H. Goldhaber argues that in the new economy, neither information nor knowledge are scarce resources and thus lack economic power to drive demand.[14] Digitalization and proliferation of social networking sites, digital media and internet platforms have led to an exponential surplus of information. However, from an economic perspective, it is scarce resources that have greater value and drive demand. Limited availability increases their worth in the marketplace. Consequently, in the situation of information surplus, it is the attention rather than information that becomes a scarce and valuable resource and drives economic activities and business strategies.

The concept of attention as an economic asset dates back to before the advent of the Internet and social media. Dallas Smythe argued that mass

---

12   Zygmunt Bauman, *Liquid Modernity* (Cambridge: Polity Press, 2000).

13   Daniel Bell, *The Coming of Post-Industrial Society: A Venture in Social Forecasting* (New York: Basic Books, 1973); Daniel Bell, "The Social Framework of the Information Society", in *The Microelectronics Revolution*, eds. Tom Forester (Oxford: Blackwell Publishing, 1980), 500–549.

14   Michael H. Goldhaber, "The Attention Economy and the Net", *First Monday*, 1997, https://journals.uic.edu/ojs/index.php/fm/article/view/519/440.

media, due to its key role in producing and managing demand through advertising, is central in the final stage of infrastructural production in contemporary capitalism.[15] Edward S. Herman and Noam Chomsky further developed this argument by claiming that the primary aim of media outlets is to generate audiences rather than content. Audiences are not just passive consumers. Instead, they are a product that is sold to advertisers, who are the true customers of media companies. The advertiser-centric business model is based on advertising as the main source of revenue. Advertisers rely heavily on an audience's response to their campaigns, which are successful only if the media can effectively capture audience attention. This, in turn, influences consumer behavior. Audiences actively participate in the marketplace but not as recipients of content, but by engaging with ads and making purchasing decisions that create demand for products and services. Attention and audience engagement are valuable commodities that have become products offered to advertisers for commercial purposes.[16] Smythe introduces the term audience commodity[17] to emphasize the active role of audiences in the media ecosystem. Instead of being passive recipients of content, audiences are seen as active participants in the economic process whose attention and engagement generate revenue for media companies and advertisers.

The economic value of attention is related to its exclusivity as people have a limited capacity to focus. Our ability to process information is limited, and in a world overflowing with data, the abundance of information leads to an attention deficit. Herbert Simon, a Nobel laureate in economics, identified this problem as early as 1971. He argues that a surplus of information results in a

---

15   Dallas W. Smythe, "Communications: Blindspot of Western Marxism", *CTheory* 1, nr 3 December (1977): 2–3.

16   D.W. Smythe, "On the Audience Commodity and its Work", in *Media and Cultural Studies: Keyworks* (Malden, MA: Blackwell Publishing, 2001), 230–55; Edward S. Herman and Noam Chomsky, *Manufacturing Consent: The Political Economy of the Mass Media* (London: Vintage books, 1988).

17   Audience commodity refers to audiences distinguished by specific, predictable traits that advertisers target using their advertising budgets. Audiences are commodified within specialized markets where advertisers can buy and sell them based on specific demographic criteria, such as age, sex, income level, family composition, urban or rural location, social class, and interests. These specifications enable advertisers to reach segments of the population more likely to engage with their advertising. Thus, audiences are treated as commodities in the market economy. Their attention and engagement become crucial for advertising effectiveness and revenue generation for media companies (Dallas W. Smythe, "Communications: Blindspot of Western Marxism", *CTheory* 1, no. 3 (1977): 4).

deficit of what information consumes, namely the attention of its recipients.[18] In other words, the more information available, the harder it becomes to focus it on specific details. Simon thus recognizes attention as a valuable resource in economic decision-making.

Similarly, Thomas H. Davenport and John C. Beck argue that in affluent societies where many resources, such as information, capital, labor, and knowledge are abundant, attention becomes a valuable asset. Nowadays, starting a business or attracting customers and investors is no longer the main challenge, because there are many of them. The real challenge is to capture and maintain the attention of customers and investors, stand out in the information-driven society and persuade them to choose specific products or services.[19] Therefore, attention is a key factor in creating competitive advantage and driving economic value.

Attention has become a valuable commodity in modern society, because, like money, it has certain characteristics that make it highly valued:

- Attention is a desirable and limited resource that everyone strives to gain and retain. Once it has been captured, we crave more. For example, marketers must attract the attention of potential customers to sell a product, while celebrities work to accumulate more fans and followers to increase their popularity and influence.
- It is a rare good. The human ability to focus on multiple things at once is limited. We can only focus on one thing at a time, making attention a finite resource.
- It can be acquired. Various strategies, such as an effective promotional campaign or the use of sensational headlines, have the power to attract an audience's attention.
- It can be monetized. Once attention has been captured, it can be linked to profitability. For example, a customer's focus on an advertisement or product often leads to a purchase, which generates revenue for businesses.
- It circulates in society. Attention can be passed from one entity to another: for example, through advertising, endorsements or recommendations of a product to friends.[20]

---

18   Herbert A. Simon, "Designing Organizations for an Information-Rich World", in *Computers, Communications, and the Public Interest*, ed. Martin Greenberger (Baltimore, MD: The Johns Hopkins Press, 1971), 41.

19   Thomas H. Davenport and John C. Beck, *Attention Economy. Understanding the New Currency of Business* (Boston, MA: Harvard Business School Press, 2001).

20   Bartosz Mika, "Ekonomia Uwagi – Gospodarczy Fundament Społeczeństwa Informacyjnego Widziany Oczami Sceptyka", *Przegląd Socjologiczny* 65, no. 3 (2016): 115.

- It is convertible into other currency, and it can be exchanged for various benefits. Engagement with online advertisements on social networking sites or online games earns virtual points that can be redeemed for goods at promotional prices.
- It is governed by supply and demand, a fundamental category of economics. As the amount of information increases, the demand for customer attention also rises, making its capture even more valuable.
- Receiving attention offers emotional rewards, such as appreciation, which further increases its social value.[21]

Attention is an invaluable resource that much like money, plays a crucial role in many aspects of socio-economic life. However, unlike money, which can be deposited in a bank and saved, attention cannot be tangibly stored or accumulated. Although it cannot be objectively measured, social networking sites have developed methods to quantify attention through metrics such as the number of likes and followers, but these indicators are subject to variability and subjectivity. Even though attention cannot be physically stored, it can be monetized and traded. The attention economy has given rise to new business models and industries that depend on capturing, monetizing and influencing users' attention. Social media platforms, marketers and influencers, often referred to as attention merchants,[22] rely heavily on users' attention and data mining to generate profit through targeted advertising. They gain a competitive edge not necessarily by offering higher quality products, but by capturing consumer attention, fostering prolonged engagement with social networks, online games or websites.[23] Facebook and Google have become dominant players in the digital sector largely through advertising revenue. Despite initial reluctance to base its business model on advertising, Google has built its lead primarily through an advertising-focused search model, which analyzes user search queries to display relevant ads. On the other hand, Facebook collects vast amounts of user data, including psychographics, personal interests and online behavior, to deliver precisely targeted advertisements. These practices have elevated

---

21   Davenport and Beck, *Attention Economy. Understanding the New Currency of Business*, 3–15; Dorota Domalewska, *Media Społecznościowe – Władza i Manipulacja. Analiza Zagrożeń Społecznych, Politycznych i Informacyjnych z Perspektywy Nauk o Bezpieczeństwie* (Warsaw: Wydawnictwo Akademii Sztuki Wojennej, 2022), 45–46.

22   Tim Wu, *The Attention Merchants: The Epic Scramble to Get Inside Our Heads* (New York: Alfred A. Knopf, 2016).

23   Richard A. Lanham, *The Economics of Attention. Style and Substance in the Age of Information* (Chicago: The University of Chicago Press, 2006).

Facebook to be one of the most significant players in the digital realm, attracting advertisers who seek to reach specific audiences with precision.[24]

The rise of attention-driven advertising models clearly illustrates the economic significance of attention. In these models, companies pay to have their content promoted to specific audiences. Products and services are tailored to maximize user engagement, which can often jeopardize users' well-being and autonomy. The goal is to retain users' attention for as long as possible. The longer consumers stay online, the more ads they are exposed to, and the greater revenue generated for advertisers and platform operators. However, human cognitive resources are not infinite. Therefore, individuals can only act rationally to a limited extent. Due to the limitations in cognitive capacities, humans face challenges in processing information. As information technology and knowledge production expand, the gap between available information and our capacity to process it widens. As a result, the availability of attention inversely correlates with the accumulation of data and knowledge. Thus, the targeted allocation of attention is becoming crucial, turning it into a resource close to currency.[25]

The key question arises: how is it possible to attract the attention of consumers who are overwhelmed by information overload? This challenge is addressed through advertising messages, influence strategies and IT tools, including algorithms. Although advertising has the potential to expose the value of a product and reach a wide audience, its effectiveness is often diminished by the heavy volume of advertising clutter surrounding the contemporary consumer. In the digital world, advertising assumes a personalized form that thanks to algorithms, reaches the customer at the right moment. The customization of messages to match the individual consumer's needs and preferences amplifies the likelihood of capturing attention for specific products or services. Additionally, the digital space has also been largely shaped by persuasive technology, designed to direct user attention. Artificial intelligence refines personalized messages to consumers, thereby influencing their attitudes and behavior. Timothy B. Nee, president of Dorman Consulting Associates, vividly compares running personalized advertising to an electronic surveillance system for convicts. Under a court order, a tracking device is

---

24   Wu, *The Attention Merchants: The Epic Scramble to Get Inside Our Heads*.

25   Davenport and Beck, *Attention Economy. Understanding the New Currency of Business*; Philipp Bachmann and Gabriele Siegert, "How to Buy, Sell, and Trade Attention: A Sociology of (Digital) Attention Markets", in *Handbook of Economic Sociology for the 21st Century*, eds. Andrea Maurer, Handbooks of Sociology and Social Research (Cham: Springer International Publishing, 2021), 147–57, https://doi.org/10.1007/978-3-030-61619-9_10.

attached to a convict's ankle and continuously monitors their activity. Mobile devices work in a similar way. The key difference is that smartphone users voluntarily consent to being constantly monitored, while the convict has no choice. Nee points out that tech giants track users more extensively than they might realize.[26]

All in all, as attention becomes an increasingly valuable commodity, users frequently find themselves relegated to passive roles. This shift is largely driven by big tech companies which prioritize capturing and retaining attention through sophisticated algorithms and targeted advertising. However, tech corporations are not the first to use technology to maximize their influence and profit as traditional media has long prioritized influence and profitability over other objectives.[27]

However, the commodification of attention can have serious consequences. In an era dominated by entertainment, sensationalism and fake news, attention is easily traded with little accountability on the part of advertisers or website operators. Individuals often pay a high price, as seen in issues such as problematic internet use or gaming addiction. Social networks, similar to the gambling industry, influence compulsive behavior, such as constant news-checking, immediate responses to notifications, and a relentless pursuit of recognition and self-affirmation in the digital environment designed to generate profits for its owners.[28] Furthermore, the ease with which public opinion can be manipulated poses a serious threat to democratic societies.

Assessing the societal impact of the attention economy requires an analysis of both direct effects of social media exposure and the substitution effect, wherein attention-grabbing content diverts attention from other activities people might have engaged in.[29] Much of such content can be classed as interruptions, such as text notifications and social media alerts that shift attention to a completely different topic. Although some interruptions can enhance

---

26   Don Jergler, "Researchers Question Privacy of Usage-Based Auto Insurance", Insurance Journal, 2013, https://www.insurancejournal.com/news/national/2013/10/02/307073.htm.

27   Neil Postman, *Amusing Ourselves to Death* (New York: Viking Penguin, 1987); Edward S. Herman and Noam Chomsky, *Manufacturing Consent: The Political Economy of the Mass Media* (London: Vintage books, 1988).

28   Roger McNamee, "I Invested Early in Google and Facebook and Regret it. I Helped Create a Monster", *Tallahassee Democrat*, 2017, https://www.tallahassee.com/story/opinion/2017/08/09/mcnamee-invested-early-google-and-facebook-and-regret-it-helped-create-monster/550111001/.

29   Stefano DellaVigna and Eliana La Ferrara, "Economic and Social Impacts of the Media", w *Handbook of Media Economics*, vol. 1 (2015), 723–68, https://doi.org/10.1016/B978-0-444-63685-0.00019-X.

problem-solving and creativity, many are counterproductive, including self-interruptions, such as browsing social media or checking email compulsively. Workers in high-tech companies are interrupted approximately every three minutes and five seconds, which can lead to stress, frustration, increased mental effort, and a feeling of time pressure. Another problem is difficulty resuming work. On average, it takes approximately 23 minutes and 15 seconds to get back to the task after an interruption.[30] This significant delay points to the problem of productivity loss caused by interruptions, a challenge in our increasingly attention-driven economy.

3   Social Media Marketing and Redefining Business Strategies

Digital transformation has revolutionized retail and business operations, bringing about more than just technological advancements. It has led to fundamental changes in business processes, value creation and product offerings.[31] Social media marketing has likewise transformed many aspects of business operations, influencing customer relationship management, brand management, advertising, and sales.[32] Effective digital marketing integrates multiple channels, both offline and online, to optimize customer engagement. This strategy involves resources for customer acquisition, seamless channel integration and strategic partnerships to recognize market demands, refine products, understand customer behavior, and enhance overall customer experience. An online presence allows companies to reach a global and diverse audience while web technologies provide numerous opportunities for businesses to enter new markets, optimize their strategies and adapt their operations to changing market conditions.

---

30   Gloria Mark, "Worker, Interrupted: The Cost of Task Switching" (2008), https://www.fast company.com/944128/worker-interrupted-cost-task-switching.

31   Darlin Apasrawirote and Kritcha Yawised, "Factors Influencing the Behavioral and Purchase Intention on Live-streaming Shopping", *Asian Journal of Business Research* 12, no. 1 (2022), https://doi.org/10.14707/ajbr.220119.

32   Ali Abdallah Alalwan, Yogesh K. Dwivedi and Nripendra P. Rana, "Factors Influencing Adoption of Mobile Banking by Jordanian Bank Customers: Extending UTAUT2 with Trust", *International Journal of Information Management* 37, no. 3 (2017): 99–110, https://doi.org/10.1016/j.ijinfomgt.2017.01.002; Nikolaos Misirlis and Maro Vlachopoulou, "Social Media Metrics and Analytics in Marketing – S3M: A Mapping Literature Review", *International Journal of Information Management* 38, no. 1 (2018): 270–76, https://doi.org/10.1016/j.ijinfomgt.2017.10.005.

Social networking platforms offer companies access to billions of users worldwide. Platforms facilitate multidirectional communication with both new and existing customers, which enables companies to interact with their audience more effectively. It is easier to engage customers and build trustworthy relationships. By building online communities, companies can inspire customer loyalty. Consequently, a customer-centric digital strategy has overtaken traditional one-way advertising methods. Platforms enhance product visibility and support effective marketing strategies. Endorsements by celebrities and influencers significantly affect consumer purchasing decisions.[33] Furthermore, alternative communication channels, such as blogs, can be easily used to show off product features and reach a diverse audience.

Using various channels for strategic brand communication can significantly boost website traffic. Sponsored content on social media platforms often directs users to company websites, encourages further exploration and potential purchases. However, a mere presence on multiple social media platforms does not guarantee success. Truly effective companies are customer-centric and agile. They use big data and predictive analytics to optimize marketing strategies and enhance user engagement. Thus, they prioritize technological processes over basic tools, which makes them flexible in the face of evolving technologies and shifting customer behavior.[34] A proactive and forward-thinking approach is necessary to stay ahead of the competition and drive continuous innovation that attracts customers.

Digital interactions provide invaluable insights into customer preferences and behavior. When data analysis is integrated with marketing efforts, it enables the creation of personalized campaigns that resonate with the target audience. An example of data-driven personalized campaigns is the use of recommendation algorithms by social media platforms such as YouTube and Tik Tok to offer personalized video suggestions. Not only does this increase viewer engagement, but it also allows the platform to tailor marketing strategies to promote specific content to specific audiences. Such data-driven strategies optimize customer relationships, foster loyalty and drive customer retention.

Recommendation algorithms require systematic collection and rapid analysis of vast amounts of customer data to operate effectively. Digitalization enables businesses not only to gather valuable information about customers,

---

33   Delonia Cooley and Rochelle Parks-Yancy, "The Effect of Social Media on Perceived Information Credibility and Decision Making", *Journal of Internet Commerce* 18, no. 3 (2019): 249–69, https://doi.org/10.1080/15332861.2019.1595362.

34   Apasrawirote and Yawised, "Factors Influencing the Behavioral and Purchase Intention on Live-streaming Shopping".

but also to gain real-time insights into market trends and operational strategies, which gives companies a competitive edge. Effective use of digital strategies helps businesses take informed decisions, tailor their marketing communication, engage customers more effectively, and find the optimal product-market fit. The implementation of data analytics also provides valuable insights for product development, develops innovative strategies and adapts to a diversified customer base.[35] Furthermore, trend analysis helps companies to gauge the popularity of certain tendencies and position their marketing strategies accordingly. Information derived from data analytics is fundamental in guiding informed business model decisions.

Although digital technology serves as a powerful tool for businesses to reach their audience and expand into different markets, it is also responsible for numerous societal challenges and threats. First, digital marketing raises ethical concerns. One of the key issues is the violation of user privacy. Recommendation systems, data analysis and personalization of marketing communications often involve collecting vast amounts of personal data, which can lead to unauthorized sharing, breaches, misuse, and compromising of individual privacy. High-profile incidents like the Cambridge Analytica scandal in 2018 have significantly raised public awareness about privacy concerns. However, consumers are willing to share their behavioral and demographic details if they believe the benefits of personalized services outweigh the potential risk to their privacy.[36] This situation creates a personalization-privacy paradox where consumers often face a dilemma between the desire for personalized experiences and the need to protect their personal data. Social exchange theory[37] helps explain the paradox: people are more likely to share resources if they expect certain advantages in return. Personal data becomes a resource that consumers exchange for personalized experiences, i.e., the perceived benefit. The appeal of personalized experiences outweighs the costs of reduced privacy. This framework, however, does not take into account the critical role of trust and perceived risk in the decision to disclose personal

---

35 Belma Rizvanović et al., "Linking the Potentials of Extended Digital Marketing Impact and Start-up Growth: Developing a Macro-Dynamic Framework of Start-up Growth Drivers Supported by Digital Marketing", *Technological Forecasting and Social Change* 186 (2023): 122128, https://doi.org/10.1016/j.techfore.2022.122128.

36 Daniele Scarpi, Gabriele Pizzi and Shashi Matta, "Digital Technologies and Privacy: State of the Art and Research Directions", *Psychology & Marketing* 39, no. 9 (2022): 1687–97, https://doi.org/10.1002/mar.21692.

37 R.M. Emerson, "Social Exchange", in *Social Psychology: Sociological Perspective*, eds. M. Rosenberg and R. Turner (New York: Basic Books, 1981), 3–24; Scarpi, Pizzi and Matta, "Digital Technologies and Privacy".

information.[38] Both trust and perceived risk can vary greatly among individuals. Trust depends on the subjective perception of the company's credibility and the security measures it employs to protect user data. On the other hand, perceived risk is related to the potential negative consequences of sharing personal data, such as unwanted marketing practices. These factors are taken into consideration when customers decide whether the perceived benefits of personalization outweigh the potential privacy costs. Therefore, if companies use personal data for personalized experiences, they need to enhance trust and reduce perceived risks to reduce the personalization-privacy paradox.

Customer profiling poses a significant threat to personal privacy even if seemingly non-sensitive data related to users' interests (affinity profiling[39]) is collected. Users may not be aware that their online behavior is being analyzed for profiling purposes. The data that is collected while not directly sensitive, can become invasive. If a user is profiled to have an "affinity" for certain cultural or religious practices, it might indirectly disclose their religious beliefs or cultural background, even if that specific data was never directly collected.[40] Users might also be misclassified, leading to incorrect assumptions about their personal traits or interests. This not only breaches their privacy but can also lead to unwanted or inappropriate targeted advertising.

Businesses are relying on increasingly more advanced computational tools, such as augmented reality, smart mirrors, AI-enabled face recognition cameras, biometric checkout systems to enhance shopping experiences. However, the use of these technologies also raises significant privacy concerns. Constant monitoring through various sensors can be perceived as invasive surveillance. The more technology and data a company uses, the more customer-related information it collects, which may raise ethical concerns such as fairness or using vulnerable information to sell a product. The former includes price discrimination. The latter involves using multiple information about the

---

38   Scarpi, Pizzi and Matta, "Digital Technologies and Privacy".

39   Affinity profiling is a technique where advertisers do not directly gather sensitive data about users, such as their personal traits or membership in protected groups. Instead, they analyze other available data to gauge the user's "affinity" or likeness to certain groups. For instance, investigating a user's membership of a religious group would breach privacy regulations (e.g., the GDPR in the European Union); however, analyzing their interest in religious practices is considered less intrusive as it does not entail collecting sensitive data (Sandra Wachter, "Affinity Profiling and Discrimination by Association in Online Behavioral Advertising", *Berkeley Technology Law Journal* 35, no. 2 (2020): 367–430).

40   Wachter.

client, including emotional analytics,[41] to target advertising and sell a product. Advertising is more impactful and meaningful when it reaches customers in a certain emotional state because emotions significantly influence consumer decision-making.[42] Emotionally engaged customers are more likely to purchase, recommend and remain loyal to a brand. Products that evoke a sense of nostalgia not only create positive emotions but also reinforce commitment to the brand. Activities related to consumption can also generate positive emotions; hence, advertising strategies frequently focus on the experience of consumption rather than the product to better resonate with consumers.[43] By understanding the emotional state of a potential customer, marketers can tailor their messages to resonate more deeply or even make use of their emotional state to pitch a product.

Customized pricing is a frequently used and highly effective strategy. It was established via shopper programs that collect data on customer demographics and purchasing habits and records. The collected data serves multiple purposes. For instance, the price of new or frequently bought products may be modified to influence purchase decisions. For durable goods, such as furniture, retailers can offer discounts to price-sensitive consumers, who are more likely to buy discounted products, and maintain full prices for price-insensitive consumers who are content paying the full price. In contrast, for sporadic purchases, like airline tickets, pricing strategies can vary based on the type of traveler. The option to purchase products in bulk can also affect their pricing.[44] Some companies diversify prices to deter customers from purchasing products from other vendors. As a result, customers located near competing businesses are offered lower prices.

---

41   Emotional analytics refers to the analysis of users' emotions based on the emotional tone of their social media interactions and the content they engage with. Basic sentiment analysis categorizes social media content into positive, negative, or neutral sentiments whereas more advanced tools can identify specific emotions like joy, anger, or sadness.

42   Marco Escadas, Marjan S. Jalali and Minoo Farhangmehr, "Why Bad Feelings Predict Good Behaviours: The Role of Positive and Negative Anticipated Emotions on Consumer Ethical Decision Making", *Business Ethics: A European Review* 28, no. 4 (2019): 529–45, https://doi.org/10.1111/beer.12237; Michel Tuan Pham and Leonard Lee, "Introduction to Special Issue: Consumer Emotions in the Marketplace", *Journal of the Association for Consumer Research* 4, no. 2 (2019): 98–101, https://doi.org/10.1086/702851.

43   Pham and Lee, "Introduction to Special Issue".

44   Xin Chen et al., "Personalized Pricing with Group Fairness Constraint", in *2023 ACM Conference on Fairness, Accountability, and Transparency* (FAccT '23: the 2023 ACM Conference on Fairness, Accountability, and Transparency, Chicago IL USA: ACM, 2023), 1520–30, https://doi.org/10.1145/3593013.3594097.

The practice of personalized pricing can raise numerous ethical concerns. Although it may be beneficial in some contexts (e.g., offering senior or student discounts), it becomes ethically questionable when prices are set based on opaque algorithms or personal data without the consumer's explicit knowledge or consent. Relying on such non-transparent methods can lead to manipulation and potential exploitation of vulnerable consumers. For instance, a customer who consistently buys luxury products might be charged higher prices under the assumption that they are less price-sensitive.

Customized pricing may also raise concerns about fairness and equity. Charging different prices for identical goods can be perceived as an unfair practice that increases inequalities. Customers with limited digital literacy might be consistently charged higher prices. Furthermore, when companies use profiling to target groups or exclude specific groups from certain product offers or differentiated prices, they may inadvertently discriminate against users based on their assumed interests. Such practices can reinforce societal biases and further marginalize certain groups.

Personalized algorithms that create individual media experiences and offer recommendations trap citizens in filter bubbles, where they are only exposed to information and ads that reinforce their existing views and status. Some internet users may see a world filled with targeted advertisements for luxury goods, which creates a sense of security and stability. Additionally, a range of promotional offers is targeted at wealthier internet users who are more likely to purchase another product.[45] Not only does this lead to discrimination against other customers and the perpetuation of inequality in society, but it also shows that companies are exerting increasing control over citizens who may not realize that automated models contribute to deepening social inequalities. This form of symbolic algorithmic violence[46] can also be seen in personalized advertising. When targeted advertising focuses on specific economic groups to promote products and services, the offerings are limited based on the economic backgrounds of customers. As a result, consumer choices are dictated by algorithms or advertising strategies rather than by personal preferences. Algorithms decide who receives job offers, loans or educational opportunities

---

45   Julia Angwin, *Społeczeństwo Nadzorowane. W Poszukiwaniu Prywatności, Bezpieczeństwa i Wolności w Świecie Permanentnej Inwigilacji* (Warsaw: Wydawnictwo Naukowe PWN, 2019), 28–31.

46   Symbolic violence refers to the imposition of certain cultural norms on others, presenting them as unquestioned, universal and valid. The actual systems of power remain hidden (Daniel Mider, "The Anatomy of Violence: A Study of the Literature", *Aggression and Violent Behavior* 18, no. 6 (2013): 702–8, https://doi.org/10.1016/J.AVB.2013.07.021).

from prestigious colleges that guarantee good employment prospects.[47] An algorithm-driven environment effectively confines individuals in boundaries set by third parties, which is a form of discrimination that intensifies prejudices and reinforces the dominance of privileged groups.

Algorithmic profiling and targeting is particularly problematic when it takes place in a digital environment because it threatens to limit the freedom of individuals, not entire groups. If discrimination is directed against a group (e.g., women or people of a certain race), its members can organize and advocate for social change. However, when an algorithm individually restricts a person based on factors that are not transparent (since algorithmic operations are complex and not widely understood), there is no way to identify people who are discriminated against for the same reasons or to organize collective protests.[48] Finally, using opaque technology makes it hard to hold companies accountable for any biases or ethical lapses in their marketing strategies.

4 Influencer Marketing

Influencers, with their large followings and considerable influence, have become a powerful channel for disseminating information, opinions and trends. They have become new kinds of endorsers who shape public attitudes.[49] As a result, a new type of marketing has emerged: influencer marketing. It is a specific type of native advertising[50] that mimics the appearance and vibe of the platform it

---

47   Turow, *Niche Envy: Marketing Discrimination in the Digital Age*; Sweeney, "Discrimination in Online Ad Delivery"; Lambrecht and Tucker, "Algorithmic Bias? An Empirical Study of Apparent Gender-Based Discrimination in the Display of STEM Career Ads"; Martinez and Kirchner, "The Secret Bias Hidden in Mortgage-Approval Algorithms".

48   Yuval Noah Harari, *21 Lessons for the 21st Century*, Reprint Edition (New York: Random House Publishing Group, 2018), 100.

49   Karen Freberg et al., "Who Are the Social Media Influencers? A Study of Public Perceptions of Personality", *Public Relations Review* 37, no. 1 (2011): 90–92, https://doi.org/10.1016/j.pubrev.2010.11.001.

50   Native advertising is a form of paid content that is designed to blend in with the digital environment; therefore, it is less intrusive than traditional advertising formats. It is usually identified as informative content so the ad experience follows the natural form and function of the user experience in which it is placed (Stéphane Matteo and Cinzia Dal Zotto, "Native Advertising, or How to Stretch Editorial to Sponsored Content Within a Transmedia Branding Era", in *Handbook of Media Branding*, eds. Gabriele Siegert et al. (Cham: Springer International Publishing, 2015), 169–85, https://doi.org/10.1007/978-3-319-18236-0_12; Charles Doyle, *A Dictionary of Marketing* (Oxford: Oxford University Press, 2016)).

appears on.[51] Influencer marketing is a type of covert advertising, where the persuasive intent behind the content is hidden, and embedded advertising, where commercial content is integrated into editorial material.[52] Influencers are very attractive because they provide high quality, positive, engaging, and useful content.[53] They are authentic and relatable, so consumers engage more with influencer-sponsored posts than with brand posts.[54] They frequently use personal stories to promote sponsored content, which helps maintain their online persona's authenticity. However, they need to carefully balance the amount of advertising, as too much sponsored content may affect the influencer's credibility and make them less authentic.

The significant impact of influencers on their followers can be understood through several psychological theories. According to the social influence theory, people often rely on others when forming their own opinions, beliefs or making decisions. Influencers, due to their perceived authority and large followings, can exert considerable influence over their audience's decisions. Their endorsements provide social proof, which encourages followers to conform to the trends they promote. Influencers are also often seen as more relatable than traditional celebrities, so followers develop a personal connection (parasocial interaction) that encourages followers to identify with influencers, which, in turn, motivates them to emulate the behavior, purchases and preferences they promote.

Another theory that further explains the impact of influencers on their followers is social learning theory.[55] People acquire patterns of behavior by observing and imitating others, particularly those they admire or see as role models. When followers see influencers using certain products or behaving in specific ways, they may be more inclined to mimic them. This tendency may be

51   Colin Campbell and Pamela E. Grimm, "The Challenges Native Advertising Poses: Exploring Potential Federal Trade Commission Responses and Identifying Research Needs", *Journal of Public Policy & Marketing* 38, no. 1 (2019): 110–23, https://doi.org/10.1177/074391 5618818576.

52   Liselot Hudders, Steffi De Jans and Marijke De Veirman, "The Commercialization of Social Media Stars: A Literature Review and Conceptual Framework on the Strategic Use of Social Media Influencers", *International Journal of Advertising* 40, no. 3 (2021): 327–75, https://doi.org/10.1080/02650487.2020.1836925.

53   Elmira Djafarova and Oxana Trofimenko, "'Instafamous' – Credibility and Self-Presentation of Micro-Celebrities on Social Media", *Information, Communication & Society* 22, no. 10 (2019): 1432–46, https://doi.org/10.1080/1369118X.2018.1438491.

54   Chen Lou, Sang-Sang Tan and Xiaoyu Chen, "Investigating Consumer Engagement with Influencer- vs. Brand-Promoted Ads: The Roles of Source and Disclosure", *Journal of Interactive Advertising* 19, no. 3 (2019): 169–86, https://doi.org/10.1080/15252019.2019 .1667928.

55   Albert Bandura, *Social Learning Theory* (Englewood Cliffs, NJ: Prentice Hall, 1977).

reinforced by feelings of envy towards the idealized lifestyles influencers show off. Moreover, fans tend to develop a one-sided connection with their idol (parasocial interaction) even though they might not know them personally. An illusion of intimacy is therefore created, which also builds a relationship of power (so-called referent power, with followers desiring to connect and establish a relationship with their idol).[56] The connection is not merely superficial; it reinforces the influencer's impact, as followers might place more trust in their recommendations simply because influencers have a credibility built on emotional bonds with their audience. The relationship also frequently feels personal and direct as influencers are more relatable, authentic and trustworthy. As a result, the influencer's recommendations are seen as authentic suggestions rather than paid endorsements, which further strengthens referent power to influence consumer behavior effectively.

Given the extensive reach and persuasive power of influencers, it is important to consider the broader implications of their endorsements. Their influence can extend beyond simple consumer choices and potentially guide public opinion and behavior in ways that have profound ethical and safety implications. There is growing concern over the content of these endorsements, particularly when influencers promote products or behavior that may undermine public health or safety. Research has shown that influencers often promote harmful behavior such as vaping and risky diet pills.[57] They also promote unhealthy food choices more frequently than healthy alternatives, which potentially affects the dietary habits of impressionable demographics such as children. In fact, children exposed to influencers promoting unhealthy foods consumed more unhealthy options. Unfortunately, endorsing healthy food products did not cause a positive change in consumption patterns.[58] Frances Haugen, a former Facebook product manager and a whistleblower, revealed that frequent use of Instagram was linked to a range of mental health issues in teenagers such as increased rates of anxiety, depression and body image concerns. The studies showed that Instagram's focus on staged lifestyles and physical appearances could lead to significant distress among young users, in particular teenage girls, who often compare themselves unfavorably to the idealized images they see on the platform.

---

56   Ann-Kristin Kupfer et al., "The Role of the Partner Brand's Social Media Power in Brand Alliances", *Journal of Marketing* 82, no. 3 (2018): 25–44, https://doi.org/10.1509/jm.15.0536.

57   Hudders, De Jans and De Veirman, "The Commercialization of Social Media Stars".

58   Anna Elizabeth Coates et al., "The Effect of Influencer Marketing of Food and a 'Protective' Advertising Disclosure on Children's Food Intake", *Pediatric Obesity* 14, no. 10 (2019): e12540, https://doi.org/10.1111/ijpo.12540.

These examples demonstrate the need for effective oversight and responsible practices in influencer marketing to minimize potential harm and promote positive, health-conscious influences. Frances Haugen's disclosures highlight the tension between public welfare and business objectives, as Meta's reluctance to make meaningful changes was reportedly due to concerns over profit and user engagement. External regulations may ensure that social networking sites prioritize user safety over financial considerations.

5   Redefining Power and Privacy under Surveillance Capitalism

Contemporary digital marketing presents a paradox: on the one hand, it empowers consumers through more symmetrical and interactive modes of communication. On the other hand, it raises ethical concerns about consumer privacy and agency due to its heavy reliance on Big Data and surveillance technologies. Social media enables surveillance of an individual potentially by all, and always by many other users.[59] However, Big Tech companies like Google, Spotify, Netflix, Apple, and Amazon not only carry out surveillance, but they can influence consumer behavior through sophisticated algorithms. They have a profound ability to define human experience on the internet by displaying, editing and recommending specific information to certain groups of people. Thus, they create unique online realities for each consumer by

---

59   Vaidhyanathan introduces the concept of the "cryptopticon" to describe a situation in which individuals are subject to surveillance by numerous other users. People are aware of being watched, but they seem not to care (Siva Vaidhyanathan, *The Googlization of Everything* (Berkeley and Los Angeles, CA: University of California Press, 2011), 111–12). This concept builds on Jeremy Bentham's architectural design, the Panopticon, which was intended for a prison structured in a circular manner around a central watchtower. Bentham theorized that this setup would lead to self-regulation among inmates as they would assume constant observation. Michel Foucault later expanded on the idea, suggesting that the Panopticon was emblematic of societal control through surveillance, where the mere possibility of observation could modify behavior. However, unlike the overt and centralized surveillance of the Panopticon, the modern "cryptopticon" operates subtly across various platforms and by numerous observers. The awareness of being watched becomes normalized. It still affects individual actions and choices, shapes societal norms and expectations but without the immediate fear or pressure typically associated with direct surveillance. The decentralized network of surveillance allows even non-conforming or deviant behaviors to find acceptance among like-minded individuals who may congregate in informal, hidden groups. In this situation, surveillance does not necessarily align behavior with mainstream societal norms but enables all kinds of behavior by connecting individuals with similar interests, regardless of their deviation from conventional standards.

capturing, channeling and managing their interactions with algorithmic systems.[60] These interactions are then used to guide consumer choices subtly, a process referred to as hypernudges.[61] Shoshana Zuboff, in turn, coined the term surveillance capitalism to describe a new economic order in which human experience has been commodified and used to influence and predict our behavior for commercial or other instrumental purposes. This is a parasitic form of "computer-centric" capitalism, where human behavior is converted into data that is then used for predicting, modifying and actively controlling individual behavior.[62] The goal is not to benefit society or individuals but to serve the economic and political needs of tech giants and their associates. The controversy arises from the fact that this immense power is not used for morally good purposes, such as combating climate change or addressing hunger in developing countries, but for commercial and political goals, of which individuals may not even be aware.

In the age of surveillance capitalism, user data, referred to as "behavioral surplus" by Zuboff, has become a prized commodity. The data encompasses user activities, interactions, search patterns, location, and even writing style. Meta collects information on user activity (e.g., posts and user metadata, content we interact with, actions taken in apps, hashtags used), people we

---

60   Aron Darmody and Detlev Zwick, "Manipulate to Empower: Hyper-Relevance and the Contradictions of Marketing in the Age of Surveillance Capitalism", *Big Data & Society* 7, no. 1 (2020): 2053951720904112, https://doi.org/10.1177/2053951720904112.

61   A nudge is "any aspect of choice architecture that alters people's behavior in a predictable way without forbidding any options or significantly changing their economic incentives" (Richard H. Thaler and Cass R. Sunstein, *Nudge* (London: Penguin Books, 2008), 6). Nudging is based on cognitive psychology experiments that have demonstrated how human decision-making often departs from the rational actor model commonly assumed in microeconomics. Instead, people rely on cognitive shortcuts and heuristics, often making decisions subconsciously and without active deliberation. For example, the way food is arranged in a cafeteria can significantly affect the choices people make, without restricting their freedom of choice. Placing healthier food options at eye level or in more accessible positions can nudge people towards choosing these products (Richard H. Thaler and Cass R. Sunstein, *Nudge*). Hypernudging is an advanced form of nudging, empowered by big data analytics. While traditional nudging tactics might be static, hypernudges are dynamic and personalized. They adjust in real-time to an individual's behavior and the broader environment (Karen Yeung, "'Hypernudge': Big Data as a Mode of Regulation by Design", *Information, Communication & Society* 20, no. 1 (2017): 118–36, https://doi.org/10.1080/1369118X.2016.1186713). For example, e-commerce platforms use hypernudging to recommend merchandise based on an analysis of past browsing, purchase history and data from similar customers. Other examples include adjusting prices, displaying urgency messages and recommendations from friends.

62   Shoshana Zuboff, *The Age of Surveillance Capitalism: The Fight for a Human Future at the New Frontier of Power* (New York: Public Affairs, 2019), 12.

interact with (even if they do not use Meta's products), and details about apps, browsers, and devices (e.g., mouse movements, incoming or outgoing GPS or Bluetooth signals, cookie data). They also acquire information from partners, contractors and third parties, including activities outside their social media platforms.[63] Similar data is collected by other platforms such as Google and X. Such a wide range of data provides insights into individual personalities, preferences and behavior. The writing style can be very revealing. The use of exclamation marks or capital letters and writing fast may indicate enthusiasm or strong emotions, while meticulousness of grammar could suggest conscientiousness. The complexity of sentence structures can hint at education level, and specialized vocabulary may point to specific interests or expertise.

Behavioral data is used not to improve the services big techs offer, but to facilitate predictive analysis aimed at behavior modification and monetization. Hence, the aim is not to enhance user experience, but to manipulate and earn profit. These predictions may then be traded to a third party – advertisers and businesses or used to one's own advantage. Knowledge becomes centralized, predominantly in the technology sector, thereby transforming markets into carefully designed digital environments where consumer behavior aligns with commercial objectives. Thereby, a new form of power is created, instrumentarian power, which comes from access to a vast amount of digital data about individuals and aims to exert influence on their behavior for the purposes of modification, prediction, monetization, and control.[64] In the context of surveillance capitalism, big data offers the capability, while shareholder value drives the ambition. Influential companies provide the drive to pursue that ambition, and an often unaware or indifferent public offers the ideal conditions for its implementation. In cyberspace, few businesses have gained such a significant influence over the social and economic activities of consumers and communities globally.[65]

According to Zuboff, the new instrumentarian power is anti-democratic, driven by corporations but in which governments and other entities may also participate in the pursuit of dominance. This new power structure threatens individual freedom of choice as our ability to make choices and decisions is increasingly minimized and controlled to "produce behavior that reliably,

---

63   Meta, "Zasady Ochrony Prywatności", 2022, https://www.facebook.com/privacy/policy.

64   Zuboff, *The Age of Surveillance Capitalism: The Fight for a Human Future at the New Frontier of Power*, 352.

65   Brett Aho and Roberta Duffield, "Beyond Surveillance Capitalism: Privacy, Regulation and Big Data in Europe and China", *Economy and Society* 49, no. 2 (2020): 187–212, https://doi.org/10.1080/03085147.2019.1690275.

definitively, and certainly leads to desired commercial results".[66] Individuals are therefore nudged towards actions that benefit corporations.

Julia Angwin lends support to Zuboff's claim regarding the shift in the power dynamic. Initially, the internet was a democratizing instrument that empowered individuals by providing access to previously unavailable information. Internet users were able to compare prices from multiple vendors, conduct independent searches for knowledge or connect with like-minded individuals worldwide. However, the balance of power is now shifting towards large institutions, both governments and corporations. They now collect vast amounts of data on everyday human activities, which gives them a considerable advantage in what Angwin calls "information wars".[67] Access to expansive datasets disproportionally empowers institutions over individuals to pursue their particular goals with previously unimaginable efficiency. The power asymmetry created by access to vast amounts of data transforms the traditional roles of consumer and producer into a more manipulative dynamic where institutions can predict and control consumer behavior with great precision. As a result, what was once a tool of empowerment has become a sophisticated mechanism of surveillance and control used by corporations to pursue their own interests. This transformation is exemplified by Google, which is creating a new form of instrumental power based on extensive data collected both directly from users through user engagement with "free" services and indirectly by mining public datasets, e.g., Google Street View cars, which extensively record local neighborhoods and collect data from public Wi-Fi networks.[68] Such practices reveal that in the paradigm of surveillance capitalism, the user essentially becomes the product,[69] the source of behavioral surplus. Here, the true customers are the institutions that use the data, often disregarding privacy, moral values and individual autonomy.

---

66   Zuboff, *The Age of Surveillance Capitalism: The Fight for a Human Future at the New Frontier of Power*, 203.

67   Angwin, *Społeczeństwo Nadzorowane. W Poszukiwaniu Prywatności, Bezpieczeństwa i Wolności w Świecie Permanentnej Inwigilacji*, 34–35.

68   Jemima Kiss, "Google Admits Collecting Wi-Fi Data through Street View Cars", *The Guardian*, 15 May 2010, https://www.theguardian.com/technology/2010/may/15/google -admits-storing-private-data.

69   To highlight deliberate actions used by corporations, Zuboff uses a more explicit term, "carcass,": "[f]orget the cliché that if it's free, 'you are the product.' You are not the product; you are the abandoned carcass. The 'product' derives from the surplus that is ripped from your life (...). The corporation asserted its rights to bypass our awareness, to take our experience and transform it into data, to claim ownership of and decisions over the uses of those data, to produce strategies and tactics that keep us ignorant" (Zuboff, *The Age of Surveillance Capitalism: The Fight for a Human Future at the New Frontier of Power*, 515).

6   Surveillance Technology in Societal Governance

The scope and complexity of surveillance have grown beyond even what Shoshana Zuboff described, where societal control is exerted by those in power, and citizens are reduced to objects of manipulation.[70] A comprehensive surveillance system through a social credit system used in China is the most comprehensive and controversial use of technology for regulating citizen behavior. A draft law was introduced in November 14, 2022 to unify the various social credit practices already implemented in many Chinese provinces. Their aim was to create a comprehensive system by integrating data from various sources in order to evaluate the financial, social and moral behavior of both individuals and businesses. For instance, pilot projects in some cities assigned scores based on factors such as financial responsibility, legal compliance and even everyday actions such as jaywalking, smoking in restricted areas or paying bills on time. Individuals with high scores received benefits like easier access to loans, priority for school admissions and discounted utilities. Conversely, those with low scores faced potential penalties like slower internet, travel restrictions and limitations on job opportunities. The corporate behavior of businesses is also evaluated for such things as legal compliance, environmental practices and social responsibility initiatives. Positive evaluations can lead to benefits such as easier access to loans and reduced bureaucratic oversight, while negative scores can result in sanctions such as increased inspections, restricted market access and public shaming.[71] The current system formalizes these local practices into a comprehensive regulatory framework, the aim of which is to assess the trustworthiness of individual citizens, businesses, governmental officials, and judicial bodies across China.

The system should not be evaluated from a Western perspective due to its unique socio-economic and cultural context. It needs to be pointed out that it has been developed in response to rapid technological and economic changes that have unsettled traditional community norms and structures. Drawing from Confucian philosophy, which values finding one's place in a social hierarchy, the system aims to strengthen social cohesion and enhance societal trust

---

70   Zuboff, *The Age of Surveillance Capitalism: The Fight for a Human Future at the New Frontier of Power*.

71   Fan Liang et al., "Constructing a Data-Driven Society: China's Social Credit System As a State Surveillance Infrastructure", *Policy & Internet* 10, no. 4 (2018): 415–53, https://doi.org /10.1002/POI3.183; Aho and Duffield, "Beyond surveillance capitalism"; Zhai Xuewei and Huang Xiaoye, *China's Social Credit. Theoretical, Empirical Research, and Countermeasures* (Abingdon: Routledge, 2023).

by promoting trustworthiness or creditworthiness (understood as moral integrity in Confucianism) to citizens and organizations.[72]

While China's approach to surveillance integrates extensive social credit systems, democratic governments are increasingly adopting surveillance practices. This was first revealed by Edward Snowden, a former employee of the U.S. intelligence agency National Security Agency, who in 2013, leaked information proving not only extensive monitoring of international communications, but also the collecting of data from video recordings, audio, photos, phone calls, and emails of Americans.[73] Governments all over the world are deploying surveillance and AI-driven technology to collect and compare data from multiple sources such as social media, driver's licenses and CCTV systems.[74] Nevertheless, the extent to which technology becomes an instrument of control varies significantly between democratic and authoritarian states. In democratic countries, the strong public resistance to mass and intrusive surveillance serves as a barrier to unrestricted monitoring and control. Hence, technologies that cannot be logically justified in a democratic context, such as full-body scanners and tracking microchips implanted in children, are likely to face significant public resistance. However, if such technologies offer apparent societal benefits with only minor inconveniences, such as ubiquitous cookie consent forms designed to protect user privacy against targeted advertising, then public resistance tends to diminish.[75] Ongoing technological advancements in mass monitoring make such technology increasingly commonly used by state institutions, as shown below.

Body-worn cameras have been increasingly adopted by law enforcement departments. They were initially introduced as an accountability mechanism for law enforcement, but the footage is largely controlled by government officials, including law enforcement departments and local prosecutors. Contrary to expectations, cameras do not prevent law enforcement from using excessive

---

72   Ariane Ollier-Malaterre, *Living with Digital Surveillance in China: Citizens' Narratives on Technology, Privacy, and Governance* (London: Routledge, 2023), https://doi.org/10.4324/9781003403876; Xuewei and Xiaoye, *China's Social Credit. Theoretical, Empirical Research, and Countermeasures.*

73   Edward Snowden, *Permanent Record* (Picador Paper, 2020).

74   For example, law enforcement agencies in the U.S., UK and Australia have been regularly using Clearview AI's biometric facial recognition technology to identify suspects through scraping billions of facial images from social media and other online sources in order to prevent and detect crime. More invasive police actions may, however, require a warrant (Marcus Smith and Seumas Miller, "The Ethical Application of Biometric Facial Recognition Technology", *AI & Society* 37, no. 1 (2022): 167–75, https://doi.org/10.1007/s00146-021-01199-9).

75   Angwin, *Społeczeństwo Nadzorowane. W Poszukiwaniu Prywatności, Bezpieczeństwa i Wolności w Świecie Permanentnej Inwigilacji*, 321.

force during interactions with civilians and they are now primarily used to collect evidence against civilians rather than to document police misconduct. There are also concerns that cameras are being used for discriminatory purposes in certain neighborhoods, during certain protests and against specific groups. When protesters are recorded during protests, the footage can serve as a mechanism to limit free speech.[76] Cameras also raise issues of privacy infringement as they may record sensitive information without the consent of the individuals being filmed.

License plate readers are another example of surveillance technology. They are used by law enforcement to photograph vehicles and automatically match license plate numbers to the license numbers and vehicle ownership information kept in law enforcement databases. During protests, readers can compromise protester anonymity, as they can collect the license plate numbers of vehicles parked near the protest venues.[77] Furthermore, the tracking of citizens' movements leads to a comprehensive record of their habits and routines, which could be exploited to reveal sensitive and personal information, such as visits to political meetings, religious institutions or employment locations. Hence, their use raises concerns about privacy and the potential misuse of surveillance data.

Intelligent video systems are another type of technology with sophisticated surveillance capabilities. Video surveillance has become an effective tool in combating crime and terrorist attacks, as well as managing crowd control. This technology includes intelligent video analysis, face recognition, population density analysis, crowd density estimation, human behavior analysis, automatic number plate recognition, and traffic flow statistics.[78] Facial recognition technology, in particular, is increasingly being used by law enforcement agencies and state actors to identify and monitor potential or suspected offenders. It is often used together with body-worn cameras and other surveillance tools to capture images and videos of individuals and then use them to identify and target individuals, for example during protests or public gatherings.[79] However, there are significant concerns about the accuracy and bias inherent in facial recognition technology. Facial recognition algorithms produce erroneous results with higher rates of false positives for women, Asians and African Americans compared to Caucasians. The faces of African American

---

76   Katelyn Ringrose and Divya Ramjee, "Watch Where You Walk: Law Enforcement Surveillance and Protester Privacy", *California Law Review Online* 11 (2020): 349–66, https://doi.org/10.15779/Z38G44HR3X.

77   Ringrose and Ramjee.

78   Fredrik Nilsson, *Intelligent Network Video: Understanding Modern Video Surveillance Systems* (Logan, UT: Jenson Books, 2016).

79   Ringrose and Ramjee, "Watch Where You Walk".

women yield the highest rates of false identifications. These false positives indicate a serious problem of bias in facial recognition technology as different algorithms have varying levels of accuracy.[80] Nevertheless, in Australia, biometric facial recognition technology compatible with drivers' licenses has been allowed for law enforcement and security purposes. It enables biometric searches of drivers' license photographs for criminal investigations and terrorist threats without warrants or individual consent.[81] Law enforcement's use of facial recognition raises many questions about who gets to control and use the technology, particularly at events like protests where subjectivity may play a role.

The use of surveillance technologies poses significant concerns about infringing individuals' privacy rights and limiting free speech. It raises conflicts between certain values such as security, privacy and autonomy showing a conflict between societal values and individual rights. An ethical problem arises regarding the collection of increasing amounts of data from non-criminal citizens. In a 2020 audit of the Los Angeles Police Department, 99.9 percent of the 320 million images stored came from vehicles not involved in a criminal investigation. The information contained in databases can reveal incredibly sensitive details about individuals, including where they work, where they live and what they protest about.[82] Hence, policymakers need to ensure that technologies serve the public good while safeguarding the freedoms of citizens. An increasing number of countries are implementing regulations to specify the extent to which these tools should be employed and governed by rigorous oversight and clear legal frameworks to prevent abuses. The AI Act introduced in the EU aims to establish comprehensive rules for the use of artificial intelligence across member states. This legislation prioritizes ethical standards, transparency and accountability to ensure safe use of AI technologies without infringing on individual rights. High-risk technologies, which have significant potential to harm safety or fundamental rights, are subject to strict requirements before they can be implemented. Examples of such technologies include biometric identification systems and AI systems used in critical infrastructure, employment, education, essential private and public services (e.g., credit scoring, loan approvals or social security benefits), law enforcement, border control management, and the justice system.

---

80   Patrick Grother, Mei Ngan and Kayee Hanaoka, "Face Recognition Vendor Test Part 3: Demographic EHOffects" (Gaithersburg, MD: National Institute of Standards and Technology, 2019), https://doi.org/10.6028/NIST.IR.8280.

81   Smith and Miller, "The Ethical Application of Biometric Facial Recognition Technology".

82   Patrick McGreevy, "LAPD Automatic License Plate Readers Pose a Massive Privacy Risk, Audit Says", *Los Angeles Times*, 13 February 2020, https://www.latimes.com/california /story/2020-02-13/privacy-risks-automatic-license-plate-readers-lapd.

CHAPTER 6

Digital Persuasion: the Power of Social Media Influencers

The evolution of cyberspace has introduced diverse forms of social interaction, driven by new engagement methods and powerful opinion leaders. This chapter examines the phenomenon of social media influencers, who significantly shape public opinion and behavior. Alongside influencers, actors such as big tech companies, advertisers and political stakeholders use online communities to advance their agendas ranging from commercial gain to political influence. The interplay among these actors proves the complexity of the digital ecosystem, which extends beyond technological frameworks to social and psychological forces that shape contemporary society, culture and politics. Therefore, understanding the roles and impacts of these stakeholders is crucial to gain insight into the evolving nature of power and influence in the interconnected world.

1 Key Stakeholders and Power Dynamics in Cyberspace

In 2023, the global population reached 8.01 billion, with 5.44 billion mobile phone users (68% of the population) and 5.16 billion internet users (64.4% of the population, an increase of 1.9% since 2022). The number of social media users worldwide is 4.76 billion, which is just under 60% of the population. On average, people spend 6 hours and 37 minutes online, which is 20 minutes less than in 2022. The decrease in time spent online can be attributed to various factors such as the post-pandemic situation, limited free time, media fatigue, subscription churn, and the cost-of-living crisis. The declining trend reflects a shift toward more deliberate and purposeful online activities, where quality replaces quantity. In terms of the reasons for going online, nearly 6 in 10 working-age internet users (57.8%) rely on online resources for information, stay connected with friends and family (53.7%), stay updated on news and current events (50.9%), and watch videos (49.7%).[1]

---

1 We Are Social, 2023, https://wearesocial.com/wp-content/uploads/2023/03/Digital-2023-Glo bal-Overview-Report.pdf.

The data suggests that the primary motivations for a significant majority of working-age internet users for going online are to access information and entertainment resources. These findings suggest several societal implications. First, they illustrate the increasing reliance on digital platforms as trusted sources of information. It is therefore important to provide reliable and accessible online resources to meet people's information needs. Companies and other online actors can use this trend to their advantage. By providing users with relevant information and entertainment, they can build relationships with customers. Second, the internet fosters online communities based on shared interests or ideas. This has far-reaching implications for both individuals and society. Social networking sites have evolved beyond their original informational and entertainment functions. They now play a powerful role in influencing opinions and behavior, which various stakeholders are eager to exploit. The most significant of these are external stakeholders who attempt to directly influence users by manipulating the platforms themselves or the content they host. They include advertisers who use the web to promote products and services as well as content producers, such as media corporations, for whom the digital market is an important area of business. There is also a large group of covert influencers, such as individual hackers, entities seeking personal gain, and even high-tech companies themselves as their business model is based on maximizing user's media experience for profit. State actors also play an important role. Policymakers can use social media to monitor user activity, influence political attitudes and decisions, and infiltrate opposition groups. This happens not only in authoritarian states, but also in democratic countries, as first noted by Edward Snowden.[2] The interference of the Russian Federation in the 2016 and 2020 U.S. election campaigns has also been well documented.[3] The way digital ecosystems function is therefore influenced by economic, political and cultural factors. Legislation regulates issues related to the operation of cyberspace, the use of artificial intelligence and cybersecurity. It also attempts to reduce negative social impacts. This, however, is a two-way street since digital ecosystems also affect the economy, politics and citizen participation.

---

2 Edward Snowden, *Permanent Record* (New York: Picador, 2020).
3 Marek Górka, "Cybertools of Political Competition", *Polish Political Science Yearbook* 47, no. 4 (2018): 628–41, https://doi.org/10.15804/ppsy2018403; Gillian Cleary, "Twitterbots: Anatomy of a Propaganda Campaign", *Symantec Threat Intelligence Blog*, 2019, https://symantec-enterprise-blogs.security.com/blogs/threat-intelligence/twitterbots-propaganda-disinformation; Aral, *The Hype Machine.*

Research shows that use of the internet is country-specific and to a large extent depends on varying levels of economic, social, digital, and cultural capital. Individuals with higher levels of these forms of capital tend to use the internet more effectively for problem-solving, while those with lower levels rely on traditional, offline strategies to find information through offline social networks.[4] The reliance on the internet as a source of information is also directly influenced by varying levels of media freedom and internet penetration across countries. This discrepancy further widens the digital divide and points to the unequal distribution of technological resources and access across different regions of the world.

Considering user engagement on social media, we can see that while individual users generate most social media content, their posts and tweets typically receive sporadic likes and rarely receive comments, which indicates minimal interaction among users. Instead, they primarily act as consumers of online content and the content they produce fails to attract widespread attention. It is the content generated by stakeholders, i.e., businesses, media companies, governments, and celebrities, which achieves broad reach and effectively engages internet users. Therefore, the internet serves as a strategic platform for these stakeholders to advance their interests. They expand their online activities by organizing online campaigns to gain voter favor, attract consumer attention and influence the opinions and attitudes of undecided citizens. The predominant arguments, viewpoints and interpretations that circulate in the online public space tend to originate from the stakeholders. Despite the rise of grassroots interactive communication tools such as social networks, the agenda is still largely determined from the top-down, similar to traditional media.[5] Although studies indicate dynamic interactions among public opinion leaders and their audiences, social media remains a part of the media apparatus used to shape public opinion, set the media agenda and further the individual interests of those broadcasting the content.[6]

---

4   Adrian Leguina and John Downey, "Getting Things Done: Inequalities, Internet Use and Everyday Life", *New Media & Society* 23, no. 7 (2021): 1824–49, https://doi.org/10.1177/1461444 8211015979.

5   Dorota Domalewska, *Media Społecznościowe – Władza i Manipulacja. Analiza Zagrożeń Społecznych, Politycznych i Informacyjnych z Perspektywy Nauk o Bezpieczeństwie* (Warsaw: Wydawnictwo Akademii Sztuki Wojennej, 2022).

6   W. Russell Neuman et al., "The Dynamics of Public Attention: Agenda-Setting Theory Meets Big Data", *Journal of Communication* 64, no. 2 (2014): 193–214, https://doi.org/10.1111/JCOM .12088; Bethany A. Conway, Kate Kenski and Di Wang, "The Rise of Twitter in the Political Campaign: Searching for Intermedia Agenda-Setting Effects in the Presidential Primary", *Journal of Computer-Mediated Communication* 20, no. 4 (2015): 363–80, https://doi.org/10 .1111/JCC4.12124.

Furthermore, the presence of popular public groups indicates that users are engaging spontaneously in public dialogue around issues that are important to them. They wish to be part of self-organized communities of interest and participate actively in democratic processes. This activity, known as cyber activism or digital activism, can take various forms. Often, the differentiation is related to the motives and areas of interest that drive protests, which can be distinguished by cultural, political and nationalist themes, or more broadly as social and political action exclusive to the internet.[7] Methods of digital activism include virtual sit-ins, DDoS attacks, online petitions, email bombings, and hashtag activism. Some internet users show a high level of activism and initiate concrete actions, whereas others might only occasionally publish original content. However, the majority of users exhibit minimal engagement: they express their positions on issues through occasional mentions and primarily engage by liking and, less frequently, commenting on specific content. This type of participation is commonly referred to as slacktivism.

Different patterns of engagement reflect the dynamics observed in the formation of self-organized protest movements. These movements often originate from a small group of radicals who mobilize and gradually influence a broader range of dedicated individuals. Their influence extends from those more inclined to mobilize around a certain idea, to those who join the movement due to its size and impact. Eventually, the movement turns into a broader societal involvement.[8] The interplay between passive and active engagement points at the power of influencers. They use their visibility to subtly guide discussions and mobilize public opinion, which can lead to significant societal impacts.

2 The Persuasive Power of Social Media Influencers

Influencers are prominent social media figures who have achieved online popularity through their engaging and compelling content. Brooke Erin Duffy defines them as "a subset of digital content creators defined by their significant online following, distinctive brand persona, and patterned relationships with

---

7   M. McCaughey and M. Ayers, *Cyberactivism: Online Activism in Theory and Practice* (New York and Oxon: Routledge, 2003); Fidèle A. Vlavo, *Performing Digital Activism: New Aesthetics and Discourses of Resistance* (New York and Oxon: Routledge, 2018); Lukas Schlogl, *Digital Activism and the Global Middle Class: Generation Hashtag* (New York and Oxon: Routledge, 2022).

8   Mark Granovetter, "Threshold Models of Collective Behavior", *American Journal of Sociology* 83, no. 6 (1978): 1420–43, https://doi.org/10.1086/226707.

commercial sponsors".[9] Numerous influencers enter the digital space with already established celebrity status, such as actors and athletes. Additionally, there are numerous content creators, so-called microcelebrities, who are known to a specific niche or community with whom they develop close, frequently intimate relationships. Close intimacy is frequently established through the disclosure of personal details, a phenomenon called the "celebrification of a private self".[10] Indeed, influencers rely on strategic self-presentation techniques, follower interactions, and the sharing of daily life experiences to enhance their online presence and visibility.

Influencers can be categorized according to three key characteristics: reach, impact and bond with followers.[11] Reach refers to the size of the follower base and their ability to connect with a large audience, either directly or indirectly. This does not necessarily mean that they need a large number of followers because nano-influencers (with fewer than 1,000 followers) and micro-influencers (1,000 to 10,000 followers) can also have a significant impact if they can indirectly reach a significant audience (so-called secondary reach). Influencers often have access to niche audiences and stakeholders that are otherwise difficult to reach. Hence, they are valuable to the industry as they can deliver messages or promote products to these audiences more effectively than traditional marketing channels.

Impact refers to an influencer's ability to influence the decision-making of followers. Influencers become opinion leaders and are frequently perceived as experts in their fields. They create an authentic identity and build an intimate bond with their fans through interaction and by publishing personal and relatable content. They openly share their emotions and daily activities, which helps create a sense of similarity, familiarity and likeability. Thereby, they foster a sense of personal connection with their followers that transcends the typical celebrity–fan relationship. The one-sided emotional bond, an illusionary relationship with a media persona, known as parasocial interaction,[12] deepens a sense of familiarity and identification with the influencer. The sense of closeness makes followers feel included in the influencers' private worlds,

---

9   Brooke Erin Duffy, "Social Media Influencers", in *The International Encyclopedia of Gender, Media, and Communication*, eds. Karen Ross et al., (Hoboken NJ: Wiley, 2020), 1, https://doi.org/10.1002/9781119429128.iegmc219.

10   Hudders, De Jans and De Veirman, "The Commercialization of Social Media Stars".

11   Hudders, De Jans and De Veirman.

12   Donald Horton and R. Richard Wohl, "Mass Communication and Para-Social Interaction", *Psychiatry* 19, no. 3 (1956): 215–29, https://doi.org/10.1080/00332747.1956.11023049.

thereby strengthening parasocial relationships.[13] Authenticity, along with shared values or attitude homophily,[14] further establishes the influencer's position not merely as a public figure but as a trusted peer or friend in the eyes of their followers.[15] The blend of personal insight, authentic sharing and shared interests distinguishes influencers from traditional celebrities and marks a cultural shift towards a more intimate and interactive form of fame that prioritizes real connection over superficial appearance or remote adoration.

Influencers are frequently regarded as trusted sources[16] by other social media users. Trust derives from influencers' ability to share personal stories, authenticity, expertise, and relatability.[17] Hence, they are not only perceived as more identifiable and credible than traditional celebrities, but they are even looked up to by their audiences.[18] By consistently presenting themselves in an authentic manner, influencers foster personal connections with their followers, who in turn value their opinions and recommendations more highly. Authentic engagement significantly boosts their influence and persuasive power, as followers increasingly rely on and respect their guidance.

Building on a foundation of trust, content creators significantly influence their audiences through content, connections and strategic presentation of their online personas. They skillfully make use of the power of visually

---

13 Parasocial interaction refers to brief, one-sided interactions where audiences engage with media figures as if they were in conversation during media consumption, despite the lack of actual two-way communication. It can evolve into a parasocial relationship, which is characterized by a more sustained emotional attachment that builds over time. As viewers regularly consume media content involving the same figures, they often develop a sense of loyalty and connection that is similar to real-life relationships (Horton and Wohl).

14 Attitude homophily is "the degree to which people tend to bond with similar others" (Karina Sokolova and Hajer Kefi, "Instagram and YouTube Bloggers Promote It, Why Should I Buy? How Credibility and Parasocial Interaction Influence Purchase Intentions", *Journal of Retailing and Consumer Services* 53 (2020): 5, https://doi.org/10.1016/j.jretconser.2019.01.011).

15 Neil O'Boyle, *Communication Theory for Humans. Communicators in a Mediated World* (Cham: Palgrave Macmillan, 2022), 142.

16 See Roobina Ohanian's (1990) model of source credibility, which suggests that expertise, attractiveness and trustworthiness are key factors shaping influencer credibility.

17 Sokolova and Kefi, "Instagram and YouTube Bloggers Promote It, Why Should I Buy?"; Loes Van Driel and Delia Dumitrica, "Selling Brands While Staying 'Authentic': The Professionalization of Instagram Influencers", *Convergence: The International Journal of Research into New Media Technologies* 27, no. 1 (2021): 66–84, https://doi.org/10.1177/1354856520902136.

18 Deborah Agostino, Michela Arnaboldi and Anna Calissano, "How to Quantify Social Media Influencers: An Empirical Application at the Teatro Alla Scala", *Heliyon* 5, no. 5 (2019): e01677, https://doi.org/10.1016/j.heliyon.2019.e01677.

appealing photos and videos shared on social media to shape perceptions and behavior. The content, whether it is a detailed economic analysis, an expert interview on global issues or a breathtaking travel destination, can influence perceptions and aspirations. Influencers invest in high-quality content production, including professional photography and editing, to enhance their credibility without sacrificing the perceived authenticity. They also make sure to maintain a consistent image and narrative to reinforce their authenticity. Consistency also applies to sponsored content, which is seamlessly integrated into their feeds to avoid disrupting the perceived authenticity. However, at the same time, influencers strive for transparency in their sponsored content and disclose partnerships to maintain their authenticity.[19]

The strategic use of content plays a key role in how content creators influence their audiences, but the digital connections they establish also become their source of power. Social networks facilitate peer-to-peer interactions and the creation of a digital community where users can connect with like-minded individuals, share experiences and support one another. These personal connections, built on trust, expertise and reliability, can offer support, affirmation and a sense of belonging. Not only do celebrities use their digital connections to enhance their reach and credibility, but also ordinary users find themselves empowered to influence others in their network. Content shared by the average Joe can be highly influential, even more so than commercial advertising. Hence, users themselves can become influencers who shape the opinions and behavior of their friends and acquaintances through their social media posts.[20] Numerous viral videos have been produced and published not by seasoned professionals but by amateur users whose authentic and unscripted moments capture the public's imagination. These spontaneous clips can make an ordinary individual momentarily famous with significant yet fleeting influence. The widespread distribution of influence reflects the broader demotic turn[21] in media and culture, which started with reality TV shows featuring ordinary individuals. It has led to a rapid cycle of celebrity creation and disposal, where

---

19   Van Driel and Dumitrica, "Selling Brands While Staying 'Authentic'".

20   Alicia Chung et al., "Adolescent Peer Influence on Eating Behaviors via Social Media: Scoping Review", *Journal of Medical Internet Research* 23, no. 6 (2021): e19697, https://doi.org/10.2196/19697.

21   The demotic turn describes the growing presence of ordinary individuals in the media who transform themselves into media content through celebrity culture, reality TV and social networking platforms. The shift is driven by an increasing demand for everyday people in reality TV shows such as Big Brother, integrating the ordinary into the daily media consumption of audiences worldwide (Graeme Turner, *Understanding Celebrity* (London: Sage, 2004).

individuals can quickly rise to fame and then just as quickly fade into obscurity. This process, exemplified by the phenomenon of "celetoids"[22] who briefly capture media attention, reflects an industrial approach to celebrity production that treats individuals as disposable commodities.

The cultural paradigm shift has not only accelerated the turnover rate of celebrities but also democratized celebrity culture, making fame seem almost attainable for many. It has encouraged a proliferation of DIY celebrities,[23] especially on the internet, where individuals seek fame through self-presentation. However, despite the democratization of media access and the expansion of celebrity culture to include a wider array of individuals, the media industry continues to control the production and consumption of celebrity, maintaining a hierarchical structure that ultimately serves its interests. This development suggests a move towards a more "demotic" rather than truly democratic turn in the cultural construction of identity and desire, emphasizing the transient and manufactured nature of modern celebrity.[24]

Social media platforms serve as a double-edged sword with both positive and negative effects on users. On the positive side, they can increase peer-to-peer support, encourage positive perceptions, shared experiences and more frequent online interactions than traditional face-to-face support groups. They offer unique benefits such as greater choice, privacy and control that traditional services may lack. The rapid dissemination of ideas and trends on social networks can affect a wide range of behavior, from fashion and music preferences to political views and social activism. This encourages users to form opinions or take action based on a broad range of exposed viewpoints and campaigns.

On the downside, social platforms can also serve as outlets for harmful content and pressures, which may promote self-harm and reinforce societal and cultural pressures, such as the need for peer acceptance and issues that might amplify parental conflicts.[25] The rapid spread of information also carries the

---

22 Celetoids are "the accessories of cultures organized around mass communications and staged authenticity. Examples include lottery winners, one-hit wonders, stalkers, whistle-blowers, sports' arena streakers, have-a-go-heroes, mistresses of public figures and the various other social types who command media attention one day, and are forgotten the next" (Chris Rojek, *Celebrity* (London: Reaktion, 2001), 20–21).

23 Graeme Turner, *Ordinary People and the Media: The Demotic Turn* (New York: Sage, 2009), 14.

24 Graeme Turner, "The Mass Production of Celebrity: 'Celetoids', Reality TV and the 'Demotic Turn'", *International Journal of Cultural Studies* 9, no. 2 (2006): 155–58, https://doi.org/10.1177/1367877906064028.

25 Chung et al., "Adolescent Peer Influence on Eating Behaviors via Social Media".

risk of spreading misinformation. Furthermore, social media is strategically used by marketers and big tech companies for financial gain. Marketers and influencers promote specific products, ideas and lifestyles to boost traffic and sales. Influencers partner with brands to create engaging content that significantly impacts consumer behavior and purchase decisions.[26] Similarly, big tech companies use this influence to extend user screen time and keep users engaged on digital platforms. By implementing algorithms and personalized content delivery mechanisms, tech giants aim to captivate users and monetize their attention. The more time users spend engaged with digital content, the more opportunities there are for targeted advertising.

From a social cybersecurity perspective, media content influence has significant implications for shaping power dynamics in cyberspace – content creators shape their followers' attitudes and decisions as well as create public discourse. It is therefore not only essential to analyze the mechanisms of online influence, but also to critically evaluate the content itself and examine the values, opinions and ideologies that influencers promote. Such an analysis is however challenging to conduct as it is difficult to determine what content other users are consuming. With personalized content delivery, where each user receives information tailored to their preferences and past behavior, it is hard to identify the content consumed by others. This issue becomes particularly complex in the case of political manipulation or for parents who are trying to monitor and safeguard their children's digital experiences.

3   The Diversity of Social Media Influencers

When a social media user gains a substantial follower base, they successfully transition from a personal to a professional online presence. They become influencers, opinion leaders who hold the persuasive power to influence others and shape public opinion. The previous section explains the complex mechanisms underlying the persuasive power of social media influencers and its profound impact on audiences. This section will categorize influencers based on their origins of recognition and reach.

High-profile celebrity influencers are prominent figures in the entertainment industry, such as movie stars, musicians, models, and TV personalities, who have a significant online presence along with a large number of followers across various social media platforms. In contrast, social media influencers

---

26   Sokolova and Kefi, "Instagram and YouTube Bloggers Promote It, Why Should I Buy?"; Van
        Driel and Dumitrica, "Selling Brands While Staying 'Authentic'".

have gained recognition through social networks and have expertise in specific areas, such as video games, fashion, sports, politics, and technology. Although they have a smaller community of followers, their impact can be remarkably powerful.[27] They are ordinary people, relatable and authentic, and not openly commodified, which enhances their authenticity and trustworthiness. Consequently, their influence tends to be more powerful because they are able to develop deeper connections with their followers.

Traditionally, high-profile celebrities were distanced from their fans; they were figures to be admired from a distance. However, advances in global communication technologies have reduced the distance, making celebrities more accessible and influential. Their original roles have extended beyond the entertainment or sports sectors. They still generate substantial revenue from product endorsements, but they also actively engage in numerous non-commercial projects such as charitable work, advocacy for social issues, promotion of pro-social and environmentally friendly behavior, and shaping public risk perception.[28] The expanded presence allows them to increase their impact. Their influence even extends to international diplomacy and participation in United Nations work.[29] Since the onset of the Russian invasion of Ukraine, numerous global celebrities have visited Ukraine to show solidarity with its people and witness firsthand their resilience during the challenging times of war. Actor and director Sean Penn has made multiple trips. Movie star Angelina Jolie, a UNICEF goodwill ambassador, traveled to Lviv in April 2022 to support children impacted by the Russian armed aggression and engage with families, volunteers and medical facilities. In the summer of 2022, Ben Stiller, acting as a UNHCR goodwill ambassador, explored Lviv, Kyiv, Irpin, and Makariv. He attended several meetings with Ukrainians displaced by the war and saw the destruction caused by the Russian military.[30] The intersection of Hollywood and politics, particularly in the United States, is a long-standing phenomenon. However, in the 21st century, global celebrities are increasingly engaging in roles such as religious advocacy, negotiation with groups such as the Taliban and involvement in global crises, including the refugee situation

---

27   Paloma Sanz Marcos, *Soy Marca, Quiero Trabajar con Influencers* (Barcelona: Profit, 2017).

28   Sejung Park, "How Celebrities' Green Messages on Twitter Influence Public Attitudes and Behavioral Intentions to Mitigate Climate Change", *Sustainability* 12, no. 19 (2020): 7948, https://doi.org/10.3390/su12197948.

29   Mark D. Alleyne, "The United Nations' Celebrity Diplomacy", *SAIS Review of International Affairs* 25, no. 1 (2005): 175–85, https://doi.org/10.1353/sais.2005.0001.

30   Visit Ukraine, "Hollywood Actors and Directors who Visited Ukraine during the War", 2024, https://visitukraine.today/blog/1511/hollywood-actors-and-directors-who-visited -ukraine-during-the-war.

in Iraq. The failed attempt by actor Jude Law to negotiate with the Taliban in Afghanistan and subsequent widespread internet discussion exemplifies the increasing influence of celebrities in global affairs.[31]

Social media influencers are a diverse group who create a wide range of content, including online diaries, stunts, fashion, comedy skits, and gaming streams, all of which attract a large follower base. They increase their popularity by regularly producing both curated and viral content, often drawing on their daily experiences. Influencers construct personas that their followers perceive as consistent, relatable, trustworthy, and attainable. They foster a relationship based on trust and rapport with their audiences.[32]

Influencers have the capacity to shape the behavior and attitudes of their followers. Indeed, word of mouth, particularly when it comes from individuals with established authority and credibility in a specific field, is one of the most effective marketing strategies.[33] Influencers take advantage of this and monetize their lives to various extents, with many focusing on promoting and selling their content, personal brands or associated products.[34] Their content is often crafted with promotional objectives in mind, allowing influencers to monetize their followings through brand-sponsored content. They also develop unique personal brands that appeal to both their audience and marketers. However, they need to carefully balance self-promotion so as not to appear inauthentic, which could undermine their credibility and impact.

A wide range of celebrities create diverse content online. Influencers can be categorized based on the specific type of influence they exert, with the most popular being entertainment figures, including musicians, actors and entertainment companies; sports athletes, who post updates related to their sporting events, training sessions and personal achievements; lifestyle influencers, who post content about their daily lives, personal experiences, and interests; fashion and beauty influencers, who share makeup tutorials, fashion hauls, or product reviews; politicians who use social media to share political messages, campaign updates and commentary on current events; influencers engaged in philanthropy and activism, who use their platforms to promote and

---

31   Chong Ju Choi and Ron Berger, "Ethics of Celebrities and Their Increasing Influence in 21st Century Society", *Journal of Business Ethics* 91, no. 3 (2010): 313–18, https://doi.org /10.1007/s10551-009-0090-4.

32   Sara McCorquodale, *Influence. How Social Media Influencers Are Shaping our Digital Future* (London and New York: Bloomsbury, 2020).

33   Sanaz Saghati Jalali and Haliyana Khalid, "Understanding Instagram Influencers Values in Green Consumption Behaviour: A Review Paper", *Open International Journal of Informatics* 7, Special Issue 1 (2019): 52.

34   McCorquodale, *Influence. How Social Media Influencers Are Shaping our Digital Future*, 8.

raise funds for charitable causes and social issues; comedy and humor influencers, who deliver funny content, including pranks, challenges and amusing commentary; educational channels, which provide content for both adults and children; gaming influencers, who produce content related to video games, including "Let's Play" videos and gaming commentary. Multiple niche influencers have also gained significant popularity in specific, specialized fields. Although their follower bases may not be as extensive as those of mainstream celebrities, niche influencers exert considerable influence in their narrow target audiences.

Sports and entertainment celebrities maintain substantial followings across multiple platforms, which makes them the most powerful figures. Their reach extends beyond their professional fields as they share personal updates and take part in activities that resonate with their followers, including personal branding and endorsements. Political figures have also learned to take advantage of the power of social media to amplify their influence beyond traditional political domains. They disseminate political messages, provide campaign updates, and engage in diplomatic discussions, thereby reaching a global audience. Content creators such as PewDiePie and MrBeast, who have primarily gained popularity through their social media presence, exemplify the potential of social platforms to elevate individuals to global fame. They engage with their followers through diverse content, ranging from comedy and gaming to philanthropic activities. The most popular social media pages do not only belong to individuals; companies and brands have also emerged as influential entities. These organizations not only promote their products or services, but they also spotlight other influencers and creators. Thereby, they contribute to the diverse ecosystem of social media influence.

All in all, social media influencers represent a diverse group not only in terms of the content they create but also their varied backgrounds. Regardless of whether they share niche or broadly appealing content, their impact is substantial. Influencers are not constrained by geographical borders, which reflects the global, diverse and dynamic nature of social media.

4   Ethical Aspects of Social Media Influencing

Influencers make decisions that affect their personal lives, families and followers. One of the many issues they must decide upon is the crucial aspect of financial and business management. They need to determine the degree to which they monetize content, collaborate with brands and participate in promotional activities. These financial decisions have far-reaching implications, as they not only shape the influencer's success and income but also influence how they are perceived and trusted by their audiences. Some influencers are very conscious of the ethics surrounding their activities.[35] Mombloggers (i.e., mothers who share their parenting experiences), in particular, make decisions that have a profound impact on their family. They may find it challenging to balance commercial practices with caregiving responsibilities. What may have started as a hobby, can turn into a lucrative business that involves sharing aspects of their children's lives online. Since they frequently monetize their content, they frequently express concerns about legal and ethical issues related to sharing pictures and stories about their children.[36] Sharing content related to their children raises ethical concerns about the commodification of children's lives and the invasion of their privacy.

Sponsored content, a common feature in influencer marketing, is a highly effective advertising strategy, in particular among impressionable children and teenagers who frequently fail to recognize that such content is sponsored.[37] The blurred lines between advertising and genuine content raises ethical concerns of potential conflicts of interest.[38] Audiences rarely recognize an entry as a paid advertisement and when they do, their perceptions of news credibility and company attitudes are more negative, as are their intentions to share and their opinions of story quality. The fact that promotional content is more influential when audiences do not identify it as an advertisement creates a conflict between influencer commitments to advertisers and their audiences.[39]

Audiences value the opinions of influencers about products and services, provided those opinions are perceived as genuine, irrespective of whether influencers receive payment from brands. To maintain their trustworthiness, influencers should disclose their relationships with brands in adherence with legal requirements and ethical practices.[40] Although endorsements do

---

35   Hudders, De Jans and De Veirman, "The Commercialization of Social Media Stars".

36   Catherine Archer, "How Influencer 'Mumpreneur' Bloggers and 'Everyday' Mums Frame Presenting Their Children Online", *Media International Australia* 170, no. 1 (2019): 47–56, https://doi.org/10.1177/1329878X19828365.

37   Marina Leban, "Unethical Behaviour of Social Media Influencers: History, Practice and Future Research", in *The SAGE Handbook of Social Media Marketing*, eds. Annmarie Hanlon and Tracy Tuten (London: Sage, 2022), 464, https://doi.org/10.4135/9781529782493.n28.

38   Mariah L. Wellman et al., "Ethics of Authenticity: Social Media Influencers and the Production of Sponsored Content", *Journal of Media Ethics* 35, no. 2 (2020): 68–82, https://doi.org/10.1080/23736992.2020.1736078.

39   Bartosz W. Wojdynski and Nathaniel J. Evans, "Going Native: Effects of Disclosure Position and Language on the Recognition and Evaluation of Online Native Advertising", *Journal of Advertising* 45, no. 2 (2016): 157–68, https://doi.org/10.1080/00913367.2015.1115380.

40   Wellman et al., "Ethics of Authenticity".

not typically damage influencers' reputation or credibility, certain groups of opinion-makers are advised to abstain from public endorsements. In journalism, a conflict of interest emerges when a journalist feels compelled to report favorably on subject due to a personal, political or financial connection.[41] To maintain impartiality, reporters reject gifts and paid services that could influence their reporting. This is done to prevent biased or skewed reporting, thereby maintaining impartiality. In the case of influencers, there is no distinct division between advertising and editorial teams; influencer marketing purposefully merges business decisions with content creation.

Influencers are also involved in unethical behavior when they promote unsustainable consumption, especially by encouraging excessive purchasing among their followers. Fashion influencers frequently post updates featuring new outfits. However, what often goes unnoticed is their practice of acquiring these products solely for the purpose of a single publication. They frequently return them to the shop afterward or simply rent clothing rather than buy it.[42] This behavior persists as influencers rely on content monetization. Thus, they need to create numerous engaging posts promoting new merchandise in order to continue attracting their followers and maintain their lucrative partnerships with brands. Publishing commercial content that is appealing to sponsors misleads followers about the true value of the goods, promotes more consumption than needed and supports a throwaway culture.

Another ethical concern related to influencer marketing is the low quality of endorsed products. Many influencers promote goods without thoroughly checking their quality. In pursuit of quick profits, content creators engage in reckless endorsements and recommend products that do not meet quality expectations. Furthermore, the prevalence of counterfeit products has become another pressing issue in influencer marketing. More than 15% of posts with branded and commercial hashtags featured counterfeit products, mostly leather goods, clothing, and footwear, a 171% increase since 2016. Counterfeit products were mostly promoted on visual platforms such as Instagram and TikTok.[43] Amazon.com filed a lawsuit against 13 individuals and businesses for selling counterfeit luxury goods on its platform. The defendants allegedly collaborated to evade anti-counterfeiting measures by promoting counterfeit

---

41   John McManus, "Serving the Public and Serving the Market: A Conflict of Interest?", *Journal of Mass Media Ethics* 7, no. 4 (1992): 196–208, https://doi.org/10.1207/s15327728 jmme0704_1.

42   Leban, "Unethical Behaviour of Social Media Influencers", 461.

43   Andrea Stroppa et al., "Instagram and Counterfeiting in 2019: New Features, Old Problems", 2019, https://ghostdata.io/report/Instagram_Counterfeiting_GD.pdf.

products on social media platforms and their own websites. They used visual content to direct customers to counterfeit items while falsely advertising generic products on the Amazon platform (Amazon, 2020).

In addition to endorsing low-quality and counterfeit products, influencers also promote unhealthy snacks and idealized body images, often using filters to enhance their photos. They often boast about their extravagant lifestyles and endorse luxurious products, inadvertently reinforcing stereotypes and materialism.[44] The volume of low-quality content is growing exponentially, with lifestyle, travel, fashion, beauty, fitness, and sports dominating the online space. As a result, there is increasing pressure on individuals to conform to the standards set by influencers. Teenagers and pre-teens, in particular, are at risk. They seek social validation through likes and comments, so they actively follow and participate in these trends. An increasing number of pre-teen girls share makeup tutorials and boys live-stream their gaming sessions, further reinforcing superficial trends.

In the pursuit of rapid popularity, aspiring influencers sometimes resort to creating fake photographs and manipulating settings or scenarios to attract greater attention and engagement. They may enhance their online presence by acquiring fake likes, followers and comments from paid websites and apps. This practice might seem a quicker and easier way to increase traffic and attract a broader audience. Additionally, some influencers may artificially inflate their follower counts through strategies such as giveaways or advertising. Although these tactics may result in an initially organic follower base, their effectiveness over the long term is uncertain.

The role of influencers in content promotion has expanded beyond traditional advertising to include more controversial topics like live streaming of gambling activities, a trend that became particularly prominent during the COVID-19 pandemic. Slot streams on platforms such as Twitch garnered substantial viewership, reaching as high as 282,551 in 2022.[45] Platforms such as Kick.com facilitate both gaming and live streaming, drawing broad audiences engaged with provocative themes like sex, alcohol, drugs, and contentious content.

Some live streams feature explicit content, including a genre known as trash streaming. This form of live video broadcasting is notable for offensive and aggressive behavior, such as violence and other socially unacceptable conduct,

---

44   Liselot Hudders and Chen Lou, "The Rosy World of Influencer Marketing? Its Bright and Dark Sides and Future Research Recommendations", *International Journal of Advertising* 42, no. 1 (2023): 151–61, https://doi.org/10.1080/02650487.2022.2137318.

45   Twitch Tracker, 2023, https://twitchtracker.com/games /498566.

often amplified by substance use. Streams are typically crude and have been criticized for normalizing violence and antisocial behavior.[46] Furthermore, various other forms of explicit content streaming, such as alcohol streaming, violence streaming, sex streaming, and daily life streaming, perpetuate harmful behavior and encourage viewer engagement with controversial content, which complicates efforts to address these issues.[47]

5   Kidfluencers: Risks Connected to Child Labor

Kidfluencers, a distinct category of social media celebrities, are young children, often of preschool age, who produce engaging content that attracts young audiences. They blend ordinary life with aspirational images thereby creating an idealized youth culture that is both accessible and appealing.[48] Their videos are frequently filmed in familiar settings like bedrooms, so they create a relatable and authentic image. By strategically branding themselves and engaging with audiences, kidfluencers promote aspirational consumption and shape the desires and cultural identities of their viewers.[49] Popular kidfluencers attract millions of subscribers, especially since children increasingly favor YouTube over traditional television.[50] Significant online followings attract major brand endorsement deals. Toy unboxing videos, for example, have become a highly popular and lucrative advertising method, which provides a genuine and interactive way to promote products to children and resonate with their interests.

---

46   Barbara Cyrek and Malwina Popiołek, "Trash Streaming: Characteristics and Methodological Guidelines", *Przegląd Kulturoznawczy*, no. 3 (53) (2022): 445–58, https://doi.org/10.4467/20843860PK.22.029.16618.

47   Dominika Bek and Malwina Popiołek, "Patostreaming-Charakterystyka i Prawne Konteksty Zjawiska", *Zarządzanie Mediami* 7, no. 4 (2019): 247–62, https://doi.org/10.4467/23540214ZM.19.016.11342.

48   Melanie Kennedy, "'If the Rise of the TikTok Dance and E-Girl Aesthetic Has Taught Us Anything, It's That Teenage Girls Rule the Internet Right Now': TikTok Celebrity, Girls and the Coronavirus Crisis", *European Journal of Cultural Studies* 23, no. 6 (2020): 1069–76, https://doi.org/10.1177/1367549420945341.

49   Gavin Feller and Benjamin Burroughs, "Branding Kidfluencers: Regulating Content and Advertising on YouTube", *Television & New Media* 23, no. 6 (2022): 3, https://doi.org/10.1177/15274764211052882.

50   Özlem Kalan, "Digital Transformation in Marketing: A Sample Review on Kid Influencer Marketing and Toy Unboxing Videos on YouTube", in *Digital Transformation in Media & Society*, eds. Ayşen Akkor, Gül Yıldız and Paul Ertürk (Istanbul: Istanbul University Press, 2020).

The rise in the popularity of kidfluencers coincides with the emergence of so-called sharenting, where parents share their lives with their children on digital platforms, often with the intention of monetizing their children's online presence. In fact, children are frequently "intentionally groomed by their microcelebrity mothers to become commodities and human billboards from birth".[51] Producing family vlogs is highly lucrative not only because parenting content has become popular, but also because kidfluencers are offered profitable endorsement contracts. The profitability of viral videos featuring children has led to a rise in the production of such content.

Unlike traditional media, social networking platforms give influencers greater control over their content, including what they share and how they present themselves. However, this autonomy also raises questions about responsibility and potential boundaries when it comes to content featuring children. Often it is the parents who manage young influencers' profiles. Consequently, parent managers engage in careful monitoring, grooming and curation of a biographical narrative for their children, with the intention of monetizing it later.[52] Typically, parents construct online identities for their children, which raises the question of how this kind of parental involvement will impact the development of children's identities as they grow older.[53]

The rise of children's content creation on platforms such as YouTube and TikTok has led to the development of specialized agencies dedicated to toy marketing. These agencies help brands connect with child influencers. An example is pocket.watch, an agency which has capitalized on child-generated digital content, including Ryan Kaj from "Ryan's World" (35.2 million subscribers and 2,400 videos). However, there are concerns about the company's exploitation of child stars and producing advertising which is deceptive to young children. Despite criticism and complaints about its practices, pocket.watch remains influential in children's digital media. The company has partnered with popular kidfluencers and expanded its reach beyond YouTube through toy lines, clothing and other products.[54]

The economic activities of child influencers raise serious concerns about potential violations of child rights. The exploitation of children in content production takes various forms. First, it involves the mismanagement of children's

---

51   Crystal Abidin, "Preschool Stars on YouTube: Child Microcelebrities, Commercially Viable Biographies, and Interactions with Technology", in *Routledge Companion to Digital Media and Children*, eds. Lelia Green et al. (London: Routledge, 2020), 226–34.

52   Abidin, 227.

53   Hudders and Lou, "The rosy world of influencer marketing?".

54   Feller and Burroughs, "Branding Kidfluencers", 8–11.

earnings by parents or caregivers, who often set up social media accounts for their children and then handle influencer deals between brands.[55] To address this issue, labor laws have been enacted to protect children from economic exploitation.[56] The Coogan Act in the U.S. requires caregivers to establish Blocked Coogan Trust Accounts, where 15% of a child performer's earnings are set aside in a trust until they reach adulthood. This provision ensures the legal protection of child performers in economic terms.

Apart from economic exploitation, kid influencers are at risk of experiencing physical or psychological abuse. Caregivers, who profit from their children's online image, may even allow exploitation during content production. Two infamous examples are the 2019 Fantastic Adventures scandal, where children featured on a YouTube channel run by Machelle Hackney Hobson suffered systematic abuse, including physical harm and mistreatment. Hobson and her adult sons faced charges related to the abuse, and the channel was taken down. Another case is the controversial YouTube channel FamilyOFive, known for its depiction of physical and emotional abuse of the family's children. The parents accepted a plea deal for child neglect charges, and although their original channel was closed down, they resumed creating content under a different name.[57] In addition to these extreme cases, there are countless instances of minor disturbances where children are frequently pressured to pose for the perfect shot or participate in activities in which they are uncomfortable. The videos may appear casual and spontaneous. Rarely do they reveal the underlying calculated performance. Nevertheless, kidfluencers often experience unseen emotional pressures, as the need to perform and maintain an engaging online persona can be overwhelming.

When children spend most of their time creating content, they miss out on activities that are typical for their age group. Kidfluencers often skip school

---

55   Julia Carrie Wong, "'It's Not Play If You're Making Money': How Instagram and YouTube Disrupted Child Labor Laws", *The Guardian*, 24 April 2019, https://www.theguardian.com /media/2019/apr/24/its-not-play-if-youre-making-money-how-instagram-and-youtube -disrupted-child-labor-laws.

56   Kalan, "Digital Transformation in Marketing: A Sample Review on Kid Influencer Marketing and Toy Unboxing Videos on YouTube", 144–46; Simone Van Der Hof et al., "The Child's Right to Protection against Economic Exploitation in the Digital World", *The International Journal of Children's Rights* 28, no. 4 (2020): 1–2, https://doi.org/10.1163/15718182-28040003.

57   Daniel Victor, "Children Taken from Maryland Couple After YouTube 'Prank' Videos", *The New York Times*, 3 May 2017; Hope Schreiber, "Couple Lost Custody of 2 Children over Prank Videos, Now They're Back on YouTube under a New Name" (Yahoo! Life, 2018), https://tinyurl.com/bdem4k5f.

and sports activities.[58] Missing crucial childhood experiences like socializing with peers and engaging in free play can disrupt their normal developmental phases. Lack of natural interactions can impede the development of social skills and emotional intelligence. Furthermore, children who are in the stages of developing their self-identity can experience significant stress and harm when exposed to widespread criticism.[59] Another factor that impedes self-identity development is the high level of parental involvement. Parents often organize their offspring's free time, impose performance expectations and shape their public personas, which constrains the children's ability to explore their interests and develop autonomy. A high level of control can significantly shape the child's experience, limit their autonomy and the natural exploration of their own identity. Parental dominance can create challenges for children who are seeking their own individuality and forming their own values. It is difficult for them to live up to inflated expectations and establish a sense of self that is independent from the carefully crafted image created by their parents.

Constant content creation and media exposure place heavy pressure on child influencers. First, they feel compelled to be likable and entertaining. They try to meet audience expectations to produce engaging content. Second, their parents often push them to perform well in order to increase their following and thus ensure a steady income. Finally, advertisers also exert pressure, expecting their videos to attract new consumers and generate revenue. Most young children lack the appropriate mechanisms to cope with such intense stress, which could potentially lead to detrimental effects on their health later in life.[60] The level of stress is additionally heightened as their increased online presence exposes them not only to constant criticism but also to cyber bullying, stalking, hate, and online harassment from other users. Since many kidfluencers reveal personal information and use their real names, they are more vulnerable to harassment. They often receive hostile comments, death threats, body shaming, and insults, which terrorize them with fears that harm or abuse will occur offline and could affect their families as well.[61] Online hostility

---

58   N. McGinnis, "'They're Just Playing': Why Child Social Media Stars Need Enhanced Coogan Protections to Save them from their Parents", *Missouri Law Review* 87, no. 1 (2022): 263.

59   Marina A. Masterson, "When Play Becomes Work: Child Labor Laws in the Era of 'Kidfluencers'", *University of Pennsylvania Law Review* 169 (2018): 595.

60   Amber Lynn, "Kidfluencing: The Mental Impacts of Posting on Social Media can have on Children and Parents", *Research Archive of Rising Scholars*, 2023, 3, https://research-arch ive.org/index.php/rars/preprint/view/537/874.

61   Taylor Lorenz, "Instagram Has a Massive Harassment Problem", *The Atlantic Daily*, 15 October 2018, https://www.theatlantic.com/technology/archive/2018/10/instagram -has-massive-harassment-problem/572890/.

creates an enormous burden that can have enduring effects on their physical and psychological health. Unfortunately, the effects are difficult to determine as to date, there have been no longitudinal studies investigating the effects of long-term online presence and online fame on children and adolescents.

Another significant risk faced by kidfluencers is the loss of their privacy. Their images often become tied to specific brands, which can attract unwanted attention, heightening their visibility and exposure. This is particularly concerning because much of the content is created in their own homes, often using their real names. Videos that capture everyday activities place them under constant scrutiny from their audiences. Persistent visibility not only invades their private space but also subjects them to continuous public judgment and commentary.

All in all, the growing trend of featuring children in online content creates various risks for young microcelebrities. It is therefore necessary to address the ethical dilemmas involved, including child exploitation in content production. Unlike child stars in traditional media, child microcelebrities are not protected by the workplace standards that prevent exploitation.[62] Social media platforms often allow parents to manage and run kidfluencer accounts, sometimes anonymously, which can lead to misuse, especially when financial gain is involved.[63] Following prolonged criticism for neglecting the problem,[64] social media platforms have begun to take measures to ensure the safety of children. They are actively closing accounts that violate ethical boundaries, and disabling comments on many videos featuring minors. Users can also report concerning content and accounts in order to provide a protective environment for children. There is also a clear need for regulatory measures to legally enforce safeguards and ensure that the rights and interests of child content creators are adequately protected.

6 The Accountability of Social Media Influencers

As already mentioned, influencers may engage in unethical behavior in order to gain public recognition, attract brands and earn fast profits. They may create

---

62 Abidin, "Preschool Stars on YouTube: Child Microcelebrities, Commercially Viable Biographies, and Interactions with Technology", 228.

63 Alex Ambrose, "Kidfluencers Recast Spotlight on Children's Rights in Digital Entertainment", *Information Technology & Innovation Foundation*, 2023, https://itif.org/publications/2023/09/05/kidfluencers-recast-spotlight-on-children-s-rights-in-digital-entertainment/.

64 Lorenz, "Instagram Has a Massive Harassment Problem".

low-quality or explicit content, produce fake photographs and fabricated settings to make their posts more attractive and engaging. Offensive comments made by influencers can also provoke widespread criticism. A notable example includes the controversial comments about slavery made by Kanye West, a renowned rapper.[65] Offensive comments spark debates over the responsibility of public figures in shaping public opinion. Strong reactions also follow when influencers or companies fail to uphold ethical standards. For example, Oatly, a popular Swedish vegan milk brand among environmentally conscious consumers, faced criticism when it sold shares to a consortium accused of rainforest destruction in the Amazon. In such instances, social media users demand greater accountability for what influencers say and publish. In both cases, fans withdrew their support, participating in what is known as cancel culture, a phenomenon featuring collective strategies and actions to culturally ostracize targets through social pressure, and bring attention to improper behavior, especially when committed by prominent figures. The consequences can include financial losses, cancelled contracts, damaged reputations, and loss of brand positioning for those who are subjected to cancellation.[66] On the one hand, cancel culture can empower consumers, allowing them to express their opinions and engage in activism for social justice by criticizing abuse of power, offensive language and harmful actions such as racism, ethnocentrism, sexual harassment, gender inequalities, and homophobia. On the other hand, cancel culture may promote the dominance of certain values and suppress diverse perspectives, including unpopular ones. It may lead to groupthink, intolerance of dissenting views and limitations on freedom of speech.[67]

Harsh comments can easily escalate to online hate. Although such negative behavior cannot be condoned, it is often perceived as a form of fair punishment for perceived ethical transgressions. When influencers engage in unethical behavior that violates social norms and is publicized online, other users may see harassing comments and hate speech as justified forms of retribution or punishment. This behavior functions as a means of publicly condemning an influencer's wrongful actions through online harassment.[68] However, digital

---

65   TMZ, "Kanye West Stirs up TMZ Newsroom over Trump, Slavery, Free Thought", 2018, https://www.tmz.com/2018/05/01/kanye-west-tmz-live-slavery-trump/.

66   Natalya Saldanha, Rajendra Mulye and Kaleel Rahman, "Cancel Culture and the Consumer: A Strategic Marketing Perspective", *Journal of Strategic Marketing* 31, no. 5 (2023): 1073, https://doi.org/10.1080/0965254X.2022.2040577.

67   Pippa Norris, "Cancel Culture: Myth or Reality?", *Political Studies* 71, no. 1 (2023): 145–74, https://doi.org/10.1177/00323217211037023.

68   Noelia Valenzuela-García et al., "Too Lucky to Be a Victim? An Exploratory Study of Online Harassment and Hate Messages Faced by Social Media Influencers", *European Journal on Criminal Policy and Research*, 2023, https://doi.org/10.1007/s10610-023-09542-0.

vigilantism may contribute to a hostile online environment rather than ensure that influencers adhere to high ethical standards.

7 The Social Impact of Social Media Influencers

Research increasingly proves the significant role of digital influencers in the lives of young people, particularly teenagers who spend a considerable time online.[69] Influencers appear approachable and relatable. The content they create is frequently filmed in familiar settings like bedrooms, depicts every-day activities and idealized lifestyles, relationships and family life. It resonates deeply with many teenagers who seek not only entertainment but also information, advice, companionship, and comfort. Followers' engagement with influencers also leads to increased purchases of products they endorse, which is frequently driven by a belief in their recommendations and a desire to mimic them.

However, the pervasive influence of social media extends beyond mere interaction with influencers or purchasing products they recommend. It contributes to serious societal issues including teen suicide, body shaming and hate attacks.[70] Social networking sites encourage negative self-comparisons and reduce well-being. Research indicates that high exposure to social media is more closely linked with negative rather than positive social comparisons.[71] Viewing profiles that portray lives in a positive and frequently idealized light tends to make users feel dissatisfied with their own lives and self-image.

---

69 Chryssoula Chatzigeorgiou, "Modelling The Impact of Social Media Influencers on Behavioural Intentions of Millennials: The Case of Tourism in Rural Areas in Greece", 2017, https://doi.org/10.5281/ZENODO.1209125; Katarzyna Garwol, "Influencers – Contemporary Authorities of the Young Generation?", *European Journal of Sustainable Development* 9, no. 4 (2020): 273–273, https://doi.org/10.14207/ejsd.2020.v9n4p273; Karima Lajnef, "The Effect of Social Media Influencers' on Teenagers Behavior: An Empirical Study Using Cognitive Map Technique", *Current Psychology* 42, no. 22 (2023): 19364–77, https://doi.org/10.1007/s12144-023-04273-1.

70 O'Boyle, *Communication Theory for Humans. Communicators in a Mediated World*, 135.

71 Jesse Fox and Megan A. Vendemia, "Selective Self-Presentation and Social Comparison Through Photographs on Social Networking Sites", *Cyberpsychology, Behavior, and Social Networking* 19, no. 10 (2016): 593–600, https://doi.org/10.1089/cyber.2016.0248; Desirée Schmuck et al., "'Looking Up and Feeling Down'. The Influence of Mobile Social Networking Site Use on Upward Social Comparison, Self-Esteem, and Well-Being of Adult Smartphone Users", *Telematics and Informatics* 42 (2019): 101240, https://doi.org/10.1016/j.tele.2019.101240.

Audiences may view themselves as inferior, especially when compared to those exposed to more negatively presented profiles.[72]

The trend of negative self-comparison further emphasizes the complex impact of influencers. Many popular microcelebrities are young, affluent, white women who conform closely to restrictive standards of beauty.[73] Next to highly visible influencers, there are countless others outside these 'ideal' criteria who fail to capture marketers' attention.

Some influencers use their platforms to address various social issues, but the majority tend to reinforce concerning trends such as dissatisfaction with one's body, increased desire for cosmetic procedures and the sexualization of youth.[74] The entertainment and celebrity culture on social media frequently celebrates a specific demographic (young, female, white, wealthy) and overlooks the diverse realities and challenges faced by young people globally, such as access to education, gender-based violence and poverty.[75] This singular narrative fails to acknowledge the variety of experiences and mundane reality. It imposes unrealistic standards and leads to skewed representations. It not only reinforces stereotypes and societal norms that prioritize certain attributes over others, but also affects self-esteem and identity. These standards are often Western-centric and rooted in affluent societies. They do not directly translate to many other cultures where different values and opportunities prevail. In many societies, young people are expected to contribute to their family's livelihood, helping with work or household responsibilities. In various regions, young people may need to assist their parents in looking after the household, working on family farms, or engaging in other forms of labor essential for family survival. This stark contrast highlights the disparity between the idealized lifestyles promoted by influencers and the everyday realities faced by many young people worldwide. Imposing Western-centric beauty and lifestyle standards can create a dissonance, leading to further alienation and unrealistic aspirations that do not align with their socio-economic circumstances.

Influencers play an important part in teenagers' lives. However, the degree to which these opinion leaders shape adolescent identities requires further investigation. A large body of research proves that microcelebrities play

---

72   Elizabeth G. Spitzer, Eric S. Crosby and Tracy K. Witte, "Looking through a Filtered Lens: Negative Social Comparison on Social Media and Suicidal Ideation among Young Adults", *Psychology of Popular Media* 12, no. 1 (2023): 69–76, https://doi.org/10.1037/ppm0000380.

73   Kennedy, "'If the Rise of the TikTok Dance and e-Girl Aesthetic Has Taught Us Anything, It's That Teenage Girls Rule the Internet Right Now'".

74   O'Boyle, *Communication Theory for Humans. Communicators in a Mediated World*, 129.

75   Kennedy, "'If the Rise of the TikTok Dance and e-Girl Aesthetic Has Taught Us Anything, It's That Teenage Girls Rule the Internet Right Now'".

a crucial role in the identity formation of teenagers, who often mimic their behavior and adopt their ideologies, which suggests a profound impact on their self-concept. Adolescents who seek a sense of self find social networking sites to be influential environments that shape their identities and self-esteem.[76] Other studies, however, provide more cautious results suggesting that teenagers perceive influencers as an integral part of digital teen culture rather than as influential figures to identify with or admire. When asked about their future aspirations, the prospect of becoming a YouTuber is often seen as more of a hobby than a profession, which shows that social networking sites still have a limited impact on young people at this stage of their identity development.[77] However, more research is needed to further investigate how influencers shape adolescent identities and the broader implications for their psychological well-being and societal norms.

---

76   Luis V. Casaló, Carlos Flavián and Sergio Ibáñez-Sánchez, "Influencers on Instagram: Antecedents and Consequences of Opinion Leadership", *Journal of Business Research* 117 (2020): 510–19, https://doi.org/10.1016/j.jbusres.2018.07.005; O'Boyle, *Communication Theory for Humans. Communicators in a Mediated World*; Lajnef, "The Effect of Social Media Influencers' on Teenagers Behavior".

77   Sue Aran-Ramspott, Maddalena Fedele and Anna Tarragó, "YouTubers' Social Functions and Their Influence on Pre-Adolescence" 26, no. 2 (2018), https://doi.org/10.3916/C57 -2018-07.

CHAPTER 7

From Overload to Overreach: the Impact of Digital Content on Society

The exponential growth in digital data has brought about information overload, where excessive content leads to stress and cognitive burdens that impair decision-making. Using algorithmic filtering to manage this overflow may compromise the integrity and objectivity of information. It may lead to a superficial consumption of content and a weakened grasp of complex subjects. The blend of information and entertainment (infotainment) flooding social media also creates content that maximizes user engagement and screen time, often at the expense of substantive discourse. This chapter also addresses the pervasive impact of hate speech and cyber bullying in digital media, emphasizing their potential to incite violence, discrimination and societal division. Cyber aggression manifests through harassment and intimidation on digital platforms, where anonymity and the lack of physical presence can exacerbate hostile interactions.

1   Information Overload

The evolution of information technology has significantly increased the volume of digital data encountered by the average internet user. Every day, about 38.77 million terabytes of data are created, with over half attributed to videos on social networks. Social media and gaming alone make up over three-quarters of internet traffic. Additionally, nearly 250 million emails are sent every minute.[1] The proliferation of information has led to a state of information overload, i.e., a situation where the amount of available data exceeds an individual's ability to process it, leading to negative feelings such as stress or confusion. The negative impact of information overload can be seen in at least three different domains. First, the excessive numbers of messages individuals receive can become overwhelming, making it hard to respond and manage related tasks. The sense of being overwhelmed arises because the volume of information that requires processing and response exceeds an individual's capacity. Essentially, the

---

[1] Fabio Duarte, "Amount of Data Created Daily (2024)", 2023, https://explodingtopics.com/blog/data-generated-per-day.

backlog of unaddressed messages and the tasks they require creates a sense of overload. Second, messages frequently interrupt ongoing activities, causing a continuous shift in attention and doing multiple things at once, which further increases the feeling of being overwhelmed. Interruptions fragment concentration, making it difficult to engage deeply with any single task. Third, people are bombarded by the vast quantity of content on social media, text messages and notifications, all demanding their attention. The overly rich media content can lead to constant consumption without a clear purpose or focus and without meaningful engagement.[2] Thus, information overload is characterized by both the excessive quantity and the poor quality of information.

Alvin Toffler was one of the first sociologists who identified the phenomenon of information overload in 1970. He described the transition from an industrial to an informational (or super-industrial, as Toffler called it) society. He also warned of the adverse psychological and societal effects resulting from an excessive amount of information. He argued that excess of information, much of it coming at a pace faster than what individuals are able to process, could lead to a state of future shock. Information overload does not empower people, but instead overwhelms them, making them feel powerless, disoriented and stressed.[3]

Indeed, the processing of vast amounts of unassimilable information leads to a significant cognitive burden. Research shows that information overload negatively impacts cognitive processes, productivity[4] and job satisfaction.[5] It reduces self-control[6] and complicates decision-making processes as individuals need more time to find the right information.[7] It also affects individuals'

---

2 P. Brey, "Foreword", in *Information Overload. An International Challenge for Professional Engineers and Technical Communicators* (Hoboken, NJ: Wiley, 2012); Neil Postman, "Informing Ourselves to Death", in *The Nature of Technology: Implications for Learning and Teaching*, eds. Michael P. Clough, Joanne K. Olson and Dale S. Niederhauser (Leiden, Boston: Brill, 2013).

3 Alvin Toffler, *Future Shock* (London: Bodley Head, 1970).

4 Derek Dean and Caroline Webb, "Recovering from Information Overload", *McKinsey Quarterly*, 2011, https://www.mckinsey.com/business-functions/people-and-organizational-performance/our-insights/recovering-from-information-overload.

5 Pengzhen Yin et al., "Coping with Mobile Technology Overload in the Workplace", *Internet Research* 28, no. 5 (2018): 1189–1212, https://doi.org/10.1108/INTR-01-2017-0016.

6 Oberiri Destiny Apuke and Bahiyah Omar, "Social Media Affordances and Information Abundance: Enabling Fake News Sharing during the COVID-19 Health Crisis", *Health Informatics Journal* 27, no. 3 (2021): 146045822110214, https://doi.org/10.1177/14604582211021470.

7 Manuel Gomez-Rodriguez, Krishna Gummadi and Bernhard Schoelkopf, "Quantifying Information Overload in Social Media and its Impact on Social Contagions", in *Proceedings of the Eighth International AAAI Conference on Weblogs and Social Media*, 2014, 170–79, https://www.aaai.org/ocs/index.php/ICWSM/ICWSM14/paper/view/8108/8117.

attitudes and emotions, leading to exhaustion, regret and dissatisfaction.[8] It causes concentration difficulties, further reducing productivity, job satisfaction and academic performance.[9] This can also be accompanied by a loss of control and feelings of being overwhelmed, with time constraints adding to the stress.

In the context of online shopping, information overload acts as a significant stressor causing tension and negative emotions, such as anxiety, which can influence purchasing decisions.[10] Consumers are bombarded with vast amounts of information, recommendations and opinions, making it difficult for them to distinguish valuable insights from noise. As a result, they may abandon shopping altogether, delay their decision-making or lose confidence in their decisions.

Cognitive overload not only impairs decision-making, but also reduces social trust. One significant manifestation of this is the sharing of fake news. Individuals overwhelmed by the sheer volume of information on social media often share content without taking time to understand it. Careless sharing of posts contributes to the rapid spread of misinformation. On the other hand, when individuals are faced with an excessive amount of information, they may find it challenging to verify its accuracy and relevance. They need to sift through vast amounts of data to find what is true or relevant. Cognitive overload leads to decision fatigue, which impedes the ability to make informed decisions. Furthermore, the constant state of uncertainty creates a general atmosphere of doubt and skepticism towards information sources, regardless of whether they are individuals, institutions or digital platforms.

The overwhelming volume of information also makes us rely on digital technology and algorithms to filter and select data. Many people are often unaware that the algorithms displaying results operate on specific criteria. Search engine results, for instance, are optimized to prioritize certain information.

---

8   Amandeep Dhir et al., "Online Social Media Fatigue and Psychological Wellbeing – A Study of Compulsive Use, Fear of Missing out, Fatigue, Anxiety and Depression", *International Journal of Information Management* 40 (2018): 141–52, https://doi.org/10.1016/J .IJINFOMGT.2018.01.012; Muhammad Asim Nawaz et al., "Overload and Exhaustion: Classifying SNS Discontinuance Intentions", http://www.editorialmanager.com/cogent psychology 5, no. 1 (2018): 1–18, https://doi.org/10.1080/23311908.2018.1515584.

9   Lingling Yu et al., "Excessive Social Media Use at Work: Exploring the Effects of Social Media Overload on Job Performance", *Information Technology and People* 31, no. 6 (2018): 1091–1112, https://doi.org/10.1108/ITP-10-2016-0237.

10   Xiaoyan Ding, Gaoshan Wang and Xin Zhang, "Do You Get Tired of Shopping Online? Exploring the Influence of Information Overload on Subjective States towards Purchase Decision", in *WHICEB 2017 Proceedings* 7, 2017, http://aisel.aisnet.org/whiceb2017/7.

As a result, search engine results are neither objective nor precise. Reliance on technology for information selection not only exacerbates the challenge of navigating through huge amounts of data but also questions the integrity and reliability of the information we consume, further complicating our search for knowledge.

The phenomenon of information overload contributes to significant qualitative changes in content consumption. The excess of irrelevant, untrustworthy, imprecise, and inauthentic content complicates the ability to find useful and reliable information that could be used for learning or making informed decisions. Due to time constraints, individuals fall for superficial or imprecise criteria while searching for information. They make shallow analyses, rely on fragmented data or content detached from context. On social networking sites, users are processing information more superficially, skimming articles instead of reading them in full. Over time, reading articles has been replaced by reading blogs, then superseded by short tweets.[11] In academia, literature reviews are often reduced to scanning abstracts without reading the full publications. However, studies show that 20% of abstracts contain significant inaccuracies, usually presenting research results in an overly positive light.[12] As users move towards more concise forms of information, they may become less critical of the content they encounter and less thoughtful in their analysis. Consequently, it is more difficult for them to get a comprehensive understanding of the topic.

Yuval Noah Harari argues that information overload is a form of 21st century censorship. He suggests that the sheer volume of data, much of it irrelevant or trivial, creates a barrier to understanding and engagement with critical issues.[13] Excess of information overwhelms individuals who are unable to discern what information is worthy of attention. As a result, people often focus on peripheral or trivial matters, effectively silencing important discussions and considerations. In essence, in an age where information is abundant and access is largely unrestricted, the true power lies in the ability to sift through the noise, know what data to ignore and focus on what is genuinely important.

11   Nicholas Carr, *The Shallows: How the Internet Is Changing the Way We Think* (London: Atlantic Books, 2010).

12   James Hartley and Lucy Betts, "Common Weaknesses in Traditional Abstracts in the Social Sciences", *Journal of the American Society for Information Science and Technology* 60, no. 10 (2009): 2010–18, https://doi.org/10.1002/asi.21102.

13   Yuval Noah Harari, *Homo Deus. A Brief History of Tomorrow* (New York: Vintage, 2017).

2   Infotainment

Finding information is the primary reason why people use the internet, followed by socializing, news consumption, entertainment, and learning practical skills.[14] The inherent desire for both knowledge and amusement has led to the development of infotainment, a prevalent form of content online, particularly on social media. Infotainment blends information with entertainment, creating a hybrid format that aims to inform and engage its audience simultaneously. The principle behind infotainment is that people are more likely to absorb and retain information when it is presented in an engaging and enjoyable manner. After all, cognitive stimulation coupled with emotional engagement makes learning more effective and information better remembered. A long speech or lecture will be better retained when enriched with anecdotes, humor and compelling narratives, as humor and light-hearted off-topic remarks tend to capture and keep the audience's attention.

Presenting information in an entertaining way has always been a part of communication, which is particularly evident in the social media domain, which is primarily geared towards entertainment. Focus on entertainment is related to the commercial nature of many platforms, whose business models are fundamentally based on developing strategies and actions that generate profits. Consequently, social media platforms continuously draw users' attention to their screens and the most effective method to extend user screen time is through providing engaging and entertaining content. This approach not only extends screen time but also increases user engagement, driving the platforms' profitability.

Social networking sites offer a personalized stream of entertainment. They cater to diverse interests and offer a wide range of content formats. Social media engage users with topics of their interest, ensuring enjoyable use of time. They help viewers to escape daily concerns as well as provide relief from anxiety and tedious routines. Entertainment plays a particularly significant role in our lives. It provides enjoyment, reduces stress and restores mental balance. It can enhance productivity, creativity and self-esteem. Social media, in particular, offers a unique form of entertainment that caters to these needs. It can fulfill our desires for emotional release and anxiety reduction.[15]

---

14   We Are Social, 2023, 63, https://wearesocial.com/wp-content/uploads/2023/03/Digital-2023-Global-Overview-Report.pdf.

15   Izzal Asnira Zolkepli and Yusniza Kamarulzaman, "Social Media Adoption: The Role of Media Needs and Innovation Characteristics", *Computers in Human Behavior* 43 (2015): 189–209, https://doi.org/10.1016/J.CHB.2014.10.050.

Given the numerous positive aspects and need for entertainment, it is paradoxical that social media entertainment might be detrimental. While extremely engaging, social media entertainment offers immediate gratification and fulfills basic human needs, it is also extremely absorbing and potentially addictive. It easily diverts attention from real-world responsibilities.[16] Both actively seeking interaction with other users and passively consuming content like memes and games contribute to this diversion. The desire for pleasure and escape from obligations fuels this behavior.[17] Personalized and easily accessible social media content often replaces real-life interaction. Platforms capture attention and offer a quick escape from the daily grind. Escapism extends to fake news and conspiracy theories, which oversimplify complex issues and divert users from seeking accurate information.

Social media promotes consumerism and hedonism through short and engaging, but very often low-quality posts filled with visual content such as photos, video clips, memes, or other graphic elements that amuse and engage users. While this keeps users hooked, it also raises their expectations for constant stimulation. Users gradually become accustomed to the level of stimuli provided and demand more intensity – they want more entertainment, more engagement, more colorful graphics and memes, and not just in fun content but also in informative pieces.

To remain competitive and maintain a viewership, news media must adjust their messages to the changing ways content is consumed and shifting audience expectations. Informative pieces have evolved – they have become increasingly shorter with headlines and leads designed to condense information into easily digestible chunks that present everything in a nutshell (readers often just skim past headlines and do not even access full articles). Neil Postman

---

16   Erin E. Hollenbaugh and Amber L. Ferris, "Facebook Self-Disclosure: Examining the Role of Traits, Social Cohesion, and Motives", *Computers in Human Behavior* 30 (2014): 50–58, https://doi.org/10.1016/J.CHB.2013.07.055; Heather Shoenberger and Edson Tandoc, "Updated Statuses: Understanding Facebook Use through Explicit and Implicit Measures of Attitudes and Motivations", *Online Journal of Communication and Media Technologies* 4, no. 1 (2014): 217–44, https://doi.org/10.29333/OJCMT/2462; Eveline Teppers et al., "Loneliness and Facebook Motives in Adolescence: a Longitudinal Inquiry into Directionality of Effect", *Journal of Adolescence* 37, no. 5 (2014): 691–99, https://doi.org/10.1016/J.ADOLESCENCE.2013.11.003.

17   Tracii Ryan et al., "The Uses and Abuses of Facebook: A Review of Facebook Addiction", *Journal of Behavioral Addictions* 3, no. 3 (2014): 133–48, https://doi.org/10.1556/JBA.3.2014.016.

argues that the infotainment approach trivializes serious discourse by turning news, politics, science, and education into mere entertainment packages.[18]

Social media takes this evolution a step further by creating a chaotic stream that blends emotions and logic, reality and fiction, truth and falsehood. All of this is presented with humor or sensational headlines, which, as Postman further argues, trivializes public discourse and prioritizes emotional appeals over fact-based arguments.[19] Complex analyses and nuanced perspectives lose their appeal. Audiences become passive consumers who prioritize excitement over substance.[20] The transition to a post-truth era is marked by the tendency of users to consume content that aligns with their own views and is easily accessible or understandable. The accuracy of the information is no longer considered important. In fact, truth and accuracy have expired. Existing beliefs and values have a greater impact on shaping public opinion than facts. Informational space, devoid of traditional gatekeepers, is saturated with user-generated content. An overwhelming influx of information often exceeds individuals' capacity for meaningful engagement.[21] As a result, critical thinking and informed decision-making are undermined, leading to a growing gap between perception and reality. The collective capacity to engage with complex issues, discern credible information and resist manipulation is diminished. As audiences become more accustomed to this mode of consumption, the distinction between entertainment and informative content blurs. As a result, it is increasingly difficult to access high-quality content.

The rise of social media as a source of political information and current events has significantly transformed how people engage with news. As a result, the shift in news consumption has brought a major change in how individuals understand the world. Social media platforms have become primary channels for disseminating and discussing political matters and global events. Their vast reach and interactive nature allow for a wider spread of information, but also raise concerns about the potential for bias.

---

18   Neil Postman, *Amusing Ourselves to Death. Public Discourse in the Age of Show Business* (London: Viking, 2005).

19   Andrew Postman, "My Dad Predicted Trump in 1985 – It's not Orwell, He Warned, It's Brave New World", *The Guardian*, 2017, https://www.theguardian.com/media/2017/feb/02/amusing-ourselves-to-death-neil-postman-trump-orwell-huxley.

20   Daniel Mider, *Partycypacja Polityczna w Internecie. Studium Politologiczne* (Warsaw: Dom Wydawniczy Elipsa, 2008).

21   Ignas Kalpokas, "Post-Truth and Information Warfare in their Technological Context", *Applied Cybersecurity & Internet Governance* 4, no. 2 (2024), https://doi.org/10.60097/ACIG/190407.

One major risk lies in algorithmic filtering. Algorithms curate content based on past user interactions. They create filter bubbles where individuals are primarily exposed to views that reinforce their existing beliefs. The echo chamber effect limits exposure to diverse information, hindering a well-rounded understanding of current affairs and increasing susceptibility to misinformation or manipulation. The ability of algorithms to shape the flow of information raises concerns about the integrity of democratic processes, which rely on an informed society. Statistics show a dramatic rise in reliance on social media for news. Social media has become a key source of news for half of U.S. adults, with Facebook being the most common platform for regular news updates, followed by YouTube. Other platforms such as Instagram, TikTok, X, and Telegram also contribute to news distribution but to a lesser extent.[22] Clearly, social media affects individual standpoints and has a profound impact on public opinion and discourse. When people rely on social media for information about current events, they allow carefully curated content and pre-programmed algorithms to significantly influence their worldviews, shape their understanding of current events, and form long-term political views. The reliance on social media for news necessitates heightened awareness and critical evaluation of the information encountered online (media literacy). Such measures are crucial to mitigate the risks of misinformation, opinion manipulation and the formation of polarized communities.

The merging of entertainment with news further complicates the audience's ability to distinguish factual from fictional content. Many of the younger generation struggle to distinguish between advertisements and actual news, and two-thirds of adults express concern over the influence of fabricated content.[23] An increasing number of audiences discuss current events mixing information derived from news sources with references to popular culture, movies and TV shows. The boundaries between real-world issues and fictional narratives become blurred. This phenomenon suggests that people's political and social understandings are shaped by a mix of both fictional and non-fictional media, without significant distinction. The key factor influencing people's perceptions and discussions is not the genre of the content but the overarching patterns of the communicated information and the mental models they help construct.[24]

---

22   Pew Research Center, "Social Media and News Fact Sheet", 2023, https://www.pewre search.org/journalism/fact-sheet/social-media-and-news-fact-sheet/.

23   California Legislative Information, "Senate Bill No. 830. Chapter 448" (2018), https://leg info.legislature.ca.gov/faces/billTextClient.xhtml?bill_id=201720180SB830.

24   Yaeli Bloch-Elkon and Brigitte L. Nacos, "News and Entertainment Media: Government's Big Helpers in the Selling of Counterterrorism", *Perspectives on Terrorism* 8, no. 5 (2014): 19–20.

The blend of entertainment and news creates a unified field of media influence, where different types of content collectively shape viewers' schemas for interpreting the social world, further challenging the ability to engage critically with information and make informed decisions.

The combined effect of very engaging entertainment and being diverted from important issues poses a significant threat: the creation of a passive, self-absorbed society. People become numb to emotions, bored by constant stimuli and ultimately dissatisfied by shallow pleasures.[25] Siva Vaidhyanathan draws attention to the danger of collective inability to engage with critical issues. He argues that our collective tendency to ignore problems breeds brutality, or at the very least, severely hampers our ability to confront it.[26] The Pew Research Center analysis reveals a significant decline in the number of Americans who closely follow the news, dropping from 51% in 2016 to 38% in 2022. Simultaneously, there is an increase in those who occasionally follow current news. This trend can be seen across all age groups, although older adults are generally more likely to follow news regularly than younger adults.[27] This is connected with the decline in trust in not only national news organizations but also in science and experts. With easy access to vast amounts of information, people often believe they know more than others, even more than the experts themselves. Self-perceived knowledge is often based on prejudices, stereotypes, generalizations, and conspiracy theories, further reinforced by heuristics and cognitive biases. This creates a widening gap between individuals and reliable knowledge, while simultaneously fostering an unwavering belief in their own competence. The internet exacerbates the issue by making shared opinions appear as facts, which, in turn, cultivates distrust, or even contempt, for experts. The erosion of trust in expertise poses a significant threat to society and security. An ignorant electorate not only elects unqualified politicians but also lacks the capacity to recognize their leaders' shortcomings due to their own lack of knowledge.[28]

Weakening public trust in experts has facilitated the rise of pseudo-experts. These self-proclaimed specialists confidently express their opinions without having the necessary qualifications, knowledge or skills that genuine experts possess. They contribute to an overabundance of information, often based on

---

25   Neil Postman, *Amusing Ourselves to Death* (New York: Viking Penguin, 1987).

26   Siva Vaidhyanathan, *Anti-Social Media. How Facebook Disconnects Us and Undermines Democracy* (Oxford: Oxford University Press, 2018), 44.

27   Naomi Forman-Katz, "Americans are following the news less closely than they used to" (Pew Research Center, 2023).

28   Tom Nichols, *The Death of Expertise. The Campaign against Established Knowledge and Why It Matters* (Oxford: Oxford University Press, 2017).

misleading or fabricated evidence.[29] Their ability to captivate and influence others with emotional appeals and catchy slogans, makes them a significant threat. They undermine informed decision-making and critical thinking. Over time, they are displacing traditional figures of authority, including intellectuals, established media outlets and politicians.

Pseudo-experts are flooding the public sphere with twisted narratives and conspiracy theories, further eroding trust in institutions and credible information sources. As they continue to offer views that diverge from or even contradict genuine expert knowledge, public suspicion towards all experts may intensify. General skepticism makes it increasingly difficult for real experts to communicate effectively with the public, especially on important issues like health, the environment and policy. Consequently, the erosion of trust in expert knowledge undermines the foundations of an informed and rational society.

The erosion of trust in expert knowledge is further compounded by the rise of pseudo-media sites, i.e., the outlets which imitate visual forms and styles of mainstream media while blending news, commentary and ideology. They contribute to information disorder by disseminating conspiracy theories and misleading content. This phenomenon is facilitated by the hybrid media system, where traditional and new media intersect, allowing for the proliferation of biased, disinformation-laden content. Furthermore, pseudo-media sites often rely on emotional manipulation and populist rhetoric to attract and engage audiences. They use sensationalist headlines and clickbait strategies to drive traffic.[30] The blend of entertainment and information distorts public discourse and makes it increasingly challenging for individuals to distinguish fact from fiction or to critically evaluate the information they consume. The proliferation of pseudo-experts and pseudo-media sites reinforces polarized viewpoints and deepens societal divides.

3   Engagement, Emotions and User Behavior

The immense volume of digital content and its immediate availability has transformed user interaction into a largely superficial engagement, characterized by low-level interactions rather than meaningful dialogue. The shallower

29   Sarah Sorial, "The Legitimacy of Pseudo-Expert Discourse in the Public Sphere", *Metaphilosophy* 48, no. 3 (2017): 304–24, https://doi.org/10.1111/META.12233.

30   Dolors Palau-Sampio, "Pseudo-Media Disinformation Patterns: Polarised Discourse, Clickbait and Twisted Journalistic Mimicry", *Journalism Practice* 17, no. 10 (2023): 2141–42, https://doi.org/10.1080/17512786.2022.2126992.

nature of interactions is a significant aspect of information overload, where the abundance of information not only competes for users' attention but also drives them towards passive consumption instead of active, thoughtful participation. Fleeting engagements prioritize the entertainment value of content. As a result, more serious issues are overshadowed by infotainment. In this context, individual users, despite their active involvement in producing and sharing content, find that their contributions have minimal impact. They actively participate on social networking sites and produce a vast amount of data. They form small communities and engage in conversations in these groups. However, despite their active participation, the impact of their contributions is limited, with low engagement levels on their posts and a predominance of passive interactions in the form of likes over substantive comments. Discussions on social media are generally ephemeral and lack broader societal impact. Although users contribute content, they rarely engage a broad audience. They engage superficially with content, often merely acknowledging posts rather than participating in meaningful exchanges. The majority of users assume the role of content consumers rather than active participants. Consequently, discussions on social media are highly dispersed and dominated by a large volume of low-resonating posts and tweets.[31] This trend points to a broader issue of information overload, where the sheer volume of available content dilutes individual messages and contributes to the challenges of infotainment.

Understanding user behavior in digital environments is crucial for two main reasons. First, it helps create safer digital spaces, where user protection against exploitation and manipulation is prioritized. Second, understanding typical user behavior helps identify anomalies that may signal security breaches. By establishing a baseline of "normal" behavior in a digital system, it is easy to detect activities that deviate from that norm. Deviations can indicate potential threats, such as unauthorized access or data breaches.

User experiences in the digital space are significantly influenced by emotional responses, triggered by both exposure to content and interactions with other users. Research comparing the brain's reaction to general internet browsing with both passive (scrolling and browsing) and active (tweeting and retweeting) engagement on social platforms reveals that social networking sites can significantly enhance feelings of personal relevance, emotional intensity and memory formation compared to general internet browsing. Passive use of social networking sites can increase the sense of personal relevance by

---

31   Dorota Domalewska, *Media Społecznościowe – Władza i Manipulacja. Analiza Zagrożeń Społecznych, Politycznych i Informacyjnych z Perspektywy Nauk o Bezpieczeństwie* (Warsaw: Wydawnictwo Akademii Sztuki Wojennej, 2022).

27%, which can rise to 51% with active engagement. Emotional activity can increase by 64% when reading feeds and up to 75% when users actively publish content. Memory-related brain activity also shows significant increases during these engagements. The findings suggest that social media has a significant impact on cognitive and emotional processes.[32] However, the results need to be interpreted with caution due to the limitations and potential biases of the neuroimaging techniques employed in such research, such as Steady State Topography (SST). More studies are needed to understand how neurological responses translate into real-world behavior, such as consumer or political decisions influenced by social media interactions.

Social networking sites enable users to express themselves by sharing comments, emoticons, hashtags, photos, and videos. Social platforms not only document enjoyable moments, trips and professional successes but also serves as tools for mood alterations. The interactive nature of social media magnifies the emotional impact of user-generated content. Positive feedback such as likes, comments and shares from their peers not only reinforces their positive emotions but also validates their experiences, which amplifies the rewarding nature of social media interactions.

Emotions experienced on social networking sites can spread contagiously. Users transmit a range of emotions, from fleeting to more persistent moods such as happiness and depression. Studies reveal that users are susceptible to both positive and negative emotions expressed in the posts they read. However, there is a disagreement among scholars regarding which type of emotion is more contagious. Some analyses indicate that positive posts expressing happiness, contentment and pride exert a greater influence than negative messages.[33] Other studies, however, conclude that negative emotions, such as sadness, elicit stronger reactions than positive ones.[34]

Emotional contagion is associated with the amount of time spent on social media, the number of platforms used, the types of content encountered, and the frequency of online interactions. Research has demonstrated a correlation between the total time spent on social media and the prevalence of negative

---

32   Steven Levy, "This Is Your Brain on Twitter", https://medium.com/backchannel/this-is-your-brain-on-twitter-caco725cea2b, 2015.

33   Emilio Ferrara and Zeyao Yang, "Measuring Emotional Contagion in Social Media", *PLOS ONE* 10, no. 11 (2015): e0142390, https://doi.org/10.1371/JOURNAL.PONE.0142390.

34   Adam D.I. Kramer, Jamie E. Guillory and Jeffrey T. Hancock, "Experimental Evidence of Massive-Scale Emotional Contagion through Social Networks", *Proceedings of the National Academy of Sciences of the United States of America* 111, no. 24 (2014): 8788–90, https://doi.org/10.1073/PNAS.1320040111.

moods.[35] Similarly, increased use of multiple social networks has been linked with symptoms of depression and anxiety.[36] The content displayed on users' newsfeeds also significantly influences their emotions because emotions expressed on social networking sites can affect others in the network, even if users are not directly interacting with the person expressing the emotion. Emotional contagion can occur through social networks without the need for in-person interaction or non-verbal cues. Even reducing negative posts led to an increase in positive posts, which suggests that textual content alone is sufficient for emotional contagion. The effects from these manipulations were small, but given the massive scale of social networks such as Facebook, even small effects can have large aggregated consequences.[37]

Despite the potential for positive emotional contagion, social media can also foster negative emotions. Online content can induce feelings of envy and reinforce feelings of dissatisfaction because users frequently perceive others as leading happier and more fulfilling lives.[38] Research by Christian Weismayer and his colleagues revealed that as social network users engage with more posts, they tend to become increasingly critical. The prevalence of negative posts and the intensity of emotions such as anger and fear escalate with both the quantity of posts consumed and the time spent on social networks. At the same time, positive moods and associated emotions, such as joy and surprise, gradually diminish.[39]

Empirical studies also show a significant increase in anxiety and lowered mood among individuals who frequently use multiple social networks.[40] Watching others' happiness and fulfilment on social media, often idealized

---

35   Anna Vannucci, Christine Mc Cauley Ohannessian and Sonja Gagnon, "Use of Multiple Social Media Platforms in Relation to Psychological Functioning in Emerging Adults", *Emerging Adulthood* 7, no. 6 (2018): 501–6, https://doi.org/10.1177/2167696818782309.

36   Brian A. Primack et al., "Use of Multiple Social Media Platforms and Symptoms of Depression and Anxiety: A Nationally-Representative Study among U.S. Young Adults", *Computers in Human Behavior* 69 (2017): 1–9, https://doi.org/10.1016/J.CHB.2016.11.013.

37   Kramer, Guillory and Hancock, "Experimental Evidence of Massive-Scale Emotional Contagion through Social Networks".

38   Hui Tzu Grace Chou and Nicholas Edge, "'They Are Happier and Having Better Lives than I Am': The Impact of Using Facebook on Perceptions of Others' Lives", *Cyberpsychology, Behavior, and Social Networking* 15, no. 2 (2012): 117–21, https://doi.org/10.1089/CYBER .2011.0324.

39   Christian Weismayer, Ulrich Gunter and Irem Önder, "Temporal Variability of Emotions in Social Media Posts", *Technological Forecasting and Social Change* 167 (2021): 120699, https://doi.org/10.1016/J.TECHFORE.2021.120699.

40   Primack et al., "Use of Multiple Social Media Platforms and Symptoms of Depression and Anxiety: A Nationally-Representative Study among U.S. Young Adults".

and amplified, can intensify negative feelings.[41] Passive users, who consume content without engaging or publishing content themselves, are particularly vulnerable to the adverse emotional impact of social networks. Simply viewing others' content can generate feelings of inferiority, jealousy and frustration as it reinforces social comparisons.[42] This phenomenon can be understood in two ways: first, extensive time spent online can lead to frustration or anger. Second, continuous comparisons with the idealized images of others can result in depression.

Emotions are deeply embedded in the business models of social networking sites. Although digital platforms are often free to use, they generate significant profits, primarily from advertising revenue. Revenue is directly linked to user engagement; the more time users spend on the platform, the more ads they are likely to see and interact with. Therefore, big tech companies aim to maximize screen time by engaging users with emotionally charged content. Posts with clear emotional undertones become more viral than others, e.g., tweets about illness that are highly emotionally charged and express feelings of joy, sadness or hope are more popular than others, whereas tweets demonstrating joy and anger are more likely to be forwarded.[43] By emotionally engaging users, social platforms capture attention and extend screen time. User attention is effectively monetized as the main source of platform revenue (attention economy) emphasizing the importance of emotions in generating economic value. This concept, known as affective capitalism, recognizes that emotions play a primary role in driving consumer behavior and market dynamics. Emotion is a force that can generate economic outcomes more rapidly and reliably than traditional economic factors.[44] First, emotional content quickly becomes viral and increased traffic translates into growing advertising revenue. Second, there is significant interplay between emotional discourse and economic practices, especially on social networking sites. This relationship is characterized by the way emotional and passionate language connects audiences and commodities through persuasion. Emotions play a crucial role in the consumer's

---

41   Chou and Edge, "'They Are Happier and Having Better Lives than I Am': The Impact of Using Facebook on Perceptions of Others' Lives".

42   Sunkyung Yoon et al., "Is Social Network Site Usage Related to Depression? A Meta-Analysis of Facebook-Depression Relations", *Journal of Affective Disorders* 248 (2019): 65–72, https://doi.org/10.1016/J.JAD.2019.01.026.

43   Jinping Wang and Lewen Wei, "Fear and Hope, Bitter and Sweet: Emotion Sharing of Cancer Community on Twitter", *Social Media + Society* 6, no. 1 (2020), https://doi.org/10.1177/2056305119897319.

44   Brian Massumi, *Parables of the Virtual: Movement, Affect, Sensation* (Durham, NC: Duke University Press, 2002), 45.

decision-making process.[45] They are often employed to justify and rationalize consumption behavior. A user may be persuaded to purchase a product or service because of an emotional connection or reaction triggered by marketing language or images. Influencers, who have established credibility and a sizeable audience, are often employed by brands to promote their products and services. They use their personal connection with their followers to drive consumer behavior. Influencers do not just advertise a product, as one might see in a traditional TV commercial. Instead, they create an emotional narrative around it. They might share a personal story about how the product boosted their confidence and helped them achieve their goals. In this way, they tap into the emotions of aspiration and self-improvement, which are powerful drivers for followers to make a purchase.

Celebrity gossip blogs are another example of using emotions for profit in a form of affective capitalism. Blogs engage readers by managing their emotions. They often ridicule or mock celebrities through snarky comments and image manipulations, creating content that is pleasurable for readers but not necessarily for the celebrities involved. Readers are encouraged to actively participate in creating the experiences they later consume, usually in the form of a buzz or conversation that follows online publications. The more interaction a post garners, the more emotionally charged it becomes. Interaction and intimacy contribute to the affective layering of the website, which, in turn, can be monetized through online advertising.[46] Furthermore, emotions, particularly humor, are used to conceal economic motivations behind these blogs, drawing the audience deeper into a cycle where their engagement is driven by affect.[47]

4   Digital Narcissism

In the digital age, where social media dominates interpersonal communication, digital narcissism has emerged as a factor that significantly affects

---

45   Annamari Vänskä, "'Cause I Wuv You!' Pet Dog Fashion and Emotional Consumption", *Ephemera. Theory and Politics in Organization* 16, no. 4 (2016): 75–97.

46   Philip Drake, "Celebrity, Reputational Capital and the Media Industries", in *Routledge Handbook of Celebrity Studies*, eds. Anthony Elliott, (London: Routledge, 2018), 271–72, https://doi.org/10.4324/9781315776774-18; Tobias Raun, "Capitalizing Intimacy: New Subcultural Forms of Micro-Celebrity Strategies and Affective Labour on YouTube", *Convergence: The International Journal of Research into New Media Technologies* 24, no. 1 (2018): 99–113, https://doi.org/10.1177/1354856517736983.

47   Anne Graefer, "The Work of Humour in Affective Capitalism: A Case Study of Celebrity Gossip Blogs", *Ephemera. Theory and Politics in Organization* 16, no. 4 (2016): 143–62.

interpersonal relationships, the wellbeing of individuals and overall social dynamics. Digital narcissism refers to the exhibition of narcissistic traits in digital environments, particularly on social media platforms.[48] Individuals with narcissistic traits often seek attention, admiration and affirmation by posting content that boasts personal achievements, physical attractiveness or unique experiences. Social media platforms may intensify narcissistic behavior by continuously emphasizing achievements and attractiveness.[49] They facilitate self-promotion and the pursuit of admiration. Narcissists use social media extensively to manage and enhance their image through frequent updates about achievements, appearance and lifestyle, which are designed to elicit admiration.[50] The findings suggest that the nature of social networking sites, which encourage users to engage in self-promotion, attracts individuals with narcissistic tendencies. Moreover, the platform may not only appeal to those already exhibiting narcissistic traits but could potentially exacerbate such traits among its users.[51]

The concept of digital narcissism has profound implications for culture and social relationships, fostering a culture that prioritizes appearance, success and popularity over genuine character and authenticity. This focus can skew younger generations' perceptions of reality and pressure them to meet the unrealistic standards often presented online. The constant pursuit of more likes, comments or followers can cause anxiety, depression and diminished self-esteem, particularly among young people. Comparison to others on

---

48   Narcissism manifests in two primary forms: clinical and subclinical. Clinical narcissism, recognized as a personality disorder, is delineated in diagnostic frameworks such as Europe's ICD-10 and America's DSM-V, and the updated ICD-11 effective from 2022. It features persistent behavior that significantly deviates from cultural norms. Symptoms include a marked sense of superiority and arrogance, a profound need for admiration, and a lack of empathy. Subclinical narcissism, viewed as a personality trait, shares features with its clinical counterpart but with milder narcissistic behavior that does not severely impact personal or social functioning. This form does not meet the criteria for a personality disorder but is notable for a less intense expression of narcissistic traits (Eve Caligor, Kenneth N. Levy and Frank E. Yeomans, "Narcissistic Personality Disorder: Diagnostic and Clinical Challenges", *American Journal of Psychiatry* 172, no. 5 (2015): 415–22, https://doi.org/10.1176/appi.ajp.2014.14060723).

49   Jean M. Twenge and W. Keith Campbell, *The Narcissism Epidemic: Living in the Age of Entitlement* (Free Press: New York, 2009).

50   Ryan et al., "The Uses and Abuses of Facebook: A Review of Facebook Addiction"; Barbara Lopes and Hui Yu, "Who Do You Troll and Why: An Investigation into the Relationship between the Dark Triad Personalities and Online Trolling Behaviours towards Popular and Less Popular Facebook Profiles", *Computers in Human Behavior* 77 (2017): 69–76, https://doi.org/10.1016/j.chb.2017.08.036.

51   Ryan et al., "The Uses and Abuses of Facebook: A Review of Facebook Addiction".

social media platforms and the pressure to uphold an idealized online persona can exacerbate anxiety disorders and depression as well as increase jealousy, inferiority and dissatisfaction with one's life.[52] Moreover, constant boasting about successes and positive life aspects can distort personal self-perception. Audiences may find it challenging to accept their own failures and limitations, which ultimately reduces genuine self-esteem and increases dissatisfaction. Furthermore, the emphasis on appearance and status promoted by social media can lead to superficial interactions and relationships.[53]

Jay Watts, on the other hand, explains how digital spaces serve as a modern 'looking glass' where individuals see and shape themselves. Digital self-construction is heavily influenced by the interactions and feedback they receive online, such as likes, comments and shares, which can often reinforce or challenge their self-perception. The digital space allows for a type of self-expression and identity exploration that is less defined by physical presence and traditional societal roles. This can be both liberating and disorienting, as it allows individuals to present idealized versions of themselves across various platforms, often simultaneously. Watts points out that while this can lead to a more fluid and multifaceted expression of self, it also raises concerns about the authenticity and stability of digital identities. Therefore, digital narcissism is not just about self-absorption or vanity; it is a broader engagement with self-esteem and self-construction that reflects deep-seated human needs and desires. Digital spaces allow for new forms of social interaction and identity play that were not possible before, reshaping traditional notions of what constitutes healthy or normative behavior.[54]

Digital narcissism requires deep understanding and intervention at both individual and societal levels due to its extensive impact. The extensive sharing of personal information by those exhibiting narcissistic traits online increases

---

52   J. Patrick Seder and Shigehiro Oishi, "Intensity of Smiling in Facebook Photos Predicts Future Life Satisfaction", *Social Psychological and Personality Science* 3, no. 4 (2012): 407–13, https://doi.org/10.1177/1948550611424968.

53   Laura E. Buffardi and W. Keith Campbell, "Narcissism and Social Networking Web Sites", *Personality and Social Psychology Bulletin* 34, no. 10 (2008): 1303–14, https://doi.org/10.1177/0146167208320061.

54   Jay Watts, "Digital Narcissism in the Consulting Room", in *Media and the Inner World: Psycho-Cultural Approaches to Emotion, Media and Popular Culture*, eds. Caroline Bainbridge and Candida Yates (London: Palgrave Macmillan UK, 2014), 168–84, https://doi.org/10.1057/9781137345547_11; Jay Watts, "Narcissism Through the Digital Looking Glass", in *Narcissism, Melancholia and the Subject of Community*, eds. Barry Sheils and Julie Walsh (Cham: Springer International Publishing, 2017), 65–89, https://doi.org/10.1007/978-3-319-63829-4_3.

their risk of falling prey to cybercrimes like phishing and fraud.[55] Politically and publicly, the behavior of digitally prominent individuals can shape public opinion and influence political discourse. It frequently promotes a focus on superficiality rather than substantive political engagement. This shift can deteriorate the quality of public debate and sway voters toward appealing yet shallow messages.

Feldman Marzochi and Fernando de Balieiro argue that social media amplifies narcissistic tendencies in political discourse, leading to intense and polarized ideological conflicts. Individuals and groups use social platforms to project their ideals and anxieties, thereby turning political engagement into a reflection of their own ego ideals and narcissistic desires.[56] Social media acts as a mirror, reflecting and reinforcing the users' views and identities. Users often engage with content that aligns with their beliefs, which social media algorithms further facilitate by creating echo chambers that selectively expose them to confirming information and similar viewpoints. This mechanism enhances users' sense of righteousness and the perceived legitimacy of their perspectives while painting opposing views as not merely different or challenging but morally and fundamentally wrong, which results in a battle of narcissistic projections. Each group or individual elevates their preferred ideologies or figures to an idealized status, like a narcissistic extension of themselves. Conversely, opposing views and those who hold them are demonized and treated as threats. This is not just a disagreement but a manifestation of a perceived threat to the existential security of their identity and values. Such demonization is often disproportionate, viewing the opposition as not only wrong but also as an existential danger to the social order and personal well-being. Polarization can escalate to a point where political opponents are no longer seen as participants in a shared democratic process but as enemies that must be opposed at all costs. Thereby an environment of conflict is created where the possibility for dialogue and compromise is gradually diminished, as each side is deeply entrenched in its narrative and views any concession as a betrayal of their identity and values.

---

55   Chris Stiff and Meike Reeves, "Careful When You Click? How the Dark Triad of Personality Can Influence the Likelihood of Online Crime Victimization", *The Journal of Psychology* 158, no. 3 (2024): 238–56, https://doi.org/10.1080/00223980.2023.2286451.

56   Samira Feldman Marzochi and Fernando De Figueiredo Balieiro, "Muralha de Espelhos: O Narcisismo Político Nas Plataformas Digitais", *Revista Brasileira de Sociologia – RBS* 9, no. 23 (2021): 121–48, https://doi.org/10.20336/rbs.766.

5   Hate Speech

The prevalence of entertaining content, including infotainment, has significantly shaped how users interact with online media, as they often prioritize engagement over depth. However, the focus on engagement carries risk. The same mechanisms that captivate users with compelling narratives and emotional appeals can also foster harmful forms of communication, such as cyber aggression, which is demonstrated in a range of negative behavior, including cyber bullying, vitriol, hate speech, and trolling. Hate speech[57] is a particularly harmful manifestation because it can incite violence, discrimination and deep-seated social divisions. It entails "all forms of expression which spread, incite, promote or justify racial hatred, xenophobia, antisemitism or other forms of hatred based on intolerance (including intolerance expressed by aggressive nationalism and ethnocentrism, discrimination and hostility against minorities, and migrants and people of immigrant origin) that undermine democratic security, cultural cohesiveness and pluralism".[58] A key aspect of this definition is that it includes "any form of expression," encompassing not only text but also images, films and any other forms of activity, particularly those prevalent on the internet. Furthermore, the definition extends to "other forms of hate based on intolerance," which covers a broad spectrum of currently recognizable and applicable forms of discrimination and prejudice, such as anti-Roma discrimination, Christianophobia, Islamophobia, misogyny, sexism, and discrimination based on sexual orientation and gender identity. It is also important that this concept allows for the inclusion of other, as yet

---

57   Hate speech definitions vary significantly across disciplines due to its complex, multidisciplinary nature, which sparks extensive academic debate. It is analyzed from various legal, political, cultural, psychological, pedagogical, linguistic, and sociological perspectives, each offering unique methodologies and frameworks. Despite these differences, several key elements are commonly found in many definitions: (1) targeting a group or its members, (2) conveying hate messages, (3) causing harm, (4) the perpetrator's intention to inflict harm or take adverse action, (5) inciting negative actions beyond the utterance itself, (6) the specific audience or group targeted, (7) a context that fosters an aggressive response, (8) the lack of any positive purpose in the message (Andrew Sellars, "Defining Hate Speech", *SSRN Electronic Journal*, 2016, https://doi.org/10.2139/ssrn.2882244). Characteristic elements of hate speech often involve generalizing negative stereotypes, attributing extremely negative traits, using demeaning and dehumanizing language, disparaging and undermining values, creating catalogues of accusations, and targeting groups based on immutable traits such as race or gender.

58   Council of Europe, "Recommendation No. R(97)20 of the Committee of Ministers to Member States on 'Hate Speech'", 1997, 106, https://rm.coe.int/1680505d5b.

unnamed forms, which, in principle, meet the criteria of harmfulness in the context of democracy, culture and pluralism.

The United Nations defines hate speech as "any kind of communication in speech, writing or behavior that attacks or uses pejorative or discriminatory language with reference to a person or a group on the basis of who they are, in other words, based on their religion, ethnicity, nationality, race, color, descent, gender or other identity factor".[59] The International Lesbian, Gay, Bisexual, Trans and Intersex Association (ILGA) describes hate speech as "public expressions which spread, incite, promote, or justify hatred, discrimination, or hostility toward a specific group, contributing to a general climate of intolerance that, in turn, makes attacks more probable against those groups".[60] This perspective emphasizes the broader societal impact of such speech, where hate and hate speech foster an environment that increases the likelihood of tensions, violence and discrimination. Discriminatory aggression is considered "a vice, evil and threat" that "fuels terror and extremism".[61] It can lead to the incitement of mass crimes or genocide[62] and for this reason, it poses a threat to democracy and human rights. Hostility often results not from actual grievances but from exaggerated or even imaginary wrongs. Fabricated issues and prejudices can distort perceptions and fuel aggressive behavior, leading to disproportionate and unfounded attacks against specific groups. Public tolerance of hate speech can further perpetuate prejudices and stereotypes, reduce acceptance of individuals or groups who are victims of hate speech, which in turn can lead to hate crimes.[63] Hate speech derives its power from its ability to degrade and dehumanize individuals and groups. It fosters an environment of exclusion, fear and division. It also undermines human rights and dignity by reinforcing biases and threatening social cohesion. It is frequently linked to the radicalization of individuals, groups or entire communities. Intolerance, which

---

59   United Nations, "United Nations Strategy and Plan of Action on Hate Speech", 2019.

60   ILGA, "Hate Crime and Hate Speech", 2016.

61   Thomas Brudholm and Birgitte Schepelern Johansen, *Hate, Politics, Law. Critical Perspectives on Combating Hate* (Oxford: Oxford University Press, 2018).

62   Roundtable Report, "Hate Speech. The Role of New Media in the Prevention of Mass Atrocities", 2014.

63   Hate crimes are criminal acts driven by bias or prejudice against specific demographic groups. Essentially, a hate crime includes two key components: (1) It is an act that constitutes an offense under criminal law, and (2) the perpetrator commits the crime based on prejudice or bias. There is a direct link between hate speech and physical violence, where the former can be a precursor to the latter. This connection justifies action to eliminate hate speech in order to counter more extreme acts of aggression.

underpins hate speech, helps spread extremist attitudes and may encourage the commission of hate crimes and other forms of criminal offenses.

The situation in Myanmar from 2012 to 2017 illustrates how hate speech can escalate into hate crime, with social media, especially Facebook, playing a central role in amplifying anti-Rohingya[64] sentiment and violence. Tensions rose due to the spread of inflammatory and false rhetoric on Facebook. Despite low internet penetration at the time, the International Crisis Group identified the significant influence of online posts in fueling tensions. This was especially evident following the crisis that was triggered by the alleged rape and murder of a Buddhist woman by Muslim men in Rakhine State in 2012. It led to the mob's brutal killing of ten Muslim bus passengers in Toungup Township and the subsequent Mandalay riots. As a result of these acts of violence, the Myanmar authorities temporarily blocked Facebook access in Mandalay. However, despite clear evidence of the dangers posed by unchecked hate speech on its platform, Meta was slow to respond to the proliferation of harmful content. The company struggled with inadequate content moderation and often failed to address reported hate speech effectively. Harmful posts remained active on the platform, which contributed to a permissive environment where anti-Rohingya sentiment was able to fester and grow. Consequently, violence against the Rohingya community increased. Online hostility and misinformation set the stage for the 2017 atrocities against the Rohingya in Rakhine State, where a coordinated campaign of violence by the Myanmar military, known as "clearance operations," was launched following attacks by the Arakan Rohingya Salvation Army (ARSA) on police posts. The military's actions, which included mass killings, arson and sexual violence, made over 700,000 Rohingya flee to Bangladesh.[65]

The tragic plight of the Rohingya community proves the devastating consequences of hate speech. However, online hate is not only harmful to the communities it targets, directly affecting their safety and well-being. Hate speech may also have disturbing effects on all those exposed. The groups that are particularly vulnerable are women, immigrants and those who suffered from past online and offline victimization,[66] Hispanics, people with higher

---

64   The Rohingya are an ethnic Muslim minority primarily residing in the Rakhine State of Myanmar.

65   Amnesty International, *The Social Atrocity. Meta and the Right to Remedy for the Rohingya* (London: Amnesty International Ltd, 2022).

66   Tuukka Savimäki et al., "Disquieted by Online Hate: Negative Experiences of Finnish Adolescents and Young Adults", *European Journal on Criminal Policy and Research* 26, no. 1 (2020): 23–37, https://doi.org/10.1007/S10610-018-9393-2.

levels of education and living alone,[67] as well as those with offline associations with racist and delinquent peers.[68] Exposure to online hate breeds anger, sadness and shame.[69] Hate speech builds social relationships based on hatred and propagates hate and intolerance.[70] Alarmingly, witnessing verbal aggressive attacks can sometimes generate a sense of pride, which sheds light on the troubling rise in extremist sentiments among internet users.[71] These findings show how deep-rooted communal narratives of hate can rationalize violence.

Hate as a tool of multi-layered narrative has been seen in the Russian–Ukrainian conflict since the 2014 occupation of Crimea and Donbas. Russian propaganda involves creating and promoting disinformation, fake news, targeting various audiences, and using the concepts of dehumanization and discrimination against the Russian-speaking population or even alleging genocide.[72] Anti-Ukrainian sentiment, which is essentially an extrapolation of pan-Russian imperialism or pan-Russianism, is strongly promoted through demonization and accusations of fascism or Nazism against Ukrainians, or by questioning the idea of a Ukrainian nation. Although this narrative also includes anti-Western and anti-American themes, it portrays them as manipulations by the 'brotherly' neighbor.[73]

Despite its offensive nature, hate speech is not a crime. It is protected under free speech laws, such as the First Amendment of the U.S. Constitution. Legal protection means that people cannot be prosecuted simply for expressing offensive views, even if these views are based on false stereotypes and offend

---

67   James Hawdon, Atte Oksanen and Pekka Räsänen, "Victims of Online Hate Groups: American Youth's Exposure to Online Hate Speech", in *The Causes and Consequences of Group Violence: From Bullies to Terrorists*, eds. James Hawdon, John Ryan and Mark Lucht (Lanham, MD: Lexington Books, 2014), 165–82; Ashley Reichelmann et al., "Hate Knows no Boundaries: Online Hate in Six Nations", *Deviant Behavior* 42, no. 9 (2020): 1100–1111, https://doi.org/10.1080/01639625.2020.1722337.

68   Nele Schils and Lieven Pauwels, "Explaining Violent Extremism for Subgroups by Gender and Immigrant Background, Using SAT as a Framework", *Journal of Strategic Security* 7, no. 3 (2014): 3, http://dx.doi.org/10.5038/1944-0472.7.3.2.

69   Matthew Williams, *The Science of Hate: How Prejudice Becomes Hate and what we Can Do to Stop It* (London: Faber & Faber, 2021).

70   Jeremy Waldron, *The Harm in Hate Speech* (Cambridge, MA: Harvard University Press, 2012); I. Jakubowska-Branicka, *Hate Narratives. Language as a Tool of Intolerance* (Berlin: Peter Lange, 2016).

71   Reichelmann et al., "Hate Knows no Boundaries: Online Hate in Six Nations".

72   Viktoriia Romaniuk, "Disinformation Narratives of Hate as a Tool of Escalating Russia's War Against Ukraine (based on Stopfake Fact-Checking Project Materials)", *Sojateadlane. Estonian Journal of Military Studies* 23, no. 2 (2023): 146.

73   Martin Kragh and Andreas Umland, "L'Imaginaire Russe anti-Ukraine: Le Cas Patrouchev", 2023, 2, https://doi.org/10.13140/RG.2.2.13319.78248.

or upset others. Although there is no specific "hate speech" exception in the First Amendment, such speech can be used as evidence in hate crime prosecutions and may influence sentencing enhancements. Similarly, in Europe, the European Commission upholds the right to freedom of expression, as stated by the European Court of Human Rights, which affirms that this right "applies not only to 'information' or 'ideas' that are favorably received or regarded as inoffensive or indifferent, but also to those that offend, shock or disturb the state or any sector of society".[74] This approach emphasizes the balance required to protect free speech and address the harmful impacts of hate speech even though interpretations of hate speech are often subjective and depend on the social context and individual perception of recipients. Chris Demaske argues that the challenge of regulating hate speech while protecting free expression involves discerning the point at which speech ceases to contribute to public debate and instead aims solely to injure or degrade based on group identity.[75] It is a complex task that requires an understanding of the broader societal impact rather than just the individual intent or content of speech. Jeremy Waldron argues that tolerance involves not only protecting minorities from physical harm but also treating them as equal members of society. Waldron thus counters the absolutist view held by proponents of the American First Amendment's perspective on freedom of speech. He maintains that hate speech should be regulated as part of our commitment to human dignity, inclusion and respect for members of vulnerable minorities.[76] This implies that true tolerance encompasses both safety and a sense of belonging for all individuals. Arguments in favor of legal and criminal regulation of hate speech before all else point to the negative consequences associated with its dissemination.[77]

Nevertheless, hate speech poses a significant threat to democratic values by promoting exclusionary and discriminatory narratives that violate principles of equality and freedom of expression. The United Nations' Strategy and Plan of Action on Hate Speech views this issue as not only a breach of certain standards and principles but also an erosion of the fundamental aspects of our collective human identity, placing efforts to combat hate speech in a specific value set and world perspective.[78] Addressing hate speech not only supports

---

74   European Commission, "The EU Code of Conduct on Countering Illegal Hate Speech Online", 2016.

75   Chris Demaske, *Free Speech and Hate Speech in the United States. The Limits of Toleration* (New York and London: Routledge, 2022).

76   Waldron, *The Harm in Hate Speech*.

77   Abigail Levin, *The Cost of Free Speech* (London: Palgrave Macmillan UK, 2010), https://doi.org/10.1057/9780230293960.

78   United Nations, "United Nations Strategy and Plan of Action on Hate Speech".

fundamental democratic values but also encourages responsibility and mutual respect. In addition, tackling the negative impact of hate speech on the mental health and well-being of its victims is crucial in order to create a safe and supportive societal environment.

6   Cyber Aggression and Cyber Bullying

Cyber aggression encompasses a range of harmful types of behavior carried out through digital means. This form of harassment and intimidation can include various actions such as teasing, spreading false information, public ridicule, making inappropriate or malicious comments, spreading rumors, and sending threats. Such behavior is common across various digital platforms, such as email, chat rooms, instant messaging, websites, and text messages.[79] It can take various forms. Depending on the relationship between the aggressor and the victim, as well as the contexts in which they interact, we can distinguish several types of cyber aggression. One type involves a power imbalance, where the aggressor uses their superior position to control or harm the victim. Another targets public figures or celebrities, who are vulnerable due to their high visibility and constant public scrutiny.[80] Bias-driven aggression targets groups based on shared characteristics like nationality, religion or political affiliation. It is often fueled by prejudices and stereotypes. In contrast, random online aggression exploits the anonymity of the internet to target individuals indiscriminately. Lastly, cyber bullying occurs in known social or professional groups, mainly affecting the victim's social interactions and mental health.[81]

Cyber bullying is a modern manifestation of traditional peer violence adapted to the digital age. It occurs in online space, where individuals use

---

79   Corinne David-Ferdon and Marci Feldman Hertz, "Electronic Media, Violence, and Adolescents: An Emerging Public Health Problem", *Journal of Adolescent Health* 41, no. 6 (2007): S1–5, https://doi.org/10.1016/j.jadohealth.2007.08.020.

80   Online aggression directed against a public figure (or a specific company) often occurs during online debates on public issues, where users express public criticism and personal indignation or respond to their dissatisfaction and frustration. Aggression manifests as vitriol in the form of malicious and angry posts. Typically, it does not involve substantive discussions but includes vulgar and aggressive comments detached from the context. In such cases, the relationship is usually asymmetric, with the aggressor being the weaker party and the victim being the person in the power position, such as a public figure (Xing Zhao and James Caverlee, "Vitriol on Social Media: Curation and Investigation", in *Social Informatics*, eds. Steffen Staab, Olessia Koltsova and Dimitry Ignatov (Cham: Springer, 2018), https://doi.org/10.1007/978-3-030-01129-1_30).

81   Jacek Pyżalski, *Agresja Elektroniczna wśród Dzieci i Młodzieży* (Sopot: GWP, 2012), 40.

electronic communication channels to exert aggression. Key features of cyber bullying include regularity, because the victim experiences ongoing and repetitive aggression over a long period; power imbalance, as perpetrators have some form of an advantage over the victim who feels powerless; and intentionality, because the aggressors' actions are deliberate and aimed at harming the victim through conscious actions.[82] Cyber bullying mainly occurs on digital platforms designed to facilitate user interaction, such as Facebook, Instagram and TikTok, as well as through text messaging and mobile messaging apps, where high user engagement provides many opportunities for cyber bullying. Online forums, chat rooms and online gaming communities are also conducive to cyber bullying because the interactive and competitive nature of these venues encourages aggressive behavior. Furthermore, digital media often allows anonymity or semi-privacy, which enables perpetrators to target victims, often without immediate repercussions. This highlights the challenges in moderating such expansive and dynamic environments.

The most common forms of cyber bullying include verbal aggression, such as name-calling in online chat rooms or posting comments in order to ridicule, annoy or frighten another person. Other forms involve sending embarrassing material, forwarding and multiplying received messages and images, making public humiliating or manipulative pictures and videos, and posting hurtful comments on other people's social networking profiles. Cyberbullies also engage in hacking into accounts and impersonating someone, blackmailing, revealing secrets, creating ridiculous websites, and deliberately ignoring someone's online activities. These actions contribute to the prevalence of cyber bullying, as they provide various ways for bullies to target their victims without the immediate consequences that might occur in face-to-face interactions.

Cyber bullying is characterized by the critical roles of its participants: the victim, perpetrator and bystander. Understanding these roles provides insight into the mechanisms governing cyber bullying and aids in developing effective intervention and prevention strategies. The victim who is the target of cyber bullying experiences negative emotional and psychological consequences such as depression or isolation, which can lead to long-term mental health issues. The perpetrator, motivated by a variety of psychological impulses including the desire to dominate or respond to personal frustrations, can act both anonymously and openly. Bystanders to cyber bullying play a key role, as their reactions can significantly influence the dynamics of the phenomenon

---

82   Dan Olweus, "School Bullying: Development and Some Important Challenges", *Annual Review of Clinical Psychology* 9, no. 1 (2013): 751–80, https://doi.org/10.1146/annurev-clinpsy -050212-185516.

by either actively supporting the victim or passively condoning further acts of violence. In interventions, bystanders need to be protected from retaliation. Confrontation with the perpetrator should be avoided. Inadequate safety measures may result in bystanders not reporting the incident in the future, being reluctant to participate in the investigation, or failing to take action to defend the victims.

Cyber bullying impacts the online reputations of all involved parties, not only the victims but also the perpetrators. The availability of digital devices around the clock allows aggressors to harass their targets continuously, leaving victims with little respite. Among young people of school age, ubiquitous mobile devices contribute to an environment where stress and anxiety extend beyond the school day and into all hours, significantly impacting victims' self-perception and interpersonal relationships. They may suffer from decreased self-esteem, difficulties in social connections, academic challenges, and health issues like headaches and sleep disturbances, with potential long-term effects including depression, anxiety and lowered self-worth.[83] For perpetrators, the consequences can include a solidification of aggressive behavior, diminished accountability and a future inclination towards antisocial attitudes. Another critical aspect is the permanence of digital actions. Unlike transient verbal or physical acts, digital communications can be indefinitely stored and shared, making it possible for hurtful messages to resurface and cause ongoing harm. Digital permanence can adversely affect the reputations of all involved, as their online behavior remains accessible to educational institutions, future employers and others, potentially influencing opportunities in higher education and the job market.[84]

Detecting cyber bullying poses significant challenges. Traditional bullying often occurs in physical spaces like schoolyards, where teachers and peers can observe and intervene. In contrast, cyber bullying happens in the digital space – often in private communities not immediately visible to adults. The hidden nature of these interactions means that parents and educators may not witness the bullying incidents, thereby complicating efforts to recognize and address the behavior effectively. The lack of observable evidence demands more sophisticated monitoring techniques and greater understanding of the

---

83 Amanda E. Fahy et al., "Longitudinal Associations Between Cyberbullying Involvement and Adolescent Mental Health", *Journal of Adolescent Health* 59, no. 5 (2016): 502–9, https://doi.org/10.1016/j.jadohealth.2016.06.006; Matteo Vismara et al., "The Current Status of Cyberbullying Research: A Short Review of the Literature", *Current Opinion in Behavioral Sciences* 46 (2022): 101152, https://doi.org/10.1016/j.cobeha.2022.101152.

84 Sameer Hinduja and Justin W. Patchin, "Bullying, Cyberbullying, and Suicide", *Archives of Suicide Research* 14, no. 3 (2010): 206–21, https://doi.org/10.1080/13811118.2010.494133.

digital spaces frequented by young people.[85] Consequently, cyber bullying is a complex issue that can silently and continually affect individuals. Vigilant monitoring and proactive measures need to be taken to detect and prevent online aggression.

First, clear and consistent safety policies need to be established in order to define the legal framework and response procedures for handling cyber bullying incidents. Creating uniform standards for responding to cyber bullying is crucial to foster a safe educational environment and provide effective intervention tools. Additionally, the advancement of technology offers valuable support in preventing cyber bullying. Tools like content filters and online activity monitoring systems are increasingly useful for schools and parents to identify and address cyber bullying incidents.

Comprehensive education for both students and staff is crucial to prevent cyber bullying and provide a safe space where all individuals feel safe and respected.[86] Modules dealing with the safe use of the internet and the analysis of the consequences of cyber bullying behavior can be included in the curriculum to significantly increase public awareness and shape attitudes toward responsible use of virtual space. To ensure digital safety for students, educational institutions must implement comprehensive strategies encompassing three key domains: technological, competency and regulatory. In the technological domain, improving infrastructural capabilities and ensuring secured access to internet resources is crucial. This involves incorporating sophisticated security measures such as advanced filtering and firewall configurations. The competency domain focuses on the ongoing professional development of teachers through targeted training sessions, preventive and educational initiatives, support mechanisms for parents, and the establishment of multidisciplinary support teams. Finally, the regulatory domain includes the formulation and enactment of safety policies and response protocols that address the procedures for managing online risks such as cyber

---

85   Robert S. Tokunaga, "Following You Home from School: A Critical Review and Synthesis of Research on Cyberbullying Victimization", *Computers in Human Behavior* 26, no. 3 (2010): 277–87.

86   Dorota Domalewska et al., "On Safe Space in Education: A Polish-Vietnamese Comparative Study", *Journal of Human Security* 17, no. 1 (2021): 35–45, https://doi.org/10.12924/johs2021.17010035; Małgorzata Gawlik-Kobylińska, Dorota Domalewska and Paweł Maciejewski, "How to Motivate Students? The Four Dimensional Instructional Design Approach in a Non-core Blended Learning Course", in *Cross Reality and Data Science in Engineering. REV 2020. Advances in Intelligent Systems and Computing, vol 1231.*, eds. Auer M. and May D. (Cham: Springer, 2021), 782–94, https://doi.org/10.1007/978-3-030-52575-0_64.

bullying, hazardous interactions and other internet abuses. These protocols should clearly outline procedures for managing and mitigating various types of online threats. Integrating the three strategies is crucial for effective risk management in digital environments.

7   The Roots of Cyber Aggression

Cyber aggression is a complex phenomenon and to understand why it occurs, we need to consider the diverse origins of aggression, including neurophysiological, psychological, situational, and socio-cultural determinants. Neurophysiological factors consider the biological and genetic predispositions that might influence aggressive behavior, involving brain chemistry and structures that predispose individuals to aggressive responses. Psychological determinants refer to individual traits, emotional regulation capabilities and personality factors, such as impulsivity, low empathy and narcissism. Situational factors address the immediate contexts or environments that trigger aggressive behavior, such as interpersonal conflicts or stressful life events. Socio-cultural determinants examine broader cultural and social norms, including media influence and prevailing cultural attitudes towards aggression.

The online environment facilitates the spread of hate speech and aggression mainly because individuals can easily bypass the social norms and constraints that typically govern face-to-face interactions. The widespread prevalence of vitriol and hate speech online can be attributed to multiple factors. First, the sense of anonymity and the perceived invisibility of other users on the internet reduce users' control over hostile incidents. This allows individuals to assume a form of social power under the guise of an avatar, which allows them to express more outrageous, obnoxious or hateful behavior without facing immediate consequences.[87] The sense of invisibility encourages online disinhibition, which may exacerbate aggression. People who may feel shy or inhibited in face-to-face interactions often become bolder in expressing aggressive or harmful opinions online. However, it should be noted that contrary to popular belief, cyber bullying is not anonymous. Typically, victims of cyber bullying know their aggressors as they frequently share the same school or online environments. Cyber bullying then persists because the victim is

---

87   Diana L. Ascher and Safiya Umoja Noble, "Unmasking Hate on Twitter: Disrupting Anonymity by Tracking Trolls", in *Free Speech in the Digital Age*, eds. Susan J. Brison and Katharine Gelber (New York: Oxford University Press, 2019), 172, https://doi.org/10.1093/OSO/9780190883591.003.0011.

easily accessible, facilitated by the "always connected" culture of modern youth using social media platforms. Hence, the perpetrator can send messages to the victim at any time, which exacerbates the scale of the problem compared to traditional bullying, where the victim could find refuge at home.

Second, people lose their inner inhibitions and feel less self-conscious and less responsible for their behavior when they are in a group.[88] Social media amplifies this effect, normalizing certain behavior amid prevailing feelings of insecurity. Anonymity also provides a sense of comfort; when the face, name and other identifying features of the aggressor are hidden, they can act in ways they would normally avoid in face-to-face interactions. The victim also often remains anonymous, or at least their reaction to the aggression cannot be seen by the aggressor. The digital environment often obscures the direct effects of actions, so perpetrators frequently underestimate the real pain and damage their actions cause. The digital separation between action and its outcomes desensitizes perpetrators and may encourage them to carry on their aggressive behavior. The absence of direct observation of victims' emotional reactions can result in the "cockpit effect," leading to a distorted perception of their impact on victims. The emotional distance from witnessing the victim's direct reactions can lead to an underestimation of the distress caused by cyber bullying, diminishing empathy and accountability. In such situations, the attack does not trigger discomfort or sympathy, which typically takes place in face-to-face interactions. In a way, the aggressors do not feel responsible for their actions. Anonymity, invisibility, asynchronicity, and the textuality of communication reduce non-verbal signals that might inhibit aggression. As a result, a sense of impunity arises, which desensitises individuals and encourages further aggression.

Online interactions also often lack clear indications of acceptable social behavior, which reduces respect for social norms, contributing to increased

---

88   According to the theory of deindividuation, individuals in groups can lose their self-restraints, thus acting in ways they would not normally as individuals. The loss of self-awareness can lead to disinhibited, impulsive and even aggressive behavior. Being in a crowd can provide anonymity and group dynamics can diminish personal responsibility. A diminished sense of accountability may cause individuals to relax their inner restraints and engage in behavior that would typically be suppressed (Leon Festinger, Albert Pepitone and Theodore M. Newcomb, "Some Consequences of De-Individuation in a Group", *Journal of Abnormal and Social Psychology* 47, no. 2 SUPPL. (1952): 382–89, https://doi.org/10.1037 /H0057906; Russell Spears, "Deindividuation", in *The Oxford Handbook of Social Influence* (Oxford: Oxford University Press, 2017), 280.

verbal aggression[89] and the indifference of other users to such attacks. Therefore, the online environment diminishes personal responsibility for defending victims of hate or discrimination, and users are indifferent to attacks on others, which reduces the likelihood of intervention or sanctions against incivility.[90] In addition, users who engage in vulgar and hateful content distance themselves (a strategy of moral distance) to avoid self-condemnation and social repercussions for supporting acts of aggression.[91] As a result, a permissive atmosphere may dominate in some communities where hate speech and other forms of online aggression proliferate. Without the usual social cues and consequences, individuals may feel free to express extreme views or engage in harmful behavior.

Aggression can also serve as a means of expressing psychological needs that go beyond mere hostility or conflict. Engaging in aggressive behavior allows individuals to vent unwanted feelings and emotions, such as frustration, anger or irritation. The internet serves as a platform for those dealing with personal issues, stress or low self-esteem to anonymously manifest aggression. This form of expression can often make the aggressor to feel more valued or significant. Another motive for cyber aggression is the desire to regain control. Psychological theories of self-efficacy suggest that individuals who feel powerless in their offline lives may seek to regain a sense of efficacy through online interactions. Anonymity and unlimited exposure allow them to assert dominance, an action that may be challenging in real-world interactions.[92] The sense of dominance correlates with aggressive attitudes online, where action inconsistency reinforces this tendency.

---

89   Raymond A. Friedman and Steven C. Currall, "Conflict Escalation: Dispute Exacerbating Elements of E-Mail Communication", *Human Relations* 56, no. 11 (2016): 1325–47, https://doi.org/10.1177/00187267035611003.

90   Emilija Gagrčin, "Your Social Ties, Your Personal Public Sphere, Your Responsibility: How Users Construe a Sense of Personal Responsibility for Intervention against Uncivil Comments on Facebook", *New Media & Society*, 2022, 1–18, https://doi.org/10.1177/1461444822 1117499.

91   Nicholas Faulkner and Ana Maria Bliuc, "Breaking Down the Language of Online Racism: A Comparison of the Psychological Dimensions of Communication in Racist, Anti-Racist, and Non-Activist Groups", *Analyses of Social Issues and Public Policy* 18, no. 1 (2018): 307–22, https://doi.org/10.1111/ASAP.12159.

92   Patti M. Valkenburg and Peter Jochen, "Online Communication Among Adolescents: An Integrated Model of Its Attraction, Opportunities, and Risks", *Journal of Adolescent Health* 48, no. 2 (2011): 121–27.

Aggression can serve as a strategy to defend one's self-image, a concept explained by social identity theory.[93] In the digital age, the online image becomes an integral part of an individual's identity, and defending the digital persona can take the form of cyber aggression. Individuals often react aggressively to real or perceived threats to their online image, viewing such defensive actions as necessary to safeguard their digital identity.[94] Protective aggression arises from the need to prevent attacks that may damage one's online presence.

Vitriol can also become a form of entertainment, a way of having fun by humiliating others. The aggressor may experience satisfaction from manipulating others' emotions and observing the outcomes of their actions. Such behavior not only provides a sense of enjoyment but also reinforces the aggressor's feeling of power and control.

Group pressure and social dynamics, particularly among teenagers, also significantly promote cyber bullying. Young people may engage in undesirable online behavior to gain group acceptance or avoid becoming targets themselves. The effect of deindividuation in online groups weakens social inhibitions, leading to behavior that is usually condemned. Hence, aggression can be an attempt to seek popularity and recognition. Additionally, other users may also strengthen the negative behavior of the aggressor. This may manifest itself as affective contagion, where users unconsciously adopt the emotions or behavior of others.[95] Critical comments on social media influence other users' behavior and intensify negative emotions. This aligns with Albert Bandura's theory of social learning[96]. However, aggressors often do not achieve broad popularity. While they are accepted by the subgroups they belong to, they are less involved in broader online communities. Their aggression is erratic, characterized by rapid, short bursts of posts and tweets with numerous hashtags and URLs,[97] reflecting the complex dynamics of online aggression and hate speech. Understanding the psychological motivations behind such

93   Henri Tajfel and John Turner, "An Integrative Theory of Intergroup Conflict", in *The Social Psychology of Intergroup Relations*, eds. William G. Austing and Stephen Worchel (Pacific Grove, CA: Brooks/Cole, 1979), 33–47.

94   Shanyang Zhao, Sherri Grasmuck and Jason Martin, "Identity Construction on Facebook: Digital Empowerment in Anchored Relationships", *Computers in Human Behavior* 24, no. 5 (2008): 1816–36, https://doi.org/10.1016/j.chb.2008.02.012.

95   Gerald Schoenewolf, "Emotional Contagion: Behavioral Induction in Individuals and Groups", *Modern Psychoanalysis* 15, no. 1 (1990): 49–61.

96   Albert Bandura, *Social Learning Theory* (Englewood Cliffs, NJ: Prentice Hall, 1977).

97   Despoina Chatzakou et al., "Mean Birds: Detecting Aggression and Bullying on Twitter", *WebSci 2017 – Proceedings of the 2017 ACM Web Science Conference*, 2017, 21, https://doi.org/10.48550/arxiv.1702.06877.

behavior and the social mechanisms that reinforce it sheds light on the complexity of causes and influencing factors that disconnect groups and break apart social media networks.

Hate and vitriol are not limited to individuals or social groups; they extend into the political sphere, where political elites frequently use malicious and hateful statements against their adversaries. They seek to damage their opponents or assert their dominance by stirring negative emotions in the public. In this situation, verbal aggression is aimed at capturing media attention and generating online engagement. It is particularly effective for attracting the attention of journalists, as positive news is often overlooked in the media.[98] However, incivility does not merely attract media and public attention. It manipulates public perception and influences the political narrative. By intensifying divisive and inflammatory language, political figures use the discourse to push their political agendas. This strategy not only reinforces existing biases and prejudices but also exacerbates social divisions and contributes to a more polarized and contentious political environment.[99]

Social media platforms, driven by business models that rely on continuous user engagement, often promote emotionally charged posts that enhance virality. Emotions are key to engaging users as they capture their attention and extend screen time. User attention is monetized and becomes the primary source of revenue for digital platforms. Posts expressing strong emotions like joy, sadness or hope, such as tweets about illness, are more popular and frequently shared.[100] Aggressive content also tends to go viral, so the media frequently amplifies aggression.[101] Conversely, users whose posts fail to elicit emotional responses see a significant drop in activity.[102] The aim is to attract the widest audience possible, which then translates into advertising

---

98   John G. Geer, "The News Media and the Rise of Negativity in Presidential Campaigns", *PS: Political Science & Politics* 45, no. 3 (2012): 423, https://doi.org/10.1017/S104909 6512000492.

99   Jakubowska-Branicka, *Hate Narratives. Language as a Tool of Intolerance.*

100   Wang and Wei, "Fear and Hope, Bitter and Sweet: Emotion Sharing of Cancer Community on Twitter".

101   Jacques Gerstlé and Alessandro Nai, "Negativity, Emotionality and Populist Rhetoric in Election Campaigns Worldwide, and Their Effects on Media Attention and Electoral Success", *European Journal of Communication* 34, no. 4 (2019): 410–44, https://doi.org/10 .1177/0267323119861875; Shupei Yuan et al., "More Aggressive, More Retweets? Exploring the Effects of Aggressive Climate Change Messages on Twitter", *New Media & Society* 26, no. 8, (2022), https://doi.org/10.1177/14614448221122202.

102   Kramer, Guillory and Hancock, "Experimental Evidence of Massive-Scale Emotional Contagion through Social Networks".

revenue.[103] Algorithmic recommendation systems, which favor emotional content, inadvertently promote sensationalist or emotionally charged publications, including hate speech. When vitriol and hate gain greater visibility, they are perceived as more acceptable. This may contribute to the normalization of harmful behavior and speech on social networking sites. Furthermore, algorithms create echo chambers and filter bubbles that limit users' exposure to diverse viewpoints, reinforce existing biases and encourage radical or extremist views. In this way, even though they are neutral tools, algorithms can inadvertently contribute to the growth and persistence of phenomena like hate speech on social media. When used intentionally, they can escalate conflicts and deepen social divisions. In the face of these challenges, there is a need to develop more sophisticated methods of content filtering and moderation that balance user engagement with the responsibility to reduce harmful content. To foster a healthier and more inclusive communication environment on social media, well-designed algorithms play a crucial role in shaping public discourse and opinion.

8 Multidisciplinary Approaches to Combating Hate Speech

Hate speech significantly disrupts social cohesion and undermines the foundational principles of democracy. It poses a serious threat to social integrity and human rights. Countering hate speech requires a multidisciplinary approach that is adopted across various sectors of society. Effective countermeasures need to cover various areas such as public awareness building and education, establishing legal frameworks, launching community initiatives, and providing victim support. Given the complexities related to globalization and multiculturalism, innovative and culturally sensitive approaches are crucial to counter hate speech effectively. Holistic educational and societal interventions need to be implemented to promote openness, tolerance, critical thinking, empathy, and responsible behavior. These efforts are essential for building a society that values mutual respect and understanding, essential for maintaining democratic integrity and social harmony.

---

103 Vian Bakir and Andrew McStay, "Fake News and the Economy of Emotions", *Digital Journalism* 6, no. 2 (2017): 154–75, https://doi.org/10.1080/21670811.2017.1345645; Sara Polak and Daniel Trottier, "Introducing Online Vitriol", in *Violence and Trolling on Social Media. History, Affect, and Effects on Online Vitriol* (Amsterdam: Amsterdam University Press, 2020), 9–24.

Addressing hate speech effectively requires an analytical approach grounded in the attitudinal framework. This approach calls for a comprehensive evaluation of every aspect of hate speech to alleviate its detrimental impacts. By viewing hate speech through this lens, we recognize it as a multifaceted phenomenon that fundamentally influences human behavior and perception through attitudinal mechanisms. Attitudes encompass cognitive components, emotional reactions, future intentions, and resultant behavior, forming mental schemas that trigger emotional responses and influence conduct.[104] Consequently, attitudes not only reflect but also shape the values upheld by communities and guide individual decisions. Attitudes encompass cognitive, emotional and behavioral components with distinct levels of complexity and intensity.[105] In the context of hate speech, the cognitive component often lacks explicit knowledge about the target group, but relies on skewed perceptions and stereotypes propagated by media and anecdotes. The emotional aspect is marked by contempt and rejection, occasionally expressing a desire to eliminate the target group based on often imaginary, negatively attributed characteristics. The behavioral component reflects actions motivated by ignorance and entrenched negative stereotypes, which may manifest itself in verbal forms such as public statements and graffiti or direct actions such as demonstrations and physical attacks.

Analyzing hate speech in the attitudinal framework points at the need for adopting a comprehensive strategy that includes moral and ethical considerations alongside legal and political measures. The integrated approach is necessary to build a just, tolerant and inclusive society. Our social and technological environments are continuously evolving, which requires ongoing analysis and regulatory adaptations. First, education plays a crucial role in countering hate speech. Educational programs, both formal and informal, should promote respect, empathy and understanding of diversity. Instruction at all levels of education should develop critical thinking and raise awareness of the consequences of hate speech. Lessons on history, culture and human rights can increase public awareness of the adverse effects of discrimination and hatred. Alongside education, effective legal regulations are also necessary. Precise legislation should criminalize the most harmful forms of hate speech while respecting freedom of expression. Precision is necessary to avoid abuse and unambiguously define the limits of acceptable criticism.

---

104   Rathus; Philip Zimbardo and Michael Leippe, *The Psychology of Attitude Change and Social Influence* (Philadelphia: Temple University Press, 1991).

105   Ryszard Holly, "Postawa (i Hasła Korespondujące)", in *Słownik Psychologiczny*, ed. Włodzimierz Szewczuk (Warsaw: Wiedza Powszechna, 1985).

Social initiatives and victim support are also of great importance. NGO s, support groups and grassroots initiatives play essential roles in educating and assisting victims and promoting intercultural dialogue. Furthermore, creating spaces for the exchange of experiences and mutual support contributes to a better understanding and a more effective response to hate speech. Strengthening a sense of community and respect for the dignity of each individual is fundamental to countering hate speech. Referring to shared values and history, as well as appreciating diverse cultural contributions, can help reduce prejudice and stereotyping. Promoting openness, tolerance and intercultural dialogue is critical to building a society where diversity is seen as an added value rather than a source of division.

An integrated approach to combating hate speech involves shaping values and fostering a sense of community. It is essential to respond to any manifestation of hate speech, wherever it occurs – in public spaces or on the internet. Silence in the face of such acts can be misinterpreted as acceptance, reinforcing prejudices and stereotypes.[106] Therefore, early intervention is critical – identifying and preventing the escalation of hate speech issues. Proactive responses range from reporting offensive content to the relevant authorities to conducting educational activities that raise public awareness of the negative consequences of hate speech. Collaborating with NGO s, community groups, educational institutions, the business sector, and public administration is vital for effectively countering discrimination and promoting a culture of tolerance. Such cooperation enables the creation and implementation of large-scale, effective anti-discrimination strategies that contribute to sustainable social change. Participating in social campaigns, organizing educational workshops, and being active in public discourse facilitates the exchange of knowledge, experiences and best practices in combating hate speech. Building bridges between different social groups is another effective strategy. Initiating and supporting activities that encourage dialogue and mutual understanding among diverse groups helps break down barriers and stereotypes. Cultural festivals, community projects and joint initiatives can serve as platforms for building sustainable and positive interpersonal relationships that enhance mutual understanding and respect.

In November 2020, an effective collaboration was demonstrated through a Europe-wide day of joint action coordinated by Europol's European Counter-Terrorism Centre. The initiative, led by Germany and involving nine countries including the Czech Republic, France, Greece, Italy, Ireland, Norway,

---

106   Humanity in Action, "Czym Jest Mowa Nienawiści", 2014, https://uprzedzuprzedzenia.org
      /czym-mowa-nienawisci/.

Spain, and the UK, targeted racist and xenophobic hate speech on the internet. Its primary aim was to curb the spread of hate crimes, racism and xenophobia online, focusing on individuals and communities disseminating hate through various media such as posts, comments and memes. Law enforcement agencies collaborated to emphasize that the internet is not beyond the law, and online anonymity does not shield individuals from legal repercussions for unlawful activities. This operation sent a definitive message against online hate, warning that such actions would lead to detection and prosecution. Subsequent initiatives have continued to build on this foundation. In April 2022, a second day of joint action led by France, now with the participation of 11 countries, focused on combating both online and offline hate speech. Most recently, in December 2023, a third joint day of action, coordinated by Spain's National Office for Combating Hate Crimes (ONDOD), involved law enforcement from Austria, France, Germany, and Italy targeting violent hate crimes. These continued efforts, supported by tangible results, prove the commitment to an ongoing, collaborative fight against hate speech and crimes.

The state should likewise foster an environment that supports the rights to freedom of expression, equality and non-discrimination. It can be achieved through various positive policy measures to combat prejudice and discrimination. Addressing the root causes of hate and meeting the needs of victims is essential. Other stakeholders, including civil society, the media and businesses, should likewise take voluntary initiatives to address the root causes of prejudice and intolerance and counteract hate speech. Lawmakers and regulators must balance the need to protect individuals from the harmful effects of hate speech with the need to preserve space for the open and free exchange of ideas. Achieving balance is challenging due to constant changes in social norms and the technological landscape. Consequently, this issue requires ongoing analysis and regulatory adaptation to evolving socio-cultural and technological conditions.

Government regulations typically set minimum standards, while platforms such as Facebook and X often implement stricter guidelines, responding more quickly to changing social norms, which evolve faster than legislation. Under social pressure and to avoid reputational risk, big tech companies can adapt their moderation rules more quickly to respond to these changes, while the legislative process is usually longer and more complex. Government regulations may thus only cover some forms of discrimination, creating gaps in legal protection. The challenges of interpreting and enforcing the law on digital platforms, along with the dynamics of changing social norms, require companies to continuously adapt their policies. What is considered hate speech varies depending on a country's cultural and legal context. Multinational companies, therefore, need to balance compliance with local laws while maintaining global standards and policies. Although platforms were initially under no obligation to regulate their content to eliminate hate speech (in line with the principle of freedom of expression), as they evolved, they recognized the need to protect against potential litigation and user dissatisfaction and controversy.

Social networks' terms and conditions (Facebook, YouTube and X) are crucial because hate and vulgarity regularly occur on social platforms. Facebook defines hate speech as "content that attacks people based on their actual or perceived race, ethnicity, national origin, religion, sex, gender or gender identity, sexual orientation, disability or disease". The platform permits instances of humor or satire that could otherwise be viewed as potential threats or attacks, as well as content that some might consider distasteful, such as jokes, stand-up comedy and song lyrics.[107] Facebook also identifies "objectionable content" as anything attacking people based on their "protected characteristics": race, ethnicity, national origin, disability, religious affiliation, caste, sexual orientation, sex, gender identity, and serious disease.[108] YouTube defines hate speech as content promoting violence or hatred against individuals or groups based on attributes such as race or ethnic origin, religion, disability, gender, age, veteran status, and sexual orientation/gender identity. The service distinguishes between criticizing a nation-state and posting malicious hateful comments about a group based solely on their ethnicity.[109] YouTube's Hate Speech Policy forbids the promotion of violence or hatred against individuals or groups based on age, caste, disability, ethnicity, gender identity and expression, nationality, race, immigrant status, religion, sex/gender, sexual orientation, victims of a major violent event and their kin, and veteran status.[110] X defines "hateful conduct" as promoting violence or directly attacking or threatening other people based on race, ethnicity, national origin, sexual orientation, gender, gender identity, religious affiliation, age, disability, or disease.[111] The service specifies categories that should not be attacked or threatened: race, ethnicity, national origin, caste, sexual orientation, gender, gender identity, religious affiliation, age, disability, or serious disease. It also forbids hateful imagery, violent threats, "wishing, hoping or calling for serious harm," and repeated slurs, tropes, or

---

107   Facebook, "What Does Facebook Consider To Be Hate Speech?", 2018, https://www.face book.com/help/.

108   Facebook; Meta, "Hate speech. In Facebook Community Standards", 2022, https://trans parency.meta.com/pl-pl/policies/community-standards/hate-speech/.

109   YouTube, "Hate Speech Policy", 2019, https://support.google.com/youtube/answer/2801939.

110   YouTube.

111   X, "Rules & Policies. Hateful Conduct", 2023, https://help.x.com/en/rules-and-policies/hateful-conduct-policy.

other content that dehumanizes, degrades, or reinforces negative stereotypes about a protected category.[112]

While the policies of social networks like Facebook, YouTube and X include clear definitions and prohibitions against hate speech and hateful conduct, their effectiveness depends on the consistent application and interpretation of these rules. The diversity of user interactions and the global reach of platforms make distinguishing harmful content from protected speech a real challenge. On top of this, social networking sites are characterized by the rapid and widespread dissemination of content, which, in the absence of traditional regulatory and gate-keeping mechanisms, allows hate speech to flourish. Ethical questions arise about the platforms' responsibilities and the balance they must maintain between freedom of expression and the protection of users from harm. As social media continues to evolve, these challenges will persist, testing the resilience of policies and the adaptability of platforms in managing the fine line between safeguarding user rights and curbing the spread of hate speech.

---

112   Twitter, "Hateful Conduct Policy", 2021, https://help.twitter.com/en/rules-and-policies/hateful-conduct-policy.

Digital Dependency: Exploring Problematic Internet Use

Problematic internet use (PIU) has become a significant social concern. It refers to a wide range of compulsive behaviors online, including excessive gaming, shopping, gambling, and social media use. To fully understand its nature, it is essential to consider the underlying psychological and behavioral mechanisms that drive this disorder. The compulsive use of the internet and gaming are not merely habits but involve profound alterations in brain structure and functionality, similar to those of substance addiction. Such compulsive use is exacerbated by the inherently addictive design of digital technologies. Features such as unlimited access, instant feedback and interactive interfaces engage users in a continuous loop of stimulation and gratification. These design elements, aimed at maximizing user engagement, exploit psychological vulnerabilities. As a result, they lead to patterns of use that can disrupt normal life activities and responsibilities.

1 Problematic Internet Use

Problematic internet use (PIU) is a social pathology that has attracted substantial scholarly attention due to its rapidly increasing prevalence and its potential to disrupt everyday life. It is a broad term that includes various digital experiences such as gaming disorder, excessive viewing of pornography or cyber sex, excessive shopping, problematic online gambling, and social media addiction. The terminology used to describe PIU is varied, encompassing various terms coined by different researchers over time, such as internet addiction,[1]

---

1   Kimberly S. Young, "Internet Addiction: The Emergence of a New Clinical Disorder", *Cyberpsychology and Behavior* 1, no. 3 (1998): 237–44, https://doi.org/10.1089/CPB.1998.1.237; Mark Griffiths, "Does Internet and Computer 'Addiction' Exist? Some Case Study Evidence", *Cyberpsychology and Behavior* 3, no. 2 (2000): 211–18; Kimberly S. Young and Carl J. Case, "Internet Abuse in the Workplace: New Trends in Risk Management", *CyberPsychology & Behavior* 7, no. 1 (2004): 105–11, https://doi.org/10.1089/109493104322820174.

internet abuse,[2] internet dependency,[3] and internet addiction syndrome.[4] Increasingly, researchers use terms such as problematic internet use (PUI);[5] defined as compulsive involvement in internet use, pathological internet use,[6] internet abuse,[7] compulsive internet use,[8] excessive internet use,[9] maladaptive

2 Mark Griffiths, "Internet Abuse in the Workplace: Issues and Concerns for Employers and Employment Counselors", *Journal of Employment Counseling* 40, no. 2 (2003): 87–96, https://doi.org/10.1002/j.2161-1920.2003.tb00859.x; Young and Case, "Internet Abuse in the Workplace".

3 Magda Javakhishvili and Alexander T. Vazsonyi, "Parental Vigilance, Low Self-Control, and Internet Dependency among Rural Adolescents", in *Child and Adolescent Online Risk Exposure* (2021), 191–208, https://doi.org/10.1016/B978-0-12-817499-9.00010-7.

4 Yi Zhang, Pan Zhang and Yu Liu, "Chinese Indigenous Intervention on Internet Gaming Disorder: A Review of Traditional Chinese Therapies": (2021 4th International Conference on Humanities Education and Social Sciences (ICHESS 2021), Xishuangbanna, China, 2021), https://doi.org/10.2991/assehr.k.211220.085; Mengyuan Huang and Weiyi Zhang, "The Mechanism and Treatment of Teenager Internet Addiction from Stress: A Review": (2021 International Conference on Public Art and Human Development (ICPAHD 2021), Kunming, China, 2022), https://doi.org/10.2991/assehr.k.220110.155.

5 Orsolya Király et al., "Preventing Problematic Internet Use during the COVID-19 Pandemic: Consensus Guidance", *Comprehensive Psychiatry* 100 (2020): 152180, https://doi.org/10.1016/j.comppsych.2020.152180; Yaron Sela et al., "Family Environment and Problematic Internet Use among Adolescents: The Mediating Roles of Depression and Fear of Missing Out", *Computers in Human Behavior* 106 (2020): 106226, https://doi.org/10.1016/j.chb.2019.106226.

6 Ran Tao et al., "Proposed Diagnostic Criteria for Internet Addiction", *Addiction* 105, no. 3 (2010): 556–64, https://doi.org/10.1111/j.1360-0443.2009.02828.x; Geoffrey Talis, "Internet Addiction", in *Substance and Non-Substance Related Addictions*, ed. Evaristo Akerele (Cham: Springer International Publishing, 2022), 99–107, https://doi.org/10.1007/978-3-030-84834-7_7.

7 Janet Morahan-Martin, "Internet Abuse: Addiction? Disorder? Symptom? Alternative Explanations?", *Social Science Computer Review* 23, no. 1 (2005): 39–48, https://doi.org/10.1177/0894439304271533; Janet Morahan-Martin, "Internet Abuse: Emerging Trends and Lingering Questions", in *Psychological Aspects of Cyberspace*, ed. Azy Barak (Cambridge University Press, 2008), 32–69, https://doi.org/10.1017/CBO9780511813740.004; Raiswa Saha et al., "Online Abuse: A Systematic Literature Review and Future Research Agenda", *International Journal of Conflict Management*, 2024, https://doi.org/10.1108/IJCMA-09-2023-0188.

8 Tahir Islam et al., "Determinants of Purchase Luxury Counterfeit Products in Social Commerce: The Mediating Role of Compulsive Internet Use", *Journal of Retailing and Consumer Services* 62 (2021): 102596, https://doi.org/10.1016/j.jretconser.2021.102596; Pey-Yan Liou, Ssu-Ching Huang and Sufen Chen, "Longitudinal Relationships between School Burnout, Compulsive Internet Use, and Academic Decrement: A Three-Wave Cross-Lagged Study", *Computers in Human Behavior* 135 (2022): 107363, https://doi.org/10.1016/j.chb.2022.107363; Okwach Alphonce Akungu, Sufen Chen and Chiu-Hung Su, "Longitudinal Association of Adolescents' Perceptions of Parental Mediations and Compulsive Internet Use", *Computers in Human Behavior* 150 (2024): 107989, https://doi.org/10.1016/j.chb.2023.107989.

9 Georgios Floros and Konstantinos Siomos, "Excessive Internet Use and Personality Traits", *Current Behavioral Neuroscience Reports* 1, no. 1 (2014): 19–26, https://doi.org/10.1007/s40473-014-0006-1; Ellen Johanna Helsper and David Smahel, "Excessive Internet Use by Young Europeans: Psychological Vulnerability and Digital Literacy?", *Information, Communication & Society* 23, no. 9 (2020): 1255–73, https://doi.org/10.1080/1369118X.2018.1563203.

internet use,[10] and dysfunctional internet use.[11] Other commonly used terms include Internet Addiction Disorder (IAD), cyber dependence, www-holism, interholism, cyber addiction, net holism or net addiction. The diversity of terms indicates the broad spectrum of internet-related compulsive behavior and the evolving understanding of this disorder. While each term highlights a different aspect of addiction, they all emphasize the syndromic nature of addiction symptoms.

Regardless of definitional debates, PIU remains a serious problem that is characterized by prolonged and intense internet use, accompanied by a perceived need to use it, which can often lead to a loss of control. It is a complex condition that involves an interplay of behavioral mechanisms and alterations in brain structure and function. The consequences can be detrimental to the individual's life, as it may cause them to neglect other aspects of life and engage in socially harmful behavior. In order to fully understand the disorder, it is essential to first explore the fundamental nature of addiction. This chapter will analyze various aspects of addiction, including its physiological, neurobiological and psychological aspects, and will lay the groundwork for a more detailed analysis of how these dimensions surface in digital settings.

Addiction is a condition in which an individual experiences a psychological and physical compulsion to perform specific activities or to take psychoactive substances. Addiction, therefore, involves situations in which an individual becomes dependent on a particular stimulus or factor. Dependence can take two forms. First, physical dependence occurs when the body has adapted to toxic substances, leading to physiological and psychological disturbances when the substances are absent. Second, psychological dependence manifests as an irresistible desire to re-engage in a particular situation or activity. The obsession causes the individual's life to become centered around the stimulus, potentially leading to the neglect or rejection of other areas of their life.

---

10   Scarlett Mattoli, Melanie Shaw and Scott Burrus, "Adult Maladaptive Internet Use, Depression, and Self-Efficacy in Hong Kong", *The International Journal of Health, Wellness, and Society* 11, no. 2 (2021): 187–207, https://doi.org/10.18848/2156-8960/CGP/v11i02/187-207; Stephen A. Rains and Robert S. Tokunaga, "The Role of Emotion in Maladaptive Internet Use: Internet Addiction, Problematic Internet Use, and Deficient Self-Regulation", in *Emotions in the Digital World*, eds. Robin L. Nabi and Jessica Gall Myrick (Oxford University Press New York, 2023), 174–92, https://doi.org/10.1093/oso/9780197520536.003.0010.

11   Giorgos Assimogiorgos et al., "Dysfunctional Internet Use by Adolescents in an Urban Environment: A Case-Control Study", *Developmental and Adolescent Health* 1, no. 4 (2021), https://doi.org/10.54088/8ujmkll; Mirko Duradoni et al., "Exploring the Relationships Between Digital Life Balance and Internet Social Capital, Loneliness, Fear of Missing Out, and Anxiety", ed. Pinaki Chakraborty, *Human Behavior and Emerging Technologies* 2024 (2024): 1–9, https://doi.org/10.1155/2024/5079719.

From a medical perspective, addiction is a chronic disorder characterized by changes in brain function, including a reduction in top-down processes and decreased prefrontal cortex activity that leads to the appearance of normally controlled behavior, a dysfunctional dopamine reward system that reinforces compulsive behavior despite its adverse consequences.[12] Addiction is a process in which there is a disruption between the reward and punishment systems, where the role of reward is amplified, and the role of punishment is diminished, thereby making an activity a source of immediate gratification. Neurotransmitters such as endorphin, dynorphin, serotonin, and dopamine, which interact with opioid receptors, play a critical role in the functioning of the reward system. In particular, dopamine plays a vital role in the addiction process. The amount of dopamine increases markedly after taking a psychoactive substance or after performing an activity.[13] It is important to remember that irrespective of the type of addiction, the feeling of pleasure or the relief of tension is caused by the same neurotransmitter.

The journey to addiction usually begins when the individual experiences initial exposure to a substance or activity, often influenced by social and environmental factors. Initial use is typically driven by the pleasure or relief it provides, mediated by the brain's reward system. As the individual repeats the behavior, positive reinforcement strengthens the habit. Over time, environmental cues and stressors further condition the individual to crave the substance or activity, leading to increased use. Eventually, this escalates to a loss of control and a perceived continuous need for the substance or activity to satisfy desires, avoid withdrawal symptoms, or cope with negative emotions.[14] The Diagnostic and Statistical Manual of Mental Disorders (DSM-5)[15] defines addiction as a mental or physical compulsion to perform specific activities or take certain substances, driven by the anticipation of their effects or to avoid the unpleasant symptoms of their absence. Similarly, the International

---

12   Harold Kincaid and Jacqueline A. Sullivan, "Medical Models of Addiction", in *What Is Addiction?*, eds. Don Ross et al. (Cambridge, MA: The MIT Press, 2010), 352–76, https://doi.org/10.7551/mitpress/9780262513111.003.0014.

13   David J. Nutt et al., "The Dopamine Theory of Addiction: 40 Years of Highs and Lows", *Nature Reviews Neuroscience* 16, no. 5 (2015): 305–12, https://doi.org/10.1038/nrn3939.

14   Robert West and Jamie Brown, *Theory of Addiction. Second Edition* (Hoboken, NJ: Wiley Blackwell, 2013).

15   American Psychiatric Association, *Diagnostic and Statistical Manual of Mental Disorders. Fifth Edition* (Arlington, VA: American Psychiatric Association, 2013), https://doi.org/10.1176/appi.books.9780890425596.

Classification of Diseases (ICD-11)[16] describes addiction as a set of physiological, behavioral and cognitive phenomena where substance use predominates over activities previously valued more highly by the individual. Addiction is thus categorized as a specific disease entity with a distinct code in the classification system. Its key manifestations include an intense desire or 'craving' for a psychoactive substance and an 'addiction memory,' which leads to a rapid resurgence of the full addiction syndrome even after prolonged abstinence.

In order to diagnose addiction, at least three out of six indicative symptoms must be present, distributed across three categories: psychopathology (intense substance craving or compulsion to take the substance and reduction or even loss of ability to control its use), pathophysiology (physiological withdrawal symptoms and tolerance changes), behavior (compulsive use, neglect of responsibilities, excessive time spent on acquiring the substance, persistent use despite the obvious harm caused), social and environmental factors (social isolation, relationship problems), cognitive symptoms (distorted thinking, rationalizing or minimizing the impact of addiction). These criteria are essential for diagnosing and recognizing psychoactive substance dependence.[17]

Spending numerous hours online, frequent use of mobile devices, and intensive involvement in digital activities have become so common that they are now topics of significant discussion among scientific communities, including psychologists, educators, psychiatrists, sociologists, and other scholars. Although phenomena involving addiction to various online activities have been observed and described since the 1990s, researchers still disagree on definitional issues and diagnostic criteria. Lack of consensus on a single, generally accepted term and scientific description stems from the multifacetedness and complexity of digital interactions and their impact on individuals' psychological, physical and social development.

The term 'addiction' related to internet use sparks controversy among researchers. Some argue that its application is inappropriate as it is traditionally reserved for substance addictions like alcohol, nicotine or drugs. Others, however, view internet addiction in the broader spectrum of behavioral or activity addictions, such as gambling addiction. In one of the earlier scholarly works on this subject, Kimberly Young defines internet addiction as "an impulse-control disorder which does not involve an intoxicant"[18] whereas

---

16   World Health Organization, "International Statistical Classification of Diseases and Related Health Problems (ICD)", 2024, https://www.who.int/standards/classifications /classification-of-diseases.

17   American Psychiatric Association, *Diagnostic and Statistical Manual of Mental Disorders. Fifth Edition*; West and Brown, *Theory of Addiction. Second Edition*.

18   Young, "Internet Addiction: The Emergence of a New Clinical Disorder", 238.

Mark Griffiths views it as an example of the technological addictions that he defined as "nonchemical (behavioral) addictions that involve human-machine interaction"[19] that can be either passive (e.g., television) or active (e.g., computer games). Based on the diagnostic criteria for pathological gambling, Young suggests that individuals may be addicted to the internet if they meet certain criteria, such as preoccupation with the internet, increasing amounts of time spent on internet activities, unsuccessful attempts to control use, restlessness or irritability when attempting to stop the activity, and use of the internet to escape problems or relieve negative mood.[20]

Young likens internet addiction to substance addiction; however, it has not been formally recognized as an addictive disorder, primarily because it does not involve a physical substance to which users can become dependent.[21] Furthermore, some clinicians argue that obsessive use of the technology often manifests as a symptom of other underlying psychiatric disorders such as depression or social anxiety.[22] Lastly, some propose that pathological internet use should be divided into different subtypes and treated as a digital version of its offline equivalent – for instance, treating online gamblers as gamblers and internet pornography addiction as compulsive sexual behavior.[23] All in all, there is opposition among researchers to categorizing internet addiction as a distinct disorder due to "insufficient peer-reviewed evidence to establish the diagnostic criteria and course descriptions to identify the behavior as a mental disorder".[24] Online gaming fits into the addiction framework and displays many behavioral similarities with other addictive behavior; therefore, Internet Gambling Disorder has been added to the appendix of the fifth edition of the Diagnostic and Statistical Manual of Mental Disorders (DSM-5) by the American Psychiatric Association (2013) as an addictive disorder warranting further study. The World Health Organization (2018) acknowledged Online Gaming Disorder in its 11th International Classification of Diseases (ICD-11). Other addictive behavior, such as cyber sexual addiction, or net compulsions,

---

19   Griffiths, "Does Internet and Computer 'Addiction' Exist? Some Case Study Evidence", 211.

20   Young, "Internet Addiction: The Emergence of a New Clinical Disorder".

21   Young.

22   Richard A. Davis, "A Cognitive-Behavioral Model of Pathological Internet Use", *Computers in Human Behavior* 17, no. 2 (2001): 187–95, https://doi.org/10.1016/S0747-5632(00)00041-8; Ronald Pies, "Should DSM-V Designate 'Internet Addiction' a Mental Disorder?", *Psychiatry (Edgmont)* 6, no. 2 (2009): 31.

23   Fionnbar Lenihan, "Computer Addiction – A Sceptical View: Invited Commentary On: Lost Online", *Advances in Psychiatric Treatment* 13, no. 1 (2007): 31–33, https://doi.org/10.1192/APT.BP.106.003004.

24   Pabasari Ginige, "Internet Addiction Disorder", in *Child and Adolescent Mental Health* (IntechOpen, 2017), https://doi.org/10.5772/66966.

is categorized as impulse disorders. The ongoing debate on the terminology and classification of internet addiction aims to better understand the phenomenon and approach diagnosis, research and the development of therapeutic interventions accordingly.

Furthermore, there is discussion on whether to view the problem collectively or focus on specific online activities. A general approach treats internet addiction as a single disorder that is characterized by compulsive use of an online activity, regardless of the specific activities involved. In this perspective, internet addiction is seen as a general tendency to use the internet excessively and harmfully. In contrast, a more specific approach recognizes that various types of online activities may trigger different types of addiction. Therefore, each type of online activity is considered a potential source of addiction, each with its own set of dynamics, psychological impacts and potential for addiction and, as such, should be assessed and analyzed individually. Individuals often develop a dependency on specific applications that serve as catalysts for their excessive use of the internet. Certain clinicians advocate for the classification of pathological internet use into distinct subcategories, treating each as an online manifestation of its offline counterpart. For instance, they propose categorizing online gamblers as gamblers and treating internet pornography addiction as a form of compulsive sexual behavior.[25]

PIU encompasses a diverse range of behaviors and issues related to impulse control, which Young divided into five distinct subtypes:

- Net-compulsions are characterized by compulsive maintenance of a continuous connection to the internet. Those affected remain online most of the time, closely monitoring online events and content, frequently engaging in obsessive online gambling, compulsive online shopping and stock trading.
- Information overload involves excessive downloading and processing of information. This includes simultaneously participating in many chat rooms and being active on many mailing lists.
- Cyber relational addiction is an addiction to online social contacts. Addicts seek support, comfort and acceptance in interactive online environments. They find a sense of belonging without the usual social risks. This over-involvement can disrupt interpersonal relationships in the real world.
- Cyber sexual addiction involves heavy viewing of pornographic content or participating in erotic online chat rooms.
- Computer addiction is characterized by a strong need to spend time in front of the computer, often involving obsessive computer game playing. For those affected, being online and having access to the computer are both

---

25   Lenihan, "Computer Addiction – A Sceptical View: Invited Commentary On: Lost Online".

optional and essential as the computer serves as a gateway to a broad online experience.[26]

Identifying individuals at risk of developing pathological internet use is crucial, as excessive computer use has been linked to increased susceptibility to smoking, alcohol abuse and drug use.[27] Moreover, comorbidity is prevalent, with numerous concurrent conditions such as depression, social anxiety disorder, OCD, ADHD, and substance use disorders including gambling, alcohol, marijuana, nicotine, and cocaine addiction, as well as eating disorders like binge eating disorder, bulimia and obesity. Specific personality traits and disorders such as impulsivity, borderline, avoidant personality, and antisocial disorders are also often associated.[28] Furthermore, comorbidities are typically correlated with the nature of internet-related issues. General internet addiction tends to be linked with common mental health disorders like anxiety, mood, eating, psychotic, and dissociative disorders, along with increased substance dependence. On the other hand, individuals with gaming addiction often experience a more extensive and severe range of comorbidities.[29] Excessive internet use is also a social issue that impacts not only individuals but also their families and society at large. It can lead to marital or family discord, reduced work productivity, legal troubles, and academic decline.[30] Given its multiple comorbidities and social consequences, it is crucial to identify individuals at risk of developing pathological internet use and help internet users develop good cyber hygiene habits.

2   Problematic Smartphone Use

Smartphones have integrated into everyday life and have become indispensable tools for many individuals. With their unlimited internet connectivity, they offer constant access to engaging content and numerous convenient and functional apps, which enrich various aspects of daily experiences.

---

26   Young and Case, "Internet Abuse in the Workplace".

27   Jennifer A. Epstein, "The Role of Parents and Related Factors on Adolescent Computer Use", *Journal of Public Health Research* 1, no. 1 (2012), https://doi.org/10.4081/JPHR.2012.E13.

28   Olatz Lopez-Fernandez and Daria J. Kuss, "Preventing Harmful Internet Use-Related Addiction Problems in Europe: A Literature Review and Policy Options", *International Journal of Environmental Research and Public Health* 17, no. 11 (2020): 3797, https://doi.org/10.3390/IJERPH17113797.

29   Lopez-Fernandez and Kuss.

30   Chien Chou and Ming Chun Hsiao, "Internet Addiction, Usage, Gratification, and Pleasure Experience: The Taiwan College Students' Case", *Computers & Education* 35, no. 1 (2000): 65–80, https://doi.org/10.1016/S0360-1315(00)00019-1.

These devices offer many pleasures, including facilitating social interaction, providing entertainment, granting access to information, offering coping mechanisms, and reinforcing one's social identity. However, overreliance on smartphones can make individuals form strong emotional attachments to their smartphones. When separated from their devices, individuals may experience a sense of unease or distress.[31] This illustrates the profound role that smartphones play in people's lives, surpassing their utilitarian functions to evoke emotional connections similar to those found in interpersonal relationships.

Excessive smartphone use is a highly complex issue. Smartphones are portable devices that combine multiple functions and providing unlimited internet access regardless of time and place. This feature adds complexity to the issue. They have a positive, creative and social aspect, and this does not always have to be associated with addiction but can rather represent a new form of behavior. It is, therefore, crucial to fully understand the issue of smartphone use among users and to identify risk factors associated with addiction, such as psychological factors affecting normative developmental stages, especially in the context of social environments such as family and school.

Problematic smartphone use is a behavioral disorder characterized by compulsive and obsessive mobile phone use. It manifests as an uncontrolled compulsion to constantly use the phone, accompanied by feeling anxious, frustrated and even aggressive when it is impossible to use the phone (e.g., due to low battery or poor signal). Symptoms of the syndrome include the constant need to have the phone nearby, never being separated from it, reluctance to turn it off even for a moment, impatiently awaiting incoming messages or calls, and constantly checking for new messages and calls. In the absence of a mobile phone, individuals may experience anxiety, irritability, sleep disturbances, and even aggression. Understanding the various forms of mobile phone addiction can help identify and treat those affected and promote healthy habits of modern technology use. The list below identifies selected types of problematic smartphone use and behavior:

- problematic texters
  - constantly checking the phone for new messages and information;
  - texting compulsively;
  - the relationship between mood and well-being is affected by the number of text messages received;
  - sometimes, texting oneself instead of real people;

---

31   Tayana Panova and Xavier Carbonell, "Is Smartphone Addiction Really an Addiction?", *Journal of Behavioral Addictions* 7, no. 2 (2018): 252–59, https://doi.org/10.1556/2006.7 .2018.49.

- gadget enthusiasts (mobile gadget enthusiasts owning and upgrading to new technologies)
  - striving to raise social status through expensive, modern devices;
  - selecting a phone based on style, color and price;
  - ostentatiously displaying the phone and its features;
  - speaking loudly to draw attention to the phone;
  - avoiding answering calls to display the ringtone;
  - forcing others to call them in public places;
- new model addicts
  - frequent purchases of new mobile phone models;
  - investing large sums in the latest models;
  - acquiring state-of-the-art devices every few months;
- gamers
  - spending many hours playing mobile games;
  - aiming to achieve the highest score and earn points;
  - frequently spending money on virtual items and game upgrades;
  - neglecting responsibilities and other activities in favor of gaming;
- fear of disconnection
  - anxiety about turning off the phone at night;
  - experiencing anxiety, irritation and sleeplessness due to lost phone connectivity;
  - keeping the phone in sight at all times;
  - feeling secure by having a spare battery;
  - ready to engage in calls or messages at any moment;
- controllers (compulsive controlling and gathering information about others and events in internet)
  - seeking to gather information about others;
  - feeling anxious when unable to control information about others;
  - recording and filming events that could compromise others;
  - verifying information;
- problematic users of social networking sites
  - constantly checking and updating social media profiles;
  - maintaining constant contact with others through messaging apps;
  - seeking approval and popularity through likes and comments;
  - losing track of time while on social media;
- internet browsers (compulsive internet browsing)
  - compulsively searching the internet for new information;
  - spending excessive time on news portals, blogs and forums;
  - struggling to limit online time;
  - becoming distracted and less efficient in daily tasks.

- online shopaholics (compulsive online shopping)
  - regularly making online purchases, even when unnecessary;
  - buying items that are not needed;
  - accumulating items from online shopping, often without using them;
  - incurring debt due to online spending;
- talkaholics (compulsive voice communication)
  - engaging in constant and lengthy phone conversations;
  - having phone conversations regardless of location and activity (multitasking).

The list contains various forms of problematic smartphone use, each with unique characteristics. This analysis not only emphasizes the complex nature of smartphone use, but also reveals broader societal and psychological trends. Excessive social media use is frequently related to a strong need for social validation and fear of disconnection. Similarly, a compulsive need to gather information reflects an underlying need to control information and be in the loop in an information-rich world. Many individuals feel pressured to display their wealth and status through technology due to strong consumer trends. These patterns of behavior reveal how individuals seek satisfaction and manage insecurities, often substituting real-life interactions and experiences with digital gratification. Understanding underlying motivations and societal implications is crucial for addressing the causes of smartphone pathological use and promoting more balanced technology use.

3   Behavioral Mechanisms and Brain Impacts

Excessive internet use may turn into a poorly controlled activity, a compulsion which ultimately results in significant distress or disruption in daily life. Obsessive use of technology is a behavioral addiction. It differs from substance dependence as it does not involve the ingestion of psychoactive intoxicants. However, it features numerous similarities with other impulse control disorders in symptoms and basic mechanisms:

- Excessive and compulsive behavior, which entails loss of control while engaging in the addictive behavior and neglecting other activities, such as work, school and relationships, despite any negative consequences it may bring.
- Negative repercussions include problems with physical and mental health, interpersonal relationships, work or school performance, and legal troubles.

- Mood modification that results from engaging in the particular activity and can be interpreted as a coping strategy such as an invigorating high or, in contrast, a calming sensation of escape.[32]
- Increased tolerance, which means that an increasing amount of the particular activity is required to achieve the effects previously experienced.
- Withdrawal symptoms that occur once the particular activity is discontinued. They might include anxiety, moodiness, sadness, and irritability.[33] Full abstinence from digital technology is impossible due to the digital-centric nature of our modern lifestyle. Unlike treating alcohol or substance abuse where complete abstinence is often sought, the same approach is not practical for internet addiction due to the ubiquity and necessity of the internet. Instead, the aim is to establish a balanced and mindful pattern of usage, a practice termed "conscious computing". This involves developing and incorporating healthier ways of using the internet and media technology.[34]
- Changes in cognitive processes and brain function and structure.

Numerous studies indicate that people suffering from internet addiction display alterations in brain structure and function, including decreased gray matter volume in the prefrontal cortex regions, including the bilateral dorsolateral prefrontal cortex, anterior cingulate cortex and orbitofrontal cortex. These regions are crucial for higher cognitive functions, and they play crucial roles in response inhibition, decision making, impulse control, expectation related to reward and punishment, and emotion – all of which are integral to the development of addictive behavior.[35] Alterations in these parts of the brain coupled with reduced gray matter volume due to abuse leads to increased impulsivity and poor decision-making, as well as difficulties with cognitive flexibility. This might contribute to compulsive drug-seeking behavior and poor decision-making despite negative consequences. Reduced function in the anterior cingulate cortex could interfere with the ability to monitor conflicts

---

32   Griffiths, "Does Internet and Computer « Addiction » Exist? Some Case Study Evidence", 211.

33   Dean Kaptsis et al., "Withdrawal Symptoms in Internet Gaming Disorder: A Systematic Review", *Clinical Psychology Review* 43 (2016): 58–66, https://doi.org/10.1016/J.CPR.2015.11.006.

34   David Greenfield, "The Addictive Properties of Internet Usage", in *Internet Addiction*, eds. Kimberly S. Young and Cristiano Nabuco De Abreu (Hoboken, NJ, USA: John Wiley & Sons, Inc., 2007), 138–39, https://doi.org/10.1002/9781118013991.ch8.

35   Saeid Sadeghi et al., "Brain Structures and Activity during a Working Memory Task Associated with Internet Addiction Tendency in Young Adults: A Large Sample Study", *PLOS ONE* 16, no. 11 (2021): e0259259, https://doi.org/10.1371/JOURNAL.PONE.0259259.

between the desire to engage in the addictive activity and the negative consequences of doing so, leading to continued use. Changes in the orbitofrontal cortex lead to altered perception of rewards and punishments, which means that heavy internet users often have an increased sensitivity to the rewarding effects of addictive activity and a decreased sensitivity to natural rewards and the negative consequences of their compulsive behavior.

Impairments have also been detected in the right temporal lobe, which is involved in language comprehension, auditory processing and social cognition.[36] Dysfunction of these functions leads to problems with memory (in particular forming and retrieving long-term memories), learning and emotional learning. Some studies indicate that internet addiction could interfere with the brain's capabilities for information retention and recall, and may even lead to a decline in verbal intelligence.[37] Additional alterations have been observed in the parietal and insula cortex, which are responsible for sensory processing, decision-making, emotions, and motor control.

Anomalies in the gray and white matter of specific brain regions, critical for memory processing, attention, perception, and learning, have been reported as well.[38] Hence, excessive internet users often exhibit reduced attention spans and struggle with tasks demanding prolonged concentration. Impaired attention may manifest as difficulty focusing or ignoring irrelevant stimuli, which can further complicate efforts to abstain from addictive behavior or substances.

Studies have also shown that overuse of the internet can lead to modifications in brain chemistry, specifically related to dopamine availability and expression.[39] Dopamine, a neurotransmitter linked with pleasure and reward, reinforces pathological usage of the particular activity. Engaging in satisfying internet activities like online gaming or social media triggers dopamine release in the brain, leading to feelings of pleasure. As this behavior continues, the

---

36   Sadeghi et al.

37   Hikaru Takeuchi et al., "Impact of Frequency of Internet Use on Development of Brain Structures and Verbal Intelligence: Longitudinal Analyses", *Human Brain Mapping* 39, no. 11 (2018): 4471–79, https://doi.org/10.1002/HBM.24286; Sadeghi et al., "Brain Structures and Activity during a Working Memory Task Associated with Internet Addiction Tendency in Young Adults: A Large Sample Study".

38   Takeuchi et al., "Impact of Frequency of Internet Use on Development of Brain Structures and Verbal Intelligence: Longitudinal Analyses".

39   Haifeng Hou et al., "Reduced Striatal Dopamine Transporters in People with Internet Addiction Disorder", *Journal of Biomedicine and Biotechnology* 2012 (2012), https://doi.org/10.1155/2012/854524; Soon Beom Hong et al., "Decreased Functional Brain Connectivity in Adolescents with Internet Addiction", *PLOS ONE* 8, no. 2 (2013): e57831, https://doi.org/10.1371/JOURNAL.PONE.0057831.

brain adjusts to the constant dopamine influx by reducing its receptors or production, which in turn requires increased internet use to experience the same level of satisfaction. The cycle of craving, tolerance and withdrawal can potentially lead to internet addiction.

Excessive internet use correlates with several neurobiological abnormalities and has serious implications for brain development and cognitive function, which explains numerous behavioral, cognitive, emotional, and biological symptoms. These neurocognitive deficits mirror those seen in individuals with substance and other behavioral dependence, such as gambling. Since they are related to motivation and self-regulation, they increase the risk of developing addictive behavior. They also contribute to relapse and poor recovery outcomes. Although brain alteration results from continued excessive engagement in the particular activity, addiction is a complex phenomenon that is correlated with personal factors, such as individual traits, and environmental factors.

4   Underlying Causes of Problematic Internet Use

Pathological internet use (PIU) occurs when individuals interact with their devices aimlessly, as a form of diversion, rather than focusing on specific tasks or objectives.[40] Much of the available literature on PIU has not found a correlation between demographic variables and abusive behavior.[41] Other authors prove that internet abuse is more prevalent among males, individuals aged

---

40   Daria J. Kuss et al., "Internet Addiction: A Systematic Review of Epidemiological Research for the last Decade", *Current Pharmaceutical Design* 20, no. 25 (2014): 4026–52, https://doi.org/10.2174/13816128113199990617; Chad Tossell et al., "Exploring Smartphone Addiction: Insights from Long-Term Telemetric Behavioral Measures", *International Journal of Interactive Mobile Technologies* 9, no. 2 (2015): 37–43, https://doi.org/10.3991/IJIM.V9I2.4300.

41   Eylem Simsek, Turkish Air Forces, and Jale Balaban Sali, "The Role of Internet Addiction and Social Media Membership on University Students' Psychological Capital", *Contemporary Educational Technology* 5, no. 3 (2014): 239–56; Hanna Maija Sinkkonen, Helena Puhakka and Matti Meriläinen, "Internet Use and Addiction among Finnish Adolescents (15–19 Years)", *Journal of adolescence* 37, no. 2 (2014): 123–31, https://doi.org/10.1016/J.ADOLESCENCE.2013.11.008; Zoi Tsimtsiou et al., "Internet Addiction in Greek Medical Students: An Online Survey", *Academic Psychiatry* 39, no. 3 (2015): 300–304, https://doi.org/10.1007/S40596-014-0273-X; Kavya Raj et al., "Problematic Use of the Internet among Australian University Students: Prevalence and Profile", *Computers in Human Behavior Reports* 8 (2022): 100243, https://doi.org/10.1016/J.CHBR.2022.100243.

16–25 with a lower educational level. Durkee et al.,[42] Kuss et al.,[43] Sariyska et al.,[44] and Raj et al.[45] found higher levels of problematic internet use among males than females. A study by Sinkkonen, Puhakka and Meriläinen discovered that males tend to experience a more significant decrease in real-life relationships, while females demonstrate a larger reduction in self-control, and the differences could even be seen with moderate overuse of the internet.[46] Research conducted by De-Sola *et al.* further explore gender disparities by connecting them to specific online behavior. Females generally spend more time looking at screens and excessively using social media and smartphone apps, whereas males exhibit a broader range of internet use. Despite showing a higher level of abusive behavior, females also displayed a higher capacity for personal care.[47]

According to Wang, Chen and Chen, there is a connection between the age at which individuals first access the internet and their susceptibility to problematic internet use.[48] Additionally, age plays a role in determining the specific online activities individuals engage in. De-Sola *et al.* found that online abuse is more prevalent among younger users, specifically those aged 16 to 25.[49] Adolescents and young adults are more likely to be involved in online gaming, whereas adults are more inclined to engage in frequent gambling.[50] Tsimtsiou revealed that playing online games increases the risk of developing dependence. Furthermore, both online gaming and using social networks

---

42   Tony Durkee et al., "Prevalence of Pathological Internet Use among Adolescents in Europe: Demographic and Social Factors", *Addiction* 107, no. 12 (2012): 2210–22, https://doi.org/10.1111/J.1360-0443.2012.03946.X.

43   Kuss et al., "Internet Addiction: A Systematic Review of Epidemiological Research for the last Decade".

44   Rayna Sariyska et al., "Self-Esteem, Personality and Internet Addiction: A Cross-Cultural Comparison Study", *Personality and Individual Differences* 61–62 (2014): 28–33, https://doi.org/10.1016/J.PAID.2014.01.001.

45   Raj et al., "Problematic Use of the Internet among Australian University Students: Prevalence and Profile".

46   Sinkkonen, Puhakka and Meriläinen, "Internet Use and Addiction among Finnish Adolescents (15–19 Years)".

47   José De-Sola et al., "Cell Phone Use Habits among the Spanish Population: Contribution of Applications to Problematic Use", *Frontiers in Psychiatry* 10 (2019): 883, https://doi.org/10.3389/FPSYT.2019.00883.

48   Cheng Cai Wang, Chun Fu Chen and Chin Tsu Chen, "Exploring the Different Aspects of Internet Leisure Use by College Students", *Information Development* 31, no. 1 (2013): 5–12, https://doi.org/10.1177/0266666913494909.

49   De-Sola et al., "Cell Phone Use Habits among the Spanish Population: Contribution of Applications to Problematic Use".

50   Lopez-Fernandez and Kuss, "Preventing Harmful Internet Use-Related Addiction Problems in Europe: A Literature Review and Policy Options".

are identified as the most addictive internet activities for young adults.[51] Individuals who use the internet for entertainment and leisure purposes are more prone to developing addictive behavior.[52]

Apart from gender and age, certain personality traits have been found to be associated with internet addiction. Introversion is associated with spending excessive time playing online games. Since individuals with introverted personalities often exhibit traits such as inward thinking and social anxiety, they often feel more secure in the virtual world. The anonymity of the online environment easily provides them with a sense of comfort and control over their interactions. Introverts find it easier to build relationships, express themselves socially, expand their social networks, and gain public support in this setting.[53] Individuals with high levels of neuroticism and impulsivity tend to abuse online engagement.[54] Neurotic individuals, characterized by emotional liability and depression, frequently express their opinions online and develop internet addiction. People who are psychotic, behavior that is aggressive, unempathetic, uncompromising, and sensation seeking, are susceptible to compulsive disorders.[55] Furthermore, individuals with symptoms of stress, anxiety, self-dissatisfaction, and alienation are more prone to developing deviant behavior.[56] Those with poor emotion regulation skills may also turn to the internet as a means of emotional relief, leading to abuse.[57]

51   Tsimtsiou et al., "Internet Addiction in Greek Medical Students: an Online Survey", 303.

52   Kuss et al., "Internet Addiction: A Systematic Review of Epidemiological Research for the last Decade"; José De-Sola et al., "Cell Phone Use Habits among the Spanish Population: Contribution of Applications to Problematic Use", *Frontiers in Psychiatry* 10 (2019): 883, https://doi.org/10.3389/FPSYT.2019.00883.

53   Yanshu Sun and Jeffrey S. Wilkinson, "Parenting Style, Personality Traits, and Interpersonal Relationships: A Model of Prediction of Internet Addiction", *International Journal of Communication* 14, no. 14 (2020): 2166.

54   Yang Zhang, "Direct and Indirect Effects of Neuroticism on Internet Addiction in College Students: A Structure Equation Modeling Analysis", *Psychological Reports* 124, no. 2 (2020): 611–26, https://doi.org/10.1177/0033294120918806.

55   Sun and Wilkinson, "Parenting Style, Personality Traits, and Interpersonal Relationships", 2166.

56   Lawrence T. Lam, "Risk Factors of Internet Addiction and the Health Effect of Internet Addiction on Adolescents: A Systematic Review of Longitudinal and Prospective Studies", *Current Psychiatry Reports* 16, no. 11 (2014): 1–9, https://doi.org/10.1007/S11920-014-0508-2; De-Sola et al., "Cell Phone Use Habits among the Spanish Population: Contribution of Applications to Problematic Use", 10.

57   Duygu Özer, Özlem Şahin Altun and Gülçin Avşar, "Investigation of the Relationship between Internet Addiction, Communication Skills and Difficulties in Emotion Regulation in Nursing Students", *Archives of Psychiatric Nursing* 42 (2023): 18–24, https://doi.org/10.1016/J.APNU.2022.12.004.

Relationships with parents and family dynamics are an important determinant of susceptibility to addiction. A common categorization of parenting styles distinguishes authoritative, authoritarian, indulgent, and negligent. Authoritative parenting, characterized by setting expectations while being supportive and understanding of a child's feelings, tends to foster independence and security in children. This parenting style has been found to be associated with lower levels of obsessive use of technology. On the other hand, other parenting styles tend to contribute to dysfunction and are associated with higher levels of internet addiction. Authoritarian parenting, which involves strict rules and punishment, often leads to negative outcomes such as depression, self-blame and rebellion in children. Indulgent parenting, also known as permissive parenting, focuses on meeting children's needs and desires without adequately addressing inappropriate behavior. This approach has been found to contribute to a child's dysfunction. Finally, neglectful parenting, typified by a lack of responsiveness to children's emotional and social needs, has been linked to various negative effects on child development. Failure to provide affection and impose punishment have detrimental effects on the child's overall development.[58]

Children who do not forge emotional bonds with their parents tend to exhibit insecurity in adulthood. Furthermore, poor family functioning, single-parent households and a family environment marked by conflict are associated with internet addiction. Rejecting, neglectful and overprotective parenting styles have been found to be highly correlated with internet abuse. Conversely, studies have indicated that individuals who experience sufficient parental care and protection tend to exhibit lower rates of internet addiction.[59]

Peer networks are another factor strongly associated with deviant behavior, particularly among adolescents. First, poor peer relationships can drive adolescents to seek fulfillment of their psychological needs. This creates a vicious circle as addictive patterns of internet use and preoccupation with online activities further deepen social withdrawal and weaken peer networks. Since dependence has a detrimental effect on communication skills and verbal intelligence, it is more challenging to establish new friendships. Second, peer group norms play a significant role, and when excessive deviant behavior becomes the norm, peer contagion contributes to developing addiction.[60] Individuals

---

58   Sun and Wilkinson, "Parenting Style, Personality Traits, and Interpersonal Relationships", 2165–66.

59   Sun and Wilkinson, 2165–66.

60   Nan Zhou and Xiao Yi Fang, "Beyond Peer Contagion: Unique and Interactive Effects of Multiple Peer Influences on Internet Addiction among Chinese Adolescents", *Computers in Human Behavior* 50 (2015): 231–38, https://doi.org/10.1016/J.CHB.2015.03.083.

adopt behavior and attitudes that align with the prevailing norms in their peer group. Adolescents, considerably influenced by their peers, are more vulnerable to peer pressure as they strive for acceptance, conformity and a sense of belonging. Consequently, if addictive behavior is accepted and encouraged in their peer group, individuals are more likely to adopt and participate in such behavior themselves.

Apart from family dynamics and peer social network, pathological internet use also tends to be a culture-specific disorder. Numerous cross-cultural studies report a higher prevalence of excessive internet use in Eastern societies, in particular China, Korea and the United Arab Emirates, whereas Western countries show no significant differences in usage.[61] Researchers attribute this phenomenon to the inherent cultural aspects found in Eastern societies, such as collectivism, interdependent self-construals and cultural motivations.[62]

Societal norms and cultural influences often shape how people interact with the internet too. In countries like India and Egypt, societal and cultural restrictions often limit women's access to the internet, leading to a gender disparity in internet use. This disparity can result in higher risks of internet addiction among men due to their more frequent internet use.[63] However, an area often overlooked in these studies is the difference in how the internet is used across various cultures, reflecting the distinct environmental and social contexts inherent to each culture. In Western cultures, internet users tend to place a greater emphasis on seeking information. They use the internet as a tool for research, education and accessing a wide range of resources. This reflects the individualistic nature of Western societies, where independence and personal autonomy are valued. Individuals in Western cultures often prioritize individual knowledge acquisition and self-improvement through online platforms. On the other hand, in Eastern cultures, the internet is frequently used to maintain and strengthen social relationships. The collectivistic values that underpin Eastern societies place a strong emphasis on interpersonal connections and group harmony. Consequently, individuals from Eastern cultures

---

61   Lopez-Fernandez Olatz, "Cross-Cultural Research on Internet Addiction: A Systematic Review", *International Archives of Addiction Research and Medicine* 1, no. 2 (2015), https://doi.org/10.23937/2474-3631/1510011; Deborah Ko and Mike Yao, "Internet Addiction: A Cross-Cultural Perspective", *The Psychology of Social Networking* 12 (2016): 141–58, https://doi.org/10.1515/9783110473858-013.

62   Dorota Domalewska et al., "Exploring Sociodemographic Factors of Problematic Internet Use: A Cross-National Study of North Macedonia and Poland", *Discover Global Society* 1, no. 1 (2023): 10, https://doi.org/10.1007/s44282-023-00009-5.

63   Wenliang Su et al., "Are Males More Likely To Be Addicted to the Internet Than Females? A Meta-Analysis Involving 34 Global Jurisdictions", *Computers in Human Behavior* 99 (2019): 95–96, https://doi.org/10.1016/J.CHB.2019.04.021.

may prioritize using the internet for social networking, communication and maintaining relationships with family, friends and communities.[64]

In almost all regions of the world, men tend to have higher internet penetration rates than women. The gender gap in global internet users increased from 11% in 2013 to 12% in 2016. Among different regions, Africa has the largest gender gap in internet use, with a difference of 23% between men and women. On the other hand, the gender gap is smallest in the Americas, with just a 2% variation. Furthermore, social norms can also contribute to limiting women's access to internet use.[65] The difference in internet use can significantly affect the development and manifestations of internet addiction across cultures.

Cultural differences play a significant role in shaping perceptions of mental health and determining appropriate treatment approaches. One example can be seen in Asian societies, where there is often a preference for local alternative medicines instead of formal mental health treatments. This preference reflects the cultural stigma attached to mental health issues. Consequently, when it comes to internet abuse, the symptoms may be interpreted and addressed differently in these cultures, leading to diverse manifestations and treatment strategies.[66] In Asian cultures, internet addiction may be viewed through the lens of excessive technology use or as a manifestation of broader behavioral issues. For instance, addictive patterns of internet use might be seen as a lack of self-discipline or as an escape from societal pressures rather than a specific addiction. The influence of culture proves the need for tailored, culturally sensitive approaches to addressing and treating internet addiction worldwide. Taking into account cultural differences can help reduce stigma, increase engagement in treatment and improve outcomes for individuals using the technology obsessively.

5   The Addictive Design of Technology

Apart from the numerous personal and socio-cultural factors described in the previous section, technology itself is inherently addictive because of several features. The internet is an accessible, affordable, interactive, and anonymous

---

64   Christopher N. Chapman and Michal Lahav, "International Ethnographic Observation of Social Networking Sites", in *Proceedings of the Conference on Human Factors in Computing Systems* (New York: Association for Computing Machinery, 2008), 3123–28, https:// doi.org/10.1145/1358628.1358818.

65   Su et al., "Are Males More Likely To Be Addicted to the Internet Than Females? A Meta-Analysis Involving 34 Global Jurisdictions", 87.

66   Ko and Yao, "Internet Addiction: A Cross-Cultural Perspective".

medium that offers a pleasurable experience. Online interactions are highly engaging, which increases the likelihood of increased use. Users tend to underestimate the time they spend playing games, browsing social networking sites, or watching short-form video clips. These activities provide numerous stimuli to the brain and, coupled with the distortion of attention as well as control and arousal-related mechanisms, they lead to losing track of time spent online. The intensity with which users can go online is only limited by technological properties, such as bandwidth or low battery. They are, however, easily overcome. Hence, the pleasure derived from engaging in online activities is easily available. Furthermore, technology use is not only socially approved, but also necessary in the modern world, which further increases continuous use.

Digital media technologies satisfy numerous human needs, which make the online experience highly rewarding. Complex interplay of accessible content, personalized experience and constant gratification contributes to compulsive use. The addictive nature of digital media derives from an interplay of multiple factors:

– Technological affordances: The internet is a rich source of engaging content. The most captivating being sexual material and video games. While such content could also be accessed before the age of the internet, its widespread availability online without time or space constraints contributes to the addictive nature of the internet. The ease and frequency of access has greatly increased its addictive potential.[67] Internet content is also highly dynamic, unpredictable and novel. Games that feature unexpected changes in speed and direction (acceleration) can offer excitement and surprises that enhance the gaming experience.[68] Social media content also has an element of surprise as users never know what picture, short video and snap posted by a friend will show up.

– The effectiveness of persuasive influence further increases when the content is tailored to the personality, needs and emotions of the user. After all, every person is different, so what is persuasive to one consumer may not necessarily influence another. For example, customizing an ad based on a user's extroversion/introversion or dominance level can significantly enhance the power of the persuasive message.

---

67   The term "God in a box" is frequently used in this context to reflect the transformative power of the internet. It illustrates the seemingly miraculous experience of instantly manifesting thoughts, curiosities or desires at the click of a button. The ease of access to a wealth of stimulating content is at the heart of the internet's power.

68   However, too much unpredictability (excessive vibration amplitude or jerking) can negatively affect player enjoyment.

- Unlike traditional media, which has clear beginning and end points, the internet offers unlimited content that is always available. The constant influx of new information and absence of time markers can be compared to the stimulating environment of a casino, where there is much stimulation, variable rewards and no time structure. The constant presence of additional content to discover (such as new links, websites, emails, images, or songs) exploits our inclination to complete unfinished tasks (the Zeigarnik effect[69]), maintaining our focus on what is incomplete, which makes the internet extremely compelling.

- Psychological engagement: The internet is a platform where users can act out fantasies and assume different identities, which is very powerful, especially when paired with the anonymity, disinhibition and ease of access the internet provides. Users can easily assume different roles, especially in games, sex chats and social networks. Additionally, social interaction, real-time competition, and the rewarding system that online games and social networking provide make them more addictive. A large number of internet addicts report feeling less inhibited online. Disinhibition seems to work regardless of the type of content consumed, be it gaming, shopping or adult material. Engaging with online content is a way to escape real-world problems and to alleviate negative emotions.

- The perception of anonymity encourages disinhibition, especially in areas such as sexual behavior, gambling, shopping, and gaming. This can put the brain into an altered state of consciousness similar to compulsive internet use, revealing hidden aspects of the personality and potentially leading to addictive behavior.

- Behavioral conditioning: The internet offers a variable number of reinforcements, which provide unpredictable and variable rewards, such as reaching a higher level in the game, receiving frequent notifications when new content is published on the site, receiving likes and comments from others. Unpredictability, combined with additional benefits such as avoidance of social anxiety, enhanced social status through assumed identities, and instant gratification reinforces the addiction cycle.

---

69   The Zeigarnik effect refers to the ability to better recall interrupted or uncompleted tasks than a completed one. The underlying idea is that people experience a kind of psychological tension when a task is interrupted or left incomplete. Tension creates cognitive discomfort that can lead to a stronger recall of the task, pushing us to complete the task to achieve cognitive closure. In the context of internet usage, this can refer to the constant influx of new information or tasks (like new emails to respond to or new posts to read), which creates a sense of "unfinished business" that compels users to stay online and complete these tasks.

- The internet makes instant gratification of desires possible, which further intensifies addiction. Facilitated by the anonymity of the internet and the short decision-making time, it can easily distort reality. The internet changes the traditional dynamics of delayed gratification and modulation of desires by providing a form of immediate fulfillment. Internet addicts, especially gamers, may view their online experiences as more real than their offline lives, which can make it difficult for them to recognize the negative effects of compulsive use.

- Social dynamics: The internet provides a controlled social environment where social influence significantly affects behavior. Many human actions do not result from logical reasoning but are to a large extent automatic, driven by unconscious choices and impulses influenced by the social environment, e.g., we use a service based on an acquaintance's recommendation, we make a change in behavior under the influence of an authority figure's advice, or we purchase a product sold by a likable person. In the world of games and social media, interactions such as likes, comments and shares act as "rewards" that stimulate activity in the brain's reward system, which leads to the release of dopamine, a hormone associated with pleasure. This reinforces the behavior that leads to addiction. Games and social media platforms make social comparison easy. Users often present the best version of their lives online, which can lead to unhealthy comparisons and anxiety. The pursuit of the "ideal" image can result in constant use of social media. Through likes, comments and shares, social media allows users to constantly seek approval from others. The need to be accepted and appreciated by the online community can lead to compulsive use of social platforms. This is further exacerbated by the inherent human desire to connect and communicate.

- Online games often encourage players to achieve higher scores and levels, creating a sense of achievement and competition.[70] Social networking sites

---

70   Edwin Locke and Gary Latham's goal-setting theory is based on the premise that the primary source of motivation is the pursuit of a goal. Setting goals for oneself or others and publicly committing to them motivates increased activity in order to achieve them, with difficult goals having a stronger impact than easy ones; however, goals that are too difficult, beyond an individual's capabilities, have a demotivating effect. In the case of computer games, players' goal-setting is further enhanced by the element of competition, such as the publication of player rankings and the organization of tournaments and tournament qualifiers (Edwin A. Locke and Gary P. Latham, "Building a Practically Useful Theory of Goal Setting and Task Motivation: A 35-Year Odyssey", *American Psychologist* 57, no. 9 (2002): 705–17, https://doi.org/10.1037/0003-066X.57.9.705). According to Mihály Csíkszentamihályi's flow theory, on the other hand, motivation depends on passion and involvement in an activity. The highest level of motivation is achieved through maximum involvement, like artists immersed in their work, who focus not on the goal, but on the

publicly display metrics such as likes and views, which also introduces an element of competition.

– The difficulty of attaining the goal is another compelling factor. The games offer different levels of difficulty, requiring players to constantly adapt and improve their skills. The balance between challenge and skill development, especially when the difficulty changes at different stages of the game, can create excitement and satisfaction, contributing to the addictive nature of video games.[71]

All in all, playing internet games, browsing social networking sites and engaging in online activities captivates users by providing an immersive, rewarding and competitive experience through high-score pursuits, dynamic difficulty levels, and instant gratification. Addictive potential is further amplified by social aspects, inherent challenges and the seemingly continuous highly engaging experience. Users' perceptions of technology can also affect their usage patterns. Moreover, the technology's affordances can enhance such perceptions and drive subsequent behavior. Twitter, for instance, is frequently perceived as a news hub, whereas Instagram is used as a self-presentation platform by various interest groups.

Finally, the increasing monetization of user attention has resulted in tech companies designing technology that is highly persuasive and addictive. Various manipulative tactics are employed to hold user attention contributing to surveillance capitalism and the commodification of personal data. The addictive potential of the internet and digital technology increases the level of compulsive use.

------

activity itself, which gives them pleasure and engages them. Transferring this theory to the reality of online games, it can be seen that achieving a high level of motivation requires maintaining a balance between the level of difficulty of the game and the player's abilities, skills and knowledge. If the game's difficulty level is higher than the player's abilities, the player often feels anxious; conversely, if the game is very easy and the difficulty level is lower than the players' abilities, they usually feel bored (Ali Alshammari, "Captology in Game-Based Education: a Theoretical Framework for the Design of Persuasive Games", *Interactive Learning Environments*, 2021, https://doi.org/10.1080/10494820.2021.1915803).

71   Greenfield, "The Addictive Properties of Internet Usage"; Osman Erol and Neşe SeviM Çirak, "What are the Factors that Affect the Motivation of Digital Gamers?", *Participatory Educational Research* 7, no. 1 (2020): 184–200, https://doi.org/10.17275/per.20.11.7.1; Niels J. Rosenquist, Fiona M. Scott Morton and Samuel Weinstein, "Addictive Technology and Its Implications for Antitrust Enforcement", *SSRN Electronic Journal*, 2021, https://doi.org/10.2139/ssrn.3787822; Deniz Cemiloglu et al., "Explainable Persuasion for Interactive Design: The Case of Online Gambling", *Journal of Systems and Software* 195 (2023): 111517, https://doi.org/10.1016/j.jss.2022.111517; Christian Montag and Jon D. Elhai, "On Social Media Design, (Online-)Time Well-Spent and Addictive Behaviors in the Age of Surveillance Capitalism", *Current Addiction Reports*, 2023, https://doi.org/10.1007/s40429-023-00494-3.

Conclusion: the Digital Ecosystem from the Perspective of Social Cybersecurity

Advanced information technology has transformed knowledge systems and social structures. It has triggered radical socio-political, economic and cultural changes and empowered individuals to play active roles in economic, social and political activities. In cyberspace, a network of relatively permanent relationships and interactions exists among entities such as individuals, groups, organizations, and institutions, which pursue various, sometimes opposing, needs and interests. The interactions, often marked by both cooperation and conflict, are driven by diverse motivations such as pleasure, profit or the articulation of political demands. The digital ecosystem is characterized by unique operating rules and dynamics that shape the variability of the different components, and their interactions with the physical world. Cyberspace's social system is composed of distinct sub-systems, including interest groups, hackers, hacktivists, private and state users, and criminal organizations. They engage in diverse areas of social action such as politics, economics and culture in cyberspace, reflecting human invention and activity.

By adopting a human-centered approach to cybersecurity, we have explored the digital ecosystem and its impact on both the individual and the broader socio-political environment. Furthermore, we have identified numerous threats in the social, political and informational spheres. Many of them are components of hybrid warfare. The concept of hybrid warfare now forms the foundation for analyzing 21st century threats, combining conventional and irregular military actions with political and informational strategies to destabilize and weaken target states. The pervasive influence of digital technology and social media has facilitated the execution of hybrid strategies and enabled the seamless integration of conventional and unconventional operations to amplify their impact. In the context of an increase in hybrid threats and the interference of various political actors in the internal processes of democratic states, some of whom are using information to manipulate society, studying cyberspace is essential for detecting traces of information warfare. The advent of social media has exponentially increased the prevalence of fake news and disinformation campaigns, facilitated by the ease of information dissemination, broad reach and the lack of gatekeeping mechanisms to ensure accuracy and reliability. Social media has significantly amplified the impact of the spread of manipulated and fabricated information on individuals and societies. Platforms such as Facebook, Weibo and TikTok play significant roles in our daily lives and impact social, emotional and cognitive functions. One of the most visible influences of social media is its ability to attract and distract attention. The algorithms that manage content on digital platforms are designed to maximize user engagement and prolong periods of content scrolling. Such sustained engagement encourages a behavior known as attention switching, where users frequently shift focus among various stimuli. This can diminish the ability to maintain concentration over long periods. Furthermore, algorithms often tailor content to user preferences and create echo chambers or filter bubbles. As a result, users are exposed to agreeable viewpoints. Encounters with diverse opinions are curtailed, and critical thinking skills are stunted. Continuous bombardment of the brain with new information fosters only superficial processing of data. It not only hinders the retention of information long-term but also makes users vulnerable to social engineering. Cyber criminals can easily exploit cognitive shifts to manipulate or deceive users. Social media also affects our interpersonal skills because virtual interactions differ significantly from face-to-face contact, which can impede the development of social behavior. The anonymity and digital distance provided by social media may reduce empathy and increase the likelihood of cyber bullying. Understanding these challenges is crucial. More conscious engagement with digital platforms can minimize potential negative effects and maximize benefits.

Hybrid terrorism employs both traditional and non-traditional tactics, including cyber operations, to destabilize targets and achieve strategic objectives. Technological advancements are increasingly being exploited by adversarial state and non-state actors to enhance the speed and scope of their communications. As a result, cyberspace has rapidly evolved into a domain for terrorist activities, including recruitment, propaganda and attacks on critical infrastructure. This phenomenon is not a revolution but rather a familiar process in political violence. It rather reflects an ongoing adaptation of tactics that blend conventional and unconventional methods to maximize impact and secure strategic benefits. Globally, increasing digitalization is fostering threats that are hybrid in nature. Although the fundamental goals of hostile actors, ranging from state adversaries to terrorist groups, remain unchanged and focused on exerting influence and power, the tools and strategies they use are continuously advancing.

Another trend that has been on the rise is the escalation of cybercrime, which can be attributed to a number of technological, economic and regulatory factors that create an environment that facilitates its proliferation. First of all, there has been an exponential growth in the number of internet-connected devices, including the expansion of the Internet of Things and the ubiquitous adoption of smartphones, tablets and computers. Rapid expansion of connected devices has dramatically increased the potential entry points for cyber criminals, which has amplified the vulnerability of both corporate and personal data systems. As organizations and individuals increasingly store data in the cloud, the opportunities for cyber attacks are multiplying. The complexity of modern IT systems, which often integrate multiple technologies, can introduce security weaknesses. Moreover, the continued use of outdated systems that lack adequate defenses against contemporary threats exacerbates these vulnerabilities. Many companies and individual users still do not have sufficient security measures in place, such as strong passwords, two-factor authentication and regular software updates. Another significant factor that affects the growth in cybercrime is the low risk of detection and prosecution, particularly when operations are conducted from jurisdictions with lax cybersecurity laws. The profitability of offenses such as ransomware, combined with the low likelihood of apprehension, makes cybercrime attractive. The variability of regulatory frameworks across countries and the often limited resources available to enforce these laws makes it more difficult to prosecute cyber criminals. The absence of international borders in cyberspace allows cyber criminals to operate from remote locations and use anonymity to shield their activities. User vulnerability plays a crucial role in the effectiveness of cyber attacks. A general lack of awareness of and insufficient education on cyber threats leave many individuals and organizations exposed to common tactics like phishing and malware. The COVID-19 pandemic has intensified this issue, as the sudden shift to remote work and education has expanded the attack surface for cyber criminals, often outpacing the implementation of robust security measures. Furthermore, the techniques used by cyber criminals have grown more sophisticated, with artificial intelligence increasingly used to automate and scale attacks. The emergence of cybercrime-as-a-service models, where tools to carry out attacks can be bought or rented, has also lowered barriers to entry, allowing novice criminals to easily access and deploy advanced tools.

Technological advancements are also rapidly transforming the job market, demanding complex skills such as creativity and critical thinking. This shift widens the digital divide, where individuals with digital skills prosper, while others face significant disadvantages. Algorithms on digital platforms can further increase inequalities by filtering content, limiting access to diverse information and reinforcing biases. Hostile online communications arouse prejudices, intolerance and societal divisions. Verbal abuse undermines rational public discourse and contributes to hybrid threats, increasing social dissatisfaction and polarization. The influence of technology and algorithms extends to societal polarization, as they create and reinforce echo chambers and filter bubbles. Political microtargeting further increases partisan divides and affects long-term political decisions.

Cyberspace and inherent cyber threats can only be understood through the analysis of the multidimensional factors that both shape and are shaped by them. It is also crucial to explore the interdependencies among the key components of the digital ecosystem: digital technology, its users and the evolving norms that arise from their interaction in cyberspace. Technologies and their use must be examined in the broader socio-political and economic contexts. This wider context not only shapes the digital space but also defines the interactions and developments in it, highlighting the importance of considering these external influences. A digital ecosystem is a complex network of individuals, organizations and technologies that interact with one another in a digital environment. It can be defined as

> an open, loosely coupled, demand-driven, domain clustered, agent-based, self-organized environment where species/agents form short- and long-term coalitions for specific purposes or goals, and everyone is proactive and responsive for its own benefit or profit. Interactions among peers in digital ecosystems may involve, besides unbridled competition, new modalities of pre-competitive and collaborative partnerships.[1]

However, the extent of this interaction is not limited to virtual spaces. The internet has become a vital infrastructure critical to the functioning of various sectors including business, education, government, and broader societal interactions. For numerous social groups, it serves as a primary environment for engagement, fulfilling a range of social needs and motivations seamlessly integrated with their real-world activities. Examples of digital ecosystems include platforms such as Facebook and X, e-commerce sites like Amazon and Alibaba, and online marketplaces such as eBay. Digital ecosystems unite a wide range of actors, technologies and external factors in establishing a dynamic and continually evolving, interactive environment. They are shaped not only by technological advances and economic dynamics but also by broader socio-political influences, cultural trends and legislative frameworks

---

1   Christian Guetl, Leila Ismail and Cary Lexar, "Track A: Foundations of Digital Ecosystems and Complex Environment Engineering", in *2013 7th IEEE International Conference on Digital Ecosystems and Technologies (DEST)* (Menlo Park, CA: Institute of Electrical and Electronics Engineers (IEEE), 2013), https://doi.org/10.1109/DEST.2013.6611308.

that ensure user protection, data security and corporate accountability. These factors collectively nurture an environment that balances innovation with regulatory oversight. Moreover, ecosystems adapt swiftly to changes in digital norms and user behavior, influenced by a macro environment notable for its well-developed service sector, a knowledge-driven economy and high levels of education. These elements contribute to the decentralization of society and the burgeoning information society. The shifting business models of organizations and the expansion of enterprises into cyberspace are propelled by economic and technological evolutions, leading to the emergence of new social, political and cultural phenomena. Legal regulations in cyberspace play a key role in shaping these interactions by establishing the conditions under which digital ecosystems operate. Legal framework is integral to the ongoing transformation in the socio-political landscape, influencing individual behavioral patterns and reinforcing the role of digital interactions in interpersonal relationships. Consequently, these factors are crucial in promoting the development of a networked society, where digital and real-world interactions are increasingly intertwined.

Drawing from Urie Bronfenbrenner's ecological systems theory, we gain a clearer perspective not only on the complex interactions between various ecosystems and with the broader context, but also on the resulting changes in human behavior and social systems.[2] The ecosystem is notable for its diversity and the active participation of every actor. As technology has become increasingly integrated into various aspects of daily life, the digital ecosystem exerts an influence on the course and consequence of human development. Urie Bronfenbrenner also argues that development cannot be separated from the complex system of relationships in the environment, which can be presented in the form of an order of systems that overlap and interact with one another:[3]

– Individuals are at the center of the ecosystem, where their actions and interactions are driven by diverse motivations and needs that shape their digital experience. Motivational factors include the perceived usefulness of technology, the enjoyment derived from digital interactions, and the impact of technology on self-perception. The needs driving individuals can be categorized into three main groups: psychological, social and informational. Psychological needs encompass respect, recognition, pleasure,

---

2   Urie Bronfenbrenner, *The Ecology of Human Development* (Cambridge, MA: Harvard University Press, 1979).

3   Urie Bronfenbrenner, "Interacting Systems in Human Development. Research Paradigms: Present and Future", in *Persons in Context: Developmental Processes*, ed. Niall Bolger (New York: Cambridge University Press, 1988), 80–81.

entertainment, and self-actualization. Social needs involve the desire for influence and interaction, facilitating community building and social networking. Information needs drive users to seek out and consume knowledge and data. Together, these needs prompt users to continue interacting with digital platforms.

– The microsystem includes the immediate digital environments with which an individual directly interacts: personal devices (such as smartphones and computers), software (including apps and operating systems) and digital platforms (such as social media sites and online games). These tools and platforms facilitate direct interactions that significantly influence users' behavior and daily experiences. The social media microsystem consists of user profiles and interactions on a specific platform such as X or Instagram. It also includes the design and features of the platform, such as algorithms that curate specific content for users, as well as the various groups and communities hosted on the platform.

– The mesosystem connects different microsystems and settings or a system of two or more microsystems. It serves as a bridge between the various digital and physical environments individuals interact with. For example, it encompasses interactions and cross-posting between multiple social media platforms, such as sharing a tweet on Facebook. It also includes how a person's interactions on social media platforms relate to their use of various websites, or how their professional tools integrate with personal communication apps. This layer examines how different digital platforms that a person engages with interact with each other, potentially creating a cohesive or disjointed digital experience. Additionally, the mesosystem incorporates the complex connections between virtual and physical microsystems. The integration of online and offline activities can significantly affect an individual's behavior. For instance, web- and text messaging-based interventions have been shown to reduce binge drinking,[4] which illustrates how digital interactions can influence offline behavior. Conversely, sharing alcohol-related content on social networking sites may increase an

---

4   Brian Suffoletto et al., "An Interactive Text Message Intervention to Reduce Binge Drinking in Young Adults: A Randomized Controlled Trial with 9-Month Outcomes", ed. Bernard Le Foll, *PLOS ONE* 10, no. 11 (2015): e0142877, https://doi.org/10.1371/journal.pone.0142877; Iain K. Crombie et al., "Text Message Intervention to Reduce Frequency of Binge Drinking among Disadvantaged Men: The TRAM RCT", *Public Health Research* 6, no. 6 (2018): 1–156, https://doi.org/10.3310/phr06060.

individual's alcohol consumption by normalizing or promoting drinking.[5] These examples draw attention to the mesosystem's role in mediating the effects of interactions across different environments on an individual's behavior.

— The exosystem consists of the connections and processes occurring between various microsystems and settings, where at least one does not directly involve the individual, but still impacts the processes in the microsystem where the individual is actively engaged.[6] This layer includes larger societal structures that influence an individual's immediate digital environment, even though the individual may not interact with these structures directly. Examples include the policies of technology companies, broadband accessibility policies, the economic strategies of businesses reliant on digital marketplaces, and the legal frameworks governing internet use and digital rights. Changes in these broader contexts can significantly affect the user's access to digital resources and the quality of their digital interactions.

— The macrosystem reflects the overarching political, cultural and social norms that influence digital ecosystems. It includes global internet trends, cultural attitudes towards technology use (like norms around social media engagement or privacy concerns), regulatory environments, business models and practices of large tech companies, and global trends and events that shape social media use, such as the COVID-19 pandemic or political upheavals. How different cultures regard data privacy, for instance, can influence the design of software and platforms used globally. User protection, data security and oversight of high-tech companies are guaranteed by legal regulations, making legislation a key factor shaping the digital ecosystem.

— The chronosystem, defined as "the influence on the person's development of changes (and continuities) over time in the environments in which the person is living".[7] It involves the dimension of time and how changes over time affect the digital ecosystem. This could be the evolution of various platforms (e.g.; the introduction of novel features such as Instagram's "Reels" or YouTube's "Shorts" have had a significant impact on how individuals engage

---

5   Eilin K. Erevik et al., "Disclosure and Exposure of Alcohol on Social Media and Later Alcohol Use: A Large-Scale Longitudinal Study", *Frontiers in Psychology* 8 (2017): 284957, https://doi.org/10.3389/FPSYG.2017.01934.

6   Jessica L. Navarro and Jonathan R.H. Tudge, "Technologizing Bronfenbrenner: Neo-ecological theory", *Current Psychology* 1 (2022): 1–17, https://doi.org/10.1007/S12144-022-02738-3.

7   Adapted from U. Bronfenbrenner, "Ecology of the Family as a Context for Human Development: Research Perspectives", *Developmental Psychology* 22, no. 6 (1986): 724.

with such platforms), the rise and fall of different technological trends (like the shift from desktop to mobile internet browsing), or societal changes that affect how technologies are used (such as changes due to the COVID-19 pandemic which led to changes in user behavior and content on social media platforms over time). Finally, life course variations and transitional periods affect digital media use and the degree to which such media is integrated into an individual's everyday routine.[8]

Adopting a socio-ecological approach helps one understand the complexity of digital ecosystems, which is a complex and dynamic system of relationships between individual users, various actors, the platform itself, and external factors, including social, economic and political factors, technological advancements and cultural trends as well as legislation. All of these factors influence human development and behavior in a unique and diverse way. In this context, the human being is at the center of the digital ecosystem, which is shown in Figure 1.

The digital ecosystem is made up of various elements such as hardware, software, networks, platforms, and people – all set in a larger political, socio-economic and cultural context. While hardware, software and networks are important components of the digital ecosystem, it is the human beings who use technologies that make it a dynamic and constantly evolving system. The social media ecosystem is built on the basis of big data analytics (data from user-generated content and network data such as recorded traffic from sites). Algorithms and the aforementioned digital technology operate beneath the surface of platforms, beyond the reach and awareness of users, creating an infrastructure that, when combined with commercial predictive and sales models, allows users to experience a personalized (yet commercialized) experience and encourages them to visit again. Social networking sites allow interaction between individual users, who share the content they produce, consume content and engage in entertainment. Thus, it is the user who is at the center of the ecosystem, placed in the cyber loop, shaping and being shaped by the digital ecosystem.

The digital ecosystem is rapidly expanding. It is driven by social practices and trends such as mass interpersonal persuasion, the attention economy, surveillance capitalism, automated decision-making, and micro-targeting of political, ideological and commercial messages. These dynamics profoundly impact individual users, affect their perceptions, decisions, actions, social relationships, politics, the economy, and, consequently, security. As a result, the

---

8   Molly Gloria Patel and Anabel Quan-Haase, "The Social-Ecological Model of Cyberbullying: Digital Media as a Predominant Ecology in the Everyday Lives of Youth", *New Media and Society*, 2022, https://doi.org/10.1177/14614448221136508.

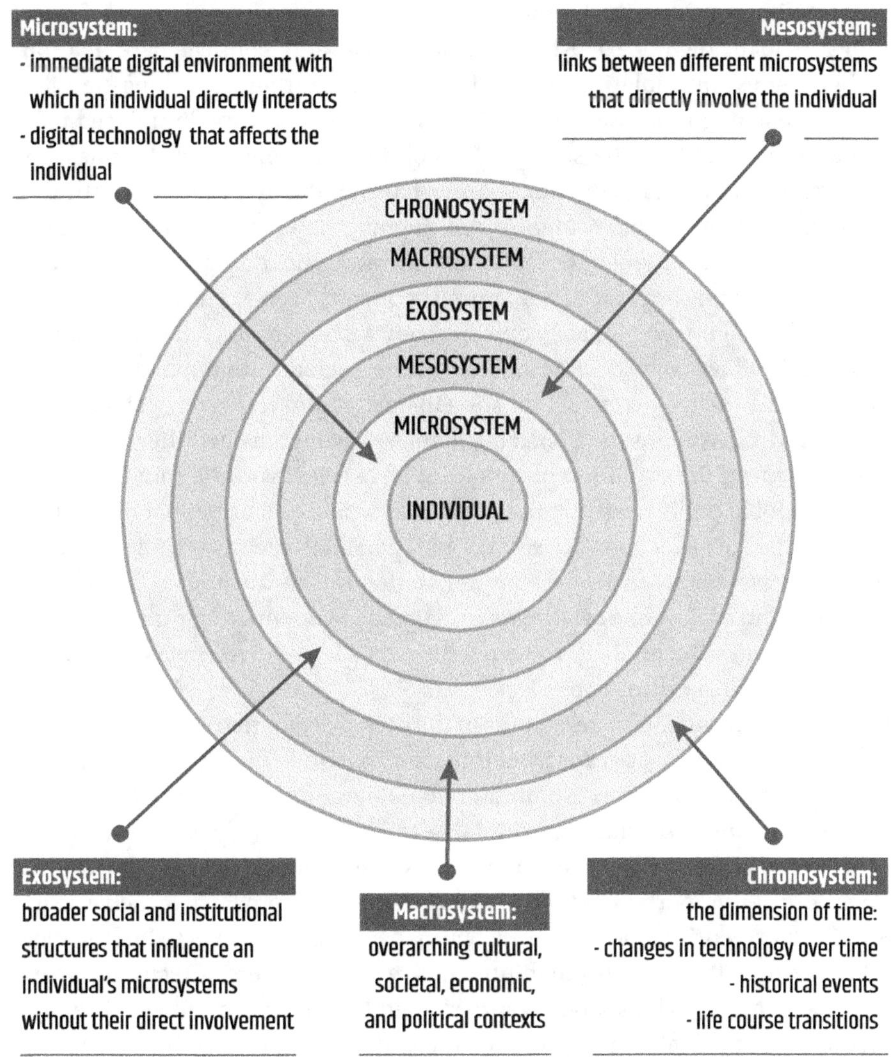

FIGURE 1   The digital ecosystem
SOURCE: BRONFENBRENNER, *THE ECOLOGY OF HUMAN DEVELOPMENT*; PATEL
AND QUAN-HAASE, "THE SOCIAL-ECOLOGICAL MODEL OF CYBERBULLYING:
DIGITAL MEDIA AS A PREDOMINANT ECOLOGY IN THE EVERYDAY LIVES OF
YOUTH"

threats present in cyberspace affect all its users, individuals, organizations, nations, and their interests.

Digital ecosystems also significantly influence the macro social, political and economic environment. They lead to qualitative changes in the social structure and potentially precipitate a crisis in democracy. Threats to democracy manifest themselves as informational threats like disinformation and socio-political threats, including entertainization of public spaces, information overload, digital exclusion, unstable civic and political participation, verbal aggression, polarization, and populism. Furthermore, long-standing and far-reaching processes such as increased consumerism, diminished trust in public institutions, the struggle for political influence, and the quest for changes in the global geopolitical order have gradually gained strength due to changes in the global economy and ongoing political, social and cultural transformations. Although these processes are amplified by social networking sites, they did not originate solely from the media, Web 2.0 technology or the activities of high-tech giants. People have always sought to gain and maintain power by influencing social groups or entire societies, manipulating public opinion and exerting control and surveillance. Rapid technological advancements and subsequent swift societal changes have intensified these practices and influenced the evolution of threats at all levels of society from individual users to global political structures and across various security domains: cybersecurity, political, economic, social, and personal security. Understanding these processes is essential for comprehending the nature and scope of informational and socio-political threats in cyberspace. Identifying threats enables the mitigation of technology's negative aspects, such as divisions, isolation and the spread of disinformation.

Human behavior and interactions in the digital ecosystem can have a significant impact on cybersecurity. Cyber threats such as phishing, social engineering attacks and malware often exploit human vulnerabilities such as trust, curiosity and ignorance. Information technologies are increasingly used as tools and channels of power and as instruments for surveillance and control purposes.[9] Therefore, it is important to take a human-centered approach to cybersecurity. Social cybersecurity looks at the way humans should be protected in the digital ecosystem. It recognizes that humans are not just users of technology, but also active agents who shape and are shaped by their environment. The protection of individuals is not just a technical issue but also involves social and cultural factors. For example, social engineering attacks are successful because they exploit the trust and social relationships between individuals. Similarly, disinformation, online harassment, problematic internet use, and polarization can be tackled more effectively by adopting a human-centered approach. Therefore, social cybersecurity integrates psychology, sociology, political science, and cybersecurity to provide comprehensive protection of individuals. It aims not only to prevent and mitigate technical threats but also to address the

---

9   Tim Stevens, *Cyber Security and the Politics of Time* (Cambridge: Cambridge University Press, 2015), 23.

underlying social dynamics that contribute to these vulnerabilities in order to build a resilient and secure digital society. The profound impact of digital ecosystems on political, social and economic processes requires a comprehensive understanding of cyber threats. An interdisciplinary approach to analyzing these threats is crucial for developing effective countermeasures. By integrating insights from social, political and informational domains, this study contributes valuable knowledge to the field of security studies, emphasizing the importance of a holistic approach to safeguarding society in the digital age.

References

AAG. "The Latest 2024 Phishing Statistics (2024)", 2024. https://aag-it.com/the-latest-phishing-statistics/.

Abidin, Crystal. "Preschool Stars on YouTube: Child Microcelebrities, Commercially Viable Biographies, and Interactions with Technology". In *Routledge Companion to Digital Media and Children*, edited by Lelia Green, Donell Holloway, Kylie Stevenson, Tama Leaver and Leslie Haddon, 226–34. London: Routledge, 2020.

Agostino, Deborah, Michela Arnaboldi and Anna Calissano. "How to Quantify Social Media Influencers: An Empirical Application at the Teatro Alla Scala". *Heliyon* 5, no. 5 (2019): e01677. https://doi.org/10.1016/j.heliyon.2019.e01677.

Aho, Brett and Roberta Duffield. "Beyond Surveillance Capitalism: Privacy, Regulation and Big data in Europe and China". *Economy and Society* 49, no. 2 (2020): 187–212. https://doi.org/10.1080/03085147.2019.1690275.

Akcinaroglu, Seden and Moyan Shi. "Exploring the Impact of Cryptocurrency on Terrorism". *Terrorism and Political Violence*, 37, no. 1 (2023): 111–135. https://doi.org/10.1080/09546553.2023.2275057.

Akungu, Okwach Alphonce, Sufen Chen and Chiu-Hung Su. "Longitudinal Association of Adolescents' Perceptions of Parental Mediations and Compulsive Internet Use". *Computers in Human Behavior* 150 (2024): 107989. https://doi.org/10.1016/j.chb.2023.107989.

Alalwan, Ali Abdallah, Yogesh K. Dwivedi and Nripendra P. Rana. "Factors Influencing Adoption of Mobile Banking by Jordanian Bank Customers: Extending UTAUT2 with Trust". *International Journal of Information Management* 37, no. 3 (2017): 99–110. https://doi.org/10.1016/j.ijinfomgt.2017.01.002.

Albaroudi, Elham, Taha Mansouri, and Ali Alameer. "A Comprehensive Review of AI Techniques for Addressing Algorithmic Bias in Job Hiring". *AI* 5, no. 1 (2024): 383–404. https://doi.org/10.3390/ai5010019.

Albertson, Bethany, and Shana Kushner Gadarian. *Anxious Politics: Democratic Citizenship in a Threatening World*. Cambridge: Cambridge University Press, 2015. https://doi.org/10.1017/CBO9781139963107.

Alexander, Julia. "The Golden Age of YouTube is over". The Verge, 2019. https://www.theverge.com/2019/4/5/18287318/youtube-logan-paul-pewdiepie-demonetization-adpocalypse-premium-influencers-creators.

Ali, Muhammad, Piotr Sapiezynski, Miranda Bogen, Aleksandra Korolova, Alan Mislove, and Aaron Rieke. "Discrimination through Optimization: How Facebook's Ad Delivery Can Lead to Biased Outcomes". *Proceedings of the ACM on Human-Computer Interaction* 3, no. CSCW (2019): 1–30. https://doi.org/10.1145/3359301.

Alleyne, Mark D. "The United Nations' Celebrity Diplomacy". *SAIS Review of International Affairs* 25, no. 1 (2005): 175–85. https://doi.org/10.1353/sais.2005.0001.

Allison, Graham T. *Destined for War: Can America and China Escape Thucydides's Trap?* Boston: Houghton Mifflin Harcourt, 2017.

Alshammari, Ali. "Captology in Game-Based Education: A Theoretical Framework for the Design of Persuasive Games". *Interactive Learning Environments*, 2021. https://doi.org/10.1080/10494820.2021.1915803.

Alyukov, Maxim. "Making Sense of the News in an Authoritarian Regime: Russian Television Viewers' Reception of the Russia–Ukraine Conflict". *Europe-Asia Studies* 74, no. 3 (2022): 337–59. https://doi.org/10.1080/09668136.2021.2016633.

Ambika, V., H.L. Gururaj and V. Janhavi. Boca Raton, Fl: CRC Press, 2024.

Ambrose, Alex. "Kidfluencers Recast Spotlight on Children's Rights in Digital Entertainment".*Information Technology & Innovation Foundation*, 2023. https://itif.org /publications/2023/09/05/kidfluencers-recast-spotlight-on-children-s-rights-in -digital-entertainment/.

American Psychiatric Association. *Diagnostic and Statistical Manual of Mental Disorders. Fifth Edition.* Arlington, VA: American Psychiatric Association, 2013. https://doi.org/10.1176/appi.books.9780890425596.

Amnesty International. *The Social Atrocity. Meta and the Right to Remedy for the Rohingya.* London: Amnesty International Ltd, 2022.

Amoroso, Edward. *Cyber Security.* New Jersey: Silicon Press, 2006.

Andersen, Jack. "Understanding and Interpreting Algorithms: Toward a Hermeneutics of Algorithms". *Media, Culture & Society* 42, no. 7–8 (2020): 1479–94. https://doi .org/10.1177/0163443720919373.

Anderson, Briony and Mark A. Wood. "Doxxing: A Scoping Review and Typology". In *The Emerald International Handbook of Technology-Facilitated Violence and Abuse,* edited by Jane Bailey, Asher Flynn and Nicola Henry, 205–26. Bingley: Emerald Publishing Limited, 2021. https://doi.org/10.1108/978-1-83982-848-520211015.

Andrew, Jonathan and Frédéric Bernard, eds. *Human Rights Responsibilities in the Digital Age: States, Companies and Individuals.* Oxford: Hart Publishing, 2021.

Angwin, Julia. *Społeczeństwo Nadzorowane. W Poszukiwaniu Prywatności, Bezpieczeństwa i Wolności w Świecie Permanentnej Inwigilacji.* Warsaw: Wydawnictwo Naukowe PWN, 2019.

Antonescu, Mihail and Ramona Birău. "Financial and Non-Financial Implications of Cybercrimes in Emerging Countries". *Procedia Economics and Finance* 32 (2015): 618–21. https://doi.org/10.1016/S2212–5671(15)01440-9.

Anwar, Memoona J., Asif Q. Gill, Farookh K. Hussain, and Muhammad Imran. "Secure Big Data Ecosystem Architecture: Challenges and Solutions". *EURASIP Journal on Wireless Communications and Networking 2021 2021:1* 2021, no. 1 (2021): 1–30. https://doi.org/10.1186/S13638-021-01996-2.

Apasrawirote, Darlin and Kritcha Yawised. "Factors Influencing the Behavioral and Purchase Intention on Live-streaming Shopping". *Asian Journal of Business Research* 12, no. 1 (2022). https://doi.org/10.14707/ajbr.220119.

Applegate, Scott. "Cybermilitias and Political Hackers: Use of Irregular Forces in Cyberwarfare". *IEEE Security & Privacy Magazine* 9, no. 5 (2011): 16–22. https://doi.org/10.1109/MSP.2011.46.

Apuke, Oberiri Destiny and Bahiyah Omar. "Social Media Affordances and Information Abundance: Enabling Fake News Sharing during the COVID-19 Health Crisis". *Health Informatics Journal* 27, no. 3 (2021): 146045822110214. https://doi.org/10.1177/14604582211021470.

Aral, Sinan, 22 January 2021. https://twitter.com/sinanaral/status/1352657222279557125.

Aral, Sinan. *The Hype Machine.* New York: Currency, 2020.

Aral, Sinan. "The Changing Face of Russia's Information War against Ukraine and other Democratic Countries: Lessons and Recommendations. Interview with Professor Sinan Aral". *Security and Defence Quarterly* 41, no. 1 (2023). https://doi.org/10.35467/SDQ/156264.

Aran-Ramspott, Sue, Maddalena Fedele and Anna Tarragó. "YouTubers' Social Functions and Their Influence on Pre-Adolescence" 26, no. 2 (2018). https://doi.org/10.3916/C57-2018-07.

Archer, Catherine. "How Influencer 'Mumpreneur' Bloggers and 'Everyday' Mums Frame Presenting Their Children Online". *Media International Australia* 170, no. 1 (2019): 47–56. https://doi.org/10.1177/1329878X19828365.

Arcos, Rubén, Irena Chiru and Cristina Ivan, eds. *Routledge Handbook of Disinformation and National Security.* Abingdon and New York: Routledge, 2024.

Arifi, Dritero and Ngadhnjim Brovina. "Kosovo Society: Coexistence, Challenges and Opportunities". In *Social Security in the Balkans – Volume 3: An Overview of Social Policy in Serbia and Kosovo*, edited by Marzena Żakowska, 224–54. Boston: Brill, 2022. https://doi.org/10.1163/9789004500068.

Arntz, Melanie, Terry Gregory and Ulrich Zierahn. "The Risk of Automation for Jobs in OECD Countries: A Comparative Analysis". OECD Social, Employment and Migration Working Papers. T. 189. OECD Social, Employment and Migration Working Papers, 2016. https://doi.org/10.1787/5jlz9h56dvq7-en.

Aronson, Elliot and Anthony Pratkanis. *Age of Propaganda: The Everyday Use and Abuse of Persuasion. Revised Edition.* New York: Henry Holt and Company, 2001.

Ascher, Diana L. and Safiya Umoja Noble. "Unmasking Hate on Twitter: Disrupting Anonymity by Tracking Trolls". In *Free Speech in the Digital Age*, edited by Susan J. Brison and Katharine Gelber, 170–88. New York: Oxford University Press, 2019. https://doi.org/10.1093/OSO/9780190883591.003.0011.

Assimogiorgos, Giorgos, Alexandros Gryparis, Eleni Panagouli, Clive Richardson, Flora Bacopoulou and Artemis Tsitsika. "Dysfunctional Internet Use by Adolescents in an

Urban Environment: A Case-Control Study". *Developmental and Adolescent Health* 1, no. 4 (2021). https://doi.org/10.54088/8ujmkll.

Astghik, Grigoryan. "Russia: Russian President Signs Anti-fake News Laws", 2019. https://www.loc.gov/item/global-legal-monitor/2019-04-11/russia-russian-presi dent-signs-anti-fake-news-laws/.

Bachmann, Philipp and Gabriele Siegert. "How to Buy, Sell, and Trade Attention: A Sociology of (Digital) Attention Markets". In *Handbook of Economic Sociology for the 21st Century*, edited by Andrea Maurer, 147–57. Handbooks of Sociology and Social Research. Cham: Springer International Publishing, 2021. https://doi.org/10 .1007/978-3-030-61619-9_10.

Bakir, Vian and Andrew McStay. "Fake News and the Economy of Emotions". *Digital Journalism* 6, no. 2 (2017): 154–75. https://doi.org/10.1080/21670811.2017.1345645.

Bandura, Albert. *Social Learning Theory*. Englewood Cliffs, NJ: Prentice Hall, 1977.

Barberà, Oscar. "All Fake? Information Disorders and the 2017 Referendum in Catalonia". In *Misinformation in Referenda*, edited by Sandrine Baume, Véronique Boillet and Vincent Martenet. London and New York: Routledge, 2020.

Bauman, Zygmunt. *Liquid Modernity*. Cambridge: Polity Press, 2000.

Bayer, Judit, Bernd Holznagel, Katarzyna Lubianiec, Adela Pintea, Josephine B. Schmitt, Judit Szakacs and Erik Uszkiewicz. "Disinformation and Propaganda – Impact on the Functioning of the Rule of Law in the EU and its Member States". Brussels: European Parliament, 2019. https://www.europarl.europa.eu/RegData/etu des/STUD/2021/653633/EXPO_STU(2021)653633_EN.pdf.

Beauvisage, Thomas, Jean-Samuel Beuscart, Samuel Coavoux, and Kevin Mellet. "How Online Advertising Targets Consumers: The Uses of Categories and Algorithmic Tools by Audience Planners". *New Media & Society*, 2023, 146144482211461. https:// doi.org/10.1177/14614448221146174.

Bechis, Francesco. "Playing the Russian Disinformation Game: Information Operations from Soviet Tactics to Putin's Sharp Power". In *Democracy and Fake News. Information Manipulation and Post-Truth Politics*, 107–18. London and New York: Routledge, 2021.

Beck, Ulrich. *Risk Society: Towards a New Modernity*. London; Newbury Park, Calif: Sage Publications, 1992.

Bek, Dominika and Malwina Popiołek. "Patostreaming-Charakterystyka i Prawne Konteksty Zjawiska". *Zarządzanie Mediami* 7, no. 4 (2019): 247–62. https://doi.org /10.4467/23540214ZM.19.016.11342.

Bell, Daniel. "The Social Framework of the Information Society". In *The Microelectronics Revolution*, edited by Tom Forester, 500–549. Oxford: Blackwell Publishing, 1980.

Bell, Daniel. *The Coming of Post-Industrial Society: A Venture in Social Forecasting*. New York: Basic Books, 1973.

Bellamy, Alex J. "Understanding and Regulating Contemporary War". *Australian Journal of Political Science* 42, no. 4 (2007): 701–9. https://doi.org/10.1080/10361140701 689214.

Berger, J.M. and Jonathon Morgan. "The ISIS Twitter Census Defining and Describing the Population of ISIS Supporters on Twitter". The Brookings Project on U.S. Relations with the Islamic World, 2015.

Beskow, David M. and Kathleen M. Carley. "Social Cybersecurity an Emerging National Security Requirement". *Military Review* 2 (2019): 117–27.

Blannin, Patrick. "Islamic State's Financing: Sources, methods and utilization". *Counter Terrorist Trends and Analyses* 9, no. 5 (2017): 13–22.

Bloch-Elkon, Yaeli and Brigitte L. Nacos. "News and Entertainment Media: Government's Big Helpers in the Selling of Counterterrorism". *Perspectives on Terrorism* 8, no. 5 (2014): 18–32.

Bouzar, Dounia, Christophe Caupenne and Sulayman Valsan. "La Métamorphose Opérée chez le Jeune par les Nouveaux Discours Terroristes". Lille: CPDSI, 2014.

Boyd-Barrett, Oliver. "MH17 as Free-Floating Atrocity Propaganda". In *Media, Ideology and Hegemony*, edited by Savaş Çoban, 267–98. The Hague: Brill, 2018. https://doi .org/10.1163/9789004364417.

Branon, Oriana. "Why Artificial Intelligence is the Future of Growth". Accenture, 2016. https://newsroom.accenture.com/subjects/technology/artificial-intelligence-pois ed-to-double-annual-economic-growth-rate-in-12-developed-economies-and -boost-labor-productivity-by-up-to-40-percent-by-2035-according-to-new-research -by-accenture.htm.

Brantly, Aaron. "Utopia Lost – Human Rights in a Digital World". *Applied Cybersecurity & Internet Governance* 1, no. 1 (2022): 1–19. https://doi.org/10.5604/01.3001.0016.1238.

Bravo, Cesar and Desilda Toska. *The Art of Social Engineering. Uncover the Secrets Behind the Human Dynamics in Cybersecurity*. Birmingham: Packt Publishing, 2023.

Brey, P. "Foreword". In *Information Overload. An International Challenge for Professional Engineers and Technical Communicators*. Hoboken, NJ: Wiley, 2012.

Bronfenbrenner, Urie. "Ecology of the Family as a Context for Human Development: Research Perspectives". *Developmental Psychology* 22, no. 6 (1986): 723–42.

Bronfenbrenner, Urie. "Interacting Systems in Human Development. Research Paradigms: Present and Future". In *Persons in Context: Developmental Processes*, edited by Niall Bolger, 25–49. New York: Cambridge University Press, 1988.

Bronfenbrenner, Urie. *The Ecology of Human Development*. Cambridge, MA: Harvard University Press, 1979.

Brudholm, Thomas and Birgitte Schepelern Johansen. *Hate, Politics, Law. Critical Perspectives on Combating Hate*. Oxford: Oxford University Press, 2018.

Brynjolfsson, Erik and Andrew McAfee. *Race Against the Machine*. Lexington, MA: Digital Frontier Press, 2011.

Bucher, Taina. *If ... Then. Algorithmic Power and Politics*. Oxford: Oxford University Press, 2018.

Buffardi, Laura E. and W. Keith Campbell. "Narcissism and Social Networking Web Sites". *Personality and Social Psychology Bulletin* 34, no. 10 (2008): 1303–14. https://doi.org/10.1177/0146167208320061.

Buzan, Barry, Ole Wæver and Jaap de Wilde. *Security: A New Framework for Analysis*. Boulder, CO: Lynne Rienner Publishers, 1998.

Buzan, Barry. *People, States and Fear: An Agenda for International Security Studies in the Post-Cold War Era*. London: Harvester Wheatsheaf, 1991.

California Legislative Information. Senate Bill No. 830. Chapter 448 (2018). https://leginfo.legislature.ca.gov/faces/billTextClient.xhtml?bill_id=201720180SB830.

Caligor, Eve, Kenneth N. Levy and Frank E. Yeomans. "Narcissistic Personality Disorder: Diagnostic and Clinical Challenges". *American Journal of Psychiatry* 172, no. 5 (2015): 415–22. https://doi.org/10.1176/appi.ajp.2014.14060723.

Campbell, Colin and Pamela E. Grimm. "The Challenges Native Advertising Poses: Exploring Potential Federal Trade Commission Responses and Identifying Research Needs". *Journal of Public Policy & Marketing* 38, no. 1 (2019): 110–23. https://doi.org/10.1177/0743915618818576.

Cardon, Dominique. "Deconstructing the Algorithm: Four Types of Digital Information Calculations". In *Algorithmic Cultures – Essays on Meaning, Performance and New Technologies*, edited by Robert Seyfert and Jonathan Roberge, 95–110. New York: Routledge, 2016.

Carley, Kathleen M. "Social Cybersecurity: An Emerging Science". *Computational and Mathematical Organization Theory* 26, no. 4 (2020): 365–81. https://doi.org/10.1007/S10588-020-09322-9.

Carr, Nicholas. *The Shallows: How the Internet Is Changing the Way We Think*. London: Atlantic Books, 2010.

Casaló, Luis V., Carlos Flavián and Sergio Ibáñez-Sánchez. "Influencers on Instagram: Antecedents and Consequences of Opinion Leadership". *Journal of Business Research* 117 (2020): 510–19. https://doi.org/10.1016/j.jbusres.2018.07.005.

Castells, Manuel. *The Internet Galaxy: Reflections on the Internet, Business and Society*. Oxford: Oxford University Press, 2002.

Cemiloglu, Deniz, Emily Arden-Close, Sarah E. Hodge and Raian Ali. "Explainable Persuasion for Interactive Design: The Case of Online Gambling". *Journal of Systems and Software* 195 (2023): 111517. https://doi.org/10.1016/j.jss.2022.111517.

Chapman, Christopher N. and Michal Lahav. "International Ethnographic Observation of Social Networking Sites". In *Proceedings of the Conference on Human Factors in Computing Systems*, 3123–28. New York: Association for Computing Machinery, 2008. https://doi.org/10.1145/1358628.1358818.

Chatzakou, Despoina, Nicolas Kourtellis, Jeremy Blackburn, Emiliano De Cristofaro, Gianluca Stringhini and Athena Vakali. "Mean Birds: Detecting Aggression and Bullying on Twitter". *WebSci 2017 – Proceedings of the 2017 ACM Web Science Conference*, 2017, 13–22. https://doi.org/10.48550/arxiv.1702.06877.

Chatzigeorgiou, Chryssoula. "Modelling The Impact of Social Media Influencers on Behavioural Intentions of Millennials: The Case of Tourism in Rural Areas in Greece", 2017. https://doi.org/10.5281/ZENODO.1209125.

Chen, Xin, Zexing Xu, Zishuo Zhao and Yuan Zhou. "Personalized Pricing with Group Fairness Constraint". In *2023 ACM Conference on Fairness, Accountability, and Transparency*, 1520–30. Chicago IL USA: ACM, 2023. https://doi.org/10.1145/3593013.3594097.

Cheng, Cecilia, Linus Chan and Chor-lam Chau. "Individual Differences in Susceptibility to Cybercrime Victimization and Its Psychological Aftermath". *Computers in Human Behavior* 108 (2020): 106311. https://doi.org/10.1016/j.chb.2020.106311.

Choi, Chong Ju and Ron Berger. "Ethics of Celebrities and Their Increasing Influence in 21st Century Society". *Journal of Business Ethics* 91, no. 3 (2010): 313–18. https://doi.org/10.1007/s10551-009-0090-4.

Chorev, Matan. "When in the Divide? Terrorism and the Future of Atlanticism". *Journal of International Affairs* 11, no. 1 (2006): 38–53.

Chou, Chien and Ming Chun Hsiao. "Internet Addiction, Usage, Gratification, and Pleasure Experience: The Taiwan College Students' Case". *Computers & Education* 35, no. 1 (2000): 65–80. https://doi.org/10.1016/S0360-1315(00)00019-1.

Chou, Hui Tzu Grace and Nicholas Edge. "'They Are Happier and Having Better Lives than I Am': The Impact of Using Facebook on Perceptions of Others' Lives". *Cyberpsychology, Behavior, and Social Networking* 15, no. 2 (2012): 117–21. https://doi.org/10.1089/CYBER.2011.0324.

Chung, Alicia, Dorice Vieira, Tiffany Donley, Nicholas Tan, Girardin Jean-Louis, Kathleen Kiely Gouley and Azizi Seixas. "Adolescent Peer Influence on Eating Behaviors via Social Media: Scoping Review". *Journal of Medical Internet Research* 23, no. 6 (2021): e19697. https://doi.org/10.2196/19697.

Chwan-Hwa, John Wu and J. David Irwin. *Introduction to Computer Networks and Cybersecurity*. Boca Faton, FL: CRC Press, 2013.

Cialdini, Robert B. *Influence, New and Expanded: The Psychology of Persuasion*. New York: HarperCollins, 2021.

Cialdini, Robert B. *Pre-Suasion: Channeling Attention for Change*. New York: Simon & Schuster, 2016.

Cifuentes-Faura, Javier. "The Role of Accountability and Transparency in Government during Disasters: The Case of Ukraine–Russia War". *Public Money & Management*, 2023, 1–10. https://doi.org/10.1080/09540962.2023.2243131.

Claverie, Bernard and François du Cluzel. "The Cognitive Warfare Concept". Innovation Hub Sponsored by NATO Allied Command Transformation, 2022. https://innovationhub-act.org/wp-content/uploads/2023/12/CW-article-Claverie-du-Cluzel-final_0.pdf.

Cleary, Gillian. "Twitterbots: Anatomy of a Propaganda Campaign". *Symantec Threat Intelligence Blog*, 2019. https://symantec-enterprise-blogs.security.com/blogs/threat-intelligence/twitterbots-propaganda-disinformation.

Clegg, Nick. "You and the Algorithm: It Takes Two to Tango", 2021. https://nickclegg.medium.com/you-and-the-algorithm-it-takes-two-to-tango-7722b19aa1c2.

Coates, Anna Elizabeth, Charlotte Alice Hardman, Jason Christian Grovenor Halford, Paul Christiansen and Emma Jane Boyland. "The Effect of Influencer Marketing of Food and a 'Protective' Advertising Disclosure on Children's Food Intake". *Pediatric Obesity* 14, no. 10 (2019): e12540. https://doi.org/10.1111/ijpo.12540.

Cobbe, Jennifer. "Algorithmic Censorship by Social Platforms: Power and Resistance". *Philosophy & Technology* 34, no. 4 (2021): 739–66. https://doi.org/10.1007/s13347-020-00429-0.

Constantinescu, Maria. "Measuring Economic Resilience for the CEE and Black Sea Countries in the Framework of Comprehensive Defense". *Security and Defence Quarterly* 44, no. 4 (2023): 55–83. https://doi.org/10.35467/sdq/175379.

Conway, Bethany A., Kate Kenski and Di Wang. "The Rise of Twitter in the Political Campaign: Searching for Intermedia Agenda-Setting Effects in the Presidential Primary". *Journal of Computer-Mediated Communication* 20, no. 4 (2015): 363–80. https://doi.org/10.1111/JCC4.12124.

Cooley, Delonia and Rochelle Parks-Yancy. "The Effect of Social Media on Perceived Information Credibility and Decision Making". *Journal of Internet Commerce* 18, no. 3 (2019): 249–69. https://doi.org/10.1080/15332861.2019.1595362.

Cormac, Rory and Richard J. Aldrich. "Grey Is the New Black: Covert Action and Implausible Deniability". *International Affairs* 94, no. 3 (2018): 477–94. https://doi.org/10.1093/ia/iiy067.

Council of Europe. "Recommendation No. R(97)20 of the Committee of Ministers to Member States on 'Hate Speech'", 1997. https://rm.coe.int/1680505d5b.

Crabtree, Charles, Matt Golder, Thomas Gschwend, and Indriði H. Indriðason. "It Is Not Only What You Say, It Is Also how You Say It: The Strategic Use of Campaign Sentiment". *The Journal of Politics* 82, no. 3 (2020): 1044–60. https://doi.org/10.1086/707613.

Craigen, Dan, Nadia Diakun-Thibault and Randy Purse. "Defining Cybersecurity". *Technology Innovation Management Review* 4, no. 10 (2014): 13–21.

Crombie, Iain K., Linda Irvine, Brian Williams, Falko F. Sniehotta, Dennis J. Petrie, Claire Jones, John Norrie, et al. "Text Message Intervention to Reduce Frequency of Binge Drinking among Disadvantaged Men: The TRAM RCT". *Public Health Research* 6, no. 6 (2018): 1–156. https://doi.org/10.3310/phr06060.

Cronin, Audrey Kurth. *Power to the People. How Open Technological Innovation Is Arming Tomorrow's Terrorists.* Oxford: Oxford University Press, 2019.

Cyrek, Barbara and Malwina Popiołek. "Trash Streaming: Characteristics and Methodological Guidelines". *Przegląd Kulturoznawczy*, no. 3 (53) (2022): 445–58. https://doi.org/10.4467/20843860PK.22.029.16618.

Darmody, Aron and Detlev Zwick. "Manipulate to Empower: Hyper-Relevance and the Contradictions of Marketing in the Age of Surveillance Capitalism". *Big Data & Society* 7, no. 1 (2020): 2053951720904112. https://doi.org/10.1177/2053951720904112.

Dastin, Jeffrey. "Amazon Scraps Secret AI Recruiting Tool that Showed Bias against Women". *Reuters*, 11 October 2019. https://www.reuters.com/article/idUSKCN1MK0AG/.

Davenport, Thomas H. and John C. Beck. *Attention Economy. Understanding the New Currency of Business.* Boston, MA: Harvard Business School Press, 2001.

David-Ferdon, Corinne and Marci Feldman Hertz. "Electronic Media, Violence, and Adolescents: An Emerging Public Health Problem". *Journal of Adolescent Health* 41, no. 6 (2007): S1–5. https://doi.org/10.1016/j.jadohealth.2007.08.020.

Davis, Richard A. "A Cognitive-Behavioral Model of Pathological Internet Use". *Computers in Human Behavior* 17, no. 2 (2001): 187–95. https://doi.org/10.1016/S0747-5632(00)00041-8.

Dean, Derek and Caroline Webb. "Recovering from Information Overload". *McKinsey Quarterly*, 2011. https://www.mckinsey.com/business-functions/people-and-organizational-performance/our-insights/recovering-from-information-overload.

DellaVigna, Stefano and Eliana La Ferrara. "Economic and Social Impacts of the Media". In *Handbook of Media Economics*, 1: 723–68. Elsevier, 2015. https://doi.org/10.1016/B978-0-444-63685-0.00019-X.

Demaske, Chris. *Free Speech and Hate Speech in the United States. The Limits of Toleration.* New York and London: Routledge, 2022.

Denning, Dorothy E. "Activism, Hacktivism, and Cyberterrorism: The Internet as a Tool for Influencing Foreign Policy". Global Problem Solving Information Technology and Tools, 2000. https://nautilus.org/global-problem-solving/activism-hacktivism-and-cyberterrorism-the-internet-as-a-tool-for-influencing-foreign-policy-2/.

De-Sola, José, Gabriel Rubio, Hernán Talledo, Luis Pistoni, Henk Van Riesen and Fernando Rodríguez de Fonseca. "Cell Phone Use Habits among the Spanish Population: Contribution of Applications to Problematic Use". *Frontiers in Psychiatry* 10 (2019): 883. https://doi.org/10.3389/FPSYT.2019.00883.

Dhir, Amandeep, Yossiri Yossatorn, Puneet Kaur and Sufen Chen. "Online Social Media Fatigue and Psychological Wellbeing – A Study of Compulsive Use, Fear of Missing out, Fatigue, Anxiety and Depression". *International Journal of Information Management* 40 (2018): 141–52. https://doi.org/10.1016/J.IJINFOMGT.2018.01.012.

Ding, Xiaoyan, Gaoshan Wang and Xin Zhang. "Do You Get Tired of Shopping Online? Exploring the Influence of Information Overload on Subjective States towards

Purchase Decision". In *WHICEB 2017 Proceedings 7*, 2017. http://aisel.aisnet.org/whiceb2017/7.

Djafarova, Elmira and Oxana Trofimenko. "'Instafamous' – Credibility and Self-Presentation of Micro-Celebrities on Social Media". *Information, Communication & Society* 22, no. 10 (2019): 1432–46. https://doi.org/10.1080/1369118X.2018.1438491.

Domalewska, Dorota, Aleksandar Jovanoski, Blagoj Nenovski, Kire Sharlamanov and Marzena Żakowska. "Exploring Sociodemographic Factors of Problematic Internet Use: A Cross-National Study of North Macedonia and Poland". *Discover Global Society* 1, no. 1 (2023): 10. https://doi.org/10.1007/s44282-023-00009-5.

Domalewska, Dorota, Małgorzata Gawlik-Kobylińska, Phuong Hoang Yen, Rebecca K. Webb and Nakonthep Thiparasuparat. "On Safe Space in Education: A Polish-Vietnamese Comparative Study". *Journal of Human Security* 17, no. 1 (2021): 35–45. https://doi.org/10.12924/johs2021.17010035.

Domalewska, Dorota. *Media Społecznościowe – Władza i Manipulacja. Analiza Zagrożeń Społecznych, Politycznych i Informacyjnych z Perspektywy Nauk o Bezpieczeństwie.* Warsaw: Wydawnictwo Akademii Sztuki Wojennej, 2022.

Dourish, Paul. "Algorithms and their Others: Algorithmic Culture in Context". *Big Data & Society* 3, no. 2 (2016). https://doi.org/10.1177/2053951716665128.

Dowództwo Komponentu Wojsk Obrony Cyberprzestrzeni. "Ukraina 2022 na Cyfrowym Froncie", 2022. https://www.wojsko-polskie.pl/woc/u/4c/d1/4cd11eaf-3567-405d-994f-f88b6b45ad0b/ukraina_2022_na_cyfrowym_froncie.pdf.

Doyle, Charles. *A Dictionary of Marketing.* Oxford: Oxford University Press, 2016.

Drake, Philip. "Celebrity, Reputational Capital and the Media Industries". In *Routledge Handbook of Celebrity Studies*, przez Anthony Elliott, 271–84. edited by Anthony Elliott. London: Routledge, 2018. https://doi.org/10.4324/9781315776774-18.

Druckman, James N., Erik Peterson, and Rune Slothuus. "How Elite Partisan Polarization Affects Public Opinion Formation". *American Political Science Review* 107, no. 1 (2013): 57–79. https://doi.org/10.1017/S0003055412000500.

Druckman, James N., Jordan Fein, and Thomas J. Leeper. "A Source of Bias in Public Opinion Stability". *American Political Science Review* 106, no. 2 (2012): 430–54. https://doi.org/10.1017/S0003055412000123.

Duarte, Fabio. "Amount of Data Created Daily (2024)", 2023. https://explodingtopics.com/blog/data-generated-per-day.

Duffy, Brooke Erin. "Social Media Influencers". In *The International Encyclopedia of Gender, Media, and Communication*, edited by Karen Ross, Ingrid Bachmann, Valentina Cardo, Sujata Moorti and Marco Scarcelli, 1–4. Hoboken, NJ: Wiley, 2020. https://doi.org/10.1002/9781119429128.iegmc219.

Dunn Cavelty, Myriam and Andreas Wenger. "Cyber Security Meets Security Politics: Complex Technology, Fragmented Politics, and Networked Science". *Contemporary Security Policy* 41, no. 1 (2020): 5–32. https://doi.org/10.1080/13523260.2019.1678855.

Dunn Cavelty, Myriam. "Is Anything ever New? – Exploring the Specificities of Security and Governance in the Information Age". In *Power and Security in the Information Age*, edited by Myriam Dunn Cavelty, Victor Mauer and Sai-Felicia Krishna-Hensel, 25–50. Aldershot: Ashgate, 2007.

Duradoni, Mirko, Elena Serritella, Franca Paola Severino and Andrea Guazzini. "Exploring the Relationships Between Digital Life Balance and Internet Social Capital, Loneliness, Fear of Missing Out, and Anxiety". Edited by Pinaki Chakraborty. *Human Behavior and Emerging Technologies* 2024 (2024): 1–9. https://doi.org/10.1155/2024/5079719.

Durkee, Tony, Michael Kaess, Vladimir Carli, Peter Parzer, Camilla Wasserman, Birgitta Floderus, Alan Apter, et al. "Prevalence of Pathological Internet Use among Adolescents in Europe: Demographic and Social Factors". *Addiction* 107, no. 12 (2012): 2210–22. https://doi.org/10.1111/J.1360-0443.2012.03946.X.

Dutch Safety Board. "Crash MH17, 17 July 2014", 2015. https://onderzoeksraad.nl/en/onderzoek/crash-mh17-17-july-2014/.

Dwork, Cynthia, and Deirdre K. Mulligan. "It's not Privacy, and It's not Fair". *Stanford Law Review* 66 (2013). https://www.stanfordlawreview.org/online/privacy-and-big-data-its-not-privacy-and-its-not-fair/.

Echevarria, Antulio J. *Globalization and the Nature of War*. Carlisle, PA: Strategic Studies Institute, 2003.

Eichensehr, Kristen E. "Ukraine, Cyberattacks, and the Lessons for International Law". *AJIL Unbound* 116 (2022): 145–49. https://doi.org/10.1017/aju.2022.20.

Emerson, R.M. "Social Exchange". In *Social Psychology: Sociological Perspective*, edited by M. Rosenberg and R. Turner, 3–24. New York: Basic Books, 1981.

ENISA. "ENISA Threat Landscape 2022". Athens: European Union Agency for Network and Information Security, 2022. https://www.enisa.europa.eu/publications/enisa-threat-landscape-2022.

ENISA. "ENISA Threat Landscape July 2022 to June 2023". Athens: European Union Agency for Network and Information Security, 2023. https://www.enisa.europa.eu/publications/enisa-threat-landscape-2023.

Epstein, Jennifer A. "The Role of Parents and Related Factors on Adolescent Computer Use". *Journal of Public Health Research* 1, no. 1 (2012). https://doi.org/10.4081/JPHR.2012.E13.

Erbschloe, Michael. *Social Engineering. Hacking Systems, Nations, and Societies*. Boca Raton, Fl: CRC Press, 2020.

Erevik, Eilin K., Torbjørn Torsheim, Cecilie S. Andreassen, Øystein Vedaa and Ståle Pallesen. "Disclosure and Exposure of Alcohol on Social Media and Later Alcohol Use: A Large-Scale Longitudinal Study". *Frontiers in Psychology* 8 (2017): 284957. https://doi.org/10.3389/FPSYG.2017.01934.

Eriksson, E. Anders. "Viewpoint. Information Warfare: Hype or Reality?" *The Nonproliferation Review* 6, no. 3 (1999): 57–64. https://doi.org/10.1080/10736709908436765.

Erol, Osman and Neşe SeviM Çirak. "What are the Factors that Affect the Motivation of Digital Gamers?" *Participatory Educational Research* 7, no. 1 (2020): 184–200. https://doi.org/10.17275/per.20.11.7.1.

Escadas, Marco, Marjan S. Jalali and Minoo Farhangmehr. "Why Bad Feelings Predict Good Behaviours: The Role of Positive and Negative Anticipated Emotions on Consumer Ethical Decision Making". *Business Ethics: A European Review* 28, no. 4 (2019): 529–45. https://doi.org/10.1111/beer.12237.

European Commission. "Ethics Guidelines for Trustworthy AI", 2019. https://digital-strategy.ec.europa.eu/en/library/ethics-guidelines-trustworthy-ai.

European Commission. "The EU Code of Conduct on Countering Illegal Hate Speech Online", 2016.

European Commission. Communication on Tackling On-line Disinformation: A European Approach, COM(2018)236 (2018). https://eur-lex.europa.eu/legal-content/EN/TXT/?uri=CELEX%3A52018DC0236.

European Commission. Joint Communication to the European Parliament and the Council. Joint Framework on Countering Hybrid Threats a European Union Response (2016). https://eur-lex.europa.eu/legal-content/EN/TXT/?uri=CELEX%3A52016JC0018.

Europol. *ChatGPT – The Impact of Large Language Models on Law Enforcement, a Tech Watch Flash Report from the Europol Innovation Lab*. Luxembourg: Publications Office of the European Union, 2023.

Facebook. "Simplifying Targeting Categories", 2020. https://www.facebook.com/business/news/update-to-facebook-ads-targeting-categories.

Facebook. "What Does Facebook Consider To Be Hate Speech?", 2018. https://www.facebook.com/help/.

Fahy, Amanda E., Stephen A. Stansfeld, Melanie Smuk, Neil R. Smith, Steven Cummins and Charlotte Clark. "Longitudinal Associations Between Cyberbullying Involvement and Adolescent Mental Health". *Journal of Adolescent Health* 59, no. 5 (2016): 502–9. https://doi.org/10.1016/j.jadohealth.2016.06.006.

Faulkner, Nicholas and Ana Maria Bliuc. "Breaking Down the Language of Online Racism: A Comparison of the Psychological Dimensions of Communication in Racist, Anti-Racist, and Non-Activist Groups". *Analyses of Social Issues and Public Policy* 18, no. 1 (2018): 307–22. https://doi.org/10.1111/ASAP.12159.

Federal Law of July 27, 2006 N 149-FZ On Information, Information Technologies and Information Protection. https://www.consultant.ru/document/cons_doc_LAW_61798/72898298ae4b1568b5dabf766b3a1bab03748c2a/.

Feller, Gavin and Benjamin Burroughs. "Branding Kidfluencers: Regulating Content and Advertising on YouTube". *Television & New Media* 23, no. 6 (2022): 575–92. https://doi.org/10.1177/15274764211052882.

Ferrara, Emilio and Zeyao Yang. "Measuring Emotional Contagion in Social Media". *PLOS ONE* 10, no. 11 (2015): e0142390. https://doi.org/10.1371/JOURNAL.PONE.0142390.

Festinger, Leon, Albert Pepitone and Theodore M. Newcomb. "Some Consequences of De-Individuation in a Group". *Journal of Abnormal and Social Psychology* 47, no. 2 SUPPL. (1952): 382–89. https://doi.org/10.1037/H0057906.

Floros, Georgios and Konstantinos Siomos. "Excessive Internet Use and Personality Traits". *Current Behavioral Neuroscience Reports* 1, no. 1 (2014): 19–26. https://doi.org/10.1007/s40473-014-0006-1.

Forman-Katz, Naomi. "Americans are following the news less closely than they used to". Pew Research Center, 2023.

Fox, Jesse and Megan A. Vendemia. "Selective Self-Presentation and Social Comparison Through Photographs on Social Networking Sites". *Cyberpsychology, Behavior, and Social Networking* 19, no. 10 (2016): 593–600. https://doi.org/10.1089/cyber.2016.0248.

Freberg, Karen, Kristin Graham, Karen McGaughey and Laura A. Freberg. "Who Are the Social Media Influencers? A Study of Public Perceptions of Personality". *Public Relations Review* 37, no. 1 (2011): 90–92. https://doi.org/10.1016/j.pubrev.2010.11.001.

Freedom House. "Freedom on the Net 2017: Manipulating Social Media to Undermine Democracy", 2017. https://freedomhouse.org/report/freedom-net/freedom-net-2017.

Freier, Nathan. "Hybrid Threats and Challenges: Describe ... Don't Define". *Small Wars Journal*, 2009.

Friedman, Raymond A. and Steven C. Currall. "Conflict Escalation: Dispute Exacerbating Elements of E-Mail Communication". *Human Relations* 56, no. 11 (2016): 1325–47. https://doi.org/10.1177/00187267035611003.

Gagrčin, Emilija. "Your Social Ties, Your Personal Public Sphere, Your Responsibility: How Users Construe a Sense of Personal Responsibility for Intervention against Uncivil Comments on Facebook". *New Media & Society*, 2022, 1–18. https://doi.org/10.1177/14614448221117499.

Gartzke, Erik. "The Myth of Cyberwar: Bringing War in Cyberspace Back Down to Earth". *International Security* 38, no. 2 (2013): 41–73. https://doi.org/10.1162/ISEC_a_00136.

Garwol, Katarzyna. "Influencers – Contemporary Authorities of the Young Generation?" *European Journal of Sustainable Development* 9, no. 4 (2020): 273–273. https://doi.org/10.14207/ejsd.2020.v9n4p273.

Gasztold, Aleksandra and Przemysław Gasztold. "The Polish Counterterrorism System and Hybrid Warfare Threats". *Terrorism and Political Violence* 34, no. 6 (2022): 1259–76. https://doi.org/10.1080/09546553.2020.1777110.

Gawlik-Kobylińska, Małgorzata and Marcin Rojek. "Artificial Intelligence in the Implementation of Didactic Principles in a Novel Mobility Platform: The Case of the eMediator Project". In *Reliability and Statistics in Transportation and Communication,* edited by Igor Kabashkin, Irina Yatskiv and Olegas Prentkovskis, 913: 617–27. Lecture Notes in Networks and Systems. Cham: Springer Nature Switzerland, 2024. https://doi.org/10.1007/978-3-031-53598-7_55.

Gawlik-Kobylińska, Małgorzata, Dorota Domalewska and Paweł Maciejewski. "How to Motivate Students? The Four-Dimensional Instructional Design Approach in a Non-core Blended Learning Course". In *Cross Reality and Data Science in Engineering. REV 2020. Advances in Intelligent Systems and Computing, vol 1231*, edited by Auer M. and May D., 782–94. Cham: Springer, 2021. https://doi.org/10.1007/978-3-030-52575-0_64.

Geer, John G. "The News Media and the Rise of Negativity in Presidential Campaigns". *PS: Political Science & Politics* 45, no. 3 (2012): 422–27. https://doi.org/10.1017/S1049096512000492.

Gerhart, Susan. "Do Web Search Engines Suppress Controversy". *First Monday* 9, no. 1 (2004). https://doi.org/10.5210/fm.v9i1.1111.

Gerstlé, Jacques and Alessandro Nai. "Negativity, Emotionality and Populist Rhetoric in Election Campaigns Worldwide, and Their Effects on Media Attention and Electoral Success". *European Journal of Communication* 34, no. 4 (2019): 410–44. https://doi.org/10.1177/0267323119861875.

Ginige, Pabasari. "Internet Addiction Disorder". In *Child and Adolescent Mental Health*. IntechOpen, 2017. https://doi.org/10.5772/66966.

Glaser, Vern L., Neil Pollock, and Luciana D'Adderio. "The Biography of an Algorithm: Performing Algorithmic Technologies in Organizations". *Organization Theory* 2, no. 2 (2021): 263178772110046. https://doi.org/10.1177/26317877211004609.

Golbeck, Jennifer, Cristina Robles, Michon Edmondson, and Karen Turner. "Predicting Personality from Twitter". *Proceedings – 2011 IEEE International Conference on Privacy, Security, Risk and Trust and IEEE International Conference on Social Computing, PASSAT/SocialCom 2011*, 149–56. https://doi.org/10.1109/PASSAT/SOCIALCOM.2011.33.

Goldfarb, Avi, Shane M. Greenstein and Catherine E. Tucker. *Economic Analysis of the Digital Economy*. Chicago: The University of Chicago Press, 2015.

Goldhaber, Michael H. "The Attention Economy and the Net". *First Monday*, 1997. https://journals.uic.edu/ojs/index.php/fm/article/view/519/440.

Gomez-Rodriguez, Manuel, Krishna Gummadi and Bernhard Schoelkopf. "Quantifying Information Overload in Social Media and its Impact on Social Contagions". In *Proceedings of the Eighth International AAAI Conference on Weblogs and Social Media*, 170–79, 2014. https://www.aaai.org/ocs/index.php/ICWSM/ICWSM14/paper/view/8108/8117.

González-Bailón, Sandra, David Lazer, Pablo Barberá, Meiqing Zhang, Hunt Allcott, Taylor Brown, Adriana Crespo-Tenorio et al. "Asymmetric Ideological Segregation in Exposure to Political News on Facebook". *Science* 381, no. 6656 (2023): 392–98. https://doi.org/10.1126/science.ade7138.

Górka, Marek. "Cybertools of Political Competition". *Polish Political Science Yearbook* 47, no. 4 (2018): 628–41. https://doi.org/10.15804/ppsy2018403.

Gottfried, Jeffrey, Amy Mitchell, Mark Jurkowitz and Jacob Liedke. "Journalists Highly Concerned about Misinformation, Future of Press Freedoms". Pew Research Center, 2022. https://www.pewresearch.org/journalism/2022/06/14/journalists-highly-concerned-about-misinformation-future-of-press-freedoms/.

Graefer, Anne. "The Work of Humour in Affective Capitalism: A Case Study of Celebrity Gossip Blogs". *Ephemera. Theory and Politics in Organization* 16, no. 4 (2016): 143–62.

Granovetter, Mark. "Threshold Models of Collective Behavior". *American Journal of Sociology* 83, no. 6 (1978): 1420–43. https://doi.org/10.1086/226707.

Green, Andrew and Lucas Lamby. "The Supply, Demand and Characteristics of the AI Workforce across OECD Countries". OECD Social, Employment and Migration Working Papers. T. 287. OECD Social, Employment and Migration Working Papers, 2023. https://doi.org/10.1787/bb17314a-en.

Greenfield, David. "The Addictive Properties of Internet Usage". In *Internet Addiction*, edited by Kimberly S. Young and Cristiano Nabuco De Abreu, 133–53. Hoboken, NJ: John Wiley & Sons, 2007. https://doi.org/10.1002/9781118013991.ch8.

Griffiths, Mark. "Does Internet and Computer 'Addiction' Exist? Some Case Study Evidence". *Cyberpsychology and Behavior* 3, no. 2 (2000): 211–18.

Griffiths, Mark. "Internet Abuse in the Workplace: Issues and Concerns for Employers and Employment Counselors". *Journal of Employment Counseling* 40, no. 2 (2003): 87–96. https://doi.org/10.1002/j.2161-1920.2003.tb00859.x.

Grobler, Marthie, Raj Gaire and Surya Nepal. "User, Usage and Usability: Redefining Human Centric Cyber Security". *Frontiers in Big Data* 4 (2021): 5. https://doi.org/10.3389/FDATA.2021.583723.

Gross, Michael L., Daphna Canetti and Dana R. Vashdi. "The Psychological Effects of Cyber Terrorism". *Bulletin of the Atomic Scientists* 72, no. 5 (2016): 284–91. https://doi.org/10.1080/00963402.2016.1216502.

Grother, Patrick, Mei Ngan and Kayee Hanaoka. "Face Recognition Vendor Test Part 3: Demographic EHOffects". Gaithersburg, MD: National Institute of Standards and Technology, 2019. https://doi.org/10.6028/NIST.IR.8280.

Gruszczak, Artur. "Hybrydowość Współczesnych Wojen – Analiza Krytyczna". In *Asymetria i hybrydowość – stare armie wobec nowych konfliktów*, edited by Witold Sokała and Bartłomiej Zapała, 9–17. Warsaw: Biuro Bezpieczeństwa Narodowego, 2011.

Grzegorzewski, Mark "Russian Cyber Operations: The Relationship between the State and Cybercriminals". In *Cyber Terrorism and Extremism as Threat to Critical Infrastructure Protection*, edited by Denis Caleta and James F. Powers, 53–64. Ljubljana: Ministry of Defence Republic of Slovenia, 2020.

Guetl, Christian, Leila Ismail and Cary Lexar. "Track A: Foundations of Digital Ecosystems and Complex Environment Engineering". In *2013 7th IEEE International Conference on Digital Ecosystems and Technologies (DEST)*, 1–1. Menlo Park, CA: Institute of Electrical and Electronics Engineers (IEEE), 2013. https://doi.org/10.1109/DEST.2013.6611308.

Hadnagy, Christopher. *Social Engineering: The Art of Human Hacking*. Hoboken, NJ: Wiley, 2012.

Hadnagy, Christopher. *Social Engineering: The Science of Human Hacking*. Hoboken, NJ: Wiley, 2018.

Hakala, Janne and Jazlyn Melnychuk. *Russia's Strategy in Cyberspace*. Riga: NATO Strategic Communication Centre of Excellence, 2021.

Hall, Jeffrey A., Natalie Pennington and Allyn Lueders. "Impression Management and Formation on Facebook: A Lens Model Approach": *New Media & Society* 16, no. 6 (2013): 958–82. https://doi.org/10.1177/1461444813495166.

Hameleers, Michael, Anna Brosius and Claes H. de Vreese. "Whom to Trust? Media Exposure Patterns of Citizens with Perceptions of Misinformation and Disinformation Related to the News Media". *European Journal of Communication*, 2022. https://doi.org/10.1177/02673231211072667.

Hansen, Lene and Helen Nissenbaum. "Digital Disaster, Cyber Security, and the Copenhagen School". *International Studies Quarterly* 53, no. 4 (2009): 1155–75. https://doi.org/10.1111/j.1468-2478.2009.00572.x.

Hansson, Sten. "Discursive Strategies of Blame Avoidance in Government: A Framework for Analysis". *Discourse & Society* 26, no. 3 (2015): 297–322. https://doi.org/10.1177/0957926514564736.

Harari, Yuval Noah. *21 Lessons for the 21st Century*. Reprint Edition. New York: Random House Publishing Group, 2018.

Harari, Yuval Noah. *Homo Deus. A Brief History of Tomorrow*. Nowy Jork: Vintage, 2017.

Harcourt, Bernard E. "Risk as a Proxy for Race: The Dangers of Risk Assessment". *Federal Sentencing Reporter* 27, no. 4 (2015): 237–43. https://doi.org/10.1525/fsr.2015.27.4.237.

Hartley, James and Lucy Betts. "Common Weaknesses in Traditional Abstracts in the Social Sciences". *Journal of the American Society for Information Science and Technology* 60, no. 10 (2009): 2010–18. https://doi.org/10.1002/asi.21102.

Hawdon, James, Atte Oksanen and Pekka Räsänen. "Victims of Online Hate Groups: American Youth's Exposure to Online Hate Speech". In *The Causes and Consequences of Group Violence: From Bullies to Terrorists*, edited by James Hawdon, John Ryan and Mark Lucht, 165–82. Lanham, MD: Lexington Books, 2014.

Helsper, Ellen Johanna and David Smahel. "Excessive Internet Use by Young Europeans: Psychological Vulnerability and Digital Literacy?" *Information, Communication & Society* 23, no. 9 (2020): 1255–73. https://doi.org/10.1080/1369118X.2018.1563203.

Henkin, Louis. "Law and Politics in International Relations: State and Human Values". *Journal of International Affairs* 44, no. 1 (1990): 183–208.

Herman, Edward S. and Noam Chomsky. *Manufacturing Consent: The Political Economy of the Mass Media*. London: Vintage books, 1988.

Hern, Alex. "TikTok's Local Moderation Guidelines Ban Pro-LGBT Content". *The Guardian*, 26 September 2019. https://www.theguardian.com/technology/2019/sep /26/tiktoks-local-moderation-guidelines-ban-pro-lgbt-content.

Herz, John H. "Idealist Internationalism and the Security Dilemma". *World Politics* 2, no. 2 (1950): 157–80. https://doi.org/10.2307/2009187.

Herzog, Lisa. "Algorithmic Bias and Access to Opportunities". In *The Oxford Handbook of Digital Ethics*, edited by C. Veliz, 413–32. Oxford: Oxford University Press, 2024.

Hill, Joshua B. and Nancy E. Marion. *Introduction to Cybercrime: Computer Crimes, Laws, and Policing in the 21st Century*. Santa Barbara, CA: Bloomsbury Publishing USA, 2016.

Hinduja, Sameer and Justin W. Patchin. "Bullying, Cyberbullying, and Suicide". *Archives of Suicide Research* 14, no. 3 (2010): 206–21. https://doi.org/10.1080/13811118.2010 .494133.

Hoffman, Frank G. *Conflict in the 21st Century: The Rise of Hybrid Wars*. Arlington, VA: Potomac Institute for Policy Studies, 2007.

Hollenbaugh, Erin E. and Amber L. Ferris. "Facebook Self-Disclosure: Examining the Role of Traits, Social Cohesion, and Motives". *Computers in Human Behavior* 30 (2014): 50–58. https://doi.org/10.1016/J.CHB.2013.07.055.

Holly, Ryszard "Postawa (i Hasła Korespondujące)". In *Słownik Psychologiczny*, edited by Włodziemierz Szewczuk. Warsaw: Wiedza Powszechna, 1985.

Hong, Soon Beom, Andrew Zalesky, Luca Cocchi, Alex Fornito, Eun Jung Choi, Ho Hyun Kim, Jeong Eun Suh, Chang Dai Kim, Jae Won Kim and Soon Hyung Yi. "Decreased Functional Brain Connectivity in Adolescents with Internet Addiction". *PLOS ONE* 8, no. 2 (2013): e57831. https://doi.org/10.1371/JOURNAL.PONE.0057831.

Horton, Donald and R. Richard Wohl. "Mass Communication and Para-Social Interaction". *Psychiatry* 19, no. 3 (1956): 215–29. https://doi.org/10.1080/00332747.1956 .11023049.

Hou, Haifeng, Shaowe Jia, Shu Hu, Rong Fan, Wen Sun, Taotao Sun and Hong Zhang. "Reduced Striatal Dopamine Transporters in People with Internet Addiction Disorder". *Journal of Biomedicine and Biotechnology* 2012 (2012). https://doi.org/10.1155 /2012/854524.

Huang, Mengyuan and Weiyi Zhang. "The Mechanism and Treatment of Teenager Internet Addiction from Stress: A Review": Kunming, China, 2022. https://doi.org/10 .2991/assehr.k.220110.155.

Hudders, Liselot and Chen Lou. "The Rosy World of Influencer Marketing? Its Bright and Dark Sides, and Future Research Recommendations". *International Journal of Advertising* 42, no. 1 (2023): 151–61. https://doi.org/10.1080/02650487.2022.2137318.

Hudders, Liselot, Steffi De Jans and Marijke De Veirman. "The Commercialization of Social Media Stars: A Literature Review and Conceptual Framework on the Strategic Use of Social Media Influencers". *International Journal of Advertising* 40, no. 3 (2021): 327–75. https://doi.org/10.1080/02650487.2020.1836925.

Humanity in Action. "Czym Jest Mowa Nienawiści", 2014. https://uprzedzuprzedzenia .org/czym-mowa-nienawisci/.

Humprecht, Edda, Frank Esser and Peter Van Aelst. "Resilience to Online Disinformation: A Framework for Cross-National Comparative Research". *The International Journal of Press/Politics* 25, no. 3 (2020): 493–516. https://doi.org/10.1177/1940161219900126.

Hyslip, Thomas S. "Cybercrime-as-a-Service Operations". In *The Palgrave Handbook of International Cybercrime and Cyberdeviance*, edited by Thomas J. Holt and Adam M. Bossler, 815–46. Cham: Springer International Publishing, 2020. https:// doi.org/10.1007/978-3-319-78440-3_36.

IBM. "Cost of a Data Breach Report", 2024. https://www.ibm.com/downloads/cas /1KZ3XE9D.

ILGA. "Hate Crime and Hate Speech", 2016.

Imana, Basileal, Aleksandra Korolova and John Heidemann. "Auditing for Discrimination in Algorithms Delivering Job Ads". In *Proceedings of the Web Conference 2021*, 3767–78. Ljubljana: ACM, 2021. https://doi.org/10.1145/3442381.3450077.

Ireton, Cherilyn. "Truth, Trust and Journalism: Why it Matters". In *Journalism, Fake News & Disinformation. Handbook for Journalism Education and Training*, edited by Cherilyn Ireton and Julie Posetti, 32–43. Paris: United Nations, 2018.

Iskandarov, Khayal and Piotr Gawliczek. "Economic Coercion as a Means of Hybrid Warfare: The South Caucasus as a Focal Point". *Security and Defence Quarterly* 40, no. 4 (2022): 47–57. https://doi.org/10.35467/sdq/151038.

Islam, Tahir, Abdul Hameed Pitafi, Naeem Akhtar and Liang Xiaobei. "Determinants of Purchase Luxury Counterfeit Products in Social Commerce: The Mediating Role of Compulsive Internet Use". *Journal of Retailing and Consumer Services* 62 (2021): 102596. https://doi.org/10.1016/j.jretconser.2021.102596.

Jackson, Richard, Marie Breen Smyth and Jeroen Gunning. *Critical Terrorism Studies: A New Research Agenda*. New York: Routledge, 2009.

Jackson, Richard. "Security, Democracy, and the Rhetoric of Counter-Terrorism". *Democracy and Security* 1, no. 2 (2005): 147–71. https://doi.org/10.1080/17419160500322517.

Jackson, Richard. *Writing the War on Terrorism: Language, Politics, and Counter-Terrorism*. Manchester; New York: Manchester University Press, 2005.

Jakubowska-Branicka, Iwona. *Hate Narratives. Language as a Tool of Intolerance*. Berlin: Peter Lange, 2016.

Jalali, Sanaz Saghati and Haliyana Khalid. "Understanding Instagram Influencers Values in Green Consumption Behaviour: A Review Paper". *Open International Journal of Informatics* 7, Special Issue 1 (2019): 47–58.

Jarvis, Lee, Stuart Macdonald and Lella Nouri. "The Cyberterrorism Threat: Findings from a Survey of Researchers". *Studies in Conflict & Terrorism* 37, no. 1 (2014): 68–90. https://doi.org/10.1080/1057610X.2014.853603.

Javakhishvili, Magda and Alexander T. Vazsonyi. "Parental Vigilance, Low Self-Control, and Internet Dependency among Rural Adolescents". In *Child and Adolescent Online Risk Exposure*, (2021): 191–208. https://doi.org/10.1016/B978-0-12-817499-9.00010-7.

Jergler, Don. "Researchers Question Privacy of Usage-Based Auto Insurance". Insurance Journal, 2013. https://www.insurancejournal.com/news/national/2013/10/02/307073.htm.

Jowett, Garth S. and Victoria O'Donnell. *Propaganda and Persuasion*. Thousand Oaks, CA: Sage, 2019.

Juurvee, Ivo, V. Sazonov, K. Parppei, E. Engizers, I. Pałasz and M. Zawadzka. "Falsification of History as a Tool of Influence". NATO Strategic Communications Centre of Excellence, 2020.

Kalan, Özlem. "Digital Transformation in Marketing: A Sample Review on Kid Influencer Marketing and Toy Unboxing Videos on YouTube". In *Digital Transformation in Media & Society*, edited by Ayşen Akkor, Gül Yıldız and Paul Ertürk. Istanbul: Istanbul University Press, 2020.

Kaldor, Mary. "In Defence of New Wars". *Stability: International Journal of Security and Development* 2, no. 1 (2013): 4. https://doi.org/10.5334/sta.at.

Kalpokas, Ignas. "Post-Truth and Information Warfare in their Technological Context". *Applied Cybersecurity & Internet Governance* 4, no. 2 (2024). https://doi.org/10.60097/ACIG/190407.

Kamphuis, Christian. "Reflexive Control". *Militaire Spectator*, 2018. https://www.militairespectator.nl/thema/strategie-operaties/artikel/reflexive-control.

Kapantai, Eleni, Androniki Christopoulou, Christos Berberidis and Vassilios Peristeras. "A Systematic Literature Review on Disinformation: Toward a Unified Taxonomical Framework". *New Media & Society* 23, no. 5 (2021): 1301–26. https://doi.org/10.1177/1461444820959296.

Kaptsis, Dean, Daniel L. King, Paul H. Delfabbro and Michael Gradisar. "Withdrawal Symptoms in Internet Gaming Disorder: A Systematic Review". *Clinical Psychology Review* 43 (2016): 58–66. https://doi.org/10.1016/J.CPR.2015.11.006.

Kaul, Inge. "Global Public Goods and Governance for Addressing Sustainability". In *The Palgrave Handbook of Development Economics*, edited by Machiko Nissanke and José Antonio Ocampo, 833–65. Cham: Springer International Publishing, 2019. https://doi.org/10.1007/978-3-030-14000-7_24.

Kaunert, Christian, Alex MacKenzie and Sarah Léonard. "Far-Right Foreign Fighters and Ukraine: A Blind Spot for the European Union?" *New Journal of European Criminal Law* 14, no. 2 (2023): 247–66. https://doi.org/10.1177/20322844231164089.

Kelion, Leo. "TikTok Suppressed Disabled Users' Videos". *BBC*, 3 December 2019. https://www.bbc.com/news/technology-50645345.

Kennedy, Melanie. "'If the Rise of the TikTok Dance and E-Girl Aesthetic Has Taught Us Anything, It's That Teenage Girls Rule the Internet Right Now': TikTok Celebrity, Girls and the Coronavirus Crisis". *European Journal of Cultural Studies* 23, no. 6 (2020): 1069–76. https://doi.org/10.1177/1367549420945341.

Kertzer, Joshua D. "Seriousness, Grand Strategy, and Paradigm Shifts in the 'War on Terror'". *International Journal: Canada's Journal of Global Policy Analysis* 62, no. 4 (2007): 961–79. https://doi.org/10.1177/002070200706200414.

Kianpour, Mazaher, Stewart James Kowalski and Harald Øverby. "Advancing the Concept of Cybersecurity as a Public Good". *Simulation Modelling Practice and Theory* 116 (2022): 102493. https://doi.org/10.1016/j.simpat.2022.102493.

Kincaid, Harold and Jacqueline A. Sullivan. "Medical Models of Addiction". In *What Is Addiction?*, edited by Don Ross, Harold Kincaid, David Spurrett and Peter Collins, 352–76. Cambridge, MA: The MIT Press, 2010. https://doi.org/10.7551/mitpress/9780262513111.003.0014.

Király, Orsolya, Marc N. Potenza, Dan J. Stein, Daniel L. King, David C. Hodgins, John B. Saunders, Mark D. Griffiths, et al. "Preventing Problematic Internet Use during the COVID-19 Pandemic: Consensus Guidance". *Comprehensive Psychiatry* 100 (2020): 152180. https://doi.org/10.1016/j.comppsych.2020.152180.

Kiss, Jemima. "Google Admits Collecting Wi-Fi Data through Street View Cars". *The Guardian*, 15 May 2010. https://www.theguardian.com/technology/2010/may/15/google-admits-storing-private-data.

Klein, Joëlle and Kamrul Hossain. "Conceptualising Human-centric Cyber Security in the Arctic in Light of Digitalisation and Climate Change". *Arctic Review on Law and Politics* 11 (2020): 1–18. https://doi.org/10.23865/arctic.v11.1936.

Ko, Deborah and Mike Yao. "Internet Addiction: A Cross-Cultural Perspective". *The Psychology of Social Networking* 12 (2016): 141–58. https://doi.org/10.1515/9783110473858-013.

Kollanyi, Bence, Philip N. Howard and Samuel C. Woolley. "Bots and Automation over Twitter during the U.S. Election". Oxford: Data Memo 2016.4., 2016. https://comprop.oii.ox.ac.uk/research/working-papers/bots-and-automation-over-twitter-during-the-u-s-election/.

Kott, Alexander, Norbou Buchler and Kristin E. Schaefer. "Kinetic and Cyber". In *Cyber Defense and Situational Awareness*, edited by Alexander Kott, Cliff Wang and Robert F. Erbacher, 62: 29–45. Advances in Information Security. Cham: Springer International Publishing, 2014. https://doi.org/10.1007/978-3-319-11391-3_3.

Kragh, Martin and Andreas Umland. "L'Imaginaire Russe anti-Ukraine: Le Cas Patrouchev", 2023. https://doi.org/10.13140/RG.2.2.13319.78248.

Kramer, Adam D.I., Jamie E. Guillory and Jeffrey T. Hancock. "Experimental Evidence of Massive-Scale Emotional Contagion through Social Networks". *Proceedings of the National Academy of Sciences of the United States of America* 111, no. 24 (2014): 8788–90. https://doi.org/10.1073/PNAS.1320040111.

Krishna Viraja, V. and Pradnya Purandare. "A Qualitative Research on the Impact and Challenges of Cybercrimes". *Journal of Physics: Conference Series* 1964, no. 4 (2021): 042004. https://doi.org/10.1088/1742–6596/1964/4/042004.

Kundi, Ghulam Muhammad, Allah Nawaz and Robina Akhtar. "Digital Revolution, Cyber-Crimes and Cyber Legislation: A Challenge To Governments In Developing Countries". *Journal of Information Engineering and Applications* 4, no. 4 (2014): 61–70.

Kupfer, Ann-Kristin, Nora Pähler Vor Der Holte, Raoul V. Kübler and Thorsten Hennig-Thurau. "The Role of the Partner Brand's Social Media Power in Brand Alliances". *Journal of Marketing* 82, no. 3 (2018): 25–44. https://doi.org/10.1509/jm.15.0536.

Kuss, Daria J., Mark Griffiths, Laurent Karila and J. Billieux. "Internet Addiction: A Systematic Review of Epidemiological Research for the Last Decade". *Current Pharmaceutical Design* 20, no. 25 (2014): 4026–52. https://doi.org/10.2174/138161281 13199990617.

Lada, Akos, Meihong Wang and Tak Yan. "How does News Feed Predict what You Want to See? Personalized Ranking with Machine Learning", 2021. https://tech.fb.com /news-feed-ranking/.

Lajnef, Karima. "The Effect of Social Media Influencers' on Teenagers Behavior: An Empirical Study Using Cognitive Map Technique". *Current Psychology* 42, no. 22 (2023): 19364–77. https://doi.org/10.1007/s12144-023-04273-1.

Lakhani, Suraj and Susann Wiedlitzka. "'Press F to Pay Respects': An Empirical Exploration of the Mechanics of Gamification in Relation to the Christchurch Attack". *Terrorism and Political Violence* 35, no. 7 (2023): 1586–1603. https://doi.org/10.1080 /09546553.2022.2064746.

Lakhani, Suraj. "Video Gaming and (Violent) Extremism: An Exploration of the Current Landscape, Trends, and Threats". Luxembourg: Publication Office of the European Union, 2021. https://home-affairs.ec.europa.eu/document/download/67db2a03 -5b45-44f2-b0e9-3b0544a08dfc_en?filename=EUIF%20Technical%20Meeting %20on%20Video%20Gaming%20October%202021%20RAN%20Policy%20 Support%20paper_en.pdf.

Lam, Lawrence T. "Risk Factors of Internet Addiction and the Health Effect of Internet Addiction on Adolescents: A Systematic Review of Longitudinal and Prospective Studies". *Current Psychiatry Reports* 16, no. 11 (2014): 1–9. https://doi.org/10.1007 /S11920-014-0508-2.

Lambrecht, Anja and Catherine Tucker. "Algorithmic Bias? An Empirical Study of Apparent Gender-Based Discrimination in the Display of STEM Career Ads". *Management Science* 65, no. 7 (2019): 2966–81. https://doi.org/10.1287/MNSC.2018.3093.

Lambrecht, Anja and Catherine Tucker. "Algorithmic Bias? An Empirical Study of Apparent Gender-Based Discrimination in the Display of STEM Career Ads". *Management Science* 65, no. 7 (2019): 2966–81. https://doi.org/10.1287/MNSC.2018.3093.

Lanham, Richard A. *The Economics of Attention. Style and Substance in the Age of Information*. Chicago: The University of Chicago Press, 2006.

Larsson, Anthony and Robin Teigland. *The Digital Transformation of Labor*. Abingdon and New York: Routledge, 2020.

Lasconjarias, Guillaume Jeffrey A. Larsen. "Introduction: A New Way of Warfare". In *NATO's Response to Hybrid Threats*, edited by Lasconjarias, G., Larsen, J.A. Rome: NATO Defense College, 2015.

Lazer, David M.J., Matthew A. Baum, Yochai Benkler, Adam J. Berinsky, Kelly M. Greenhill, Filippo Menczer, Miriam J. Metzger, et al. "The Science of Fake News". *Science* 359, no. 6380 (2018): 1094–96. https://doi.org/10.1126/SCIENCE.AAO2998.

Leban, Marina. "Unethical Behaviour of Social Media Influencers: History, Practice and Future Research". In *The SAGE Handbook of Social Media Marketing*, przez Annmarie Hanlon and Tracy Tuten, 456–69. London: Sage, 2022. https://doi.org/10.4135/9781529782493.n28.

Leguina, Adrian and John Downey. "Getting Things Done: Inequalities, Internet Use and Everyday Life". *New Media & Society* 23, no. 7 (2021): 1824–49. https://doi.org/10.1177/14614448211015979.

Lehne, Stefan. "After Russia's War Against Ukraine: What Kind of World Order?", 2023. https://carnegieeurope.eu/research/2023/02/after-russias-war-against-ukraine-what-kind-of-world-order?lang=en¢er=europe.

Lenihan, Fionnbar. "Computer Addiction – A Sceptical View: Invited Commentary On: Lost Online". *Advances in Psychiatric Treatment* 13, no. 1 (2007): 31–33. https://doi.org/10.1192/APT.BP.106.003004.

Levin, Abigail. *The Cost of Free Speech*. London: Palgrave Macmillan UK, 2010. https://doi.org/10.1057/9780230293960.

Levy, Steven. "This Is Your Brain on Twitter". https://medium.com/backchannel/this-is-your-brain-on-twitter-cac0725cea2b, 2015.

Lewis, James A. "Assessing the Risks of Cyber Terrorism, Cyber War and Other Cyber Threats". Center for Strategic and International Studies, 2002.

Li, Yuchong and Qinghui Liu. "A Comprehensive Review Study of Cyber-Attacks and Cyber Security; Emerging Trends and Recent Developments". *Energy Reports* 7 (2021): 8176–86. https://doi.org/10.1016/j.egyr.2021.08.126.

Liang, Fan, Vishnupriya Das, Nadiya Kostyuk and Muzammil M. Hussain. "Constructing a Data-Driven Society: China's Social Credit System As a State Surveillance Infrastructure". *Policy & Internet* 10, no. 4 (2018): 415–53. https://doi.org/10.1002/POI3.183.

Lindstaedt, Natasha. *Human Security in Disease and Disaster*. London and New York: Routledge, 2022.

Liou, Pey-Yan, Ssu-Ching Huang and Sufen Chen. "Longitudinal Relationships between School Burnout, Compulsive Internet Use, and Academic Decrement: A Three-Wave

Cross-Lagged Study". *Computers in Human Behavior* 135 (2022): 107363. https://doi .org/10.1016/j.chb.2022.107363.

Locke, Edwin A. and Gary P. Latham. "Building a Practically Useful Theory of Goal Setting and Task Motivation: A 35-Year Odyssey". *American Psychologist* 57, no. 9 (2002): 705–17. https://doi.org/10.1037/0003-066X.57.9.705.

Loiseau, Hugo, Daniel Ventre and Hartmut Aden, eds. *Cybersecurity in Humanities and Social Sciences: A Research Methods Approach.* Hoboken, NJ: Wiley, 2020.

Lopes, Barbara and Hui Yu. "Who Do You Troll and Why: An Investigation into the Relationship between the Dark Triad Personalities and Online Trolling Behaviours towards Popular and Less Popular Facebook Profiles". *Computers in Human Behavior* 77 (2017): 69–76. https://doi.org/10.1016/j.chb.2017.08.036.

Lopez-Fernandez, Olatz and Daria J. Kuss. "Preventing Harmful Internet Use-Related Addiction Problems in Europe: A Literature Review and Policy Options". *International Journal of Environmental Research and Public Health* 17, no. 11 (2020): 3797. https://doi.org/10.3390/IJERPH17113797.

Lorenz, Taylor. "Instagram Has a Massive Harassment Problem". *The Atlantic Daily*, 15 October 2018. https://www.theatlantic.com/technology/archive/2018/10/insta gram-has-massive-harassment-problem/572890/.

Lou, Chen, Sang-Sang Tan and Xiaoyu Chen. "Investigating Consumer Engagement with Influencer- vs. Brand-Promoted Ads: The Roles of Source and Disclosure". *Journal of Interactive Advertising* 19, no. 3 (2019): 169–86. https://doi.org/10.1080 /15252019.2019.1667928.

Luhn, Alec. "MH17: Vast Majority of Russians Believe Ukraine Downed Plane, Poll Finds". *The Guardian*, 30 July 2014. https://www.theguardian.com/world/2014/jul/30 /mh17-vast-majority-russians-believe-ukraine-downed-plane-poll.

Lynn, Amber. "Kidfluencing: The Mental Impacts of Posting on Social Media can have on Children and Parents". *Research Archive of Rising Scholars*, 2023. https:// research-archive.org/index.php/rars/preprint/view/537/874.

Macdonald, Stuart, Lee Jarvis and Simon M. Lavis. "Cyberterrorism Today? Findings From a Follow-on Survey of Researchers". *Studies in Conflict & Terrorism* 45, no. 8 (2022): 727–52. https://doi.org/10.1080/1057610X.2019.1696444.

MacFarlane, S. Neil and Yuen Foong Khong. *Human Security and the UN: A Critical History.* Bloomington: Indiana University Press, 2006.

Madio, Leonardo and Martin Quinn. "Content Moderation and Advertising in Social Media Platforms. Marco Fanno Working Papers – 297". University of Padova, 2023. https://econpapers.repec.org/paper/padwpaper/0297.htm.

Maniszewska, Katarzyna. *Towards a New Definition of Terrorism. Challenges and Perspectives in a Shifting Paradigm.* Cham: Springer, 2024.

Marcellino, William, Christian Johnson, Marek N. Posario and Todd C. Helmus. *Foreign Interference in the 2020 Election. Tools for Detecting Online Election Interference.*

Santa Monica, CA: RAND Corporation, 2020. https://www.rand.org/pubs/research_reports/RRA704-02.html.

Marcus, Bernd, Franz MacHilek and Astrid Schütz. "Personality in Cyberspace: Personal Web Sites as Media for Personality Expressions and Impressions". *Journal of Personality and Social Psychology* 90, no. 6 (2006): 1014–31. https://doi.org/10.1037/0022-3514.90.6.1014.

Marcus, George E. and Michael B. MacKuen. "Anxiety, Enthusiasm, and the Vote: The Emotional Underpinnings of Learning and Involvement during Presidential Campaigns". *American Political Science Review* 87, no. 3 (1993): 672–85. https://doi.org/10.2307/2938743.

Mark, Gloria. "Worker, Interrupted: The Cost of Task Switching". Fast Company, 2008. https://www.fastcompany.com/944128/worker-interrupted-cost-task-switching.

Marsili, Marco. "Guerre à la Carte: Cyber, Information, Cognitive Warfare and the Metaverse". *Applied Cybersecurity & Internet Governance* 2, no. 1 (2023): 1–11. https://doi.org/10.60097/ACIG/162861.

Marsili, Marco. "The War on Cyberterrorism". *Democracy and Security* 15, no. 2 (2019): 172–99. https://doi.org/10.1080/17419166.2018.1496826.

Martel, Cameron, Gordon Pennycook and David G. Rand. "Reliance on Emotion Promotes Belief in Fake News". *Cognitive Research: Principles and Implications* 5, no. 1 (2020): 1–20. https://doi.org/10.1186/S41235-020-00252-3.

Martinez, Emmanuel and Lauren Kirchner. "The Secret Bias Hidden in Mortgage-Approval Algorithms". *The Markup*, 2021. https://themarkup.org/denied/2021/08/25/the-secret-bias-hidden-in-mortgage-approval-algorithms.

Marzochi, Samira Feldman and Fernando De Figueiredo Balieiro. "Muralha de Espelhos: O Narcisismo Político Nas Plataformas Digitais". *Revista Brasileira de Sociologia – RBS* 9, no. 23 (2021): 121–48. https://doi.org/10.20336/rbs.766.

Masakowski, Yvonne R. and J.M. Blatny. "Mitigating and Responding to Cognitive Warfare". NATO Science and Technical Organization, 2023.

Massumi, Brian. *Parables of the Virtual: Movement, Affect, Sensation.* Durham, NC: Duke University Press, 2002.

Masterson, Marina A. "When Play Becomes Work: Child Labor Laws in the Era of 'Kidfluencers'". *University of Pennsylvania Law Review* 169 (2018): 577–607.

Matteo, Stéphane and Cinzia Dal Zotto. "Native Advertising, or How to Stretch Editorial to Sponsored Content Within a Transmedia Branding Era". In *Handbook of Media Branding*, edited by Gabriele Siegert, Kati Förster, Sylvia M. Chan-Olmsted and Mart Ots, 169–85. Cham: Springer International Publishing, 2015. https://doi.org/10.1007/978-3-319-18236-0_12.

Mattoli, Scarlett, Melanie Shaw and Scott Burrus. "Adult Maladaptive Internet Use, Depression, and Self-Efficacy in Hong Kong". *The International Journal of Health, Wellness, and Society* 11, no. 2 (2021): 187–207. https://doi.org/10.18848/2156-8960/CGP/v11i02/187-207.

Matusitz, Jonathan. "The Role of Intercultural Communication in Cyberterrorism". *Journal of Human Behavior in the Social Environment* 24, no. 7 (2014): 775–90. https://doi.org/10.1080/10911359.2013.876375.

Matz, Sandra C., Michal Kosinski, Gideon Nave and David J. Stillwell. "Psychological Targeting as an Effective Approach to Digital Mass Persuasion". *Proceedings of the National Academy of Sciences of the United States of America* 114, no. 48 (2017): 12714–19. https://doi.org/10.1073/PNAS.1710966114.

McCaughey, M. and M. Ayers. *Cyberactivism: Online Activism in Theory and Practice.* New York and Oxon: Routledge, 2003.

McCorquodale, Sara. *Influence. How Social Media Influencers Are Shaping our Digital Future.* London and New York: Bloomsbury, 2020.

McCoy, Jennifer and Murat Somer. "Transformations Through Polarizations and Global Threats to Democracy". *The Annals of the American Academy of Political and Social Science* 681, no. 1 (2018): 8–22. https://doi.org/10.1177/0002716218818058.

McCrisken, Trevor. "Ten Years on: Obama's War on Terrorism in Rhetoric and Practice". *International Affairs* 87, no. 4 (2011): 781–801. https://doi.org/10.1111/j.1468-2346.2011.01004.x.

McGinnis, N. "'They're Just Playing': Why Child Social Media Stars Need Enhanced Coogan Protections to Save them from their Parents". *Missouri Law Review* 87, no. 1 (2022): 247–67.

McGreevy, Patrick. "LAPD Automatic License Plate Readers Pose a Massive Privacy Risk, Audit Says". *Los Angeles Times*, 13 February 2020. https://www.latimes.com/california/story/2020-02-13/privacy-risks-automatic-license-plate-readers-lapd.

McIntyre, Lee. *Post-Truth.* Cambridge, MA: The MIT Press, 2018. https://doi.org/10.7551/mitpress/11483.001.0001.

McManus, John. "Serving the Public and Serving the Market: A Conflict of Interest?" *Journal of Mass Media Ethics* 7, no. 4 (1992): 196–208. https://doi.org/10.1207/s15327728jmme0704_1.

McNamee, Roger. "I Invested Early in Google and Facebook and Regret it. I Helped Create a Monster". *Tallahassee Democrat*, 2017. https://www.tallahassee.com/story/opinion/2017/08/09/mcnamee-invested-early-google-and-facebook-and-regret-it-helped-create-monster/550111001/.

Meaker, Morgan. "Russia Blocks Facebook and Twitter in a Propaganda Standoff". Wired, 2022. https://www.wired.com/story/russia-ukraine-social-media/.

Mearsheimer, John J. *The Great Delusion: Liberal Dreams and International Realities.* New Haven and London: Yale University Press, 2018.

Mearsheimer, John J. *The Tragedy of Great Power Politics.* New York: Norton, 2001.

Mejias, Ulises A. and Nikolai E. Vokuev. "Disinformation and the Media: The Case of Russia and Ukraine". *Media, Culture & Society* 39, no. 7 (2017): 1027–42. https://doi.org/10.1177/0163443716686672.

Meta. "Hate speech. In Facebook Community Standards", 2022. https://transparency .meta.com/pl-pl/policies/community-standards/hate-speech/.

Meta. "Zasady Ochrony Prywatności", 2022. https://www.facebook.com/privacy/policy.

Meyerend, Daniel. "The Algorithm Knows I'M Black: From Users to Subjects". *Media, Culture & Society* 45, no. 3 (2023): 629–45. https://doi.org/10.1177/01634437221140539.

Mider, Daniel. "The Anatomy of Violence: A Study of the Literature". *Aggression and Violent Behavior* 18, no. 6 (2013): 702–8. https://doi.org/10.1016/J.AVB.2013.07.021.

Mider, Daniel. *Partycypacja Polityczna w Internecie. Studium Politologiczne.* Warszawa: Dom Wydawniczy Elipsa, 2008.

Mika, Bartosz. "Ekonomia Uwagi – Gospodarczy Fundament Społeczeństwa Informacyjnego Widziany Oczami Sceptyka". *Przegląd Socjologiczny* 65, no. 3 (2016): 111–29.

Miron, Marina and Rod Thornton. "The Use of Cyber Tools by the Russian Military: Lessons from the War against Ukraine and a Warning for NATO?" *Applied Cybersecurity & Internet Governance* 3, no. 1 (2024). https://doi.org/10.60097/ACIG/190142.

Misirlis, Nikolaos and Maro Vlachopoulou. "Social Media Metrics and Analytics in Marketing – S3M: A Mapping Literature Review". *International Journal of Information Management* 38, no. 1 (2018): 270–76. https://doi.org/10.1016/j.ijinfomgt.2017 .10.005.

Montag, Christian and Jon D. Elhai. "On Social Media Design, (Online-)Time Well-Spent and Addictive Behaviors in the Age of Surveillance Capitalism". *Current Addiction Reports*, 2023. https://doi.org/10.1007/s40429-023-00494-3.

Mooij, Annelieke. *Regulating the Metaverse Economy: How to Prevent Money Laundering and the Financing of Terrorism.* SpringerBriefs in Law. Cham: Springer Nature Switzerland, 2024. https://doi.org/10.1007/978-3-031-46417-1.

Morahan-Martin, Janet. "Internet Abuse: Addiction? Disorder? Symptom? Alternative Explanations?" *Social Science Computer Review* 23, no. 1 (2005): 39–48. https://doi .org/10.1177/0894439304271533.

Morahan-Martin, Janet. "Internet Abuse: Emerging Trends and Lingering Questions". In *Psychological Aspects of Cyberspace,* edited by Azy Barak, 32–69. Cambridge University Press, 2008. https://doi.org/10.1017/CBO9780511813740.004.

Moy, Wesley R. and Kacper Gradon. *COVID-19 Effects of Russian Disinformation Campaigns.* Homeland Security Affairs Journal, Special COVID-19 Issue, 2020. https:// www.hsaj.org/resources/uploads/2020/12/hsaj_Covid192020_COVID19EffectsRus sianDisinformationCampaigns.pdf.

Mueller, Milton. *Will the Internet Fragment? Sovereignty, Globalization, and Cyberspace.* Cambridge: Polity Press, 2017.

Münkler, Herfried. *Die Neuen Kriege. 6. Aufl.* Reinbek bei Hamburg: Rowohlt, 2003.

Nader, Karim. "Dating through the Filters". *Social Philosophy and Policy* 37, no. 2 (2020): 237–48. https://doi.org/10.1017/S0265052521000133.

Nai, Alessandro, Yves Schemeil and Jean Louis Marie. "Anxiety, Sophistication, and Resistance to Persuasion: Evidence from a Quasi-Experimental Survey on Global Climate Change". *Political Psychology* 38, no. 1 (2017): 137–56. https://doi.org/10.1111/POPS.12331.

NATO STO. "Military Aspects of Countering Hybrid Warfare: Experiences, Lessons, Best Practices. Volume 2: Information and Influence". NATO STO, 2024.

NATO. "BI-SC Input for a New NATO Capstone Concept for The Military Contribution to Countering Hybrid Threats". Brussels: NATO, 2010.

Navarro, Jessica L. and Jonathan R.H. Tudge. "Technologizing Bronfenbrenner: Neo-ecological theory". *Current Psychology* 1 (2022): 1–17. https://doi.org/10.1007/S12144-022-02738-3.

Nawaz, Muhammad Asim, Zakir Shah, Ali Nawaz, Fahad Asmi, Zameer Hassan and Junaid Raza. "Overload and Exhaustion: Classifying SNS Discontinuance Intentions". http://www.editorialmanager.com/cogentpsychology 5, no. 1 (2018): 1–18. https://doi.org/10.1080/23311908.2018.1515584.

Neuman, W. Russell, Lauren Guggenheim, S. Mo Jang and Soo Young Bae. "The Dynamics of Public Attention: Agenda-Setting Theory Meets Big Data". *Journal of Communication* 64, no. 2 (2014): 193–214. https://doi.org/10.1111/JCOM.12088.

Newman, Edward. "Critical Human Security Studies". *Review of International Studies* 36, no. 1 (2010): 77–94. https://doi.org/10.1017/S0260210509990519.

Newman, Edward. "The 'New Wars' Debate: A Historical Perspective Is Needed". *Security Dialogue* 35, no. 2 (2004): 173–89. https://doi.org/10.1177/0967010604044975.

Newman, Nic, Richard Fletcher, Antonis Kalogeropoulos, David A.L. Levy and Rasmus Kleis Nielsen. *Reuters Institute Digital News Report 2017*. Oxford: Reuters Institute for the Study of Journalism, 2017.

Nichols, Tom. *The Death of Expertise. The Campaign against Established Knowledge and Why It Matters*. Oxford: Oxford University Press, 2017.

Nilsson, Fredrik. *Intelligent Network Video: Understanding Modern Video Surveillance Systems*. Logan, UT: Jenson Books, 2016.

Nisbet, Erik C. and Olga Kamenchuk. "The Psychology of State-Sponsored Disinformation Campaigns and Implications for Public Diplomacy". *The Hague Journal of Diplomacy* 14, no. 1–2 (2019): 65–82. https://doi.org/10.1163/1871191X-11411019.

Noam, Eli. "Inequality and the Digital Economy". In *Digitized Labor. The Impact of the Internet on Employment*, 117–40. Cham: Palgrave Macmillan, 2018. doi: 10.1007/978-3-319-78420-5.

Noble, Safiya Umoja. *Algorithms of Oppression: How Search Engines Reinforce Racism*. New York: New York University Press, 2018.

Nobles, Calvin, Sharon L. Burton and Darrell Norman Burrell. "Cybercrime as a Sustained Business" In *Advances in Information Security, Privacy, and Ethics*, edited by Festus Fatai Adedoyin and Bryan Christiansen, 98–120. IGI Global, 2023. https://doi.org/10.4018/978-1-6684-7207-1.ch005.

Norris, Pippa. "Cancel Culture: Myth or Reality?" *Political Studies* 71, no. 1 (2023): 145–74. https://doi.org/10.1177/00323217211037023.

Nunes, Ashley. "Automation Doesn't Just Create or Destroy Jobs – It Transforms Them". *Harvard Business Review*, 2021. https://hbr.org/2021/11/automation-doesnt-just-create-or-destroy-jobs-it-transforms-them.

Nutt, David J., Anne Lingford-Hughes, David Erritzoe and Paul R.A. Stokes. "The Dopamine Theory of Addiction: 40 Years of Highs and Lows". *Nature Reviews Neuroscience* 16, no. 5 (2015): 305–12. https://doi.org/10.1038/nrn3939.

Nye, Joseph S. *Understanding International Conflicts: An Introduction to Theory and History.* New York: Harper Collins, 1993.

O'Boyle, Neil. *Communication Theory for Humans. Communicators in a Mediated World.* Cham: Palgrave Macmillan, 2022.

O'Neil, Cathy. *Weapons of Math Destruction.* New York: Crown, 2016.

OECD. "AI Principles Overview", 2019. https://oecd.ai/en/ai-principles.

OECD. *OECD Employment Outlook 2023: Artificial Intelligence and the Labour Market.* OECD. Paris: OECD, 2023. https://doi.org/10.1787/08785bba-en.

Ohanian, Roobina. "Construction and Validation of a Scale to Measure Celebrity Endorsers' Perceived Expertise, Trustworthiness, and Attractiveness". *Journal of Advertising* 19, no. 3 (1990): 39–52.

Olatz, Lopez-Fernandez. "Cross-Cultural Research on Internet Addiction: A Systematic Review". *International Archives of Addiction Research and Medicine* 1, no. 2 (2015). https://doi.org/10.23937/2474-3631/1510011.

Ollier-Malaterre, Ariane. *Living with Digital Surveillance in China: Citizens' Narratives on Technology, Privacy, and Governance.* London: Routledge, 2023. https://doi.org/10.4324/9781003403876.

Olweus, Dan. "School Bullying: Development and Some Important Challenges". *Annual Review of Clinical Psychology* 9, no. 1 (2013): 751–80. https://doi.org/10.1146/annurev-clinpsy-050212-185516.

Özer, Duygu, Özlem Şahin Altun and Gülçin Avşar. "Investigation of the Relationship between Internet Addiction, Communication Skills and Difficulties in Emotion Regulation in Nursing Students". *Archives of Psychiatric Nursing* 42 (2023): 18–24. https://doi.org/10.1016/J.APNU.2022.12.004.

Palau-Sampio, Dolors. "Pseudo-Media Disinformation Patterns: Polarised Discourse, Clickbait and Twisted Journalistic Mimicry". *Journalism Practice* 17, no. 10 (2023): 2140–58. https://doi.org/10.1080/17512786.2022.2126992.

Panova, Tayana and Xavier Carbonell. "Is Smartphone Addiction Really an Addiction?" *Journal of Behavioral Addictions* 7, no. 2 (2018): 252–59. https://doi.org/10.1556/2006.7.2018.49.

Pappalardo, D. "'Win the War before the War?': A French Perspective on Cognitive Warfare". War on the Rocks, 2022. https://warontherocks.com/2022/08/win-the-war-before-the-war-a-french-perspective-on-cognitive-warfare/.

Paquet-Clouston, Masarah and Sebastián García. "On the Motivations and Challenges of Affiliates Involved in Cybercrime". *Trends in Organized Crime*, 2022. https://doi.org/10.1007/s12117-022-09474-x.

Pariser, Eli. *The Filter Bubble. How the New Personalized Web is Changing What We Read and How We Think*. London: Penguin Books, 2011.

Park, Sejung. "How Celebrities' Green Messages on Twitter Influence Public Attitudes and Behavioral Intentions to Mitigate Climate Change". *Sustainability* 12, no. 19 (2020): 7948. https://doi.org/10.3390/su12197948.

Parket, Landelijk. "Update in Criminal Investigation MH17 Disaster", 2018.

Patel, Molly Gloria and Anabel Quan-Haase. "The Social-Ecological Model of Cyberbullying: Digital Media as a Predominant Ecology in the Everyday Lives of Youth". *New Media and Society* 26, no. 9 (2022). https://doi.org/10.1177/14614448221136508.

Pearson, Elizabeth. "Online as the New Frontline: Affect, Gender, and ISIS-Take-Down on Social Media". *Studies in Conflict & Terrorism* 41, no. 11 (2018): 850–74. https://doi.org/10.1080/1057610X.2017.1352280.

Pennycook, Gordon and David G. Rand. "Lazy, not Biased: Susceptibility to Partisan Fake News is Better Explained by Lack of Reasoning than by Motivated Reasoning". *Cognition* 188 (2019): 39–50. https://doi.org/10.1016/J.COGNITION.2018.06.011.

Pennycook, Gordon and David G. Rand. "The Psychology of Fake News". *Trends in Cognitive Sciences* 25, no. 5 (2021): 388–402. https://doi.org/10.1016/J.TICS.2021.02.007.

Pew Research Center. "Social Media and News Fact Sheet", 2023. https://www.pewresearch.org/journalism/fact-sheet/social-media-and-news-fact-sheet/.

Pham, Michel Tuan and Leonard Lee. "Introduction to Special Issue: Consumer Emotions in the Marketplace". *Journal of the Association for Consumer Research* 4, no. 2 (2019): 98–101. https://doi.org/10.1086/702851.

Pies, Ronald. "Should DSM-V Designate 'Internet Addiction' a Mental Disorder?" *Psychiatry (Edgmont)* 6, no. 2 (2009): 31.

Pilipets, Elena and Susanna Paasonen. "Nipples, Memes, and Algorithmic Failure: NSFW Critique of Tumblr Censorship". *New Media & Society* 24, no. 6 (2022): 1459–80. https://doi.org/10.1177/1461444820979280.

Pisano, Paola, Luca Macis and Marco Tagliapietra. "Insights from Practice: Applying the Integrated Gradient methodology to help explain AI predictions", 2024. https://www.unesco.org/en/articles/insights-practice-applying-integrated-gradient-methodology-help-explain-ai-predictions.

Polak, Sara and Daniel Trottier. "Introducing Online Vitriol". In *Violence and Trolling on Social Media. History, Affect, and Effects on Online Vitriol*, 9–24. Amsterdam: Amsterdam University Press, 2020.

Postman, Andrew. "My Dad Predicted Trump in 1985 – It's Not Orwell, He Warned, It's Brave New World". *The Guardian*, 2017. https://www.theguardian.com/media/2017/feb/02/amusing-ourselves-to-death-neil-postman-trump-orwell-huxley.

Postman, Neil. *Amusing Ourselves to Death*. New York: Viking Penguin, 1987.

Postman, Neil. "Informing Ourselves to Death". In *The Nature of Technology: Implications for Learning and Teaching*, edited by Michael P. Clough, Joanne K. Olson and Dale S. Niederhauser. Leiden, Boston: Brill, 2013.

Primack, Brian A., Ariel Shensa, César G. Escobar-Viera, Erica L. Barrett, Jaime E. Sidani, Jason B. Colditz and A. Everette James. "Use of Multiple Social Media Platforms and Symptoms of Depression and Anxiety: A Nationally-Representative Study among U.S. Young Adults". *Computers in Human Behavior* 69 (2017): 1–9. https://doi.org/10.1016/J.CHB.2016.11.013.

Public Dialog. "Raport: Fake News z Perspektywy Polskich Dziennikarzy", 2017. http://publicdialog.home.pl/www_logotomia/wp-content/uploads/2018/07/Raport_Badanie-fake-news-23-05-2017.pdf.

Pyżalski, Jacek. *Agresja Elektroniczna wśród Dzieci i Młodzieży*. Sopot: GWP, 2012.

Rains, Stephen A. and Robert S. Tokunaga. "The Role of Emotion in Maladaptive Internet Use: Internet Addiction, Problematic Internet Use, and Deficient Self-Regulation". In *Emotions in the Digital World*, edited by Robin L. Nabi and Jessica Gall Myrick, 174–92. New York: Oxford University Press, 2023. https://doi.org/10.1093/oso/9780197520536.003.0010.

Raj, Kavya, Rebecca Segrave, Jeggan Tiego, Antonio Verdéjo-Garcia and Murat Yücel. "Problematic Use of the Internet among Australian University Students: Prevalence and Profile". *Computers in Human Behavior Reports* 8 (2022): 100243. https://doi.org/10.1016/J.CHBR.2022.100243.

Rathus, Spencer. *Psychologia Współczesna*. Gdańsk: GWP, 2004.

Raun, Tobias. "Capitalizing Intimacy: New Subcultural Forms of Micro-Celebrity Strategies and Affective Labour on YouTube". *Convergence: The International Journal of Research into New Media Technologies* 24, no. 1 (2018): 99–113. https://doi.org/10.1177/1354856517736983.

Reichelmann, Ashley, James Hawdon, Matt Costello, John Ryan, Catherine Blaya, Vicente Llorent, Atte Oksanen, Pekka Räsänen and Izabela Zych. "Hate Knows no Boundaries: Online Hate in Six Nations". *Deviant Behavior* 42, no. 9 (2020): 1100–1111. https://doi.org/10.1080/01639625.2020.1722337.

Rękawek, Kacper. *Foreign Fighters in Ukraine: The Brown-Red Cocktail*. Routledge Studies in Fascism and the Far Right. London; New York: Routledge, 2023.

Reporters Without Borders. "Russia", 2024. https://rsf.org/en/country/russia.

Reuters. "Russian Competition Watchdog Opens Case against Google over YouTube Curbs". *reuters.com*, 2021. https://www.reuters.com/technology/russian-competition-watchdog-opens-case-against-google-over-youtube-curbs-2021-04-19/.

Richey, Mason. "Contemporary Russian Revisionism: Understanding the Kremlin's Hybrid Warfare and the Strategic and Tactical Deployment of Disinformation". *Asia Europe Journal* 16, no. 1 (2018): 101–13. https://doi.org/10.1007/s10308-017-0482-5.

Rid, Thomas. *Active Measures. The Secret History of Disinformation and Political Warfare*. London: Profile Books Ltd., 2020.

Riisalo, Tiit. "Artificial Intelligence Is Part of the Next Chapter in Estonia's Digital Story", 2023. https://tinyurl.com/25zftmp7.

Ringrose, Katelyn and Divya Ramjee. "Watch Where You Walk: Law Enforcement Surveillance and Protester Privacy". *Californa Law Review Online* 11 (2020): 349–66. https://doi.org/10.15779/Z38G44HR3X.

Rizvanović, Belma, Aneesh Zutshi, Antonio Grilo and Tahereh Nodehi. "Linking the Potentials of Extended Digital Marketing Impact and Start-up Growth: Developing a Macro-Dynamic Framework of Start-up Growth Drivers Supported by Digital Marketing". *Technological Forecasting and Social Change* 186 (2023): 122128. https://doi.org/10.1016/j.techfore.2022.122128.

Rojek, Chris. *Celebrity*. London: Reaktion, 2001.

Romaniuk, Viktoriia. "Disinformation Narratives of Hate as a Tool of Escalating Russia's War Against Ukraine (based on Stopfake Fact-Checking Project Materials)". *Sojateadlane. Estonian Journal of Military Studies* 23, no. 2 (2023): 143–57.

Rosenberger, Laura. "Disinformation Disorientation". *Journal of Democracy* 31, no. 1 (2020): 203–7.

Rosenquist, Niels J., Fiona M. Scott Morton and Samuel Weinstein. "Addictive Technology and Its Implications for Antitrust Enforcement". *SSRN Electronic Journal*, 2021. https://doi.org/10.2139/ssrn.3787822.

Rosenzweig, Paul. "Cybersecurity, the Public/Private 'Partnership,' and Public Goods". SSRN Scholarly Paper. Rochester, NY, 2011. https://papers.ssrn.com/abstract=1923869.

Rosińska, Klaudia. *Fake News. Geneza, Istota, Przeciwdziałanie*. Warsaw: PWN, 2021.

Roundtable Report. "Hate Speech. The Role of New Media in the Prevention of Mass Atrocities", 2014.

Roy, Senjooti and Liat Ayalon. "Age and Gender Stereotypes Reflected in Google's 'Autocomplete' Function: The Portrayal and Possible Spread of Societal Stereotypes". *The Gerontologist* 60, no. 6 (2020): 1020–28. https://doi.org/10.1093/GERONT/GNZ172.

Ruckenstein, Minna and Julia Granroth. "Algorithms, Advertising and the Intimacy of Surveillance". *Journal of Cultural Economy* 13, no. 1 (2020): 12–24. https://doi.org/10.1080/17530350.2019.1574866.

Rudner, Martin. "Electronic Jihad: The Internet as Al Qaeda's Catalyst for Global Terror". *Studies in Conflict & Terrorism* 40, no. 1 (2017): 10–23. https://doi.org/10.1080/1057610X.2016.1157403.

Ryan, Tracii, Andrea Chester, John Reece and Sophia Xenos. "The Uses and Abuses of Facebook: A Review of Facebook Addiction". *Journal of Behavioral Addictions* 3, no. 3 (2014): 133–48. https://doi.org/10.1556/JBA.3.2014.016.

Sadeghi, Saeid, Hikaru Takeuchi, Bita Shalani, Yasuyuki Taki, Rui Nouchi, Ryoichi Yokoyama, Yuka Kotozaki, et al. "Brain Structures and Activity during a Working Memory Task Associated with Internet Addiction Tendency in Young Adults: A Large Sample Study". *PLOS ONE* 16, no. 11 (2021): e0259259. https://doi.org/10.1371/JOURNAL.PONE.0259259.

Saha, Raiswa, Sakshi Ahlawat, Umair Akram, Uttara Jangbahadur, Amol S. Dhaigude, Pooja Sharma and Sarika Kumar. "Online Abuse: A Systematic Literature Review and Future Research Agenda". *International Journal of Conflict Management*, 2024. https://doi.org/10.1108/IJCMA-09-2023-0188.

Salahdine, Fatima and Naima Kaabouch. "Social Engineering Attacks: A Survey". *Future Internet* 11, no. 4 (2019): 89. https://doi.org/10.3390/fi11040089.

Saldanha, Natalya, Rajendra Mulye and Kaleel Rahman. "Cancel Culture and the Consumer: A Strategic Marketing Perspective". *Journal of Strategic Marketing* 31, no. 5 (2023): 1071–86. https://doi.org/10.1080/0965254X.2022.2040577.

Salminen, Mirva, Gerald Zojer and Kamrul Hossain. "Comprehensive Cybersecurity and Human Rights in the Digitalising European High North". In *Digitalisation and Human Security*, edited by Mirva Salminen, Gerald Zojer and Kamrul Hossain, 21–55. New Security Challenges. Cham: Springer International Publishing, 2020. https://doi.org/10.1007/978-3-030-48070-7_2.

Samuelson, Paul A. "The Pure Theory of Public Expenditure". *The Review of Economics and Statistics* 36, no. 4 (1954): 387. https://doi.org/10.2307/1925895.

Santos, Fernando P., Yphtach Lelkes and Simon A. Levin. "Link Recommendation Algorithms and Dynamics of Polarization in Online Social Networks". *Proceedings of the National Academy of Sciences* 118, no. 50 (2021): e2102141118. https://doi.org/10.1073/pnas.2102141118.

Sanz Marcos, Paloma. *Soy Marca, Quiero Trabajar con Influencers*. Barcelona: Profit, 2017.

Sariyska, Rayna, Martin Reuter, Katharina Bey, Peng Sha, Mei Li, Ya Fei Chen, Wei Yin Liu, et al. "Self-Esteem, Personality and Internet Addiction: A Cross-Cultural Comparison Study". *Personality and Individual Differences* 61–62 (2014): 28–33. https://doi.org/10.1016/J.PAID.2014.01.001.

Savimäki, Tuukka, Markus Kaakinen, Pekka Räsänen and Atte Oksanen. "Disquieted by Online Hate: Negative Experiences of Finnish Adolescents and Young Adults". *European Journal on Criminal Policy and Research* 26, no. 1 (2020): 23–37. https://doi.org/10.1007/S10610-018-9393-2.

Savolainen, Laura. "The Shadow Banning Controversy: Perceived Governance and Algorithmic Folklore". *Media, Culture & Society* 44, no. 6 (2022): 1091–1109. https://doi.org/10.1177/01634437221077174.

Scarpi, Daniele, Gabriele Pizzi and Shashi Matta. "Digital Technologies and Privacy: State of the Art and Research Directions". *Psychology & Marketing* 39, no. 9 (2022): 1687–97. https://doi.org/10.1002/mar.21692.

Schils, Nele and Lieven Pauwels. "Explaining Violent Extremism for Subgroups by Gender and Immigrant Background, Using SAT as a Framework". *Journal of Strategic Security* 7, no. 3 (2014): 3. http://dx.doi.org/10.5038/1944-0472.7.3.2.

Schlegel, Linda and Rachel Kowert, eds. *Gaming and Extremism. The Radicalization of Digital Playgrounds*. London and New York: Routledge, 2024.

Schlogl, Lukas. *Digital Activism and the Global Middle Class: Generation Hashtag*. New York and Oxon: Routledge, 2022.

Schmuck, Desirée, Kathrin Karsay, Jörg Matthes and Anja Stevic. "'Looking Up and Feeling Down'. The Influence of Mobile Social Networking Site Use on Upward Social Comparison, Self-Esteem, and Well-Being of Adult Smartphone Users". *Telematics and Informatics* 42 (2019): 101240. https://doi.org/10.1016/j.tele.2019.101240.

Schoenewolf, Gerald. "Emotional Contagion: Behavioral Induction in Individuals and Groups". *Modern Psychoanalysis* 15, no. 1 (1990): 49–61.

Schreiber, Hope. "Couple Lost Custody of 2 Children over Prank Videos, Now They're Back on YouTube under a New Name". Yahoo! Life, 2018. https://tinyurl.com/bdem4k5f.

Seder, J. Patrick and Shigehiro Oishi. "Intensity of Smiling in Facebook Photos Predicts Future Life Satisfaction". *Social Psychological and Personality Science* 3, no. 4 (2012): 407–13. https://doi.org/10.1177/1948550611424968.

Segalin, Crisitina, Alessandro Perina, Marco Cristani and Alessandro Vinciarelli. "The Pictures We Like Are our Image: Continuous Mapping of Favorite Pictures into Self-Assessed and Attributed Personality Traits". *IEEE Transactions on Affective Computing* 8, no. 2 (2017): 268–85. https://doi.org/10.1109/TAFFC.2016.2516994.

Sela, Yaron, Merav Zach, Yair Amichay-Hamburger, Moshe Mishali and Haim Omer. "Family Environment and Problematic Internet Use among Adolescents: The Mediating Roles of Depression and Fear of Missing Out". *Computers in Human Behavior* 106 (2020): 106226. https://doi.org/10.1016/j.chb.2019.106226.

Sellars, Andrew. "Defining Hate Speech". *SSRN Electronic Journal*, 2016. https://doi.org/10.2139/ssrn.2882244.

Seppälä, Päivi and Magdalena Małecka. "AI and Discriminative Decisions in Recruitment: Challenging the Core Assumptions". *Big Data & Society* 11, no. 1 (2024): 20539517241235872. https://doi.org/10.1177/20539517241235872.

Shahbaz, Funk, Vesteinsson Slipowitz, Grothe Baker and Weal Vepa. "Freedom on the Net 2021". Freedom House, 2021. freedomonthenet.org.

Shandler, Ryan, Michael L. Gross, Sophia Backhaus and Daphna Canetti. "Cyber Terrorism and Public Support for Retaliation – A Multi-Country Survey Experiment". *British Journal of Political Science* 52, no. 2 (2022): 850–68. https://doi.org/10.1017/S0007123420000812.

Sharma, Karishma, Yizhou Zhang and Yan Liu. "COVID-19 Vaccine Misinformation Campaigns and Social Media Narratives". *Proceedings of the International AAAI*

Conference on Web and Social Media 16 (2022): 920–31. https://doi.org/10.1609/icwsm.v16i1.19346.

Shehata, Adam and Jesper Strömbäck. "Learning Political News from Social Media: Network Media Logic and Current Affairs News Learning in a High-Choice Media Environment". *Communication Research* 48, no. 1 (2018): 125–47. https://doi.org/10.1177/0093650217749354.

Shin, Donghee. "Embodying Algorithms, Enactive Artificial Intelligence and the Extended Cognition: You Can See as Much as You Know about Algorithm": *Journal of Information Science*, 2021. https://doi.org/10.1177/0165551520985495.

Shoenberger, Heather and Edson Tandoc. "Updated Statuses: Understanding Facebook Use through Explicit and Implicit Measures of Attitudes and Motivations". *Online Journal of Communication and Media Technologies* 4, no. 1 (2014): 217–44. https://doi.org/10.29333/OJCMT/2462.

Sikkut, Siim, Ott Velsberg and Kristo Vaher. "#KrattAI: The Next Stage of Digital Public Serviced in #eEstonia", 2020. https://e-estonia.com/wp-content/uploads/2020-april-facts-ai-strategy.pdf.

Simon, Herbert A. "Designing Organizations for an Information-Rich World". In *Computers, Communications, and the Public Interest*, edited by Martin Greenberger, 37–72. Baltimore, MD: The Johns Hopkins Press, 1971.

Simon, Judith, Gernot Rieder and Jason Branford. "The Philosophy and Ethics of AI: Conceptual, Empirical and Technological Investigations into Values: CEPE/IACAP 2021: Introduction to Topical Collection". *Digital Society* 3, no. 1 (2024): 10, s44206-024-00094-2. https://doi.org/10.1007/s44206-024-00094-2.

Simons, Greg, Yuriy Danyk and Tamara Maliarchuk. "Hybrid War and Cyber-Attacks: Creating Legal and Operational Dilemmas". *Global Change, Peace & Security* 32, no. 3 (2020): 337–42. https://doi.org/10.1080/14781158.2020.1732899.

Simsek, Eylem, Turkish Air Forces and Jale Balaban Sali. "The Role of Internet Addiction and Social Media Membership on University Students' Psychological Capital". *Contemporary Educational Technology* 5, no. 3 (2014): 239–56.

Sinkkonen, Hanna Maija, Helena Puhakka and Matti Meriläinen. "Internet Use and Addiction among Finnish Adolescents (15–19 Years)". *Journal of Adolescence* 37, no. 2 (2014): 123–31. https://doi.org/10.1016/J.ADOLESCENCE.2013.11.008.

Smith, Marcus and Seumas Miller. "The Ethical Application of Biometric Facial Recognition Technology". *AI & Society* 37, no. 1 (2022): 167–75. https://doi.org/10.1007/s00146-021-01199-9.

Smythe, Dallas W. "Communications: Blindspot of Western Marxism". *CTheory* 1, no. 3 (1977): 1–27.

Smythe, Dallas W. "On the Audience Commodity and its Work". In *Media and Cultural Studies: Keyworks*, 230–55. Malden, MA: Blackwell Publishing, 2001.

Snowden, Edward. *Permanent Record*. New York: Picador, 2020.

Snyder, Peter, Periwinkle Doerfler, Chris Kanich and Damon McCoy. "Fifteen Minutes of Unwanted Fame: Detecting and Characterizing Doxing". In *Proceedings of the 2017 Internet Measurement Conference*, 432–44. London: ACM, 2017. https://doi.org/10.1145/3131365.3131385.

Sokolova, Karina and Hajer Kefi. "Instagram and YouTube Bloggers Promote It, Why Should I Buy? How Credibility and Parasocial Interaction Influence Purchase Intentions". *Journal of Retailing and Consumer Services* 53 (2020): 101742. https://doi.org/10.1016/j.jretconser.2019.01.011.

Solos, Wein K. and Joel Leonard. "On the Impact of Artificial Intelligence on Economy". *Science Insights* 41, no. 1 (2022): 551–60. https://doi.org/10.15354/si.22.re066.

"Sonicwall Cyber Threat Report: Charting Cybercrime's Shifting Frontlines". Sonicwall, 2023. https://www.sonicwall.com/2023-cyber-threat-report/.

Sorial, Sarah. "The Legitimacy of Pseudo-Expert Discourse in the Public Sphere". *Metaphilosophy* 48, no. 3 (2017): 304–24. https://doi.org/10.1111/META.12233.

Spears, Russell. "Deindividuation". In *The Oxford Handbook of Social Influence*, 279–97. Oxford: Oxford University Press, 2017.

Spencer, Scott. "Upcoming Update to Housing, Employment, and Credit Advertising Policies", 2020. https://blog.google/technology/ads/upcoming-update-housing-employment-and-credit-advertising-policies/.

Spitzer, Elizabeth G., Eric S. Crosby and Tracy K. Witte. "Looking through a Filtered Lens: Negative Social Comparison on Social Media and Suicidal Ideation among Young Adults." *Psychology of Popular Media* 12, no. 1 (2023): 69–76. https://doi.org/10.1037/ppm0000380.

Staciwa, Katarzyna "Wykorzystanie Seksualne Dzieci w Cyberprzestrzeni: Analiza Akt Postępowań Karnych ze Szczególnym Uwzględnieniem Roli Biegłych Powołanych w tych Postępowaniach". Warsaw: NASK Państwowy Instytut Badawczy, 2023.

Stevens, Tim. *Cyber Security and the Politics of Time*. Cambridge: Cambridge University Press, 2015.

Stiff, Chris and Meike Reeves. "Careful When You Click? How the Dark Triad of Personality Can Influence the Likelihood of Online Crime Victimization". *The Journal of Psychology* 158, no. 3 (2024): 238–56. https://doi.org/10.1080/00223980.2023.2286451.

Stoilova, Mariya, Sonia Livingstone and Daniel Kardefelt-Winther. "Global Kids Online: Researching Children's Rights Globally in the Digital Age". *Global Studies of Childhood* 6, no. 4 (2016): 455–66. https://doi.org/10.1177/2043610616676035.

Stroppa, Andrea, Davide Gatto, Lev Pasha and Bernardo Parrella. "Instagram and Counterfeiting in 2019: New Features, Old Problems", 2019. https://ghostdata.io/report/Instagram_Counterfeiting_GD.pdf.

Stump, Jacob L. and Priya Dixit. *Critical Terrorism Studies: An Introduction to Research Methods*. London; New York, NY: Routledge, 2013.

Su, Wenliang, Xiaoli Han, Cheng Jin, Yan Yan and Marc N. Potenza. "Are Males More Likely to Be Addicted to the Internet Than Females? A Meta-Analysis Involving 34 Global Jurisdictions". *Computers in Human Behavior* 99 (2019): 86–100. https://doi.org/10.1016/J.CHB.2019.04.021.

Subramanian, Samanth. "Inside the Macedonian Fake-News Complex", 2017. https://www.wired.com/2017/02/veles-macedonia-fake-news/%oA.

Suffoletto, Brian, Jeffrey Kristan, Tammy Chung, Kwonho Jeong, Anthony Fabio, Peter Monti and Duncan B. Clark. "An Interactive Text Message Intervention to Reduce Binge Drinking in Young Adults: A Randomized Controlled Trial with 9-Month Outcomes". Edited by Bernard Le Foll. *PLOS ONE* 10, no. 11 (2015): e0142877. https://doi.org/10.1371/journal.pone.0142877.

Sühr, Tom, Sophie Hilgard and Himabindu Lakkaraju. "Does Fair Ranking Improve Minority Outcomes? Understanding the Interplay of Human and Algorithmic Biases in Online Hiring". In *Proceedings of the 2021 AAAI/ACM Conference on AI, Ethics and Society*, 989–99. Virtual Event USA: ACM, 2021. https://doi.org/10.1145/3461702.3462602.

Sun, Yanshu and Jeffrey S. Wilkinson. "Parenting Style, Personality Traits, and Interpersonal Relationships: A Model of Prediction of Internet Addiction". *International Journal of Communication* 14 (2020): 23.

Swami, Viren, Martin Voracek, Stefan Stieger, Ulrich S. Tran and Adrian Furnham. "Analytic Thinking Reduces Belief in Conspiracy Theories". *Cognition* 133, no. 3 (2014): 572–85. https://doi.org/10.1016/J.COGNITION.2014.08.006.

Swart, Joëlle. "Experiencing Algorithms: How Young People Understand, Feel about, and Engage with Algorithmic News Selection on Social Media". *Social Media + Society* 7, no. 2 (2021): 1–11. https://doi.org/10.1177/20563051211008828.

Sweeney, Latanya. "Discrimination in Online Ad Delivery". *Communications of the ACM* 56, no. 5 (2013): 44–54. https://doi.org/10.48550/arxiv.1301.6822.

Szpunar, Magdalena. *Kultura Algorytmów*. Kraków: Wydawnictwo Uniwersytetu Jagiellońskiego, 2019.

Szpyra, Ryszard. "Russian Information Offensive in the International Relations". *Security and Defence Quarterly* 30, no. 3 (2020): 31–48. https://doi.org/10.35467/SDQ/124436.

Taddeo, Mariarosaria. "Is Cybersecurity a Public Good?" *Minds and Machines* 29, no. 3 (2019): 349–54. https://doi.org/10.1007/s11023-019-09507-5.

Tajfel, Henri and John Turner. "An Integrative Theory of Intergroup Conflict". In *The Social Psychology of Intergroup Relations*, edited by William G. Austing and Stephen Worchel, 33–47. Pacific Grove, CA: Brooks/Cole, 1979.

Takeuchi, Hikaru, Yasuyuki Taki, Kohei Asano, Michiko Asano, Yuko Sassa, Susumu Yokota, Yuka Kotozaki, Rui Nouchi and Ryuta Kawashima. "Impact of Frequency of Internet Use on Development of Brain Structures and Verbal Intelligence:

Longitudinal Analyses". *Human Brain Mapping* 39, no. 11 (2018): 4471–79. https://doi.org/10.1002/HBM.24286.

Talis, Geoffrey. "Internet Addiction". In *Substance and Non-Substance Related Addictions*, edited by Evaristo Akerele, 99–107. Cham: Springer International Publishing, 2022. https://doi.org/10.1007/978-3-030-84834-7_7.

Tao, Ran, Xiuqin Huang, Jinan Wang, Huimin Zhang, Ying Zhang and Mengchen Li. "Proposed Diagnostic Criteria for Internet Addiction". *Addiction* 105, no. 3 (2010): 556–64. https://doi.org/10.1111/j.1360-0443.2009.02828.x.

Taori, Rohan and Tatsunori B. Hashimoto. *Data Feedback Loops: Model-driven Amplification of Dataset Biases.* In Proceedings of the 40th International Conference on Machine Learning, 2023. https://proceedings.mlr.press/v202/taori23a.html.

Teppers, Eveline, Koen Luyckx, Theo A. Klimstra and Luc Goossens. "Loneliness and Facebook Motives in Adolescence: a Longitudinal Inquiry into Directionality of Effect". *Journal of Adolescence* 37, no. 5 (2014): 691–99. https://doi.org/10.1016/J.ADOLESCENCE.2013.11.003.

"Terrorist on Telegram". The Counter Extremism Project, 2017. https://www.counterextremism.com/terrorists-on-telegram.

Thaler, Richard H. and Cass R. Sunstein. *Nudge.* London: Penguin Books, 2008.

Thomas, Timothy "Russia's Reflexive Control Theory and the Military". *Journal of Slavic Military Studies* 17 (2004): 237–56. https://doi.org/10.1080/13518040490450529.

Thorson, Kjerstin, Kelley Cotter, Mel Medeiros and Chankyung Pak. "Algorithmic Inference, Political Interest, and Exposure to News and Politics on Facebook". *Information, Communication & Society* 24, no. 2 (2021): 183–200. https://doi.org/10.1080/1369118X.2019.1642934.

TMZ. "Kanye West Stirs up TMZ Newsroom over Trump, Slavery, Free Thought", 2018. https://www.tmz.com/2018/05/01/kanye-west-tmz-live-slavery-trump/.

Toffler, Alvin. *Future Shock.* London: Bodley Head, 1970.

Tokunaga, Robert S. "Following You Home from School: A Critical Review and Synthesis of Research on Cyberbullying Victimization". *Computers in Human Behavior* 26, no. 3 (2010): 277–87.

Tossell, Chad, Philip Kortum, Clayton Shepard, Ahmad Rahmati and Lin Zhong. "Exploring Smartphone Addiction: Insights from Long-Term Telemetric Behavioral Measures". *International Journal of Interactive Mobile Technologies* 9, no. 2 (2015): 37–43. https://doi.org/10.3991/IJIM.V9I2.4300.

Tsimtsiou, Zoi, Anna Bettina Haidich, Dimitris Spachos, Stamatia Kokkali, Panagiotis Bamidis, Theodoros Dardavesis and Malamatenia Arvanitidou. "Internet Addiction in Greek Medical Students: an Online Survey". *Academic Psychiatry* 39, no. 3 (2015): 300–304. https://doi.org/10.1007/S40596-014-0273-X.

Tumber, H. and Silvio Waisbord. "Media, Disinformation, and Populism. Problems and Responses". In *The Routledge Companion to Media Disinformation and Populism.* Abingdon-on-Thames: Routledge, 2021.

Turner, Graeme. "The Mass Production of Celebrity: 'Celetoids', Reality TV and the 'Demotic Turn'". *International Journal of Cultural Studies* 9, no. 2 (2006): 153–65. https://doi.org/10.1177/1367877906064028.

Turner, Graeme. *Ordinary People and the Media: The Demotic Turn.* New York: Sage, 2009.

Turner, Graeme. *Understanding Celebrity.* London: Sage, 2004.

Turow, Joseph. *Niche Envy: Marketing Discrimination in the Digital Age.* Cambridge, MA: MIT, 2008.

Twenge, Jean M. and W. Keith Campbell. *The Narcissism Epidemic: Living in the Age of Entitlement.* Free Press: New York, 2009.

Twitch Tracker, 2023. https://twitchtracker.com/games /498566.

Twitter. "Hateful Conduct Policy", 2021. https://help.twitter.com/en/rules-and-policies/hateful-conduct-policy.

U.S. Senate. "Report of the Select Committee on Intelligence United States Senate on Russian Active Measures Campaigns and Interference in the 2016 U.S. Election. Vol. 1: Russian Efforts against Election Infrastructure with Additional Views", 2020. https://www.intelligence.senate.gov/sites/default/files/documents/Report_Volume1.pdf.

Ullman, Richard H. "Redefining Security". *International Security* 8, no. 1 (1983): 129–53. https://doi.org/10.2307/2538489.

UNCTAD. *Digital Economy Report 2019. Value Creation and Capture: Implications for Developing Countries.* Geneva: United Nations, 2019.

UNDP Report. "Human Development Report 1994". New York, NY: Oxford University Press, 1994.

UNESCO. "Recommendation on the Ethics of Artificial Intelligence". UNESCO, 2021. https://unesdoc.unesco.org/ark:/48223/pf0000381137.

UNESCO. *School Violence and Bullying: Global Status Report.* UNESCO, 2017. https://doi.org/10.54675/POIV1573.

UNICRI. *Algorithms and Terrorism: The Malicious Use of Artificial Intelligence for Terrorist Purposes. A Joint Report by UNICRI and UNCCT,* (Turin: United Nations Interregional Crime and Justice Research Institute, 2021). https://unicri.it/News/Algorithms-Terrorism-UNICRI-UNOCCT.

United Nations. "Tenth United Nations Congress on the Prevention of Crime and the Treatment of Offenders, Vienna 10–17 April 2000", 2000. https://www.unodc.org/documents/congress//Previous_Congresses/10th_Congress_2000/017_ACONF.187.10_Crimes_Related_to_Computer_Networks.pdf.

United Nations. "United Nations Strategy and Plan of Action on Hate Speech", 2019.

Vaidhyanathan, Siva. *Anti-Social Media. How Facebook Disconnects Us and Undermines Democracy.* Oxford: Oxford University Press, 2018.

Vaidhyanathan, Siva. *The Googlization of Everything.* Berkeley and Los Angeles, CA: University of California Press, 2011.

Valenzuela-García, Noelia, Diego J. Maldonado-Guzmán, Andrea García-Pérez and Cristina Del-Real. "Too Lucky to Be a Victim? An Exploratory Study of Online Harassment and Hate Messages Faced by Social Media Influencers". *European Journal on Criminal Policy and Research*, 2023. https://doi.org/10.1007/s10610-023-09542-0.

Valkenburg, Patti M. and Peter Jochen. "Online Communication Among Adolescents: An Integrated Model of Its Attraction, Opportunities, and Risks". *Journal of Adolescent Health* 48, no. 2 (2011): 121–27.

Van Der Hof, Simone, E. Lievens, I. Milkaite, V. Verdoodt, T. Hannema and T. Liefaard. "The Child's Right to Protection against Economic Exploitation in the Digital World". *The International Journal of Children's Rights* 28, no. 4 (2020): 833–59. https://doi.org/10.1163/15718182-28040003.

Van Driel, Loes and Delia Dumitrica. "Selling Brands While Staying 'Authentic': The Professionalization of Instagram Influencers". *Convergence: The International Journal of Research into New Media Technologies* 27, no. 1 (2021): 66–84. https://doi.org/10.1177/1354856520902136.

Vannucci, Anna, Christine Mc Cauley Ohannessian and Sonja Gagnon. "Use of Multiple Social Media Platforms in Relation to Psychological Functioning in Emerging Adults". *Emerging Adulthood* 7, no. 6 (2018): 501–6. https://doi.org/10.1177/2167696818782309.

Vänskä, Annamari. "'Cause I Wuv You!' Pet Dog Fashion and Emotional Consumption". *Ephemera. Theory and Politics in Organization* 16, no. 4 (2016): 75–97.

Velseberg, Ott. "Estonia's AI Vision: Building a Data-Driven Society and Government", 2024. https://apolitical.co/solution-articles/en/estonias-ai-vision-building-a-data-driven-society-and-government.

Vesselkov, Alexandr, Benjamin Finley and Jouko Vankka. "Russian Trolls Speaking Russian: Regional Twitter Operations and MH17". In *12th ACM Conference on Web Science*, 86–95. Southampton: ACM, 2020. https://doi.org/10.1145/3394231.3397898.

Vicente, Álvaro. "How Radicalizing Agents Mobilize Minors to Jihadism: a Qualitative Study in Spain". *Behavioral Sciences of Terrorism and Political Aggression* 14, no. 1 (2022): 22–48. https://doi.org/10.1080/19434472.2020.1800063.

Victor, Daniel. "Children Taken from Maryland Couple After YouTube 'Prank' Videos". *The New York Times*, 3 May 2017.

Visit Ukraine. "Hollywood Actors and Directors who Visited Ukraine during the War", 2024. https://visitukraine.today/blog/1511/hollywood-actors-and-directors-who-visited-ukraine-during-the-war.

Vismara, Matteo, Nicolaja Girone, Dario Conti, Gregorio Nicolini and Bernardo Dell'Osso. "The Current Status of Cyberbullying Research: A Short Review of the Literature". *Current Opinion in Behavioral Sciences* 46 (2022): 101152. https://doi.org/10.1016/j.cobeha.2022.101152.

Vlavo, Fidèle A. *Performing Digital Activism: New Aesthetics and Discourses of Resistance.* New York and Oxon: Routledge, 2018.

Volkoff, Vladimir. *Dezinformacja: Oręż Wojny*. Warsaw: Delikon, 1991.

Von Solms, Rossouw and Johan Van Niekerk. "From Information Security to Cyber Security". *Computers & Security* 38 (2013): 97–102. https://doi.org/10.1016/J.COSE .2013.04.004.

Vosoughi, Soroush, Deb Roy and Sinan Aral. "The Spread of True and False News Online". *Science* 359, no. 6380 (2018): 1146–51. https://doi.org/10.1126/SCIENCE .AAP9559.

Wachter, Sandra. "Affinity Profiling and Discrimination by Association in Online Behavioral Advertising". *Berkeley Technology Law Journal* 35, no. 2 (2020): 367–430.

Waldron, Jeremy. *The Harm in Hate Speech*. Cambridge, MA: Harvard University Press, 2012.

Wallner, Claudia. "The Global Far Right and the War in Ukraine: Initial Reactions and Enduring Narratives". Global Center on Cooperative Security, 2023. https://www .jstor.org/stable/resrep48741.

Waltz, Kenneth N. "Structural Realism after the Cold War". *International Security* 25, no. 1 (2000): 5–41. https://doi.org/10.1162/016228800560372.

Wang, Cheng Cai, Chun Fu Chen and Chin Tsu Chen. "Exploring the Different Aspects of Internet Leisure Use by College Students". *Information Development* 31, no. 1 (2013): 5–12. https://doi.org/10.1177/0266666913494909.

Wang, Jinping and Lewen Wei. "Fear and Hope, Bitter and Sweet: Emotion Sharing of Cancer Community on Twitter". *Social Media + Society* 6, no. 1 (2020). https://doi .org/10.1177/2056305119897319.

Wardle, Claire and Hossein Derakhshan. *Information Disorder: Toward an Interdisciplinary Framework for Research and Policy Making*. Strasbourg: Council of Europe, 2017.

Wasiuta, Olga and Sergiusz Wasiuta. "Militarne i Niemilitarne Metody Prowadzenia Wojny Hybrydowej Rosji przeciwko Ukrainie". *Visnyk of the Lviv University. Series International Relations* 39, no. 3–17 (2016).

Wasiuta, Olga. "Zagrożenia Hybrydowe". In *Vademecum Bezpieczeństwa Informacyjnego. Tom 2*, edited by Olga Wasiuta and Rafał Klepka, 637–43. Kraków: Uniwersytet Pedagogiczny im. Komisji Edukacji Narodowej w Krakowie, 2019.

Watts, Jay. "Digital Narcissism in the Consulting Room". In *Media and the Inner World: Psycho-Cultural Approaches to Emotion, Media and Popular Culture*, edited by Caroline Bainbridge and Candida Yates, 168–84. London: Palgrave Macmillan UK, 2014. https://doi.org/10.1057/9781137345547_11.

Watts, Jay. "Narcissism Through the Digital Looking Glass". In *Narcissism, Melancholia and the Subject of Community*, edited by Barry Sheils and Julie Walsh, 65–89. Cham: Springer International Publishing, 2017. https://doi.org/10.1007/978-3-319 -63829-4_3.

We Are Social, 2023. https://wearesocial.com/wp-content/uploads/2023/03/Digital-2023-Global-Overview-Report.pdf.

Weimann, Gabriel. "Terrorist Migration to Social Media". *Georgetown Journal of International Affairs* 16, no. 1 (2015): 180–87.

Weimann, Gabriele and Roy Dimant. "The Metaverse and Terrorism: Threats and Challenges". *Terrorism and Counter-Terrorism Studies* 17, no. 1 (2023). https://doi.org/10.19165/ELIM4426.

Weismayer, Christian, Ulrich Gunter and Irem Önder. "Temporal Variability of Emotions in Social Media Posts". *Technological Forecasting and Social Change* 167 (2021): 120699. https://doi.org/10.1016/J.TECHFORE.2021.120699.

Weissmann, Mikael. "Hybrid Warfare and Hybrid Threats Today and Tomorrow: Towards an Analytical Framework". *Journal on Baltic Security* 5, no. 1 (2019): 17–26. https://doi.org/10.2478/JOBS-2019-0002.

Wellman, Mariah L., Ryan Stoldt, Melissa Tully and Brian Ekdale. "Ethics of Authenticity: Social Media Influencers and the Production of Sponsored Content". *Journal of Media Ethics* 35, no. 2 (2020): 68–82. https://doi.org/10.1080/23736992.2020.1736078.

West, Robert and Jamie Brown. *Theory of Addiction. Second Edition*. Hoboken, NJ: Wiley Blackwell, 2013.

Wheeler, S. Christian, Richard E. Petty and George Y. Bizer. "Self-Schema Matching and Attitude Change: Situational and Dispositional Determinants of Message Elaboration". *Journal of Consumer Research* 31, no. 4 (2005): 787–97. https://doi.org/10.1086/426613.

White, Kalia. "Report: Drug Mixing Killed Fake-News Writer Paul Horner". *USA Today*, 2017. https://eu.usatoday.com/story/news/nation-now/2017/12/06/report-drug-mixing-killed-fake-news-writer-paul-horner/928412001/.

Williams, Matthew. *The Science of Hate: How Prejudice Becomes Hate and What We Can Do to Stop It*. London: Faber & Faber, 2021.

Wilson, Anne E., Victoria Parker and Matthew Feinberg. "Polarization in the Contemporary Political and Media Landscape". *Current Opinion in Behavioral Sciences* 34 (2020): 223–28. https://doi.org/10.1016/J.COBEHA.2020.07.005.

Wojdynski, Bartosz W. and Nathaniel J. Evans. "Going Native: Effects of Disclosure Position and Language on the Recognition and Evaluation of Online Native Advertising". *Journal of Advertising* 45, no. 2 (2016): 157–68. https://doi.org/10.1080/00913367.2015.1115380.

Wong, Julia Carrie. "'It's Not Play If You're Making Money': How Instagram and YouTube Disrupted Child Labor Laws". *The Guardian*, 24 April 2019. https://www.theguardian.com/media/2019/apr/24/its-not-play-if-youre-making-money-how-instagram-and-youtube-disrupted-child-labor-laws.

World Health Organization. "ICD-11 for Mortality and Morbidity Statistics", 2018. https://icd.who.int/dev11/l-m/en.

World Health Organization. "International Statistical Classification of Diseases and Related Health Problems (ICD)", 2024. https://www.who.int/standards/classifica tions/classification-of-diseases.

Wóycicki, Kazimierz, Marta Kowalska and Adam Lelonek. "Rosyjska Wojna Dezinfor-macyjna przeciwko Polsce". Warsaw: Fundacja im. Kazimierza Pułaskiego, 2017.

Wu, Tim. *The Attention Merchants: The Epic Scramble to Get Inside Our Heads*. New York: Alfred A. Knopf, 2016.

Wyatt, Austin. "Examining Supply Chain Risks in Autonomous Weapon Systems and Artificial Intelligence". *Applied Cybersecurity & Internet Governance* 2, no. 1 (2023): 1–21. https://doi.org/10.60097/ACIG/162874.

Wysokińska, Zofia. "A Review of the Impact of the Digital Transformation on the Global and European Economy". *Comparative Economic Research. Central and Eastern Europe* 24, no. 3 (2021): 75–92. https://doi.org/10.18778/1508-2008.24.22.

X. "Rules & Policies. Hateful Conduct", 2023. https://help.x.com/en/rules-and-policies /hateful-conduct-policy.

Xuewei, Zhai and Huang Xiaoye. *China's Social Credit. Theoretical, Empirical Research, and Countermeasures*. Abingdon: Routledge, 2023.

Yarkoni, Tal. "Personality in 100,000 Words: A Large-Scale Analysis of Personality and Word Use among Bloggers". *Journal of Research in Personality* 44, no. 3 (2010): 363–73. https://doi.org/10.1016/J.JRP.2010.04.001.

Yeung, Karen. "'Hypernudge': Big Data as a Mode of Regulation by Design". *Information, Communication & Society* 20, no. 1 (2017): 118–36. https://doi.org/10.1080/1369118X .2016.1186713.

Yin, Pengzhen, Carol X.J. Ou, Robert M. Davison and Jie Wu. "Coping with Mobile Technology Overload in the Workplace". *Internet Research* 28, no. 5 (2018): 1189–1212. https://doi.org/10.1108/INTR-01-2017-0016/FULL/HTML.

Yoon, Sunkyung, Mary Kleinman, Jessica Mertz and Michael Brannick. "Is Social Net-work Site Usage Related to Depression? A Meta-Analysis of Facebook-Depression Relations". *Journal of Affective Disorders* 248 (2019): 65–72. https://doi.org/10.1016/J .JAD.2019.01.026.

Young, Kimberly S. "Internet Addiction: The Emergence of a New Clinical Disorder". *Cyberpsychology and Behavior* 1, no. 3 (1998): 237–44. https://doi.org/10.1089/CPB .1998.1.237.

Young, Kimberly S. and Carl J. Case. "Internet Abuse in the Workplace: New Trends in Risk Management". *CyberPsychology & Behavior*, 7, no. 1 (2004): 105–11. https://doi .org/10.1089/109493104322820174.

YouTube. "Hate Speech Policy", 2019. https://support.google.com/youtube/answer /2801939.

Youyou, Wu, Michal Kosinski and David Stillwell. "Computer-Based Personality Judgments Are More Accurate than Those Made by Humans". *Proceedings of the*

National Academy of Sciences of the United States of America 112, no. 4 (2015): 1036–40. https://doi.org/10.1073/PNAS.1418680112.

Yu, Lingling, Xiongfei Cao, Zhiying Liu, and Junkai Wang. "Excessive Social Media Use at Work: Exploring the Effects of Social Media Overload on Job Performance". *Information Technology and People* 31, no. 6 (2018): 1091–1112. https://doi.org/10.1108/ITP-10-2016-0237.

Yuan, Shupei, Yingying Chen, Sophia Vojta and Yu Chen. "More Aggressive, More Retweets? Exploring the Effects of Aggressive Climate Change Messages on Twitter". *New Media & Society* 26, no. 8 (2022). https://doi.org/10.1177/14614448221122202.

Żakowska, Marzena and Dorota Domalewska. "Factors Determining Polish Parliamentarians' Tweets on Migration". *Czech Journal of Political Science* 3 (2019): 200–216. https://doi.org/10.5817/PC2019-3-200.

Żakowska, Marzena and Dorota Domalewska. "Social Security in the Balkans". In *Social Security in the Balkans – Volume 1: An Overview of Social Policy in Croatia, Albania, Bosnia and Hercegovina, Greece, Romania and Bulgaria*, edited by Marzena Żakowska and Dorota Domalewska, 1–8. Leiden, Boston: BRILL, 2021. https://doi.org/10.1163/9789004466579.

Żakowska, Marzena and Dorota Domalewska. "Social Security in the Balkans: Lessons and Recommendations". In *Social Security in the Balkans – Volume 3. An Overview of Social Policy in Serbia and Kosovo*, edited by Marzena Żakowska, 257–64. Boston, Leiden: Brill, 2022. https://doi.org/10.1163/9789004500068_011.

Zarouali, Brahim, Tom Dobber, Guy De Pauw and Claes De Vreese. "Using a Personality-Profiling Algorithm to Investigate Political Microtargeting: Assessing the Persuasion Effects of Personality-Tailored Ads on Social Media". *Communication Research* 49, no. 8 (2022): 1066–91. https://doi.org/10.1177/0093650220961965.

Zhang, Yang. "Direct and Indirect Effects of Neuroticism on Internet Addiction in College Students: A Structure Equation Modeling Analysis". *Psychological Reports* 124, no. 2 (2020): 611–26. https://doi.org/10.1177/0033294120918806.

Zhang, Yi, Pan Zhang and Yu Liu. "Chinese Indigenous Intervention on Internet Gaming Disorder: A Review of Traditional Chinese Therapies": Xishuangbanna, China, 2021. https://doi.org/10.2991/assehr.k.211220.085.

Zhao, Shanyang, Sherri Grasmuck and Jason Martin. "Identity Construction on Facebook: Digital Empowerment in Anchored Relationships". *Computers in Human Behavior* 24, no. 5 (2008): 1816–36. https://doi.org/10.1016/j.chb.2008.02.012.

Zhao, Xing and James Caverlee. "Vitriol on Social Media: Curation and Investigation". In *Social Informatics*, edited by Steffen Staab, Olessia Koltsova and Dimitry Ignatov. Cham: Springer, 2018. https://doi.org/10.1007/978-3-030-01129-1_30.

Zhou, Nan and Xiao Yi Fang. "Beyond Peer Contagion: Unique and Interactive Effects of Multiple Peer Influences on Internet Addiction among Chinese Adolescents". *Computers in Human Behavior* 50 (2015): 231–38. https://doi.org/10.1016/J.CHB.2015.03.083.

Zięba, Ryszard. *The Euro-Atlantic Security System in the 21st Century*. Global Power Shift. Cham: Springer International Publishing, 2018. https://doi.org/10.1007/978-3-319-79105-0.

Zimbardo, Philip and Michael Leippe. *The Psychology of Attitude Change and Social Influence*. Philadelphia: Temple University Press, 1991.

Zimmermann, Verena and Karen Renaud. "Moving from a 'Human-as-Problem' to a 'Human-as-Solution' Cybersecurity Mindset". *International Journal of Human-Computer Studies* 131 (2019): 169–87. https://doi.org/10.1016/j.ijhcs.2019.05.005.

Zolkepli, Izzal Asnira and Yusniza Kamarulzaman. "Social Media Adoption: The Role of Media Needs and Innovation Characteristics". *Computers in Human Behavior* 43 (2015): 189–209. https://doi.org/10.1016/J.CHB.2014.10.050.

Zuboff, Shoshana. *The Age of Surveillance Capitalism: The Fight for a Human Future at the New Frontier of Power*. New York: Public Affairs, 2019.

Żuk, Piotr and Paweł Żuk. "'Euro-Gomorrah and Homopropaganda': The Culture of Fear and 'Rainbow Scare' in the Narrative of Right-Wing Populists Media in Poland as Part of the Election Campaign to the European Parliament in 2019". *Discourse, Context & Media* 33 (2020): 100364. https://doi.org/10.1016/J.DCM.2019.100364.

Index